The Earthbound Farm Organic Cookbook

Food to Live By

by Goodman *with* Linda Holland *and* Pamela McKinstry

Earthbound Farm.
ORGANIC

To Drew,
my wonderful partner in all things—
love, parenting, and business.

And to our amazing children,
Marea and Jeffrey,
this cookbook is first and foremost
my gift to you.

Library of Congress Cataloging-in-Publication Data is available.
ISBN-13: 978-0-7611-3899-0; ISBN-10: 0-7611-3899-4 (alk. paper)
ISBN-13: 978-0-7611-4389-5; ISBN-10: 0-7611-4389-0 (hc)

Cover design by Paul Hanson
Front and back cover photographs by Patrick Tregenza
Author photograph by Tom O'Neal
Book design by Paul Hanson and Lisa Hollander
Food photography by Patrick Tregenza
Food styling by Diane Gsell
Lifestyle photography by Anne Hamersky, Greig Cranna, and Tom O'Neal

Workman books are available at special discounts when purchased in bulk for premiums
and sales promotions as well as for fund-raising or educational use.
Special editions or book excerpts can also be created to specification.
For details, contact the Special Sales Director at the address below.

Workman Publishing Company, Inc.
225 Varick Street
New York, NY 10014-4381

Printed in the U.S.A.
Food to Live By is printed on recycled paper with soy-based inks.
First printing October 2006
10 9 8 7 6 5 4 3 2 1

Acknowledgments

So many people poured their hearts and time into this book, determined to make it extra special. Thanks to every one of them for their important contributions. Linda Holland first proposed this project a few years ago, perhaps without realizing exactly what she was getting us all into. She spent countless hours tasting, testing, and telling the Earthbound Farm story through recipes. Chef Pamela McKinstry, a longtime Earthbound Farm culinary accomplice, worked tirelessly and without complaint, developing hundreds of delicious recipes. Her biggest challenge was to create recipes for the many classic Goodman family dishes whose steps had never been written down, just made by instinct time and time again.

We have been extremely fortunate to work with creative, devoted, and gifted photographers who collectively helped bring the beauty and vitality of this food and our farm to life. Thanks to Anne Hamersky, our lifestyle photographer, whose camera lens sometimes seemed magically guided by Farm Stand elves. Thanks to Patrick Tregenza, our food photographer, and Diane Gsell, his wife and our food stylist. Together, they created astonishingly beautiful photographs of our recipes and raw ingredients. Thanks to Greig Cranna, who captured the beauty of our fields and farm landscapes; and to Tom O'Neal, who has been photographing our family for over a dozen years and has created so many images we treasure. Janna Jo Williams, our Farm Stand event manager, proved to be a brilliant prop gatherer and stylist. And her gathering wouldn't have been possible without Mark Marino and his dedication to growing the most beautiful flowers and produce in our Carmel Valley fields.

Many thanks to Samantha Cabaluna and Hillary Fish for their valuable assistance with copy editing and coordinating this project, and to two wonderful writers, Ronni Sweet and Lia Huber, who helped me express myself in the introduction and various essays, respectively. I am grateful to my generous and genius friend Darryle Pollack, who stayed up until two in the morning (twice) to help me improve some of the most important sections. And appreciation to Jerry Takigawa, a wise man and gifted designer, who came up with the line, "Food to live by," which captures the essence of Earthbound Farm so perfectly that it became our tag line and, now, the title of this book.

Our wonderful employees in our Carmel marketing office spent months tasting and testing these recipes, and everyone at the Farm Stand and Organic Kitchen supported this project beyond the call of duty (emergency tofu baking and chai making, etc.). Sheila Dixon did us the big favor of testing many recipes—especially the desserts—and we incorporated many of her suggestions. My biggest recipe tasting "thank you" goes to my husband, Drew. Because of his great palate (and my expanding waistline), I constantly counted on him to try "just one more" variation of yet another recipe. Drew and our children, Marea and Jeffrey, were usually ready with assistance, patience, and humor—providing me with what I needed most in this project and everything else I do.

In addition to Chef Pamela McKinstry, many talented people made significant contributions to this collection of recipes. Thanks to Nate Johnson, Julie Love, Matthew Millea, Kari Murray, Ingrid Rohrer, Josie Rowe, Kenny Fukumoto, Sarah La Casse, Cal Stamenov, Craig von Foerster, and Ron Powell. And thanks, also, to my mother-in-law, Kathy Goodman, and my sister-in-law, Jill Goodman.

As a first-time author, I am very lucky—and grateful—for the assistance and enthusiasm from everyone at Workman Publishing. Most notably, Suzanne Rafer, our incredible editor, who has been our steadfast partner and guiding light throughout, and Peter Workman, a most impressive man with such strong, clear vision. Thanks to our entire Workman team: Paul Hanson, Lisa Hollander, David Schiller, Barbara Mateer, Melanie Bennitt, Barbara Peragine, Helen Rosner, Ron Longe, Katie Workman, Sarah Henry, and all the dedicated sales people who have been so excited about this book. And many thanks to Angela Miller for her wisdom in bringing us all together.

I want to express my deep appreciation to the entire Earthbound Farm family—all the employees who work so very hard to bring our fresh organic food to market every day, as well as our partners and growers. A heartfelt "thank you" to each and every one of you.

Thanks to all my girlfriends who provided so much encouragement and support during this process—and who help brighten my life no matter what I get myself into—especially to Trudy Anderson (help with indecision), Teresa Basham (makeup goddess), and Ruth Rubin (cheerleader sister).

Drew and I are blessed with incredible families that have supported us through every step of this remarkable journey. I especially want to acknowledge our parents, Edith and Mendek Rubin and Jim and Kathy Goodman, because Earthbound Farm would not be here without their many contributions. I am ever grateful for their boundless love and encouragement. When you have parents who believe in you so completely, you feel like you can do anything—even write a cookbook!

Contents

A delicious recipe tribute to the crop that got Earthbound Farm started. Begin the day with warm Raspberry Corn Muffins spread with fresh Apricot Raspberry Jam, and end it with creamy Raspberry-Lemon Crèmes Brûlées or Red Raspberry Ice Cream. What could be better?

E njoy a full array of tempting, innovative soups any time of the year. Choices include Summer Harvest Soup, Sweet Corn Chowder, Golden Tomato Gazpacho, Tuscan White Bean Stew, Roasted Winter Squash Soup, Hearty Cauliflower Bisque, and Simply Chicken Soup.

T here's nothing like a selection of fresh leafy greens to enhance a meal. And they shine in Spring Mâche Salad with Kohlrabi, Radishes, and Peas; Baby Greens Salad with Grilled Figs and Walnuts; Grilled Caesar Salad; Roasted Beet and Arugula Salad; Farm Stand Greek Salad, and more.

S izzling Steak and the Goodman Family Olive Sauce, Merlot-Braised Short Ribs with Cipollini Onions, Maple-Brined Pork Chops, Lamb Curry with Saffron Couscous, Kathy's Rosemary-Roasted Chicken, and Spicy Chicken Lettuce Wraps are just a small sampling of the surefire winners in this chapter.

A lthough there are no USDA standards for organic seafood, there

are still plenty of reasons to enjoy the health benefits of flavorful fish dishes like Ginger Lime Salmon, Roasted Halibut in Mediterranean Green Sauce, and Seared Tuna with a Fennel-Coriander Crust. And for shellfish lovers, there's Grilled Shrimp with Tropical Salsa, a savory Monterey Cioppino, and more.

Inviting pasta dishes to add to your repertoire include Grilled Vegetable Lasagna, Ziti with Ratatouille, and Creamy Macaroni and Three Cheeses. Plus prepare a luscious "Wild" Mushroom Ragout with Polenta, Stir-Fried Tofu with Green Beans and Shiitake Mushrooms, and a Fresh Tomato Pizza.

Roasted Balsamic Artichokes, Sautéed Ginger Baby Bok Choy, Summer Corn Pudding, Blue Cheese Smashed Potatoes, Garlicky String Beans, Creamed Parmesan Spinach, and Provençal Tomato, Eggplant, and Zucchini Tian—are a few of the sides that are so good, you may just want to make a meal of them.

Great dishes to start the day include Earthbound Farm's Famous Maple Almond Granola, Apple Nut Pancakes, Spanish Egg "Soufflé Cake," a Classic Omelet, and Mama Fries. And when you have the urge to bake, enjoy a Cinnamon Walnut Coffee Cake.

Nothing ends a meal better than something sweet—and there's something here for everyone: Chocolate Lover's Brownies, Farm Stand Carrot Cake, Cranberry-Pumpkin Bread Pudding, Strawberry Rhubarb Crumble, Fresh Peach Pie, and a Cherry Panna Cotta. And, the recipe for the bestselling Earthbound Farm Ginger Snaps!

Chapter 10:

A selection of homemade stocks, sauces, vinegars, and other staples to keep on hand in the pantry and refrigerator.

The Time Is Ripe for Organic!

The seeds of this cookbook were planted more than twenty-two years ago when my husband, Drew, and I began growing organic raspberries in our two and a half-acre garden and selling them from a roadside stand. But for many reasons, a cookbook featuring organic ingredients was not really feasible until fairly recently. For one thing, organic foods were just not available to most people twenty years ago. If you wanted organic, you had to shop in small health food stores or at seasonal farm stands, or you had to grow it yourself. And choosing organic produce was often a sacrifice—it was smaller in size, less attractive, and much more expensive.

When we started Earthbound Farm in 1984, common sense told us that chemicals used in conventional farming couldn't be good for us, and we knew we had to find a better way. Organic was our answer and soon became our passion. In those early days, we had personal contact with everyone who bought our produce. We were committed to providing our customers with the purest food possible, and we eagerly told them why our organic farming methods were better for their health and the health of the planet.

But getting the word out was slow going. Organic wasn't on the radar back then, and there wasn't much reporting in the media about the potential dangers of conventional chemicals or the benefits of organic foods.

Times have certainly changed! Today, organic products are synonymous with premium quality, better taste, and optimum health: the very best food possible. Virtually every supermarket carries organic food, and you can find

The Earthbound Farm sign welcomes visitors to our Carmel Valley Farm Stand.

organic alternatives to most conventionally produced foods.

This huge turnaround is a true revolution. And the story of Earthbound Farm—our incredible growth from a small backyard garden to the largest grower of organic produce in the world—is part of the story of that revolution.

the story of

Earthbound Farm

1984
Drew and I started Earthbound Farm on a two-and-a-half-acre plot in Carmel Valley, California. Our first crop: raspberries.

1986 We sold our first packages of prewashed organic salad mix.

1992 We opened our roadside Farm Stand in Carmel Valley.

Although our company has grown far beyond what we could ever have imagined, Drew and I still feel a personal commitment to everyone who buys an Earthbound Farm product. So it is with great enthusiasm that I offer this book of recipes our family has developed and loved over the years, as well as our customers' favorites from the Organic Kitchen at our Farm Stand in Carmel Valley, California.

An Unspoken Hunger . . . and an Unexpected Career

The beginnings of my career in organic farming (and now cookbook writing) were not auspicious. First of all, I was born and bred in New York City—not the typical training ground for a future farmer! Second, my wonderful parents nourished me with lots of love but not lots of fresh foods. I don't remember many meals cooked from scratch when I was growing up. Like many American families in the sixties and seventies, we ate a lot of TV dinners.

My clearest memory of living in Manhattan as a teenager is lying on my bed and looking out the window of my eleventh-floor apartment at the buildings across the street. All I saw was concrete—no blue sky, no trees, no grass, no flowers. Nature was an elevator ride down to the ground floor and a walk to Central Park. I craved fresh air and the sights and smells of nature, and going away to college seemed the best way to find them. I was accepted for early admission at the

University of Vermont after my junior year in high school, so in 1980, at the age of sixteen, I headed off to college and the countryside.

Vermont was gorgeous! There were farms everywhere, and the agriculture students at the university ran a store that sold really fresh milk and homemade ice cream. One summer I shared a house with some friends and I shopped and worked at the local food co-op. I can still vividly picture the huge bins of grains and piles of fresh produce—the raw ingredients of prepared food! One of my friends taught me how to bake bread. It was an amazing experience, shopping for the flour and yeast, kneading the dough, watching it rise, and finally, the incredible smell and taste of bread just out of the oven. Wholesome fresh food satisfied a profound hunger I never even realized was there.

Getting to the West Coast by Traveling More Than 7,000 Miles East

After a year and a half in Vermont, I spent the last semester of my sophomore year studying in Gujarat, India. While there, I decided to transfer to the University of California at Berkeley and majored in the political economy of industrial societies. I was planning on a career in international relations, and hoped to help make the world a better place through conflict resolution at the international level.

In 1983, while I was at Berkeley, I met—or rather, re-met—my future husband, Drew Goodman, who was an environmental studies major at the University of California, Santa Cruz. Drew and I had lived a block away from each other in Manhattan, and we had attended the same high school (three years apart), but we were only slightly acquainted. Three thousand miles away from our Manhattan roots we discovered we had so much in common. Before long, we were a couple in love, and ready to start a life together.

After I graduated, Drew and I found a house on two and a half acres in rural Carmel Valley where we could work off the rent doing property improvements while I spent a year or so preparing for graduate school. I knew that I needed to be bilingual to be accepted into any graduate program in international relations, and this setup would afford me the time to study Spanish and prepare for the GRE. And since our property included an acre and a half of raspberries, we planned to farm and sell them by the side of the road. Added to money I could make babysitting, we figured the raspberries would cover most of our expenses, as long as we lived frugally.

Seduced by the Land

We definitely earned our rent removing a dilapidated barn, a rundown storage shed, an abandoned goose pond, and an unused hog pen. But, moving to the farm was a romantic adventure, too. Our small plot included apple, fig, orange, and Meyer lemon trees, as well as pineapple guava bushes, grapevines, and of course, the raspberries. And the long driveway leading to this bounty was lined with almond, walnut, apricot, and plum trees. For me, this was a real Garden of Eden—more than I had dreamed of finding back when all I could see from my Manhattan window was concrete.

Drew at our original farm, which included a perennial herb garden and lettuce patch.

Drew and I embraced farm life. We spent our days like an old-fashioned pioneer couple—rising with the sun, feeding the chickens, gathering the eggs, tending the crops until heat and physical fatigue sent us inside for a meal and siesta, then working the land until dark. We stomped the grapes and made juice, then wine, then vinegar. During the off-season, I spent my free time blissfully learning to cook. We savored the restful rhythm of nature, living in utter contentment, far removed from caffeine-fueled nights spent studying for exams. We were soothed, charmed, and seduced by the land and the lifestyle. I told myself, "Next year I'll go to grad school." Next year came and went, then the next, and the next.

1998 We were farming on 5,800 acres of certified organic farmland, making Earthbound the largest grower of organic produce in the United States.

2006 We're farming 30,000 acres and offering more than 100 products.

Organic Just Felt Right

When we first moved onto the property, we knew absolutely nothing about farming. The previous owner gave us a quick course in raspberry horticulture, teaching us how to add chemical fertilizers to the drip irrigation lines and to apply dormant sprays twice a year to kill funguses and insects. But when the time came for us to follow the procedures, we couldn't bring ourselves to do it. We hated the way the chemicals smelled and instinctively knew they weren't healthy for us, our future customers, or the environment. And because we were literally farming our own backyard, the potential impact was clear. We had to find a better way.

Since this was the early eighties, we didn't have the option of Internet research. So we studied Rodale's *Encyclopedia of Organic Gardening* and applied the methods to our little plot, learning to successfully grow our berries without toxic pesticides or synthetic fertilizers. Once we had met the requirements, we were proud to receive organic certification from CCOF (California Certified Organic Farmers).

The more we learned about organic farming, the more committed we became. It was a natural evolution. We lived on our farmland, so there was no barrier between the health of the land and our own health.

Earthbound Farm Is Born

Sometimes a big arrow appears in your life, pointing you in the right direction. Ours showed up in 1984. It was painted on a plywood sign that we set out on Carmel Valley Road, pointing down our tree-lined driveway. Under the arrow were hand-painted red letters that shouted RASPBERRIES. Waiting for any customers who pulled over was a folding table with a metal cashbox and flats of baskets filled with deep-red, aromatic berries.

Because we insisted on selling our berries within twenty-four hours of picking them, we often had more raspberries than customers. So I became an inventive cook by necessity. Some days I sold raspberry muffins or raspberry jam or raspberry vinegar. And through my experimentation, I found joy and fulfillment in creating something delicious from the bounty we had coaxed from our beautiful land.

> *Sometimes a big arrow appears in your life, pointing you in the right direction.*

Me at our original farm, which was filled with salad greens and bordered by artichokes.

One day Drew and I decided it was time to name our fledgling business. We were walking up the driveway to post our raspberry sign when I suggested a name, "What about Earth Born Farm?" Not hearing me clearly, Drew asked, "Earthbound?" That was it. Earthbound Farm. The name said it all: We are all bound to the earth and interconnected, sharing responsibility for stewardship of its finite resources. The name felt just right, even though calling our small plot of land a farm was a bit of a stretch.

A hand-painted sign proudly announces how our produce is grown.

Our First Backyard Babies

Making a living by farming meant finding ways to uncover new ground— and new crops. We had to be innovative. We discovered that we could sell our raspberries more efficiently by delivering to local restaurants rather than waiting long hours for customers to come down our driveway. As we built our relationships with the chefs, we asked what other types of specialty crops we

might be able to grow for them. Our first endeavor was culinary herbs. These helped, but we still weren't making ends meet.

A friend mentioned that chefs in San Francisco were buying baby heads of lettuce for the same price as full-size heads. Amazing! If Drew and I could sell baby lettuces to local chefs, we might really be able to make a living from our land. It was the perfect solution for our limited acreage. We could plant lettuces closer together and harvest them sooner, allowing us to make more intensive use of the land and increase our sales.

We searched seed catalogs for beautiful heirloom lettuces, like rose-tinged Perella Red, frilly green Tango, delicate oak leaf, and ruby-tipped Lollo Rossa. When the baby lettuces were three to four inches tall, we harvested them, packed mixed cases of twenty-four mini heads, and delivered them to local restaurants. The chefs loved them! Encouraged, we tested Asian greens, like bok choy, tat soi, and mizuna, which were nearly unknown outside the Asian community. We harvested these, too, as babies. Once they passed our taste test, we had the chefs sample them. If the chefs liked them, they were added to our garden. Our backyard baby produce business flourished, primarily because the chef at a popular Carmel restaurant bought most of our crops as fast as we could grow them.

Drew with my dad, Mendek Rubin, stringing support wires for new rows of raspberries.

Tending to our garden beds.

Rows of baby lettuce grow with our handmade hoop greenhouse in the background.

Hand-harvesting baby arugula.

Bagging a Revolutionary Idea

At that time, Drew and I were working fourteen-hour days, and we developed a bad habit of eating pizza and other quick take-out foods. Ironically, we were growing delicious healthy greens right outside our kitchen window, but were not eating them ourselves! By the end of the day we were too exhausted to harvest, cut, and wash the greens for dinner. So we started a new tradition. Each Sunday evening, we harvested, washed, and dried enough greens for the week and made a bottle of vinaigrette using fresh juice from our Meyer lemon trees. We divided the mixed greens among resealable plastic bags, one for each day of the week. We were amazed that the greens were as fresh and delicious on Saturday as they had been on Monday!

Drew and my dad figure out how to wash some of our first salad mixes.

We thought, "This is such a fantastic product. Wouldn't it be great if it were available in stores?" At that time, neither prewashed salads nor specialty salads were available in grocery stores. Heads of iceberg lettuce were ubiquitous, and most people experienced the delightful tastes and textures of mixed baby greens only in a handful of cutting-edge, upscale restaurants.

But we didn't act on our idea. After all, our little business was humming along. Then in 1986, the chef who purchased the majority of our produce left suddenly and was replaced by a chef who brought in his own suppliers. Literally overnight, Drew and I found ourselves with few customers and rows and rows of baby greens that had to be harvested within a two-day window or they would no longer be babies and our crop would be lost. We had nothing to lose—so we decided to test our bagged salad idea.

We harvested, washed, dried, and bagged our organic mixed baby greens, then added a hand-drawn label. Both Drew and I went on sales calls, taking sample bags to locally owned grocery and natural food stores in the Monterey and San Francisco Bay areas. We were both a bit nervous about approaching the produce managers. We knew our salads would not be an easy sale—no one was

selling prewashed, bagged salad. Many produce managers had never even seen the type of salad mix we were hoping they'd sell! Some offered to try our product only if we guaranteed the sale. We agreed that we would not charge for any bags they were left with.

Much to the produce managers' surprise, shoppers snapped up our bagged greens. Our problem was not taking back unsold produce. Instead, our biggest challenge became keeping up with the demand.

Washing and packaging small batches of lettuces in our kitchen was labor intensive and time consuming. We needed a better system, and we needed help. So my father, an inventor and brilliant tinkerer, with a knack for solving mechanical problems, designed our first salad production line. My father and Drew searched the junkyards for pipes and pulleys. Soon they had constructed a three-sink washing system that we installed in our shed. We also set up a packaging assembly line in the best space we had on the farm—our living room.

The final design was simple and efficient. We would fill a huge mesh basket with greens, dunk and swirl them in the first sink, haul out the basket with the rope and pulley system, then repeat the washing process in the second and third sinks. For our drying system, we used restaurant salad spinners, and absorbed any leftover moisture by shaking the salad in giant terry cloth sacks made

> ## *"We had nothing to lose— so we decided to test our bagged salad idea."*

from bath towels. Last stop for the clean salad was our living room assembly line, where my father set up a system to weigh, bag, and label the final product.

We hired one employee, then another, and yet another. At some point we realized that organic farming was no longer a stopgap while we were waiting to launch our professional careers; it *was* our career. Drew and I each remember a particular moment when this reality became undeniable. For Drew, it was while driving a truckload of salads up to San Francisco. For me, it was admitting to myself, "My living room is a salad processing plant. I must be in the organic salad business!"

It turns out that we were the first people to successfully market bagged salads to retail stores. We had no idea we were making food history. And, of course, we also had no idea that eventually Earthbound Farm organic salads, fruits, and vegetables would be sold in more than eighty percent of the supermarkets across the United States. Who could foresee that our company one day would be processing more than thirty million salad servings a week?

The Business Outgrows the Living Room

Our family was expanding along with the business. Our daughter, Marea, was born in February of 1990, and our son, Jeffrey, in December of 1992. Motherhood

Drew, with help from his sister, Jill Goodman, fills bags of salad during the first season we were marketing our salad bags.

inspired me to learn more about the benefits of a healthy diet, and I became even more committed to organic foods.

By 1992, our home was overloaded—not only with two children, but as the headquarters for a three-million dollar business. It was time to move. We bought a thirty-two acre farm in nearby Watsonville, California, and built a 9,000-square-foot salad processing facility. Earthbound moved in July 1992. We thought that our Watsonville farm and facility would last us forever, but it turned out to be more of a launching pad than a resting place.

The Club Store Catapult

At a trade show in 1992, Drew met the produce buyers from a fast-growing club store chain, and he set up a meeting at our offices. We showed them our operation, which was very primitive compared to what it is today. After they had seen the farm and processing plant, we discussed

selling our salads in their stores. During the meeting, my six-week-old son began to cry, and I had no choice but to nurse him. I thought to myself, "Well, that does it. There's no way these businessmen are going to want to work with us."

I was wrong. We got their business, and our sales went through the roof. This deal also dramatically expanded our customer base. Previously, restaurants bought most of our salads. The club store chain was the driving force that launched Earthbound Farm into the world of large-scale retail sales. Once our salads proved to be a success for the club stores, several major supermarket chains wanted to carry them as well.

Ironically, most of our early customers were more interested in the novelty of specialty salads than they were in the fact that they were organic. Nonetheless, we were committed to organic methods and continued to farm that way. Riding the new demand for specialty salads enabled us to take organic produce mainstream long before there was a major demand for organic food. I've always been proud that Earthbound Farm has never been a follower in the organic trend. From the beginning, we've been a leader.

More quickly than we anticipated, our Watsonville processing facility and existing farmland were insufficient to meet the new demand. We knew we needed help. We were at a point where we needed more top-quality organic farmland. We also needed partners who knew more than we did about farming on a large scale.

The importance of establishing an organic land base can't be underestimated. Organic certification requires a three-year transition period, during which the land

Jeffrey (age 2), showing off his fresh-picked carrots with his sister, Marea (age 5).

must be farmed organically but the crops sold as conventional. The ability to acquire new farmland and make the transition to organic has always been a prerequisite for the growth of our business.

The City Kids Meet the Farm Boys, and the Farm Gets Bigger

Partnerships in 1995 with Mission Ranches and with Tanimura & Antle in 1999—both multigeneration, family-owned farming businesses from the Salinas Valley—enabled us to keep on growing. Many more consumers were choosing organic as they became aware of and concerned about the environmental and health effects of pesticides. I'll never forget asking one of our new partners what he loved most about organic farming. He answered by telling me his "pants story." When he farmed conventionally, he would come home from working in the fields all day and when his kids ran to greet him, he would push them away because he never knew what might be on his pants. After changing to organic farming methods, that was no longer necessary. Now, he relishes the joy of his children greeting him with big hugs as soon as he gets home. He no longer worries about pesticides on his pants. . . or in the food he produces.

Organic Is More Than a Business, It's Our Passion

For Drew and me, our idyllic days on the raspberry farm often seem far away. Now, we operate at a hectic pace running a large business. We are constantly

Drew and me filling a box of fresh produce.

battling the variables of weather, pests, and other factors that make providing a consistent supply of quality organic produce even more difficult than its conventional counterpart. Our days are filled with the many challenges of bringing fresh organic produce to mainstream markets.

But our rewards have also deepened over the years. I get enormous satisfaction from knowing that we're making a positive contribution to our world: We're producing the healthiest food possible and growing it in a way that helps keep the environment healthy, too. I also witness the pride of our many employees, who take personal satisfaction in working for a company that supports health and the preservation of the environment in a really big way.

If someone asked me what I'm most proud of in my life, I would definitely answer, "My children." And they always come first in everything I do. But in a very real way, Earthbound Farm is my child as well. And making sure that Earthbound Farm stays true to our original vision is protecting the health and future of my children—and all our children.

Striving to bring delicious organic food and an understanding of its tremendous value to as many people as we possibly can has been a way of life for Drew and me for more than twenty-two years. And Earthbound Farm has become an unexpected vehicle to fulfill some of my original dreams to make the world a better place. I believe that our individual destinies are like the seed of a plant: Blown to the right place, it digs into the earth, reaches toward the sunlight, and grows into its full potential. Earthbound Farm has been the ideal soil for my passions to develop and take root. And this cookbook is fed by those passions.

Drew taking a break with the kids in the wheel of our tractor.

The Carmel Valley Farm Stand and Organic Kitchen

When I was a teenager, my family would sometimes go to the countryside in the summer to escape the heat of New York City. And one result of those sunny weekends on Long Island is I fell in love with farm stands. We'd stop at rickety little roadside stands, buy potatoes and sweet corn, and cook them as soon as we got home. They tasted alive and fresh, with an earthy, sweet flavor. The experience of standing right next to rows of vegetables growing in the fields, and then eating them soon after they were picked, stirred a deep connection in me. What was on the plate became more than just food—it was part of a much richer experience.

It was exactly that connection that Drew and I wanted to share when we opened Earthbound Farm's Farm Stand in 1992. As Earthbound Farm grew, and our customer base and farmland extended farther and farther away from us, the stand became our way of maintaining a direct connection with our customers and the land.

The Farm Stand sits on sixty fertile acres in the beautiful countryside of Carmel Valley. Rows and rows of organic vegetables, fruit, and flowers surround the Farm Stand itself, a charming building with wooden floors and a wide veranda. Buckets of flowers line the path to the entrance, and a woodchip path leads to a children's garden, a pick your own herb garden, and a chamomile-carpeted, river-rock labyrinth.

To enrich the organic experience, we added America's third certified organic kitchen to the Farm Stand in July 2003. Our Organic Kitchen features an all-organic salad bar and fresh organic soups, prepared meals, and bakery treats, as well as organic coffees, teas, and smoothies. Just outside the Farm Stand there's a sunny picnic area where people enjoy food from the Organic Kitchen, if they're not making their way home with their family's evening meal. Our Farm Stand customers have embraced the farm-fresh gourmet theme of the menu, which changes seasonally to showcase freshly harvested produce at its peak. Many of the recipes in this book were developed in the Organic Kitchen.

An old Ford flatbed holds organic flowers outside of our Farm Stand.

Because of the time and expense involved in the certification process, there are very few certified organic restaurants in the United States. For us, the commitment is important. Our customers have confidence that every dish is made with organic ingredients. And the Organic Kitchen is a natural extension of our passion to spread the benefits of organic food.

The Farm Stand has evolved organically, so to speak, over the years through suggestions from customers and our own experiences. Take the herb garden, for example. We always seemed to be either out of a particular herb that someone was looking for or stocking way too much of ones that people suddenly weren't buying. So we created a pick your own herb garden where people can snip just the amount they need from the dozens of herb varieties. There are several kinds of basil, chamomile, lemon verbena, rosemary—almost any herb you can think of is growing in the garden.

Our Saturday events, held during the warmer months, include workshops, walks, and other ways to entertain and educate our visitors and stir the connection between the land and food that I had felt at those country farm stands so long ago. You can walk with "Farmer Mark" (Mark Marino, who manages our Carmel Valley farm) through the fields on Harvest Walks, filling baskets with produce you pick yourself, while learning about what you're harvesting—how it was grown and how to prepare it.

Aerial photo of our organic corn maze.

Kids on a farm tour display a big head of just-picked red leaf lettuce.

Sometimes customer suggestions lead to something new. In one case, it was a popular demand by my own family and friends. They loved the ginger snaps and maple almond granola I made at home—in fact, I had to bake several batches a week just to keep everyone satisfied. I thought I'd share them with our customers (not to mention save myself hours in the kitchen), so when we opened the Farm Stand, I hired a local bakery to make them for us. Our family favorites blossomed into local favorites, which you can now order on our Web site or make yourself from the recipes in this book. Warning: They can both become addictive.

Drew and I are deeply committed to spreading the organic message to the next generation, so we wanted our Farm Stand to be a special place for kids, whether they visit the children's garden, river rock labyrinth, or just help their parents shop for dinner. Each year, hundreds of kids on school trips roam through the fields and dig in the dirt, taste fresh vegetables, hunt for good bugs (beneficial insects) and learn about organic farming. Possibly the most popular season for kids of any age is autumn, when they scour the pumpkin patch and wander through our "a-maze-ing" corn maze.

Even with all the activities and shelves of organic products, crafts, and gifts to tempt visitors, the Farm Stand's foundation will always be our fresh organically grown produce. And the

Organic Kitchen chefs get much of their inspiration from the bounty that blooms just outside.

My own urge to make something out of a bumper crop always ends up on our dinner table or in jars or in our freezer. A glance at basil drooping under its own weight inspires me to blend batches of pesto. A tree covered with apples sends me to the kitchen to make an apple crisp, and when the thickets are ripe with raspberries . . . don't even get me started.

Different inspirations help create other Organic Kitchen recipes. Several talented chefs have interpreted our harvest in their unique ways, and it's always a treat when we bring home some of their dishes. I've included our family favorites in this book—mine is the Grilled Tahini Chicken with Eggplant and Mushrooms over Soba Noodles, and Drew's choice is Farm Stand Spinach Cannelloni.

There are still more sources for Organic Kitchen recipes. An idea may come from taking a Harvest Walk and just seeing which plants are in season at the time. Sometimes I'll run across a recipe in a magazine and tinker with it to fit my taste. Or I'll ask the Kitchen to try a new spin on an old standby. I love muffins, and the Organic Kitchen makes delicious carrot cake, so Carrot Cake Muffins are now one of our most popular treats.

I hope you will discover your own favorites from the array of tastes and treats in this book. And come visit the Farm Stand in person if you're ever near Carmel Valley. The Farm Stand and its Organic Kitchen have become an integral part of our lives and our community. In a way, the Farm Stand completes the circle we began right down the road and perfectly fulfills the name we chose for our farm—binding us to the land, to the sustenance that comes from it, and ultimately, to each other.

Here I am with a big basket of fresh-picked apples, probably heading off to bake a crisp . . .

Four Food Choices I Live By

I strongly believe that the food I buy to serve in my home should support the health of my family and our environment. While I'm usually flexible, these are the four food choices that I try not to compromise on.

1. I refuse to buy products containing partially hydrogenated oils. Many of the nonorganic processed foods on the grocery shelves—especially baked goods, breakfast cereals, and snack foods—contain partially hydrogenated oils. These processed oils extend the shelf life of the products that contain them. Partially hydrogenated oils are also what make most margarines and vegetable shortenings solid. The bad news is that partially hydrogenated oils are the main source of trans fatty acids (or trans fats) in our diet. Research shows that trans fats have harmful effects on cholesterol levels and increase the risk of heart disease. They may also harm the immune system and cell membranes, increasing the risk of inflammation and cancer. The good news is that the FDA now requires manufacturers to list trans fats on nutrition labels for products packaged for retail sale, making it easier to avoid them. Unfortunately, the law does not require that trans fat levels be disclosed for food-service products, such as baked goods and movie theater popcorn, both of which often contain this unhealthy fat.

2. I refuse to buy conventional strawberries. The one conventional produce item I absolutely won't buy is strawberries. Government reports show that conventional strawberries are one of the produce items most likely to have pesticide residues. Before conventional strawberry fields are planted, they are often fumigated with the destructive chemical methyl bromide. This pesticide is linked to neurological disorders, respiratory problems, and cancer in the farmworkers and people who live close to the fields. As if that weren't bad enough, methyl bromide seriously depletes the ozone layer, making it one of the worst pesticides for our planet. Fortunately, many people worldwide are working to eliminate its use.

3. Whenever possible, I only buy meats, poultry, and dairy products from livestock that has been humanely raised without antibiotics or added growth hormones. Animals raised in crowded conditions are more likely to get sick, so they are routinely given antibiotics as a preventative measure. This overuse has created antibiotic-resistant bacteria, making human and animal illnesses caused by these bacteria harder to treat. Additionally, many conventionally raised cows and sheep are fed natural and synthetic growth hormones, which are linked to some cancers. The most publicized bovine growth hormone is called rBST or rBGH and is used to increase milk production in dairy cows. Fortunately, more and more concerned farmers are raising livestock in humane conditions without antibiotics or added growth hormones. You can find their products labeled "raised without antibiotics," "no hormones administered," "rBGH-free," or "rBST-free." I buy organic meat, poultry, and dairy whenever it's available, because in addition to being free of antibiotics and growth hormones, organic livestock is fed organic feed.

4. I don't buy products sweetened with artificial sweeteners. The safety of artificial sweeteners has long been a subject of debate. Here, I go with my gut instinct and stay far away from them. I don't ever buy or drink diet sodas or chew sugar-free gum. I believe that if you can't afford the calories, it's much healthier to train your palate to enjoy unsweetened beverages.

Why We're Committed to Organic Foods and Farming

When we started Earthbound Farm in 1984, most people thought organic farming was "hippie farming"—it might work on a small plot of land, but it could never be relied on to feed the world. Today, Drew and I feel very proud that we have helped prove that organic farming is definitely viable on a large scale. Earthbound Farm has demonstrated that successful farming does not require an arsenal of potentially dangerous chemicals. We've combined time-honored organic farming techniques with the latest agricultural technology. And the result is organic produce that is not only affordable but also high quality—as good, if not better, than its conventional counterparts.

When farmers began routinely using powerful synthetic pesticides and fertilizers, these chemicals revolutionized agriculture, improving yields and significantly reducing crop loss to pests. However, we've come to see that conventional farming is far from perfect. Over time, pests have become more resistant to pesticides, requiring more and stronger chemicals. Soil quality has deteriorated, requiring more synthetic fertilizers. And diseases have become more prevalent, requiring the regular application of soil fumigants. It's a chemical treadmill that is not only unhealthy for people and the environment,

it's also becoming less effective and more and more costly for conventional farmers. As an increasing number of us seek to protect our health from the effects of too many chemicals in our air, water, and food supply, many of us are thrilled to have organic options readily available.

Red chard thrives in our rich organic soil.

A Healthy Choice for All

Avoiding even small amounts of dangerous chemicals whenever possible is a good idea for everyone. And for children, the benefits of organic foods are even more important because of their specific nutritional needs and vulnerabilities. Children are at a greater risk from some pesticides for several reasons. Their internal organs are still developing and maturing; their enzymatic, metabolic, and immune systems may provide less natural protection than those of an adult. Plus, they eat more food per

Radicchio, its deeply-colored leaves marbled with bold white veins.

pound of body weight than adults. That means they're also eating proportionally more of whatever is on or in their food. On average, children are exposed to about five different pesticides every day through food and drinking water.

The USDA's own Pesticide Data Program (PDP) has analyzed pesticides in nearly 200,000 samples of food since 1993, focusing on the foods most often consumed by children. While the program has found measurable pesticide residues on 75 to 80 percent of the conventional produce tested, it found residues on 90 percent or more of the conventional apples, peaches, pears, and strawberries, all commonly consumed by children. And there's new scientific evidence showing that these pesticides are present inside the womb and even in the umbilical cord blood of newborns.

Drew's and my instinctive aversion to chemicals when we first started farming seems right, although there's not much conclusive research available about the effects that small amounts of powerful chemicals might have on people. There is, however, a growing body of animal research. It suggests that even minute traces of some chemicals can have harmful effects.

Choosing organic food is a logical way to reduce your family's exposure to chemicals. As bestselling author and Harvard-trained physician Dr. Andrew Weil wrote, "The pesticides in use on conventional crops are suspect. The bottom line is: They can't be good for us. The only question is, *How bad are they?* I'm afraid the answer might be pretty bad. The pesticides we use against insects,

Jeffrey (age 4) with an armload of just-picked baby root vegetables.

SERVING AS A CATALYST FOR POSITIVE CHANGE

Earthbound Farm wants nothing less than to help change the way America farms and the way America eats. Our land base has grown to more than 30,000 acres of organic farmland—much of which has made the transition from conventional to organic farming. Annually, Earthbound Farm's organic farming has a notable impact on the environment. In 2006 alone, Earthbound Farm's organic farming practices will have

■ eliminated the use of 313,000 pounds of toxic and persistent pesticides.

■ conserved nearly 1,600,000 gallons of petroleum by not using petroleum-based pesticides and fertilizers.

■ avoided the use of nearly 10,000,000 pounds of synthetic fertilizers.

And it gets even better: Organic farming can help slow global warming! According to a Rodale Institute study, organic farming actually helps curb the ozone-depleting greenhouse gases that cause global warming. The soils on organic farms are much higher in organic matter, which pulls carbon dioxide (a greenhouse gas) out of the atmosphere and holds it in the soil. The conventional farming fields studied have not been shown to have this effect. Based on our 2006 farming acreage, Earthbound Farm's organic fields are removing more than 55,000 tons of carbon dioxide from the atmosphere each year— equal to taking approximately 11,000 cars off the road.

worms, and microorganisms are poisons, and most of them are poisons for us as well as the pests."

A Healthier Choice for Our Environment

Most people choose organic food to protect their health. One important aspect of personal health that often is not factored into the equation is our natural environment. But it matters. If the environment is polluted or thrown out of balance, then our health will unavoidably be at risk, so it's important to understand just how much kinder organic farming is to the environment.

Organic farming keeps toxic and persistent chemicals out of the air, water, and soil. It promotes a healthy, balanced ecosystem and encourages biodiversity while also helping to reduce soil erosion. It's safer for the people who farm the land, as well as for the homes, schools, and businesses nearby.

Some of the biggest environmental problems caused by conventional farming are topsoil erosion and toxic runoff. One third of our nation's topsoil has eroded due to modern industrialized farming practices. And the pesticide- and fertilizer-heavy runoff from farmland into rivers, lakes, and streams takes a toll on wildlife. A recent study conducted by Stanford University found that intensification of agricultural production in the last sixty years has resulted in substantial nitrogen pollution and ecological damage. Water supplies have been contaminated, creating adverse health effects, and biological "dead zones" have been created at the mouths of major rivers, which dump the nitrogen fertilizer

A field of romaine is interplanted with rows of alyssum, which attracts beneficial insects that help to keep pest insects in check.

runoff into the ocean (the mouth of the Mississippi is a good example, where runoff has had a devastating impact on the ocean environment). The use of organic fertilizers reduces these adverse effects.

The Foundation of Organic Farming

Many people think of organic in terms of what it doesn't have: no pesticides, no hormones, no genetically modified organisms (GMOs). And while that's all true, it's only a part of the story. A prerequisite for successful organic farming is the building of fertile, nutrient-rich soil to grow healthy plants that are more resistant to disease. Instead of becoming more depleted the more it's farmed, organic soil becomes healthier and richer year after year. And because we don't use toxic chemicals that linger in the environment for years, our soil is full of microorganisms and earthworms that keep plants healthy and less susceptible to disease.

Whether farming on our small 60-acre farm in Carmel Valley or on our largest farm of 680 acres in King City, California, Earthbound Farm uses the same methods, creating a farming environment that complements the local ecology and protects the land, air, and water from exposure to agricultural chemicals. By focusing so intently on the soil, the fertility of our fields increases each year. Here are some of the important practices that organic farmers use to build that strong foundation of healthy soil.

Compost. We use good compost to nourish our crops, recycling plant and sometimes animal waste materials and turning them into nature's best plant food, which contains high-quality organic matter and beneficial microorganisms. Microorganisms (bacteria, fungi, nematodes, protozoa) in the soil break down the raw components of compost, which generates heat. Before compost can be applied to a field, it must reach and maintain an internal temperature of 131° to 149 °F for at least five days

12 Fruits & Vegetables it Is Important to Buy Organically

These twelve produce items consistently have the highest pesticide residues when tested by the USDA and the FDA.

Fruits

Apples

Cherries

Imported grapes

Nectarines

Peaches

Pears

Strawberries

Vegetables

Carrots

Celery

Potatoes

Spinach

Sweet bell peppers

USDA ORGANIC CERTIFICATION

On October 21, 2002, the United States Department of Agriculture (USDA) launched its National Organic Program (NOP). The NOP standards govern organic certification of farming and processing operations, detailing the methods, practices, and substances that can be used in producing and handling organic crops. It also created a uniform definition of organic foods with standardized product labeling guidelines (see box, facing page). Prior to the establishment of the NOP, there was no consistent definition of the term "organic," only a network of private and public organic certification agencies with varying standards. The establishment of the USDA program assures the integrity of the organic label for consumers of organic food. When you buy food labeled as "organic," you can be sure that it was produced using strict organic production and handling methods that were certified by an accredited USDA certifying agency. In addition to ensuring that domestically produced organic products have met these stringent standards, the USDA requires that in order to be sold in the United States

as organic, any food produced overseas must be certified by a USDA-approved certifier, in accordance with the same stringent standards.

Today, in the simplest terms, food that meets the organic standards has been grown and produced with:

■ no harmful conventional pesticides.

■ no fertilizers made with synthetic ingredients or sewage sludge.

■ no genetically modified organisms (GMOs).

■ no ionizing radiation.

■ clear and appropriate buffers between organic fields and nearby conventional farms.

■ specific labeling and record keeping to ensure organic integrity.

■ a three-year transition period for fields that have been farmed conventionally.

■ an annual inspection by a USDA-accredited independent organic certifier.

USDA ORGANIC LABELING RULES

To help consumers identify which products have been grown or produced in accordance with the National Organic Program (NOP) standards, the USDA developed these important labeling categories.

Products that may bear the USDA Organic Seal:

■ **100 PERCENT ORGANIC**

■ **ORGANIC:** Made with 95 percent organic ingredients

Products that may not bear the seal, but contain organic ingredients:

■ **MADE WITH ORGANIC INGREDIENTS:** The product must contain at least 70 percent organic ingredients. "Made with organic corn," for example, might be on the display panel of tortilla chips made with organic corn, but nothing else organic.

■ If a product contains less than 70 percent organic ingredients, the ingredient list may denote which products are organic, but there can be no organic claim on the display panel.

---

to kill any disease-causing bacteria and weed seeds it may contain.

Cover crops. A cover crop is grown to enrich the soil, not to sell. Austrian field peas, bell beans, and vetch are all great cover crops because they pull nitrogen out of the atmosphere and fix it in the soil while they are growing. When the crops have matured, we till them under, which adds even more organic matter to the soil so plants can easily absorb nutrients.

Crop rotation. An important aspect of organic farming is crop rotation. Rather than planting the same crop over and over in the same place, we rotate what we grow in a given field. Every crop needs its own special set of nutrients from the soil. When the same crop is repeatedly planted in the same place, the nutrients that a particular crop needs become used up. So we rotate crops as much as possible, choosing crops with nutritional needs that complement each other, thus keeping the soil healthy and nutrient rich.

Natural fertilizers. When we fertilize our crops, we add either natural minerals or fertilizers, such as fish emulsion, to make more nutrients available for the plants to absorb while they grow. This plant food is absorbed very slowly and steadily, as opposed to the quick burst of nitrogen provided by the synthetic, petroleum-based fertilizers used in conventional farming. Slower growth, the result of the slower absorption of nutrients, creates stronger plants and, according to recent university research, enhances nutritional content in some crops.

Because of all this effort, even someone with no farming experience will notice a big difference between a handful of soil from an organic farm and a handful of soil from a conventional farm. Organic soil's texture, color, and even smell reveal an appealing richness.

Farmer Mark Marino is pleased with his perfect baby carrots.

The Challenges of Farming

Organic farmers deal with same challenges common to all farmers—such as pests, weeds, and diseases—without the use of strong agricultural chemicals. In addition to our healthy soils, here are some ways we try to protect our crops.

Insects. Our main strategy in combating harmful pests is to practice avoidance. We plant the crops where we don't expect the insects to be. But when pest insects inevitably catch up, we build up populations of beneficial insects that prey on the pests that eat our crops. Some of our favorite "beneficials" are ladybugs, hover flies, lacewings, and damsel bugs. To attract the beneficials, we plant a certain percentage of our fields with flowers that provide a very nice home for these beneficials. We also plant trap crops—attractive plants that lure pest insects away from the crops we want to sell. Of course, this reduces the amount of land planted with cash crops and is one of the reasons organic farming is more costly than conventional farming.

A farmer with rainbow chard.

Finally, crop rotation helps us stay one step ahead of the pests, too. If we keep moving crops, the pests are less likely to concentrate in one area long enough to damage them.

For the most part, the beneficials do a great job. Still, it can be nerve-racking as the farmer waits for nature to take its course. Imagine standing in the middle of a field of young romaine lettuce—a huge part of your income—and seeing that it's covered with aphids. Usually after a week or so, the beneficials have done their job, the aphids are gone, and the crop is ready to harvest. But when the beneficials don't win, the farmer loses, too, and the crop must be tilled rather than sold.

Weeds. Controlling weeds without herbicides takes a lot of time and is very costly. It costs conventional farmers a lot less to use herbicidal weed killers than organic farmers spend on more labor-intensive weed control methods.

One of the ways we tackle weeds is preirrigation: We go into a field and water it, before we plant it, so the weed

ADDITIONAL ORGANIC RESOURCES

For details about the National Organic Program standards (all five-hundred plus pages), visit the NOP Web site at: www.ams.usda.gov/nop/indexIE.htm

For summaries of scientific research related to organic farming and food, visit The Organic Center Web site, www.organiccenter.org

Natural Resources Defense Council: www.nrdc.org

Children's Health Environmental Coalition: www.checnet.org

Environmental Working Group's food information site: www.foodnews.org

seeds germinate. When they produce tiny sprouts, we can use a propane-torch flame-weeder to burn the weed shoots or till them under with a tractor. Cover crops also help stifle weed growth. Once the crop is growing in the field, we rely primarily on tractor cultivation and hand weeding. Like many things in organic agriculture, the longer the land is farmed, the more weed control improves. By using all these techniques, eventually the weed population starts to decline.

Diseases. Since organic farmers don't use powerful chemicals like fungicides and fumigants to combat diseases, we practice preventative measures, which we think are the best medicine anyway. Our best defense against plant diseases goes back to the foundation of organic farming. Healthy soils create conditions that discourage the development of devastating plant diseases. And crop rotation helps keep the crops out of the grasp of diseases, too. If we keep moving crops, the diseases that are attracted to certain crops won't build up in the fields.

We originally embraced organic farming because of its many benefits for the health of people and the environment. Today, we're even more committed to organic food and farming and we're proud to be the largest grower of organic produce in the world. Our mission is to bring the benefits of organic food to as many people as possible and to serve as a catalyst for positive change. We hope this cookbook helps us to further that mission by sparking your interest in the many benefits of choosing organic food, including its exceptionally delicious flavors.

Harvesting dinosaur kale.

WHY AN ORGANIC COOKBOOK?

Eating organically is so much easier today than it was twenty years ago. And this cookbook was written to show you just how easy. The vast majority of ingredients used in these recipes are available organically—and you may be surprised by how wide and varied the range is. Every day, new organic products are being added to the grocery shelves. For example, when we began writing this cookbook, organic buttermilk was not yet available, but by the time we were a year into our recipe development, it was on the market. More and more people are discovering the great taste and health benefits of organic food, and purchases of organic products are soaring. Manufacturers are rushing to satisfy consumer demand, so even if you don't find an organic ingredient today, keep an eye out for new arrivals.

Of course, any of these dishes will be delicious made with conventional ingredients, but even one change, like choosing organic butter for your fresh corn on the cob, is a big step in the right direction. Here you'll find information and resources that will allow you to make more informed decisions about the food you buy and serve your family. Small changes in your food choices can make a big difference. Every time you choose organic, you are reducing your exposure to toxic pesticides, supporting a cleaner environment, and treating yourself to the most delicious food available. That's why organic is truly food to live by!

Food
to Live
By

Chapter 1

It All Began with Raspberries

I have a soft spot in my heart for raspberries. The ruby berries were the first crop my husband, Drew, and I ever grew, and they will always be one of my favorite fruits. When perfectly ripe, raspberries have a unique sweet-tart taste and delicate texture that seem to melt in your mouth. I'm so devoted to raspberries, we've given them a chapter of their own.

During our first few years, Drew and I spent June through October harvesting raspberries from dawn until dusk. For our fledgling roadside stand to be successful, we had to find every ripe berry, carefully lifting each thorny branch to discover any that were hiding underneath the leaves. It takes patient, gentle hands to pick the soft berries without crushing them. Even a half-pint basket fills slowly when the berries are so small.

I was also teaching myself how to cook during these early years. Raspberries were often my main ingredient as I looked for creative ways to avoid wasting a single one. Although a few of my cooking experiments were disasters, some turned out to be fabulous, and I continue to make them to this day.

Corn muffins made with raspberries were one of my biggest successes. Customers stopping at our stand for a basket of berries would buy my freshly baked muffins to enjoy on the way home. Decades later, some of those early customers still reminisce about the muffins' moist, natural sweetness. Raspberry jam was another best-seller that I continue to make every year for my family. Raspberries have so much natural pectin that all they need is sugar and low, slow cooking to turn the fruit into a jam we enjoy all year long.

Of course, raspberries are equally at home on a dessert plate. For a special event, our friend Sarah's Chocolate Soufflés with Raspberry Sauce is our all-time favorite. Or for an easy, healthy treat, my mom's recipe for frozen raspberry yogurt churns out rosy pink with lovely berry bits.

Fresh, ripe raspberries are beautiful, fragrant, and flavorful.

Facing Page:
A gorgeous mix of red and yellow raspberries.

Our original raspberry stand is long gone, but three rows of raspberry bushes still grow behind our house. Now berry picking is a way to relax with my family after work. Even our dog, Jack, joins us. He seems to be able to smell which berries are ripe and has taught himself to pull the berries off the low-hanging branches with his tongue and eat them.

Some of our bushes were transplanted to the Carmel Valley fields beside our Farm Stand, where they continue to thrive. After all these years, our loyal customers still buy baskets of our organic raspberries and a muffin from the Farm Stand's Organic Kitchen to nibble on the road. I hope you'll enjoy our raspberry muffins as much as they do and discover other fresh ideas for bringing this succulent berry into your own life.

Jack, our dog, enjoys raspberries as much as we do.

Raspberry Corn Muffins

Drew and I grew and sold organic raspberries during our early farming years, and I often baked raspberry muffins using any berries we had left over. Through my kitchen window, I could see customers driving up to our raspberry stand, and I'd quickly wash the flour from my hands before going outside to greet them. If their timing was right, in addition to baskets of fresh raspberries, they could buy a still-warm, invitingly moist corn muffin, loaded with fresh raspberries, to eat on the way home. **MAKES 12 STANDARD-SIZE MUFFINS**

Butter for greasing the muffin cups
   (unless using cupcake liners)
1¹/₂ cups unbleached, all-purpose flour
1 cup finely ground yellow cornmeal
1 tablespoon baking powder
¹/₂ teaspoon baking soda
¹/₂ teaspoon salt
1 teaspoon ground cinnamon
2 large eggs
¹/₂ cup honey
¹/₄ cup sugar
1 cup buttermilk
6 tablespoons (³/₄ stick) unsalted butter,
   melted
1 half-pint (about 1¹/₄ cups) fresh
   raspberries or frozen (unthawed)
   unsweetened raspberries

1. Position a rack in the center of the oven and preheat the oven to 400°F. Butter 12 standard-size muffin cups or line them with cupcake liners.

2. Place the flour, cornmeal, baking powder, baking soda, salt, and cinnamon in a large bowl and whisk to combine well.

3. Place the eggs, honey, sugar, buttermilk, and melted butter in a small bowl and whisk to combine well. Add the egg mixture to the flour mixture and stir with a rubber spatula until just combined. Gently fold in the raspberries. Do not overmix the batter or the muffins will be tough. Spoon the batter into the prepared muffin cups, filling them almost to the brim.

4. Bake the muffins until they are golden brown and a toothpick inserted in the center of one comes out clean, 20 to 25 minutes.

5. Place the muffin pan on a wire rack and let the muffins cool for about 10 minutes. Remove the muffins from the pan and serve warm. The muffins taste best the day they are made but, if necessary, they can be stored in an airtight container for up to 2 days. Reheat them in a microwave for about 10 seconds or in a preheated 350°F oven for 5 to 10 minutes.

Freezing Farm-Fresh Berries

Sometimes too much of a good thing is great! If you have more berries than you can eat, freeze them. Frozen raspberries, strawberries, or blueberries are wonderful for making smoothies, baked goods, or ice cream year round. To freeze your own berries, spread them in a single layer on a baking sheet lined with paper towels, and place them in the freezer. When the berries are frozen solid, transfer them to a freezer bag or airtight container. The berries will remain loose instead of freezing into a solid mass, so you can scoop out just the amount you need.

Picking perfect ripe and juicy red raspberries.

Whole Wheat Pastry Flour

Whole wheat flour is more nutritious and has more fiber than white flour because the bran and germ are not removed during milling. However, baking with regular whole wheat flour produces baked goods that are heavier and more dense than those made with white all-purpose flour. The good news is that whole wheat pastry flour is becoming more widely available. While it still isn't as light as all-purpose white flour, it is close in texture and taste, making it appropriate for baking all but the most delicate pastries, quick breads, and cakes.

Bees pollinate the lupin at our Carmel Valley farm.

Raspberry Pecan Muffins

If you want a morning sweet, muffins are delicious, and healthier than most breakfast pastries. These raspberry and pecan muffins, flecked with golden citrus zest, are especially delicate, using canola oil as a lighter alternative to butter. In fact, they are so light, you may eat two before you realize it. **MAKES 12 STANDARD-SIZE MUFFINS**

Butter, for greasing the muffin cups
    (unless using cupcake liners)
1 1/2 cups whole wheat pastry flour
    (see sidebar, this page) or unbleached
    all-purpose flour
3/4 cup sugar, plus 1 tablespoon for
    topping
2 teaspoons baking powder
1/2 teaspoon baking soda
1/2 teaspoon salt
1 large egg
1 cup buttermilk
1/4 cup canola oil
1 teaspoon grated lemon or orange zest
    (see box, page 14)
2/3 cup (from 1 half-pint) fresh
    raspberries or frozen (unthawed)
    unsweetened raspberries
1/4 cup chopped pecans, toasted
    (see box, page 98)

1. Position a rack in the center of the oven and preheat the oven to 375°F. Butter 12 standard-size muffin cups or line them with cupcake liners.

2. Place the flour, 3/4 cup of sugar, baking powder, baking soda, and salt in a large bowl and whisk to combine well.

3. Place the egg, buttermilk, oil, and zest in a small bowl and whisk to combine well. Add the egg mixture to the flour mixture and stir with a rubber spatula until just combined. Gently fold in the raspberries and pecans. Do not overmix the batter or the muffins will be tough. Spoon the batter into the prepared muffin cups, filling them two-thirds full. Sprinkle the remaining 1 tablespoon of sugar evenly over the batter.

4. Bake the muffins until they are golden brown and a toothpick inserted in the center of one comes out clean, 20 to 25 minutes.

5. Place the muffin pan on a wire rack and let the muffins cool for about 10 minutes. If you are not serving the muffins immediately, remove them from the pan and let them finish cooling on the rack. The muffins taste best the day they are made but, if necessary, they can be stored in an airtight container for up to 2 days. If desired, reheat them in a microwave for about 10 seconds or in a preheated 350°F oven for 5 to 10 minutes.

Raspberry Cream Scones

You'll love these tender and flaky scones, with just a whisper of almond extract. The trick to making a tender scone is a light touch: Handle the dough as little as possible. You can use this basic recipe to create your own signature scones by substituting a total of two-thirds of a cup of other fruits or nuts for the raspberries. Experiment with your favorites—fresh blueberries or strawberries, chopped nuts, or dried fruits like apricots, cranberries, or cherries are all good. If you prefer vanilla extract, by all means, substitute it for the almond. Or, use orange zest instead of lemon. There's no limit to the flavor combinations you can create. Scones freeze well, so consider making a double batch (see Note, page 8). **MAKES 6 SCONES**

Any kind of fresh berries are delicious in these scones.

Note: If you only need a few scones, freeze the extra dough. Place them unbaked and unglazed on a baking sheet lined with parchment paper or waxed paper, then put them in the freezer. When frozen solid, transfer the scones to a plastic bag or airtight container. The night before you want to serve them, place the scones on a baking sheet in the refrigerator to thaw. Glaze and bake the scones according to Steps 5 to 7. If the scones are cooler than room temperature when you put them in the oven, add a few additional minutes to the baking time.

**Butter for greasing the baking sheet
   (unless using parchment paper)
2 cups unbleached all-purpose flour
$^1/_3$ cup sugar, plus 2 tablespoons
   for topping
1 tablespoon baking powder
2 teaspoons grated lemon zest
   (see box, page 14)
$^1/_4$ teaspoon salt
4 tablespoons ($^1/_2$ stick) unsalted
   butter, cut into bits and chilled
1 large egg
$^1/_2$ cup heavy (whipping) cream,
   plus 2 tablespoons for the glaze
1 teaspoon pure almond extract
$^3/_4$ cup (from 1 half-pint) fresh
   raspberries or frozen (unthawed)
   unsweetened raspberries**

1. Position a rack in the center of the oven and preheat the oven to 400° F. Lightly butter a baking sheet or line it with parchment paper.

2. Place the flour, $^1/_3$ cup of sugar, baking powder, lemon zest, and salt in a large bowl and whisk to combine well. Add the chilled butter. Using a pastry blender, 2 knives, or your fingers, blend the butter into the mixture until it is crumbly and well combined.

3. Place the egg, cream, and almond extract in a small bowl and whisk to combine well. Add the egg mixture to the flour mixture and stir with a rubber spatula until just barely combined. Gently fold in the raspberries. Do not overmix the dough or the scones will be tough.

4. Turn out the dough, along with any loose dry bits, onto a lightly floured work surface and pat into a disk about 1½ inches thick. Cut the dough with a

Freshly baked scones or cookies pair perfectly with freshly brewed tea.

knife into 6 pie-shaped wedges and place them on the prepared baking sheet.

5. Brush the scones with the remaining 2 tablespoons of cream and sprinkle them with the remaining 2 tablespoons of sugar.

6. Bake the scones until they are golden brown and firm to the touch, 15 to 20 minutes.

7. Place the baking sheet on a wire rack and let the scones cool for about 10 minutes. Serve the scones warm or at room temperature. The scones taste best the day they are made but, if necessary, they can be stored in an airtight container for up to 2 days. Reheat them in a microwave for about 10 seconds or in a preheated 350°F oven for 5 to 10 minutes.

Favorite Raspberry Jam

When summertime brings more raspberries than my family can possibly eat fresh, I know it's time to make jam. I put up dozens of jars that we'll enjoy for months to come. On jam-making days, the whole family helps pick berries. It's a time-consuming process because raspberries are so small and delicate, so the more hands the better. In my kitchen, I transform the berries into a luscious, thick jam that just can't be compared to store-bought versions. After filling the jars, I pour the jam that's left over into a bowl for everyone to enjoy. Fresh and still warm, it's delicious on bread or by the spoonful. Throughout the year, we enjoy its summery burst of flavor with every jar we open.

Because raspberries have more natural pectin than strawberries and blueberries, only sugar and slow cooking are needed for them to thicken into jam. This recipe is very easy, and it can be multiplied or divided depending on the amount of berries you have available. **MAKES ABOUT 8 HALF-PINTS OR 4 PINTS**

Raspberry jam helps preserve a taste of summer for year-round enjoyment.

16 cups (about 13 half-pints)
    fresh raspberries
8 cups sugar

1. Place the berries and sugar in a large, heavy-bottomed pot and bring to a simmer over medium-high heat. Reduce the heat to low and slowly simmer, uncovered, stirring frequently, until the jam is thick, about 50 minutes. For seedless jam, carefully pass the hot jam through a sieve, 1 to 2 cups at a time, pressing down gently on it with a wooden spoon or spatula to extract all the jam.

Scrape out the seeds before adding more jam. Repeat until all of the jam has been strained.

2. Spoon the hot jam into sterilized canning jars and seal them following the manufacturer's directions. You will need 8 half-pint or 4 pint jars. If you are not using sealed canning jars, let the jam cool completely and transfer it to clean containers with tight-fitting lids. The containers of jam will keep, covered and refrigerated, for up to 2 months.

A rainbow of sweet summer berries: blackberries, Red Heritage raspberries, Kiwi Gold (blush) raspberries, and Anne (golden) raspberries.

Apricot Raspberry Jam

Raspberry jam becomes even more luscious when there are silky bits of apricot mixed in. The color of this jam is spectacular, with the subtle golden glow of the stone fruit tinted by the ruby red berries. The apricot skins give the jam a nice texture, so don't peel organic ones. **MAKES ABOUT 7 HALF-PINTS**

1½ pounds ripe apricots, preferably
    Blenheim, pitted and finely chopped
    (about 3 cups)
6 cups (about 5 half-pints) fresh
    raspberries
1 tablespoon fresh lemon juice
1 box (1¾ ounces) powdered fruit
    pectin (such as Sure-Jell)
4¼ cups sugar

1. Place the apricots, raspberries, and lemon juice in a large, heavy-bottomed, nonreactive pot and bring to a boil over high heat.

2. Add the pectin and stir to blend thoroughly. Add the sugar and, while stirring constantly, allow the jam to come to a full rolling boil. Cook the jam until it thickens, about 1 minute.

3. Remove the jam from the heat and skim off any foam. Spoon the hot jam into sterilized canning jars and seal them following the manufacturer's directions. You will need 7 half-pint jars. If you are not using sealed canning jars, allow the jam to cool completely and transfer it to clean containers with tight-fitting lids. The containers of jam will keep, covered and refrigerated, for up to 2 months.

Cornmeal Breakfast Pancakes
with Raspberry Maple Syrup

The orange and cinnamon in these surprisingly delicate cornmeal pancakes make them a special treat. Whipping the egg whites is the secret to making these pancakes so light. They are more time-consuming than the Banana Walnut Pancakes (see page 284), so save these for a lazy weekend morning treat. The pancakes are just sturdy enough to hold a few toasted nuts or thinly sliced strawberries or banana. Sprinkle some nuts or fruit onto the batter once you pour the pancakes on the griddle and flip the pancakes carefully. **MAKES ABOUT 12 PANCAKES**

$^3/_4$ cup unbleached all-purpose flour
$^1/_2$ cup finely ground yellow cornmeal
$^1/_3$ cup sugar
$^1/_2$ teaspoon baking powder
$^1/_2$ teaspoon baking soda
$^1/_4$ teaspoon freshly grated nutmeg or
    ground nutmeg
$^1/_4$ teaspoon ground cinnamon
$^1/_8$ teaspoon salt
2 teaspoons finely grated orange zest
    (see box, page 14)
$^1/_4$ cup fresh orange juice
2 large eggs, separated
$^1/_3$ cup buttermilk
3 tablespoons canola oil, plus more for
    brushing the griddle
Raspberry Maple Syrup (recipe follows)

1. Preheat the oven to 200°F and place serving plates on the rack to warm.

2. Place the flour, cornmeal, sugar, baking powder, baking soda, nutmeg, cinnamon, salt, and orange zest in a large bowl and whisk to combine.

3. Place the orange juice, egg yolks, buttermilk, and oil in a medium-size bowl and whisk to combine well.

4. Beat the egg whites with an electric mixer at high speed until they form soft peaks, 3 to 4 minutes. Or, beat the egg whites by hand in a metal bowl; it may take longer for soft peaks to form.

5. Pour the buttermilk mixture into the flour mixture and stir with a rubber spatula until just combined. Fold in the egg whites. Do not overmix or the batter will deflate.

6. Heat a griddle or large skillet over medium-low heat until a few drops of water sizzle when splashed on the surface.

7. Brush some oil on the griddle. Spoon the batter onto the griddle to form pancakes that are about 3 inches in diameter. Spread the batter a bit with the back of the spoon so the batter is even and cook the pancakes until small bubbles begin to appear on the surface, $1^1/_2$ to 2 minutes.

8. Carefully flip the pancakes and cook until the other side is brown, $1^1/_2$ to 2 minutes. Transfer the pancakes to a warmed plate and serve with warm

Raspberry Maple Syrup. Of course, the pancakes taste best hot off the griddle, but they can be held for up to 15 minutes in the warm oven if needed.

Raspberry Maple Syrup

*P*ure maple syrup flavored with raspberries is delicious on pancakes, but it's just as yummy as a topping for ice cream or yogurt. Plus, it's so easy to make that you hardly need a recipe. The proportion of berries to syrup is just a suggestion—use more or less based on what you have on hand. Blueberries, strawberries, or blackberries can be substituted for the raspberries, or you can create your own mixed-berry blend. **MAKES ABOUT 1¹/₂ CUPS**

    1 cup pure maple syrup
    1¹/₄ cups (about 1 half-pint) fresh raspberries or frozen (unthawed or thawed) unsweetened raspberries

1. Place the syrup and raspberries in a small saucepan and bring to a simmer over medium heat. Cook, stirring occasionally and crushing the berries with the back of a wooden spoon, until the syrup is warmed through, about 5 minutes.

2. To remove the seeds, carefully pass the syrup through a sieve, pressing down gently on the raspberries with the wooden spoon or a spatula to extract all the liquid and fruit. Discard the seeds.

3. If you are not serving the syrup now, it may be refrigerated, covered, for up to 2 weeks. Before serving, reheat it in a small saucepan over medium heat for about 5 minutes.

Buying Raspberries

Fresh raspberries are typically sold in half-pint containers that hold about 1¹/₄ cups of berries.

Frozen raspberries sold in a bag have been individually quick frozen so that they are easy to pour and measure. A twelve-ounce bag holds about 3 cups of berries.

Raspberry Applesauce

I'm fortunate to have a yard loaded with fruit trees, including many apple trees. Making applesauce is a great way for me to use a bumper crop of delicious apples. But great varieties are so readily available, you don't need an apple tree to make fresh applesauce. I make big batches of it, using an adjustable apple peeler/corer with a hand crank to save time (see page 345). One day I experimented by adding some raspberries to the sauce. It was fabulous! This meal-size version takes just a few minutes to prepare. One of my favorite breakfasts is the rosy-red applesauce mixed with plain yogurt and topped with Earthbound Farm's Famous Maple Almond Granola (see page 278). **MAKES ABOUT 2 CUPS**

4 medium-size crisp, sweet-tart apples,
     such as Fuji, McIntosh, or
     Gravenstein, peeled and diced
     (about 4 cups)
1¼ cups (about 1 half-pint) fresh
     raspberries or frozen (unthawed or
     thawed) unsweetened raspberries
½ cup sugar, or more to taste
1 teaspoon fresh lemon juice

1. Place the apples and 1½ cups of water in a large nonreactive saucepan and bring to a simmer over high heat. Reduce the heat to medium and let simmer until the apples are soft, about 15 minutes.

2. Add the raspberries and sugar and cook, stirring frequently, until the apples are soft, about 5 minutes. Break up any remaining large chunks of apple with the back of a wooden spoon. The applesauce should be thick.

3. Remove the pan from the heat and allow the sauce to cool slightly. Add the lemon juice. Taste the applesauce and add more sugar, if necessary. If you are not planning on serving the applesauce immediately, cover and transfer it to a clean container. It can be refrigerated for up to 5 days. Serve the applesauce warm, at room temperature, or chilled.

A tin tub of freshly picked berries ensures there will be plenty to snack on and to turn into a summery berry dessert.

Raspberry Poached Pears

*S*ummer *markets bursting with peaches, melons, and berries make planning a fruit dessert easy. But winter also has its stars! Pears are one of my favorite winter fruits, with many wonderful varieties becoming readily available. Try this light and simple dessert when pears are at their peak and peaches are a distant memory. Of course, fresh, local raspberries will be out of season, but don't reach for expensive, imported berries. Frozen raspberries work just fine. Any leftover poaching syrup makes a spicy-sweet raspberry topping for vanilla ice cream or yogurt. It can also be frozen into intensely flavorful Popsicles or ice cubes, which will add a colorful burst of flavor to lemonade, ginger ale, or sparkling water.* **SERVES 6**

4 cups (from 4 half-pints) fresh
     raspberries or frozen (thawed or
     unthawed) unsweetened raspberries
2 cups sugar
Zest of 1 orange, removed in wide strips
     (see box, page 14)
Zest of ½ lemon, removed in wide strips

1 vanilla bean (see sidebar, page 361),
     split lengthwise
1 stick (2 to 3 inches long) cinnamon
1 whole star anise
6 ripe firm-textured pears, such as
     Anjou, Bosc, or Bartlett
Fresh lemon juice (optional)

COOKING TIP

how to zest citrus fruits

The zest is the colorful exterior of the citrus peel; it contains essential oils, which add an intense flavor and aroma to food. When zesting, use a light touch so you remove only the zest and leave behind the bitter white pith.

It's always wise to wash citrus fruit before removing the zest, but if your fruit is not organic, it's especially important since the peel may contain harmful pesticides. Fortunately, nearly all pesticides and bacteria can be removed by lightly scrubbing the outside of the citrus, using a vegetable brush and a few drops of mild, unscented dish detergent in a bowl of cool water. Rinse the fruit well under running water, dry it, and zest away!

For wide zest strips: Use a vegetable peeler to remove the zest in fat strips. Then, use a knife to slice or mince the zest into whatever size you need. There's no need to buy a special zesting tool, unless you want to.

For thin zest strips: Use a zester to cut the zest away from the fruit in narrow strips. Zesters come in two varieties: those that cut ¼-inch-wide strips and those that remove tiny threadlike strips. When investing in a zester, look for one with a head that can cut both.

For grated zest: The smallest holes on a box grater will give you the finest zest. If you have a fine Microplane grater, you'll find that it is exceptionally sharp and removes zest easily. Just keep your knuckles out of the way!

Similar to the Pink Lady variety, these heirloom apples are almost ready for harvest.

1. Select a large, deep saucepan that will just barely hold the pears. Pour 5 cups of water into the saucepan and add the raspberries, sugar, orange zest, lemon zest, vanilla bean, cinnamon stick, and star anise. Bring the poaching liquid to a simmer over medium-high heat, stirring occasionally until the sugar has dissolved.

2. Meanwhile, peel the pears with a vegetable peeler or small paring knife. If there are stems, leave them attached. Remove the core from the bottom end of each pear with a melon baller or spoon. Cut a thin slice off the bottom of the pears so that they will stand upright.

3. Add the pears to the pan with the poaching liquid; they should be submerged. Reduce the heat to low and let the pears simmer slowly until they are just tender, about 30 minutes. Remove the pan from the heat and let the pears cool in the poaching liquid. When they are cool, remove the pears from the liquid and set them aside.

4. Remove the vanilla bean from the poaching liquid and strain the liquid through a sieve, pressing down on the berries to extract all of the liquid from the fruit. Discard the raspberry seeds, citrus zest, cinnamon stick, and star anise. Scrape the seeds from the vanilla bean into the poaching liquid, then discard the pod or rinse and dry to save for another use (see page 361).

5. Transfer the poaching liquid to a medium-size saucepan and bring it to a boil over medium-high heat. Let the liquid boil until it is reduced by about half, 10 to 15 minutes. Taste the poaching liquid and add lemon juice if needed to balance the sweetness.

6. Serve the pears at room temperature, placed upright in shallow dessert bowls and drizzled with the reduced poaching liquid.

Raspberry-Lemon Crèmes Brûlées

Floating red raspberries in a rich, lemony custard provides a fresh twist on the classic vanilla crème brûlée. Save this recipe for the months when raspberries are in season (frozen berries will release too much liquid, preventing the custard from setting up properly). Everyone can enjoy the crisp sugar topping with each spoonful if you serve the custards in shallow six-ounce porcelain ramekins (like individual quiche dishes). To make the caramelized crust, you'll need a propane or butane gas kitchen torch to quickly melt the sugar; using an oven broiler would cause the delicate berries to overheat. But if you don't have a torch, skip the crust and you'll have raspberry-lemon custards. Served with Earthbound Farm Gingersnaps (see page 320), they'll be just as delicious. **SERVES 6**

A fresh Meyer lemon is juicy, aromatic, and sweeter than other varieties.

2 cups (from 2 half-pints) fresh
    raspberries
2 cups heavy (whipping) cream
¼ cup whole milk
4 large egg yolks, lightly beaten
About ¾ cup sugar
Grated zest of 3 lemons (see box, facing page)

1. Position a rack in the center of the oven and preheat the oven to 325°F.

2. Evenly divide the raspberries among six 6-ounce quiche dishes or ramekins, arranging them in a single layer. Set the dishes in a baking pan.

3. Pour the cream and milk in a small saucepan and bring to a simmer over medium heat.

4. Place the egg yolks, ½ cup of the sugar, and the lemon zest in a medium-size bowl and whisk to combine. Add about ½ cup of the hot cream mixture to the egg mixture and whisk to combine. Slowly add the remaining cream mixture to the egg mixture and stir until the sugar dissolves. Pour the custard into the dishes of raspberries, dividing it evenly among them.

5. Prepare a water bath by pouring hot water to a depth of about ¼ inch into the baking pan holding the dishes. Tightly cover the baking pan with aluminum foil.

6. Transfer the baking pan to the oven and bake the custards until the center of each is just barely set, 35 to 45 minutes.

7. Remove the baking pan from the oven. Uncover the pan carefully, allowing the steam to escape slowly, then set the pan on a wire rack to cool for 15 minutes.

8. Remove the custards from the water bath and refrigerate them, uncovered, until they are thoroughly chilled, about 2 hours. Wrap the custards in plastic wrap and return them to the refrigerator to set, for at least 4 hours or overnight.

9. When ready to serve, caramelize the tops of the custard. Unwrap the dishes and place them on a baking sheet. Evenly sprinkle 1 to 2 teaspoons of sugar over each custard. Heat the sugar with a propane or butane kitchen torch until browned and crisp but not burned. Serve the crèmes brûlées within an hour so the topping stays brittle, holding them at room temperature until ready to serve.

Sarah's Chocolate Soufflés
with Raspberry Sauce

My all-time favorite dessert—a sinfully dark chocolate soufflé served with glistening raspberry sauce and whipped cream—was created by our friend Sarah LaCasse, owner of Catering-by-the-Sea in Carmel. Drew and I first met Sarah as newlyweds when she was the chef at one of Carmel's finest restaurants. Dining there was expensive, so we'd have to save up for an anniversary or birthday splurge, but it was worth the scrimping. While other dishes on the menu were tempting, we always ordered filet mignon with fresh horseradish and scalloped potatoes, followed by Sarah's amazing chocolate soufflé. Soufflés have an intimidating reputation, but Sarah's turn out perfectly without a lot of fuss. Just be sure to use ceramic dishes with perfectly straight sides, which support the soufflés as they rise above the rim during baking. You'll need six eight-ounce baking dishes. **SERVES 6**

Note: The soufflé batter can be made in advance, through Step 6 and refrigerated, covered, for up to 3 days. Let it return to room temperature before proceeding with Step 7.

4 tablespoons unsalted butter (½ stick), plus butter for greasing the soufflé dishes

½ cup granulated sugar, plus more for dusting inside of the soufflé dishes

6 ounces high-quality bittersweet chocolate, chopped

⅓ cup unbleached all-purpose flour

1¾ cups whole milk

2 tablespoons heavy (whipping) cream

¼ cup bourbon

6 large eggs, separated

Confectioners' sugar, for garnish

Simple Raspberry Sauce (recipe follows)

Sweetened Whipped Cream (page 389)

*Golden raspberries
have a sweet and gentle
fruity flavor.*

1. Position a rack in the lower third of the oven and set a baking sheet on it. Preheat the oven to 400°F.

2. Generously butter six 8-ounce soufflé dishes and dust them with granulated sugar, shaking out any excess. Set the soufflé dishes aside.

3. Pour water to a depth of ¹/₂ inch in a saucepan or the bottom of a double boiler and bring it to a boil over high heat. Reduce the heat to low so that the water just barely simmers.

4. Place the chocolate in a medium-size metal or heatproof glass mixing bowl or the top of a double boiler and set it over the barely simmering water. Cook, stirring frequently, until the chocolate melts, about 5 minutes. Remove the melted chocolate from the heat and set it aside.

5. Place the 4 tablespoons of butter in a medium-size saucepan and melt it over medium heat. Add the flour and whisk until smooth, then add the milk and cream. Cook, stirring constantly, until the mixture starts to thicken, 1 to 2 minutes. Slowly add the ¹/₂ cup of granulated sugar, stirring constantly until very thick, about 3 minutes. Remove the saucepan from the heat and let the batter cool for 5 minutes.

6. Add the bourbon to the milk mixture. Whisk the egg yolks lightly in a bowl and slowly add them to the milk mixture, whisking constantly to thoroughly combine. Add this mixture to the melted chocolate and stir to combine.

7. Beat the egg whites with an electric mixer at high speed until they form stiff, shiny peaks, 4 to 5 minutes.

8. Whisk about one fourth of the egg whites into the chocolate mixture. Carefully fold in the remaining whites using a rubber spatula, working quickly and gently to incorporate them without deflating. Evenly divide the soufflé batter among the prepared soufflé dishes.

9. Transfer the soufflé dishes to the oven, arranging them on the baking sheet so they do not touch. Bake the soufflés until they rise 1 inch above the rim of the dish and the smell of chocolate fills the kitchen, 18 to 22 minutes.

10. Remove the soufflés from the oven and dust them with confectioners' sugar by sifting it through a sieve. Serve the soufflés immediately with bowls of Simple Raspberry Sauce and Sweetened Whipped Cream on the side.

Simple Raspberry Sauce

Raspberry sauce makes a luxurious topping, not just for Sarah's chocolate soufflés, but also for ice cream, cake, or waffles. No one will guess that it's so fast and easy to prepare. **MAKES ABOUT 1 ¹/₄ CUPS**

2¹/₂ cups (about 2 half-pints)
   fresh raspberries or frozen (thawed)
   unsweetened raspberries
1 tablespoon fresh lemon juice
¹/₂ cup confectioners' sugar

Combine the berries, lemon juice, and confectioners' sugar in a blender or food processor and puree until smooth. For a smoother sauce, strain it through a sieve, pressing down on the berries with a spoon or rubber spatula to extract all of the liquid from the fruit. Discard the seeds. The raspberry sauce can be refrigerated, covered, for up to 2 days or frozen for up to 2 months. Let it thaw overnight in the refrigerator. It can be served chilled or at room temperature.

Farm Stand Frozen Raspberry Yogurt

You'll love that this frozen treat has an amazingly rich texture, reminiscent of ice cream, but has very little fat. Its intense berry flavor and deep rose color come from draining most of the liquid from the yogurt overnight and replacing it with raspberry puree. Strawberries or blackberries would work just as well. This is an excellent opportunity to use frozen berries if you don't have a berry patch in your backyard. **MAKES ABOUT 1 1/2 QUARTS**

4 cups (32 ounces) low-fat plain yogurt
4 cups (from 4 half-pints) fresh
   raspberries or thawed frozen
   unsweetened raspberries
3/4 cup sugar
1/4 cup corn syrup, preferably dark
   (see sidebar, this page)
Grated zest of 1 lemon (see box, page 14)
Juice of 1 lemon

1. Line a colander with a single layer of damp cheesecloth and place the colander in a large bowl. Spoon the yogurt into the cheesecloth, then cover the bowl and colander with plastic wrap. Refrigerate the yogurt for at least 6 hours or overnight.

2. Meanwhile, combine the raspberries, sugar, and 1/2 cup of water in a medium-size saucepan and bring to a simmer over medium heat. Cook, stirring occasionally, until the sugar dissolves and the raspberries soften, about 5 minutes. Allow the raspberry mixture to cool to room temperature.

3. Strain the raspberry mixture through a sieve into a medium-size bowl, pressing down on the berries with a spoon or rubber spatula to extract all of the liquid from the fruit. Discard the seeds. Refrigerate the raspberry puree, covered, until ready to use.

4. Discard the liquid from the yogurt that has accumulated in the large bowl. Place the drained yogurt in the bowl and discard the cheesecloth. Add the strained raspberries, corn syrup, and lemon zest and juice to the yogurt and whisk until

Live Yogurt Cultures

In an ideal world, we'd eat yogurt everyday because it's full of protein, calcium, and B vitamins. Live yogurt cultures help the digestive and immune systems function at their best. Yogurt cultures can survive when frozen in a home or grocery store freezer, but when you cook yogurt, you lose some of its health benefits. Some companies heat their yogurt to prolong its shelf life, killing the cultures, so make sure the label of the yogurt you buy states that it contains living or active cultures. There are different types of yogurt cultures and each provides a different range of health benefits. Many yogurt brands contain two types of live cultures, but if three or even more are listed, so much the better.

smooth. Refrigerate the yogurt mixture, covered, until thoroughly chilled, at least 2 hours.

5. Place the yogurt mixture in the bowl of an ice cream maker and churn following the manufacturer's instructions.

Transfer the yogurt to an airtight container and freeze for at least 2 hours before serving. For longer storage, place a piece of plastic wrap directly on the surface of the yogurt to prevent ice crystals from forming. The yogurt can be frozen for up to 2 weeks.

Red Raspberry Ice Cream

We churned out this decadent ice cream at the Farm Stand one summer day when we had a surplus of ripe red berries. It was a delicious success. The base is made from a cooked egg custard, giving it a divine richness that spotlights the intense raspberry flavor without being overly sweet. You can also use this custard base with other fruit purees, such as strawberries, peaches, or mango. Frozen fruit works as well as fresh, so this is a treat you can enjoy year-round. **MAKES ABOUT 1 1/2 QUARTS**

1 1/2 cups whole milk
1 1/2 cups heavy (whipping) cream
6 large egg yolks
3/4 cup sugar
Pinch of salt
4 cups (from 4 half-pints) fresh raspberries or frozen (thawed) unsweetened raspberries
2 teaspoons pure vanilla extract

1. Pour the milk and cream into a medium-size saucepan. Cook the mixture over medium heat, stirring occasionally, until small bubbles form around the edge of the pan, just before the mixture comes to a boil. Immediately remove the saucepan from the heat.

2. Place the egg yolks, sugar, and salt in a medium-size bowl and whisk to combine. Add a little of the cream mixture to the egg mixture, whisking constantly. Then slowly whisk in the remaining cream mixture.

3. Return the cream mixture to the saucepan and cook over medium heat, stirring constantly, until it thickens slightly and coats the back of a wooden spoon, 5 to 10 minutes. Do not allow the mixture to boil or it will curdle.

4. Fill a large bowl with ice cubes and set it aside.

5. Strain the custard mixture through a sieve into a medium-size bowl. Set the bowl in the ice bath to quickly reduce the temperature, stirring the custard occasionally to dissipate the heat.

6. Place the raspberries in a bowl and crush them with a spoon or rubber spatula. Strain the berries through a sieve, pressing down on them with the spoon or spatula to extract as much fruit as possible. Discard the seeds.

7. Add the raspberry puree and the vanilla to the custard and stir to combine. Refrigerate the ice cream mixture, covered, until it is thoroughly chilled, at least 4 hours.

8. Place the ice cream mixture in the bowl of an ice cream maker and churn following the manufacturer's instructions.

9. Transfer the ice cream to an airtight container and freeze it for at least 2 hours before serving. For longer storage, place a piece of plastic wrap directly on the surface of the ice cream to prevent ice crystals from forming. Covered tightly, the ice cream can be frozen for up to 2 weeks.

Quick and Easy Frozen Raspberry Yogurt

Rosy pink, not too sweet, and flecked with raspberry, this super-easy dessert always reminds me of visits home during my college years. While my mother didn't cook much when I was growing up, she became very interested in healthy eating during the 1980s. Instead of a rich dessert, she made this frozen yogurt treat and served it topped with walnuts. These days, I make it for my own kids because it's healthier than ice cream and just as delicious. The soft texture doesn't last when stored in the freezer, so we enjoy eating it all right away. **MAKES ABOUT 3 CUPS**

2 cups (16 ounces) nonfat plain
   yogurt
1/3 cup maple syrup
1 cup (from 1 half-pint) fresh
   raspberries or thawed frozen
   unsweetened raspberries
Toasted walnuts (see box, page 98),
   chopped, for garnish

1. Place the yogurt and maple syrup in a medium-size bowl and stir to combine.

2. Place the yogurt mixture in the bowl of an ice cream maker and start to churn following the manufacturer's instructions. Add the raspberries and continue to churn until the mixture freezes, 15 to 30 minutes. The soft berries will break up so that the yogurt turns pink.

3. Serve the softly frozen yogurt immediately, topped with walnuts.

Farm Stand Raspberry Lemonade

We throw a Raspberry Revelry Festival at our Farm Stand every July to celebrate Earthbound Farm's beginnings as a small raspberry farm, and to enjoy the multitude of delicious treats that can be made from our favorite berry. No drink is more perfect for this mid-summer celebration than blushing pink raspberry lemonade; it's as pretty as it is refreshing. The color and sweetness comes from homemade raspberry syrup. If you have leftover syrup, use it to add raspberry flavor to sparkling water, smoothies, fruit juices, poached fruits, or ice cream. **MAKES 4 SERVINGS; 8 OUNCES EACH (CAN BE DOUBLED)**

FOR THE RASPBERRY SYRUP
1 cup sugar
1¼ cups (about 1 half-pint) fresh
    raspberries, or frozen (thawed or
    unthawed) unsweetened raspberries

FOR THE LEMONADE
¾ cup freshly squeezed lemon juice,
    or more to taste
4 lemon slices or 4 mint sprigs,
    for garnish

1. Make the raspberry syrup: Place the sugar and 1 cup of water in a small saucepan and bring to a simmer over high heat, stirring occasionally, until the sugar is dissolved, about 3 minutes. Add the raspberries and let the mixture come to a boil. Reduce the heat to low and cook until berries are completely soft, about 3 minutes. Allow the syrup to cool to room temperature.

2. Strain the syrup through a sieve, pressing down on the berries with a spoon or rubber spatula to extract all the liquid from the fruit. Discard the seeds. (If not using now, the syrup can be refrigerated, covered, for up to 2 weeks or frozen for up to 3 months.)

3. Make the lemonade: Place 1 cup of the raspberry syrup and ¾ cup of the lemon juice in a large serving pitcher. Add 2 cups ice-cold water and stir to combine. Taste and add more syrup or lemon juice, if needed.

4. Just before serving, fill 4 tall glasses with ice cubes or crushed ice. Pour the lemonade into the glasses, top each with a lemon slice, and serve immediately.

This is my daughter, Marea, when she was three, pitching in to push a cart of freshly cut flowers at our Farm Stand.

Chapter 2

Soups

Why do we crave soup on a wintry day? Perhaps it's the wholesome aroma rising from the bowl as we hold it to warm our hands, or maybe it's the chunks of vegetables in a rich broth we long for. Regardless, enjoying soup requires us to slow down and relish it slowly, spoonful by spoonful.

My son, Jeffrey, displays fresh picked green and yellow wax beans.

When my children have the sniffles, I don't need a scientific study to convince me that a bowl of Simply Chicken Soup is just what they need to feel better. To nurture myself, I'll warm up a bowl of split pea soup with bits of ham, or when I'm feeling homesick for a taste of New York City, I'll make matzoh ball soup. Some of the best-loved soups are the ones we enjoyed growing up.

Making soup is also liberating and creative. When my son, Jeffrey, was nine or ten, he decided he wanted soup for dinner. But not just any soup—he wanted to make it just the way he liked it. So we went to the supermarket where he prowled the aisles, searching for ingredients that called out to him. He filled our cart with chicken, parsnips, lentils, onions, potatoes, parsley, celery, and garlic. His enthusiasm accelerated in the kitchen as he peeled, chopped, and cooked, rarely asking for my advice. While his creation simmered, he smelled our spice bottles, selectively sprinkling a little of this and a little of that into the pot.

But what excited him most was enjoying the soup without having to avoid carrots. I'd been cleaning out his soup bowl for years without realizing the significance of the orange chunks on the bottom of the bowl. I had always assumed that a good vegetable soup required carrots, but Jeffrey's soup was fabulous without them. From his success, I learned that there are no hard-and-fast rules for making soup, as long as you use delicious ingredients and trust your nose and taste buds to guide you.

I like to think that the person who first said "waste not, want not" was a soup lover. A vegetable soup provides a satisfying way to use potatoes that are a little soft, the handful of spinach in the bottom of the bag, or a leftover onion half. When your garden is overflowing with tomatoes, it's time to make a big pot of tomato soup and freeze it for the

Facing Page:
Tuscan White Bean Stew (page 54).

winter months. A half-dozen ears of corn can become corn chowder; even the cobs go into the pot to make a flavorful broth. Soup is one of my favorite solutions to the creative challenge of ensuring that no food goes to waste.

As you browse through our soup recipes, I hope you will be reminded of old favorites and introduced to some new ones. Most of all, I hope you are inspired to create your own delicious soups that will nurture and nourish you and those you love.

Summer Harvest Soup

Transform summer's vegetable bounty into this incredibly beautiful soup with bursts of red, green, yellow, and orange drifting in a pale amber broth. Just be sure to pay close attention to the cooking time for each vegetable and add the fresh herbs at the last minute so they retain their vibrant colors. If you're missing a vegetable or two, don't worry. While the soup tastes best on the day it's made, if you need to make it in advance, reduce the cooking times so the vegetables don't overcook when reheated. Then add the tomatoes and herbs just before you're ready to serve the soup.

SERVES 6

Note: If preparing the soup ahead of time, stop after completing Step 3. The soup can be refrigerated, covered, for 3 days. Just before serving, bring the soup to a simmer and continue with Step 4.

2 tablespoons olive oil
1 large leek, both white and light green parts, rinsed well and thinly sliced (about 1 cup)
1 small fennel bulb, thinly sliced (about 1 cup)
1 bay leaf
2 cloves garlic, thinly sliced
1/2 cup dry white wine
7 cups Blond Chicken Stock (page 372) or Shiitake Vegetable Stock (page 377)
3 small carrots, sliced 1/4 inch thick (about 3/4 cup)
1/2 cup trimmed and sliced (1-inch pieces) green beans
1/2 cup trimmed and sliced (1-inch pieces) yellow wax beans

1 cup diced (1/2-inch dice) baby summer squash
1 cup diced (1/2-inch dice) baby zucchini
1/2 cup fresh shelled English peas
1/2 cup fresh corn kernels (from 1 ear; see box, page 29)
2 cups diced (1/2-inch dice) vine-ripened tomatoes
2 tablespoons coarsely chopped fresh basil
1 tablespoon fresh thyme leaves
1/4 cup chopped fresh flat-leaf parsley
Salt and freshly ground black pepper
Freshly shaved Parmesan cheese or Emerald Green Pesto (page 192), or store-bought pesto, for garnish (optional)

1. Heat the olive oil in a large, heavy pot over low heat. Add the leek, fennel, and bay leaf and cook, stirring occasionally, for 3 minutes. Add the garlic and cook, stirring frequently, until the vegetables are soft and fragrant but not browned, about 5 minutes.

2. Add the wine, increase the heat to medium-high, and cook until the wine is almost evaporated, about 5 minutes. Add the chicken stock and bring to a simmer.

3. Add the carrots, green beans, and yellow beans and let simmer for 5 minutes. Add the summer squash, zucchini, peas, and corn and let simmer until the vegetables are just tender, about 5 minutes. Do not overcook or the bright vegetable colors will be lost (see Note, page 26).

4. Add the tomatoes, basil, thyme, and parsley and let simmer until heated through, about 1 minute. Season the soup with salt and pepper to taste. Discard the bay leaf. Serve the soup immediately, garnished with ribbons of Parmesan or a dollop of pesto, if desired.

Sweet Corn Chowder

Only sweet, fresh corn rivals vine-ripened tomatoes in summertime popularity. This flavorful chowder is full of bits of smoky bacon and chunks of new potatoes. Using the stripped corn cobs to make the herb-scented broth that serves as the base for the chowder intensifies the hearty soup's delicious corn flavor. Although nothing beats the flavor of garden-fresh corn, you can substitute frozen corn kernels in a pinch if you enhance the flavor with vegetable broth instead of water when you simmer the herbs and potatoes.

SERVES 6 TO 8

C O O K I N G   T I P

cutting corn from the cob

Cutting corn kernels off the cob can be messy, but you can help contain the flying kernels by placing the cobs in a deep-sided roasting pan or large bowl first. Before you start, shuck the corn, leaving the stalk attached to use as a "handle" and remove the silk. Set the pan or bowl on a work surface and hold the ear against the bottom of the pan at a 45-degree angle. Cut down along the side of the cob with a sharp knife, removing a few rows of kernels. Turn the cob and continue cutting until all the kernels are removed. Finally, using the dull edge of the knife, scrape down the length of the cob on all sides to collect the flavorful milky juices.

Farmer Mark Marino checks to see if the corn is ready for harvest.

6 ears fresh corn, shucked and
    silk removed
1/4 pound thick-sliced bacon
    (2 or 3 slices), cut in 1/4-inch dice
1 medium-size yellow onion, minced
    (about 1/4 cup)
2 ribs celery, minced
Olive oil (optional)
5 cups homemade Shiitake Vegetable
    Stock (page 377) or store-bought
    low-sodium chicken stock or water
1 bay leaf
1 sprig fresh thyme, plus 1 tablespoon
    fresh thyme leaves, for garnish
2 cups peeled and diced (1/2-inch
    dice) Yukon Gold or waxy potatoes
    (such as White Rose)
1 1/2 cups half-and-half
1 teaspoon salt
1/2 teaspoon freshly ground white pepper

1. Cut the kernels off the corn cobs (see box, page 29). You should have 3 to 4 cups of kernels. Set aside the kernels and cobs.

2. Place the bacon in a large, heavy saucepan and cook over medium heat, stirring occasionally, until crisp, 5 to 10 minutes. Remove the bacon with a slotted spoon and set it aside on paper towels to drain.

3. Add the onion and celery to the bacon fat in the saucepan and cook over medium heat, stirring occasionally, until the vegetables are soft, about 10 minutes. (If you prefer, drain the bacon fat from the saucepan and replace it with 2 tablespoons of olive oil before adding the onion and celery.)

4. Place the corn cobs in the saucepan with the onion mixture. Add the stock,

FARM FRESH

corn on the cob

There's an old saying that you should put the water on to boil before you harvest the corn. That's because the sugar in the kernels of traditional corn varieties starts turning into starch as soon as the ears are picked. This transformation is much slower in the new corn hybrids; their sweetness lasts for days rather than hours. However, some people think the supersweet varieties are too sweet and lack true corn flavor. It's a matter of personal taste—try different varieties and see which type appeals to you.

Even with the new hybrids, fresher is always better. When buying corn, look for moist husks with shiny, brown silk spilling out the end. White or pale yellow silk means that the corn isn't ready for picking, while dark brown, dried-out silks indicate old corn. Try to resist the urge to open every ear because the kernels begin to dry out once the husk is pulled away. Generally, you can tell if the kernels are mature by the diameter of the unopened ears: the fatter the ear the more mature the kernels. Avoid ears with big, dimpled kernels, which will taste mealy and starchy. Organic corn hasn't

been treated with harmful chemical pesticides, so you may find an occasional worm nibbling the tip of an ear. Don't fret. It's easy to cut off the damaged end, and there will be plenty left for you. When you take home the ears of corn, leave them in the husk and store them in a plastic bag in the refrigerator. Just before cooking, shuck the ears and pull off the silk. To remove any stray silk, rinse the ear under running water while rubbing it with your hands. Unlike most vegetables, corn becomes tougher as it cooks, so keep your eye on the clock while it is boiling—it will be done in two to four minutes.

bay leaf, thyme sprig, and potatoes. Bring the mixture to a boil over high heat, then reduce the heat to medium and let simmer until the potatoes are just barely tender, about 20 minutes. Turn off the heat, cover the pan, and let the mixture steep at room temperature, for 20 minutes.

5. Remove and discard the bay leaf, thyme sprig, and corn cobs. Add the drained bacon, corn kernels, and the half-and-half to the chowder. If you want a thicker consistency, remove about 2 cups of chowder from the saucepan and coarsely puree it in a blender, then add the puree back to the remaining chowder.

6. Reheat the chowder slowly over low heat, stirring occasionally, until it is warmed through, then season it with the salt and pepper. Serve the chowder hot, garnished with the thyme leaves.

Heirloom Tomato Soup

From July through October, we harvest amazingly beautiful organic heirloom tomatoes from our warmest California growing regions and proudly display a bountiful array at our Farm Stand. This soup celebrates their arrival. Slow, gentle simmering distills the tomato flavor to its delicious essence—a wonderful payoff for minimal work. Try it when tomatoes are at their peak of flavor. They can even be a little too soft for slicing. While the soup is only as good as the tomatoes, if they are a bit too acidic, a teaspoon or two of sugar will make a big difference in taste. If you use several varieties of vine-ripened tomatoes, the soup will taste even better. It freezes beautifully, so make enough during the dog days of summer to tide you over the long winter months. **SERVES 4 TO 6**

5 pounds heirloom tomatoes,
    such as German Johnson or
    Brandywine, or other flavorful
    tomatoes
Salt and freshly ground black pepper
1 to 2 teaspoons sugar (optional)
Parmesan Croutons (page 90) or
    freshly shaved Parmesan cheese,
    for garnish

1. If you have a food mill (see sidebar, this page), rinse the tomatoes and cut them into large wedges without removing the skins and seeds.

If you don't have a food mill, you'll have to remove the skins and seeds now: Fill a large bowl with ice water and set it close to the stove. Bring a large pot of water to a boil. Using a slotted spoon,

Using a Food Mill

Long before the days of blenders and food processors, cooks used food mills (also called vegetable mills) to make pureed soups, sauces, and baby food. Food mills have one big advantage over the modern-day appliances: You don't have to peel or seed soft fruits and vegetables; the food mill takes care of that step for you. For example, to puree tomatoes, place cooked tomatoes— skins, seeds, cores, and all—in the top of the food mill. As you turn the handle, the mill blade forces the tomatoes through a slotted disk. The pureed tomatoes drop into the bowl and the skins, seeds, and cores are left behind. For occasional home use, you can find basic food mills for less than $30, and they are a low-tech time-saver.

lower the tomatoes into the boiling water for 1 minute to loosen the skins. Remove the tomatoes and plunge them into the ice water, letting them cool enough to handle. Using a paring knife, cut out and discard the tomato cores and slip off the skins. Cut the tomatoes in half crosswise and discard the seeds. Cut large tomatoes into wedges.

2. Place the tomatoes in a large, heavy-bottomed saucepan and add ½ cup of water. Cover the pan and cook the tomatoes over medium heat, stirring frequently, until they have completely softened, 15 to 20 minutes. Adjust the heat if necessary so the tomatoes do not scorch, but do not add any more water;

it will dilute the flavor. Remove the saucepan from the heat and uncover it. Let the tomatoes cool, stirring occasionally to dissipate the heat, about 15 minutes.

3. If you have a food mill, use it to puree the tomatoes until smooth, discarding the skins and seeds that remain in the bowl. Or, if you've already removed the skin and seeds, puree the tomatoes in batches in a food processor or blender just until smooth. If the tomatoes are overprocessed, they will become foamy. Don't worry: The foam will dissipate during cooking and will not affect the taste or appearance of the finished soup.

4. Transfer the tomato puree to a large, clean pot and reheat it gently, uncovered, over low heat. If the soup is too thin, let it simmer until the flavor is concentrated, 10 to 15 minutes.

5. Season the soup with salt and pepper to taste. If the soup is too acidic, add 1 to 2 teaspoons of sugar to taste. If you are not planning on serving the soup immediately, let it cool to room temperature. It can be refrigerated, covered, for up to 5 days or frozen for up to 6 months. Serve the soup hot, garnished with the Parmesan Croutons or shaved Parmesan.

Our first beautiful heirloom tomatoes of the summer. Their smell alone makes your mouth water.

Golden Tomato Gazpacho

Delicately flavored, this gazpacho is a seductive summer starter. Luscious yellow and orange heirloom tomatoes, teamed with a hint of licorice-flavored fennel, set the soup apart from the familiar red gazpacho. If you like spicy soups, add a finely diced jalapeño pepper or a few shakes of Tabasco sauce before serving. The gazpacho keeps well in the refrigerator for up to five days; it's a great make-ahead party soup.

SERVES 8

5 pounds ripe, flavorful yellow or orange
   tomatoes, such as **Yellow Brandywine**
1 small fennel bulb sliced (about 1 cup),
   fronds chopped for garnish
1/2 cup coarsely chopped scallions,
   white part only
3 cloves garlic, peeled
3 cups peeled and coarsely chopped
   hothouse (seedless English) cucumber
2 cups coarsely chopped yellow
   bell pepper
3 cups Blond Chicken Stock (page 372)
   or Shiitake Vegetable Stock
   (page 377)
2 tablespoons extra-virgin olive oil
1 tablespoon Champagne vinegar or
   Tarragon Vinegar (page 381), or
   more to taste
2 tablespoons sugar, or more to taste
2 teaspoons salt, or more to taste
1/4 teaspoon freshly ground white pepper,
   or more to taste
Chopped fresh dill, for garnish
Parmesan Croutons (optional; page 90)

1. Fill a large bowl with ice water and set it close to the stove. Bring a large pot of water to a boil. Using a slotted spoon, lower the tomatoes into the boiling water for 1 minute to loosen the skins. Remove the tomatoes and plunge them into the ice water, letting them cool enough to handle. Using a paring knife, cut out and discard the tomato cores and slip off the skins. Cut the tomatoes in half crosswise and discard the seeds.

2. Place the tomatoes in a food processor and pulse the machine until they are coarsely pureed. Transfer the tomatoes to a large nonreactive bowl.

3. Place the fennel bulb, scallions, and garlic in the food processor and pulse until finely chopped. Add the cucumber and process until just beginning to liquefy. Transfer the cucumber mixture to the bowl with the tomatoes.

4. Place the bell pepper in the food processor and process until coarsely pureed. Add the pepper puree to the bowl with the tomatoes.

5. Add the stock, olive oil, vinegar, sugar, salt, and white pepper to the bowl with the tomatoes and stir to combine well. Refrigerate the soup, covered, until the flavors develop, at least 4 hours.

6. Before serving, taste the chilled gazpacho and adjust the seasonings, adding more sugar, salt, white pepper, and/or another tablespoon of vinegar as needed. Serve the soup well chilled, garnished with the fennel fronds, dill, and croutons, if using.

Using Fresh & Dried Herbs in the Kitchen

There's a place for both fresh and dried herbs in your kitchen. The flavor of fresh herbs is more subtle and vibrant than dried ones, so fresh herbs are usually added toward the end of the cooking time. Dried herbs add a deeper flavor that is released during long, slow simmering.

Of course, there are times of the year when certain fresh herbs are not readily available. As a rule of thumb, use about 1 teaspoon of dried herb for every 1 tablespoon of fresh herb called for in a recipe.

Ginger Carrot Soup

The natural sweetness of carrots spiked with orange, ginger, and a whisper of nutmeg makes this soup beautifully delicious. The carrots give the soup a rich, full-bodied texture, as well as a big helping of health-enhancing antioxidants and vitamin A. Whether you enjoy this soup hot or cold, the intense carrot flavor and brilliant orange color will make it memorable. **SERVES 4**

2 tablespoons canola oil or olive oil
1 small yellow onion, coarsely chopped
 (about ¹/₂ cup)
1 piece (3 inches long) fresh ginger,
 peeled and coarsely chopped
 (about ¹/₄ cup)
1¹/₄ pounds carrots, sliced ¹/₄-inch thick
 (about 4 cups)
About 5 cups Shiitake Vegetable Stock
 (page 377) or store-bought
 low-sodium vegetable broth
¹/₂ cup fresh orange juice
Pinch of ground nutmeg
Coarse (kosher) salt and freshly ground
 black pepper
Homemade Crème Fraîche (page 389)
 or sour cream, for garnish

1. Heat the oil in a large saucepan over medium heat. Add the onion and ginger and cook, stirring occasionally, until soft and fragrant, about 5 minutes.

2. Add the carrots, stock, and orange juice. Increase the heat to medium-high and bring to a boil. Reduce the heat to low, cover the pan, and let simmer until the carrots are very tender, about 45 minutes.

3. Using an immersion blender, puree the soup in the saucepan. (Or, let the soup cool slightly, then puree it in a blender or food processor.) If you prefer a smoother texture, strain the pureed soup through a sieve.

4. Add the nutmeg to the soup and season it with salt and pepper to taste. If the soup is too thick, thin it with some water or more stock.

5. To serve the soup warm, reheat it gently over medium-low heat. To serve the soup chilled, refrigerate it, covered, until cold, at least 6 hours or up to 5 days. Garnish the soup with a spoonful of crème fraîche and a light sprinkle of nutmeg before serving. If desired, you can create a swirl pattern in the soup by dragging the tip of a knife or fork through the crème fraîche in a circular motion.

French Sorrel Soup

We use so many fresh herbs in our Organic Kitchen that we're constantly running out to the herb cutting garden for more. French sorrel is one of our favorites because we love its tangy, lemony taste. This creamy soup, with its mellow leek and potato, provides the perfect backdrop for sorrel's distinctive bright flavor, and the green romaine lettuce keeps the soup's color vibrant. Plus, it's equally delicious served warm on a nippy spring evening or chilled on a hot summer day. **SERVES 4**

Note: When selecting sorrel, keep in mind that young, tender leaves have a more subtle flavor than larger ones. If you have mature leaves, use only about 3 packed cups and, if necessary, adjust the tanginess of the soup with a bit of honey at the end. For a simple garnish, slice a few extra sorrel leaves into thin ribbons and sprinkle them over the soup at the last minute. You can substitute baby spinach, but the soup won't have the same lemony flavor.

2 tablespoons (¼ stick) unsalted butter
1 medium-size leek, white part only, rinsed well and thinly sliced
1 tablespoon fresh thyme leaves
4 cups Blond Chicken Stock (page 372) or Shiitake Vegetable Stock (page 377)
1 medium-size Yukon Gold or waxy potato (such as White Rose), peeled and cut into ½-inch dice
4 cups chopped romaine lettuce
8 ounces young sorrel leaves, rinsed and stems removed (about 6 cups, packed; see Note)
½ cup heavy (whipping) cream or half-and-half

Coarse (kosher) salt and freshly ground black pepper
Honey (optional)
Freshly grated Parmesan cheese, for garnish

1. Melt the butter in a large saucepan over medium-low heat. Add the leek and thyme and cook, stirring occasionally, until soft but not browned, about 5 minutes.

2. Add the chicken stock and potato. Increase the heat to medium-high and bring to a simmer. Reduce the heat to low, cover the pan, and let simmer until the potato is tender, about 10 minutes.

F A R M   F R E S H

sorrel

Sorrel is a tart lemony tasting herb with green arrow-shaped leaves that are about 3 to 6 inches long when mature. You're most likely to find sorrel leaves in large bunches at the farmers' market from spring through fall alongside greens like kale, arugula, and watercress. You may also find small packages of sorrel in the produce aisle of specialty food stores with other herbs.

Sorrel's intense, tangy flavor packs a powerful punch. It's usually cooked with mild ingredients, like potatoes or fish, but it is lovely eaten raw in salads, too. Its bright green leaves take on a grayish hue when cooked, so it's nice to combine sorrel with other greens that keep their green color, such as spinach. When you want a milder flavor, choose small, young sorrel leaves or use fewer mature leaves in your recipe.

3. Add the lettuce and let simmer, uncovered, for 10 minutes. Add the sorrel and cook until the lettuce and sorrel are soft, about 5 minutes longer.

4. Using an immersion blender, puree the soup in the saucepan. Or, let the soup cool slightly, then puree it in a blender or food processor and return it to the saucepan. Add the cream and season with salt and pepper to taste. If the soup is too tart, add ¼ teaspoon of honey, or more to taste.

5. To serve the soup warm, reheat it slowly over medium-low heat but do not let it boil. To serve the soup chilled, refrigerate it, covered, until cold, at least 4 hours or up to 3 days. Serve the soup garnished with Parmesan cheese.

Iced Ginger Melon Soup

Chilled soups are very refreshing on a steamy summer day—especially a soup like this one, featuring green melon laced with lime and crystallized ginger, and garnished with mint. Even after a couple of hours in the refrigerator, it has a faint bubbly sparkle, thanks to the carbonated soda. This deliciously versatile soup is easily transformed into a cocktail or dessert. Sip it as a chilled soup from a martini glass as a first course teaser. Add a splash of vodka and a handful of crushed ice, followed by a whirl in the blender, and you have a cocktail. Churned in an ice cream freezer, the soup becomes a light melon sorbet!

SERVES 4

1 medium-size green-fleshed melon,
    such as honeydew or Galia,
    cubed (about 3 cups)
1 tablespoon coarsely chopped
    crystallized ginger
2 tablespoons fresh lime juice or
    lemon juice, or more to taste
1 cup sparkling lemonade, lemon soda,
    or lemon-lime soda, chilled
Honey (optional)
Fresh mint leaves, for garnish

1. Place the melon cubes and ginger
in a blender or food processor and puree
until smooth.

2. Transfer the puree to a medium-size
bowl. Add the lime juice and lemonade
and stir to blend. Taste for sweetness,
adding honey as needed.

3. Pour the soup into martini glasses or
wine goblets and place some mint leaves
on top of each portion. Refrigerate the
soup until well chilled, 1 to 2 hours and
serve cold.

*This Earliqueen melon has
a deliciously sweet orange
flesh.*

F A R M   F R E S H

melons

The season for sweet, juicy melons
peaks during the warmest summer
months. Melons don't get sweeter
after they are picked; the best ones
ripen on the vine.

Use your nose when picking
out muskmelons, cantaloupes, and
honeydews. These melons are
fragrant when ripe and will usually
give a little when pressed near the
blossom end (the opposite end from
the stem). Most of the orange-

fleshed melons we call cantaloupes
in the United States are a type of
muskmelon. They range from the
green-fleshed Galia to the orange-
fleshed Ambrosia and Persian
varieties. True cantaloupes and
muskmelons are highly fragrant
and keep only one or two weeks.
Honeydews, which fall in a different
category, are less aromatic but keep
weeks longer.

While yellow-fleshed
watermelons are a tasty novelty,
the traditional red-fleshed varieties

are rich in lycopene, with even
more of this health-promoting
antioxidant than raw tomatoes!
You can identify a ripe watermelon
because it will have a yellowish
patch on its bottom where it rested
against the ground and will be
heavy for its size.

Before cutting into any melon,
scrub it with a soft vegetable brush
and water so that any bacteria
or residual pesticides won't be
transferred to the flesh when you
slice it.

A Field Guide to Winter Squash

Every fall, our Carmel Valley Farm Stand overflows with colorful winter squashes. While some varieties are best for decoration, these varieties taste as good as they look. Baking softens the tough flesh, turning some decadently rich and sweet, and others, nutty and mild. All are delicious.

kabocha, *also called Japanese squash, averages two to three pounds. It has a rich, honey-sweet flavor, and has a custard-like consistency when cooked.*

acorn, *a small, popular squash that weighs about one to three pounds, has a brilliant orange, slightly fibrous flesh with a sweet taste. It has a very tough rind; varieties may be green, white, golden, and multicolored.*

buttercup *is a medium-size squash weighing three to five pounds; it has orange flesh with a super-sweet, buttery-rich flavor that's delicious baked.*

delicata *is an heirloom squash that weighs in at around one pound. Its creamy flesh tastes similar to sweet potatoes; unlike most other winter squashes, its tender skin is edible.*

spaghetti squash *has pale-yellow flesh that, when cooked, separates into long spaghetti-like strands, with a mild, slightly nutty flavor. Some varieties have orange-colored flesh, which is high in beta carotene.*

blue hubbard, *a giant that can grow to fifty pounds or more, is usually sold pre-cut into large hunks. Its firm, yellow flesh has a fine texture, making it perfect for pies.*

butternut, *another popular squash, usually weighs two to five pounds. Its buttery-textured orange flesh has a nutty, sweet flavor.*

jarrahdale *is an unusual Australian heirloom pumpkin that weighs about six to ten pounds. It has thin skin and delicious flesh that is very mild and slightly sweet.*

sweet dumpling, *a small squash weighing only about a half pound, has sweet and tender deep-orange flesh. The small size is perfect for baking individual servings.*

Roasted Winter Squash Soup

When the air turns autumn crisp, you'll find our Farm Stand surrounded by mountains of winter squashes and pumpkins. We grow more than thirty varieties, including white Luminas, green acorns, striped turbans, and speckled chilacayotes. We also feature these showy squashes on our Organic Kitchen's menu. This is the soup our customers always ask for in the fall, praising its velvety texture and the intriguing nutty flavor. Roasting brings out the natural sweetness and intensifies the flavors of winter squash. Plus, it's easy to scoop out the squash flesh from its tough rind once it's baked, so you don't have to peel it first. **SERVES 4 TO 6**

In the fall, visitors to our Farm Stand are delighted by our annual totem poles of pumpkins and winter squash. Why don't they topple? They are threaded on a metal pole that's staked into the ground.

3 to 3¹/2 pounds winter squash
    (such as butternut squash or
    Hubbard squash), cut in half
    and seeds removed
2 tablespoons olive oil, plus more for
    brushing on the vegetables
Coarse (kosher) salt
1 medium-size garlic head
2 large leeks, both white and light green
    parts, rinsed well and thinly sliced
    (about 2 cups), or 1 cup thinly sliced
    yellow onions
¹/2 cup thinly sliced carrots
6 cups Blond Chicken Stock (page 372)
    or store-bought low-sodium chicken
    broth
¹/4 cup firmly packed light brown sugar
Freshly ground black pepper
4 tablespoons (¹/2 stick) butter,
    for garnish
¹/4 cup toasted hazelnuts (see box,
    page 98), chopped, for garnish

1. Position a rack in the center of the oven and preheat the oven to 375°F.

2. Brush the cut surfaces of the squash with olive oil and sprinkle salt over them.

Place the squash, cut side down, on a rimmed baking sheet.

3. Cut the top ¹/2 inch off the garlic head and discard or reserve for another use. Remove the loose, outer layers of the paperlike skin, leaving the head intact. Brush the garlic with olive oil and wrap it in heavy-duty aluminum foil or a double layer of regular aluminum foil. Place the garlic on the baking sheet with the squash.

4. Bake the squash and garlic until the squash flesh feels tender when the tip of a knife is inserted into it, 45 to 55 minutes. Remove the baking sheet from the oven and let the squash and garlic cool.

5. Heat the 2 tablespoons of olive oil in a large, heavy pot over medium-low heat. Add the leeks and carrots and cook, stirring occasionally, until the vegetables soften, 10 to 15 minutes.

6. Scoop out the squash flesh and add it to the pot with the leek mixture. Discard the squash rind.

7. Squeeze the garlic pulp from the papery skins. Add half of the roasted garlic pulp to the pot. Set the remaining garlic aside for another use (see Note) and discard the garlic skins.

8. Add the stock to the pot and stir to combine. Increase the heat to high and bring to a boil. Reduce the heat to low and let the soup simmer until the flavors meld, about 20 minutes.

9. Using an immersion blender, puree the soup in the pot. Or let the soup cool slightly, then puree it in a blender or food processor and return it to the pot. If you prefer a smoother texture, strain the pureed soup through a sieve. If you are not planning on serving the soup at this time, let it cool to room temperature. It can be refrigerated, covered, for up to 5 days.

10. Reheat the soup gently over medium-low heat. Stir in the brown sugar and season with salt and pepper to taste.

11. Place a small skillet over medium heat. When it is hot, add the butter and let cook until it turns a nutty brown, about 5 minutes. Watch the butter carefully so that it doesn't burn.

12. Ladle the soup into warm bowls. Drizzle some of the browned butter over each serving and sprinkle the hazelnuts on top.

Garlic right from the field with their long stems still attached for braiding.

Note: Roasted garlic is delicious spread on toasted baguette slices to accompany the soup.

Hearty Cauliflower Bisque

Leeks and fresh thyme enhance, but don't hide, the delicate flavor of cauliflower in this creamy soup. Blended to a coarse puree, the soup is casual and comforting. Or, you can make the bisque smooth and elegant by passing it through a sieve and serving it with a drizzle of truffle oil. Whether your style is simple or fancy, choose colorful bowls to set off the creamy color of this flavorful bisque so it will appeal to all your senses. **SERVES 4 TO 6**

2 tablespoons ($^{1}/_{4}$ stick) unsalted butter
3 medium-size leeks, both white and
    light green parts, rinsed well and
    thinly sliced (about 1$^{1}/_{2}$ cups)
2 pounds fresh cauliflower florets (from
    3 to 4 pounds whole cauliflower)
    coarsely chopped (about 6 cups)

4 cups Blond Chicken Stock (page 372) or
    Shiitake Vegetable Stock (page 377)
1$^{1}/_{2}$ cups whole or low-fat milk
2 tablespoons fresh thyme leaves
$^{1}/_{2}$ cup half-and-half
Salt and freshly ground white pepper
White truffle oil (optional), for garnish

Note: The cauliflower cooking time can be reduced by cutting the florets into small pieces. However, do not increase the cooking temperature to speed things up, because the milk may curdle.

1. Melt the butter in a large saucepan over medium-low heat. Add the leeks and cook until soft, 5 to 6 minutes.

2. Add the cauliflower, stock, and 1 cup of the milk. Increase the heat to medium-high and bring the soup just to a simmer. Reduce the heat to low, cover the pan, and let simmer very gently until the cauliflower is tender, about 45 minutes (see Note).

3. Turn off the heat, add 1 tablespoon of the thyme leaves, and stir to combine. Cover the pan and let the soup steep for at least 15 minutes.

4. Using an immersion blender, puree the soup in the saucepan. Or, let the soup cool slightly, then puree it in a blender or food processor, and return it to the saucepan. If you prefer a smoother texture, strain the pureed soup through a sieve.

5. Add the remaining ½ cup of milk and the half-and-half to the soup and stir to combine. If the soup is too thick, thin it with more milk or half-and-half or some water. Season the soup with salt and white pepper to taste. If you are not planning on serving the soup at this time, let it cool to room temperature. It can be refrigerated, covered, for up to 3 days.

6. Reheat the soup gently over low heat but do not let it boil. Ladle the soup into warm bowls, garnishing it with a drizzling of truffle oil, if desired, and the remaining 1 tablespoon of thyme leaves.

Earthbound's Janna Jo Williams shows a group of school children just how great basil smells out in the field.

Simply Chicken Soup

Whenever my family has the sniffles, I cook up a big pot of this delicious soup. As the chicken and vegetables cook, they fill the house with an inviting bouquet that can coax even the most reluctant appetite out from under the covers. The broth gets its full-bodied richness from a long, slow simmering. I often skin the chicken before I cook it to reduce the amount of fat in the broth, especially if I'm serving it right away. My family likes to eat the chicken with the broth, so I remove the breast meat early, as soon as it is cooked through, and then add it back at the end. This nourishing soup is enjoyed equally by healthy, hearty appetites, especially when matzoh balls, egg noodles, or white rice are added. **SERVES 6**

1 stewing or roasting chicken,
    5 to 6 pounds, cut into quarters,
    plus the neck and back, if available
1 bunch fresh flat-leaf parsley, plus
    2 tablespoons chopped parsley
    (optional), for garnish
3 medium-size parsnips, peeled and
    cut into 2-inch pieces
4 large carrots, peeled and cut into
    2-inch pieces
5 ribs celery, cut into 2-inch pieces
3 large onions, peeled and quartered
Coarse (kosher) salt and freshly ground
    black pepper
My Matzoh Balls (optional; recipe
    follows)

1. Rinse the chicken well and trim off any excess fat. Place the chicken in a large soup pot and add just enough cool water to cover it by 2 inches. Bring the water to a boil over high heat, then reduce the heat to low. Using a large spoon, skim off any foam that accumulates on the surface.

2. Add the bunch of parsley and the parsnips, carrots, celery, and onions. Let the soup simmer for 30 minutes, then remove the chicken breast pieces. Set them aside to cool.

3. Continue simmering the soup and when the breasts are cool enough to handle, remove the breast meat from the bones. Return the skin and bones to the pot. Refrigerate the meat, covered, until serving time.

4. Let the soup simmer gently, uncovered, until the broth is rich and flavorful, 2½ to 3 hours total.

5. Strain the soup through a sieve into a large, clean pot and discard the solids,

reserving any of the meat from the thighs and legs, if desired. Season the soup to taste with salt and pepper. (If you are making the soup in advance, see Note.)

6. Let the fat rise to the surface of the soup, then skim it off with a metal spoon or ladle. Shred the reserved chicken meat and add it to the soup. Add the matzoh balls, if using. Bring the soup to a simmer over medium-high heat and cook until the chicken and matzoh balls are warmed through, about 5 minutes. Serve hot, garnished with the chopped parsley, if desired.

My Matzoh Balls

In New York City there are great delis where I can satisfy my cravings for matzoh ball soup, but here in central California I need to make my own. I add baking powder to make the matzoh balls light and tender, so as good as they are, they're not appropriate for Passover. Any other time of the year, they turn Simply Chicken Soup (this page) from simply delicious to splendidly satisfying. **SERVES 6**

½ cup store-bought matzoh meal or
    Do-It-Yourself Matzoh Meal
    (page 386)
1 teaspoon baking powder
1 teaspoon coarse (kosher) salt
2 large eggs, beaten
2 tablespoons canola oil or schmaltz
    (melted chicken fat)
2 tablespoons Blond Chicken Stock
    (page 372), store-bought low-sodium
    chicken broth, or water

1. Place the matzoh meal, baking powder, and salt in a medium-size bowl and whisk to combine.

Note: If you are not serving the soup within 2 hours, set the soup pot in a larger pot or bowl filled with ice water and stir the soup occasionally as it cools. Once the soup reaches room temperature, refrigerate it, covered, until the fat solidifies on the surface. Remove the fat with a spoon and discard it. The soup and reserved chicken meat can be refrigerated together, covered, for up to three days or frozen for up to three months.

A great soup combines a variety of interesting flavors.

2. Place the eggs, oil, and chicken stock in a small bowl and whisk to combine.

3. Add the egg mixture to the matzoh meal and stir to combine. Cover the bowl with plastic wrap and refrigerate it until chilled, about 30 minutes.

Flowering garlic chives.

4. Pinch off enough of the batter to roll, between the palms of your hands, into a 1-inch ball. The batter will be very sticky. Place the matzoh ball on a plate. Repeat until all of the remaining batter has been used. You should have about 20 matzoh balls.

5. Bring a large saucepan of salted water to a boil over high heat. Working in two batches if needed to avoid overcrowding the pan, add the matzoh balls and reduce the heat to low. Cover the pan and let simmer gently until the matzoh balls double in size and float to the top of the water, about 20 minutes. Remove the matzoh balls from the water with a slotted spoon and place them on a platter. They will keep, covered, in the refrigerator for 3 days.

Preparing Lemongrass

Lemongrass is an Asian grass that's used like an herb. The fragrance and taste are similar to lemon, but without the sour bite. It has a long, thin, reedy stalk with a plump base. You'll find lemongrass in the produce section of Asian markets, specialty food stores, or well-stocked supermarkets. To prepare lemongrass, cut off and discard the root end and the reedy top, leaving about six inches of usable stalk. Remove and discard the dry outer leaves, usually one or two layers, to reveal the flavorful, pale inner core, which can be sliced, minced, or crushed, as needed. Lemongrass is tough and fibrous, so crushed stalks are usually discarded before serving.

Lemongrass-Coconut Chicken Soup

The pungent, hot flavors of Thailand, cooled with citrus-scented lemongrass and coconut milk, are the inspiration for this easy to make soup. It begins with a flavor-packed broth infused with ginger and hot peppers. Kaffir lime leaves and salty Thai fish sauce can be found in Asian markets, but even without them, you'll still have an explosion of flavors in your bowl. You can make the soup base several days ahead and, just before serving, add the chicken breast—or if you prefer, shrimp or tofu. If you want to stray from tradition, add half a cup of fresh corn kernels for a bit of irresistible crunch and sweetness. If you are hesitant about the peppery-hot flavors, cut back on the amount of Asian chile sauce and remove the seeds from the serrano pepper. But you'll be surprised how the lime juice and herbs quench the fiery heat in this flavorful soup. **SERVES 4 TO 6**

3 cups Blond Chicken Stock (page 372)

2 cans (about 13½ ounces each) light
   coconut milk (see Note)

½ cup minced lemongrass (about 3 stalks;
   see sidebar, facing page)

1 piece (3 inches long) fresh ginger,
   peeled and coarsely chopped
   (about ¼ cup)

½ serrano or jalapeño pepper, sliced

1½ teaspoons Asian chile garlic sauce,
   or ½ teaspoon dried red pepper flakes

4 whole cloves garlic, peeled and
   lightly crushed

2 tablespoons Thai or Vietnamese
   fish sauce (optional)

2 fresh or frozen Kaffir lime leaves
   (optional; see sidebar, this page), sliced

1 whole skinless, boneless chicken breast
   (about 12 ounces), cut into ½-inch
   cubes; or 12 ounces peeled and
   deveined medium-size shrimp;
   or 12 ounces extra-firm tofu,
   cut into ½-inch cubes

2 tablespoons fresh lime juice

Salt (optional)

¼ cup strips of fresh basil
   (preferably Thai basil), for garnish

2 tablespoons coarsely chopped
   fresh cilantro, for garnish

1. Place the stock, coconut milk,
lemongrass, ginger, serrano pepper,
chile sauce, garlic, fish sauce, and Kaffir
lime leaves, if using, in a large saucepan
and stir to combine. Bring the stock
mixture to a simmer over high heat.
Reduce the heat to low and let simmer,
uncovered, until the flavors release,
about 15 minutes. Turn off the heat,
cover the saucepan, and let the soup
base steep for 30 minutes.

2. Strain the soup base through a sieve
into a clean saucepan or bowl and discard
the solids. It can be refrigerated, covered,
for up to 3 days.

3. Reheat the soup base, uncovered, over
medium heat until it begins to simmer.
Add the chicken, shrimp, or tofu and
simmer gently until it is cooked through,
about 5 minutes for chicken, 1½ to 2
minutes for shrimp or tofu.

4. Add the lime juice and season with
salt, as needed. Pour the soup into warm
bowls, garnish each serving with some of
the basil and cilantro, and serve at once.

Note: Light coconut
milk has considerably
less fat than regular,
so I like to use it in
this dish. Of course,
regular coconut milk
can be substituted,
if you wish.

Kaffir Lime Leaves

Glossy, dark green
Kaffir lime
leaves are often used
in Thai recipes to add
a floral and citrus
aroma and taste. You
can usually find them
with the refrigerated
herbs in Asian
markets or specialty
food stores. Kaffir
lime leaves are
available both fresh
and dried, but the
fresh leaves have a
more intense flavor
and scent. Fresh
leaves, wrapped
tightly in plastic
wrap, can be stored
in the freezer for
up to six months.

Miso

Miso is a type of thick bean paste that you'll find in the refrigerated section of specialty food stores, health food stores, and Asian markets.

Miso is made from soybeans and is very nutritious. Traditionally, the beans are allowed to ferment for a few months or up to several years. These variables influence the color and flavor, resulting in the dozens of regional varieties that are available in Japan. However, in most American stores, the selection is limited to just a few.

Light-colored miso (white or golden) is the most mildly flavored and is used for delicate soups and sauces. Darker-colored miso (red, reddish brown, or dark brown) has been fermented longer and has a stronger flavor that's more appropriate for heavier dishes or richly flavored soups.

Miso Soup
with Udon Noodles

In Japan, many people sip a bowl of miso soup for breakfast, but in the United States we usually enjoy it as a light first course before a Japanese dinner. Traditional miso soup recipes blend the miso with a seaweed and fish stock. This atypical version uses a flavorful vegetable stock instead, creating a soup base that is robust and easy to make. The addition of Asian udon *noodles makes the soup substantial enough for a light lunch.* Udon *are Asian noodles, which may be round or flat. They are made from wheat or corn flour and look similar to linguine or spaghetti. Tamari is similar to soy sauce, only it has a richer taste and is slightly thicker.* **SERVES 6**

8 cups Shiitake Vegetable Stock
   (page 377)
1 tablespoon toasted sesame oil
2 teaspoons minced garlic
1 tablespoon grated peeled fresh ginger
1 large carrot, thinly sliced on an angle
3 tablespoons red miso
   (see sidebar, this page)
$\frac{1}{2}$ cup thinly sliced scallions,
   including white and 3 inches
   of green
About 2 ounces dried udon noodles,
   or linguine, cooked according to
   package directions
Soy sauce or tamari

1. Pour the stock into a large saucepan and let come to a boil over high heat.

2. Meanwhile, heat the sesame oil in a small skillet over low heat. Add the garlic and ginger and cook, stirring frequently, until the garlic is soft and fragrant but not browned, about 2 minutes.

3. When the stock is boiling, add the garlic mixture and the carrot. Lower the heat to medium-low and let simmer until the carrot is tender, about 10 minutes.

4. Add the miso and whisk to combine. Add the scallions and udon noodles and cook until heated through, 2 to 3 minutes. Do not let the soup boil or it will become cloudy. Season the soup with soy sauce to taste. Serve hot.

Mediterranean Lentil Soup

I make sure my athletic kids have some protein with virtually every meal, but I also want to reduce the amount of meat we eat. Serving lentils or beans is a great way to accomplish both goals. Lentils have the added bonus of being much quicker to cook than "real" beans (lentils are actually legumes and related to peas), so no soaking is required. This nutritious soup has a bit of everything—leafy greens, starchy potatoes, antioxidant-rich tomatoes—not to mention those protein-rich lentils. **SERVES 6 TO 8**

Note: If your potatoes are young, unblemished, and thin-skinned, there's no need to peel them.

1 tablespoon olive oil
1 medium-size yellow onion, cut into
    $^1/_4$-inch dice (about $^3/_4$ cup)
1 celery rib, thinly sliced
2 small carrots, thinly sliced
2 cloves garlic, minced
1$^1/_2$ cups French green lentils, rinsed
8 cups Blond Chicken Stock (page 372)
    or Shiitake Vegetable Stock
    (page 377), or store-bought low-
    sodium chicken or vegetable broth
1 bay leaf
$^1/_2$ teaspoon dried oregano
$^1/_2$ teaspoon dried basil
$^1/_4$ teaspoon dried red pepper flakes
1 teaspoon salt
$^1/_2$ teaspoon freshly ground black pepper
1 can (14 ounces) diced tomatoes,
    with their juice
3 medium-size Yukon Gold or waxy
    potatoes (such as White Rose;
    see Note), cut in $^1/_4$-inch dice
    (about 2 cups)
1 tablespoon fresh lemon juice, or
    1 tablespoon red wine vinegar
2 packed cups fresh spinach or chard,
    well rinsed, stems removed, and large
    leaves cut into 1-inch wide ribbons
Freshly grated Parmesan cheese
    (optional), for garnish

1. Heat the olive oil in a large, heavy pot over medium heat. Add the onion, celery, and carrots and cook, stirring frequently, for 5 minutes. Add the garlic and cook until the onion and garlic are soft but not browned, 1 minute longer.

2. Add the lentils and stock. Increase the heat to high and bring to a boil. Reduce the heat to low and let simmer until the lentils soften, about 20 minutes.

3. Add the bay leaf, oregano, basil, pepper flakes, salt, pepper, tomatoes, and potatoes. Let the soup simmer until the potatoes are tender, about 20 minutes longer.

4. Just before serving, remove and discard the bay leaf. Add the lemon juice and spinach to the soup and let simmer gently just until the spinach wilts, about 2 minutes (adding the lemon juice and greens just before serving helps the color of the greens stay bright). If you like a thinner soup, add more stock or some water. Serve the soup hot, garnished with Parmesan cheese, if desired.

Silky Black Bean Soup

If you have a well-stocked pantry and a few aromatic vegetables in the fridge, you can make this easy and delicious soup on the spur of the moment. Although you could take the time to soak and cook dried beans and make homemade stock, no one will be the wiser when you use canned beans and store-bought broth. What they will notice is that this soup is filling and flavorful. **SERVES 4**

2 tablespoons olive oil

1 rib celery, coarsely chopped

1 small carrot, coarsely chopped

$1/2$ cup coarsely chopped yellow onion

$1/4$ cup coarsely chopped green or
   red bell pepper

1 tablespoon minced garlic

$1^{1}/_{2}$ teaspoons dried cumin

1 teaspoon dried oregano

1 teaspoon chili powder

$3^{1}/_{2}$ cups store-bought low-sodium
   vegetable broth

2 cans (15 ounces each) black beans,
   drained

Coarse (kosher) salt and freshly ground
   black pepper

Soft goat cheese, for garnish

Finely chopped chives, for garnish

1. Heat the olive oil in a large, heavy pot over medium heat. Add the celery, carrot, onion, and bell pepper. Cook the vegetables, stirring frequently, until they soften and begin to brown slightly, 8 to 10 minutes. Add the garlic, cumin, oregano, and chili powder and cook, stirring frequently, until fragrant, about 2 minutes.

2. Add the stock and black beans and increase the heat to high. Bring the soup to a boil, then reduce the heat to low,
cover the pan, and let simmer until the flavors meld, 15 to 20 minutes.

3. Using an immersion blender, puree the soup in the saucepan. Or, let the soup cool slightly, then puree it in a blender or food processor and return it to the pot. Season the soup with salt and pepper to taste.

4. Gently reheat the soup over medium-low heat. Serve hot, garnished with a dollop of goat cheese and a sprinkling of chives.

Cultivating a field of cilantro.

Portuguese Kale Soup

Caldo verde (kale soup) is so popular in Portugal that some call it the national dish. Coupled with beans and hearty winter vegetables like carrots, potatoes, and onion, kale makes a full meal in a bowl. Vegetarians will love this soup made with vegetable stock, but as meat eaters, we like the Portuguese tradition of adding slices of the pork sausage called chouriço *(pronounced* sure-E-soo*)—or any other spicy smoked pork sausage.* **SERVES 6 TO 8**

¹/₄ cup olive oil
1 large yellow onion, cut into ¹/₂-inch dice (about 1 cup)
1 medium-size carrot, cut into ¹/₂-inch dice (about ¹/₂ cup)
4 cloves garlic, minced
About 8 cups Blond Chicken Stock (page 372) or Shiitake Vegetable Stock (page 377)
2 cups diced Yukon Gold or waxy potatoes (such as White Rose, see Note), cut in ¹/₂-inch dice
1 teaspoon herbes de Provence or dried thyme
1 bunch kale
1 can (28 ounces) diced tomatoes, with their juice

1 can (about 14 ounces) white beans, such as cannellini, drained
¹/₂ pound smoked pork sausage, such as chouriço, chorizo, or kielbasa (optional), cut into ¹/₄-inch slices
Coarse (kosher) salt and freshly ground black pepper

1. Heat the olive oil in a large, heavy pot over medium-low heat. Add the onion and carrots and cook until the vegetables soften, 5 to 10 minutes. Add the garlic and cook, stirring often, until fragrant, about 2 minutes.

2. Add the stock, potatoes, and *herbes de Provence* to the pot and bring to a boil over

Ornamental kale is dramatically beautiful, as (left to right) these White Nagoya, White Peacock, and Red Nagoya kales illustrate.

FARM FRESH

kale

Kale provides a much-welcomed change of pace for wintry meals. There are many varieties, each with a distinctive look. The leaves may be flat or curly, with edges that are smooth or jagged. Some types of kale have creamy pale leaves, while others are deep green, blue-green, or purple. Regardless of the shape or color, the flavor will be similar, with a pleasantly bitter taste that seems to improve when grown in frosty weather.

Like other members of the cabbage and broccoli family, kale is also a nutritious source of calcium and iron, as well as antioxidants, such as vitamin C and beta-carotene, which may protect against cancer.

Tiny baby kale enlivens a salad mix, but as this leafy green matures, it's better cooked. Discard any tough stems and ribs, and rinse the kale well before cooking. Young kale only needs a brief sauté or stir-fry; mature kale is a perfect addition to soup because it tastes best when slowly cooked until tender.

high heat. Reduce the heat to low and let simmer gently until the potatoes are partially cooked, about 15 minutes.

3. Meanwhile, rinse the kale and remove and discard the tough stems. If the kale leaves are flat, cut them crosswise into 1-inch-wide ribbons. If the leaves are curly, tear them into bite-size pieces.

4. Add the kale, tomatoes, beans, and sausage, if using, to the soup and cook until the potatoes and kale are tender, 5 to 10 minutes.

5. If the soup is too thick, thin it with more stock or some water. Season the soup with salt and pepper to taste and serve hot. Any leftover soup can be refrigerated, covered, for up to 5 days.

Note: If your potatoes are young, unblemished, and thin-skinned, there's no need to peel them.

Savory Split Pea Soup
with Ham and Pancetta

I regularly crave this hearty soup loaded with smoky bits of ham and pancetta. It's both comforting and satisfying. Splashes of sherry and balsamic vinegar add a deep, mellow richness that balances out the slightly sweet and salty ham. A sprinkling of thyme or parsley just before serving dresses the soup up nicely. With a couple of minor adjustments, vegetarians will love this soup, too—use vegetable stock instead of chicken and leave out the pancetta and ham. **SERVES 6**

2 tablespoons olive oil
³/₄ cup finely diced pancetta (about 3 ounces)
1 medium-size yellow onion, finely diced (about ³/₄ cup)
1 celery rib, finely diced (about ¹/₄ cup)
2 small carrots, finely diced (about ¹/₂ cup)
1 bay leaf
2 cloves garlic, minced
2 cups dried split green peas, rinsed
3 cups Blond Chicken Stock (page 372), or store-bought low-sodium chicken broth
1 teaspoon salt, or more to taste
1 teaspoon dried thyme

1 cup diced (¹/₄-inch dice; about 5 ounces) smoked ham, such as Black Forest (see Note, page 54)
1 tablespoon balsamic vinegar or red wine vinegar
3 tablespoons sherry, or to taste (optional)
Fresh thyme leaves or chopped flat-leaf parsley, for garnish

1. Heat the olive oil in a large, heavy pot over medium heat. Add the pancetta and cook until it softens and begins to color, about 3 minutes. Add the onion, celery, carrots, and bay leaf and cook, stirring frequently, until the vegetables soften, 8 to 10 minutes. Add the garlic and cook until fragrant, about 1 minute longer.

Our Carmel Valley foreman, Manuel Sumano, checks to be sure our irrigation is functioning properly.

Note: If you buy the ham at the deli counter, ask for it to be sliced ¼ inch thick to make dicing it easier.

2. Add the split peas, stock, and 3½ cups of water to the pot and bring to a boil over high heat. Reduce the heat to low, cover the pot, and let simmer slowly, stirring occasionally for 30 minutes.

3. Add the salt and thyme and continue cooking, partially covered, until the split peas are tender and have begun to break down slightly, about 30 minutes. Remove and discard the bay leaf. If you are not

planning on serving the soup at this time, let it cool to room temperature. It can be refrigerated, covered, for up to 3 days or frozen for 2 months.

4. Add the ham and let simmer until warmed through, about 5 minutes. Remove the soup from the heat and stir in the vinegar and sherry, if using. Serve the soup hot, sprinkled with fresh thyme leaves.

Tuscan White Bean Stew
with Rosemary

When the mercury hovers near freezing, this hearty stew of white beans and vegetables scented with rosemary will warm you from the inside out. It's no wonder that the Tuscans developed a reputation far and wide as bean eaters. Their secret to making this humble dish memorable is a long, slow simmer and a flavorful stock. The cooking time will vary depending on the freshness of the beans. Even dry beans continue to lose moisture as they sit on the store shelf, so the older they are, the longer they will need to cook to become tender. It's best to shop for beans in a busy store that will likely have a brisk turn over.

This stew is a little soupy, but if you prefer a thicker stew, puree about a cup of the beans and add it back to the pot. You'll enjoy this as a side dish with pork or lamb or as a bowlful of soupy stew with crusty bread and an arugula salad.

SERVES 4 AS A STEW OR 6 AS A SIDE DISH

2 tablespoons olive oil

$1/2$ cup diced ($1/4$-inch dice)
    yellow onion

1 small carrot, peeled and cut into
    $1/4$-inch dice

$1/3$ cup diced ($1/4$-inch dice) celery

$1/3$ cup finely diced bacon
    (from about 2 thick-cut slices)

1 tablespoon minced garlic

About 5 cups Blond Chicken Stock
    (page 372), or store-bought low-
    sodium chicken broth

$1^3/4$ cups dried cannellini beans
    (12 ounces; see Note), picked
    over and rinsed

2 ripe Roma (plum) tomatoes,
    cut into $1/4$-inch dice

1 tablespoon chopped fresh rosemary,
    or 1 teaspoon dried rosemary

1 teaspoon good-quality balsamic
    vinegar (see sidebar, page 87)

Coarse (kosher) salt and freshly
    ground black pepper

1. Heat the olive oil in a large, heavy pot over medium-high heat. Add the onion, carrot, and celery and cook, stirring frequently, until the vegetables begin to lightly brown and soften, 5 to 8 minutes.

2. Add the bacon and cook until it begins to brown, about 5 minutes. Add the garlic and cook, stirring constantly, until fragrant, about 1 minute.

3. Add the stock, beans, tomatoes, and rosemary and increase the heat to high. The liquid should cover the beans by about an inch. Add more stock or water if necessary. Bring the stock to a boil. Reduce the heat to low, cover the pot, and let simmer gently, stirring occasionally, until the beans are tender, 2 to 3 hours depending on the age of the beans. Check the pot occasionally to make sure the liquid is simmering gently but not boiling. If necessary, add water so that the beans remain just covered with liquid.

4. Add the balsamic vinegar and season the stew with salt and pepper to taste. Serve hot.

Note: For a shorter cooking time, presoak the beans by placing them in a medium-size bowl and adding 4 cups of cold water. Cover the bowl with plastic wrap and refrigerate it for about 8 hours. Test the softness of the soaked beans by squeezing one between your fingers. If the soaked bean gives slightly to the pressure, the beans should become tender when cooked 1 to $1^1/2$ hours. Before cooking, drain the beans into a colander and rinse them. Then follow the recipe, but use 4 cups of chicken stock instead of 5 cups. The liquid in the pot should just cover the presoaked beans.

Foggy Day Chili

*M*onterey County's spectacular beauty attracts visitors from all over the world, but many are surprised to discover that along the Central California coast even many summer days are often cooled by fog. Fortunately, it is sunnier inland at our Farm Stand. So while shopkeepers in foggy Carmel do a brisk sweatshirt business, we dish up bowls of our mildly spicy chili to warm visitors who have escaped to the Carmel Valley sun. This chili is quick to prepare. It's great with a slice of buttered Farm Stand Corn Bread. If you like your chili spicier, add some dried red pepper flakes at the end. The chili tastes even better reheated, and it freezes well, so you may want to make a double batch. **SERVES 6**

A traditional combination— chili and corn bread.

2 tablespoons canola or olive oil

1 medium-size yellow onion,
cut into $1/4$-inch dice
(about $3/4$ cup)

1 tablespoon minced garlic

$1^1/2$ pounds lean ground beef

1 tablespoon ground cumin

1 tablespoon chili powder

2 teaspoons dried oregano

1 can (15 ounces) black beans,
undrained

1 can (15 ounces) pinto beans,
undrained

1 can (28 ounces) crushed or
diced tomatoes, with their juices

1 teaspoon salt, or more to taste

Freshly ground black pepper

Dried red pepper flakes
(optional)

Freshly grated cheddar cheese
(optional), for garnish

Sour cream (optional), for garnish

Farm Stand Corn Bread
(recipe follows)

1. Heat the oil in a large, heavy pot over medium-low heat. Add the onion and cook for 5 minutes. Add the garlic and cook until the onion and garlic are soft but not browned, about 1 minute longer. Add the beef, and break up the meat with a wooden spoon.

2. Increase the heat to medium-high and add the cumin, chili powder, and oregano. Cook, stirring frequently, until the meat is browned and cooked through, about 7 minutes.

3. Add the black beans, pinto beans, and tomatoes, with their liquids, and bring the chili to a boil. Reduce the heat to low, cover the pot, and let the chili simmer, gently stirring occasionally until thickened and the flavors are concentrated, about 45 minutes.

4. Add the salt, then taste for seasoning, adding more salt as needed and black pepper and red pepper flakes, if using, to taste. Serve the chili hot with bowls of grated cheese and sour cream on the side, for garnish, if desired, and corn bread. If you are not planning on serving the chili at this time, let it cool to room temperature. It can be refrigerated, covered, for up to 3 days or frozen for up to 3 months.

Farm Stand Corn Bread

We serve this hearty corn bread at our Farm Stand alongside spicy chili and wintry soups. I like it best hot from the oven, or quickly warmed in the microwave later. The flavor and texture of the corn bread are so satisfying that it can turn a simple bowl of soup and salad into a meal. **MAKES ONE 9 BY 13-INCH CORN BREAD**

Butter for greasing the pan
3 large eggs
8 tablespoons (1 stick) unsalted
   butter, melted and cooled slightly
1$\frac{1}{2}$ cups half-and-half
$\frac{1}{2}$ cup heavy (whipping) cream
2 cups fine yellow cornmeal
2 cups unbleached all-purpose flour
2 teaspoons salt
1 tablespoon baking powder
$\frac{1}{4}$ cup sugar
1 cup fresh corn kernels
   (from 2 ears; see box, page 29),
   or 1 cup frozen (unthawed;
   see Note) or well-drained
   canned corn kernels
$\frac{3}{4}$ cup (about 3 ounces) freshly
   grated sharp cheddar cheese

1. Position a rack in the lower third of the oven and preheat the oven to 400°F. Butter a 9 by 13–inch baking pan and set it aside.

2. Break the eggs into a medium-size bowl and whisk until just combined. Add the butter, half-and-half, and cream and whisk well.

Note: If you use frozen corn, remove any bits of ice that may be mixed in with the kernels.

Children of all ages have great fun in our organic corn maze.

3. Place the cornmeal, flour, salt, baking powder, and sugar in a large bowl and whisk to combine well.

4. Add the egg mixture to the cornmeal mixture and stir with a rubber spatula until partially combined. Add the corn kernels and cheese and stir until just combined. Do not overmix the batter or the corn bread will be tough.

5. Spoon the batter into the prepared baking pan and smooth the surface (the batter will be very thick).

6. Bake the corn bread until it is lightly golden and a toothpick inserted in the center comes out clean, 25 to 35 minutes. Serve warm. The corn bread tastes best the day it's made, but if necessary, it can be stored in an airtight container for up to 3 days. Reheat it in a microwave for about 10 seconds or in a preheated 350°F oven for 5 to 10 minutes.

Mexican Albondigas Soup

Meatballs—albondigas in Spanish—are the main attraction in this hearty soup. An egg and a little cream bind lean ground beef with some garlic, cumin, thyme, and oregano for a rich texture and taste. If you prefer, ground turkey or pork would work just as well. The meatballs simmer in a chicken broth enriched with carrots and a leek, and are spiked with jalapeño peppers. Our customers prefer their soup on the tame side, but it's easy to turn up the heat by adding more chili powder or by leaving in the jalapeño seeds. This is Mexican home-style cooking at its best, because it gives you the chance to use whatever is on hand—zucchini, potato, celery, or corn would all be nice additions. So would a handful of baby spinach. **SERVES 6 TO 8**

FOR THE MEATBALLS

1 tablespoon olive oil

1/2 cup finely diced yellow onion
(1/4-inch dice or smaller)

1 teaspoon minced garlic

1/2 teaspoon ground cumin

1/2 teaspoon dried thyme

1/2 teaspoon dried oregano

1 large egg

1/4 cup heavy (whipping) cream

1/2 cup fresh bread crumbs

1 pound lean ground beef

1/2 teaspoon coarse (kosher) salt

1/4 teaspoon freshly ground black pepper

FOR THE SOUP

2 tablespoons olive oil

4 medium-size carrots, thinly sliced
(about 2 cups)

1 large leek, both white and light green
parts, rinsed well and thinly sliced
(about 1 cup), or 1 cup diced yellow
onions (1/4-inch dice)

1 tablespoon minced garlic

2 jalapeño peppers, stemmed, seeded,
and thinly sliced

1 cup diced fresh or canned tomatoes,
with their juice

10 cups Blond Chicken Stock
(page 372), Dark Chicken Stock
(page 373), or store-bought
low-sodium chicken broth

1 teaspoon chili powder

Coarse (kosher) salt and freshly
ground black pepper

1/2 cup finely chopped fresh cilantro,
for garnish

1. Make the meatballs: Heat the olive oil
in a small skillet over medium-low heat.
Add the onion and cook until soft, 5 to 10
minutes. Add the garlic and the cumin,
thyme, and oregano and cook, stirring
frequently, until the garlic is soft and
fragrant, 2 to 3 minutes.

Autumn is the time to
spread seeds for cover crops
that will replenish the
nutrients in the soil.

2. Place the egg and the cream in a small bowl and whisk until combined. Add the bread crumbs and stir to combine.

3. Place the beef in a medium-size bowl. Add the onion mixture, the egg mixture, and the salt and pepper and mix with your hands to combine. Form the beef mixture into 1-inch meatballs and place them on a platter. Refrigerate the meatballs, covered with plastic wrap, for at least 1 hour or as long as overnight. (The meatballs can also be frozen at this point for up to 2 months. Let them thaw in the refrigerator overnight before proceeding with the recipe.)

4. Make the soup: Heat the 2 tablespoons of olive oil in a large, heavy pot over medium-low heat. Add the carrots and leek and cook, stirring occasionally, until the vegetables are soft, 5 to 10 minutes.

Add the garlic and the jalapeños and cook, stirring constantly, until the garlic is soft but not browned, about 2 minutes.

5. Add the tomatoes, stock, and chili powder. Increase the heat to medium-high and bring the soup to a boil, then reduce the heat to medium and let simmer for 10 minutes.

6. Add the meatballs and adjust the heat so that the soup simmers gently, uncovered, until the meatballs are cooked through, 8 to 10 minutes.

7. Season the soup with salt and pepper to taste. Serve the soup hot, garnished with the chopped cilantro. Any leftover soup can be refrigerated, covered, for up to 3 days.

Chapter 3

Leafy Green Salads

I'm passionate about salads. Decades of eating two, and sometimes three, salads a day hasn't dimmed the joy they bring me one bit. The word *savor* pops into my mind when I think of salads. I eat them slowly and let each bite reveal its wholly unique combination of textures and flavors. Salads are beauty in a bowl, vitality captured; they make me feel alive and healthy.

My intimate connection with greens began in the mid-1980s when my husband, Drew, and I began growing gourmet greens to supply to local chefs. During a time when a salad usually meant a wedge of watery iceberg smothered with bottled ranch dressing, Drew and I were scouring seed catalogs for exotic varieties of Asian, European, and heirloom greens. Discovering new greens and experimenting with blends was like unearthing precious treasures to me—and it still is. It's a treat for the senses, from the way lolla rosa's ruffles look like they've been dipped in Burgundy wine to the crisp crunch frisée adds to a bite.

My creativity with salads really soared when we began washing and bagging our greens, making them readily available for meals throughout the week. When all I had to do was grab a handful of salad, I suddenly had the time to experiment with dressings and toppings. It seems others felt the same way. Within a few years, the demand for our beautiful baby greens was so great that grocery stores around the United States began stocking their shelves with Earthbound Farm bags. Today you can take your pick from beautiful spring mix, spicy argula, tender baby spinach, or nutty little leaves of mâche. Nearly every time we introduce a blend, it becomes my new favorite for weeks.

The salads in this chapter are meant to rouse your own imagination, offering you ideas to build on. There are unusual combinations, like the strawberry and tarragon salad and the roasted beet and arugula salad that's made with walnuts and feta cheese. I've included tips to familiarize you with some uncommon salad ingredients, such as kohlrabi, persimmons, and edible flowers, to embolden you to break from the routine.

A pristine field of organic broccoli.

Facing Page:
Preparing the Baby Spinach Salad with Creamy Herb Dressing (page 74).

You'll also find delicious vinaigrettes and creamy dressings, along with suggestions for pairing them with salad greens. Lighter dressings, like the Sierra Mar Shallot Vinaigrette, work well with delicate mixed baby greens. Romaine, a sturdier lettuce, holds up to the thicker Buttermilk Blue Cheese Dressing. Several, like my Lemon Vinaigrette with Dijon mustard and garlic, make a great everyday dressing for any green.

I hope this chapter will inspire you to conduct your own salad experiments. There are no hard-and-fast rules to follow. Just let what catches your eye or your curiosity have its way. The goal is a salad that is so delicious you too will savor each and every bite.

Spring Mâche Salad
with Kohlrabi, Radishes, and Peas

Mark Marino, our Carmel Valley farm manager, describes his job as growing "art supplies" for cooks. The versatile green mâche is one of our favorites. Team it with sweet young peas, peppery radishes, and crisp kohlrabi (see box, page 66), and you create a salad that's a work of art, celebrating the best of the spring garden. If you have some steamed asparagus spears on hand, add those too. And, if you are lucky enough to find very fresh, young English peas, don't even bother to blanch them; their tender sweetness will shine through just the way they are. **SERVES 4 AS A SIDE SALAD**

A heaping bowl of mixed baby greens looks at home among the dandelion greens, carrots, and basil.

$1/2$ cup fresh shelled English peas
     (from $1/2$ pound unshelled peas)
4 ounces (about 1 cup) fresh sugar snap
     peas, stems and any strings removed
$3^1/2$ ounces (about 5 cups) mâche
     (see box, page 67), carefully
     rinsed and dried, if needed
1 tablespoon packed fresh tarragon leaves
1 tablespoon packed fresh chervil or dill
About $1/4$ cup Lemon Vinaigrette
     (page 97)
1 small kohlrabi, peeled and cut into
     matchstick-size pieces
2 radishes, trimmed and thinly sliced

1. Fill a large bowl of water with ice cubes and set aside.

2. Bring a small pot of water to a boil over high heat. Add the English peas (unless they are very young and tender) and sugar snap peas and cook them until crisp-tender, about 1 minute. Immediately drain the peas in a colander and then plunge the colander into the bowl of ice water to stop the cooking. When the peas have cooled, drain them again.

3. Just before serving, place the mâche, tarragon, and chervil in a large salad bowl and toss to combine. Add 2 tablespoons of the Lemon Vinaigrette. Toss to lightly coat the leaves, then taste, adding up to 1 tablespoon more of the vinaigrette if needed. Transfer the dressed greens to a platter or individual salad plates.

4. Place the English peas, sugar snap peas, kohlrabi, and radishes in the salad bowl and toss with 1 tablespoon of the vinaigrette. Arrange the vegetables on the greens. Serve immediately.

kohlrabi

Kohlrabi is round like a turnip and has a taste similar to a cabbage, only more sweet and mild. It tastes best when grown in cool weather; hot temperatures make the flesh strong tasting and woody. Look for it in farmers' markets during the spring and fall.

At first glance, you may think kohlrabi is a root vegetable, but it's not. The round edible base grows on top of the soil and has thick, leafy stems curving out from its sides. There are green- and purple-skinned varieties; both have a creamy white center. A young kohlrabi, smaller than a tennis ball, is crisp-tender when peeled and eaten raw. It adds a delicious crunch to salads. Larger, mature kohlrabi often has a woody texture, so it tastes best cooked. Try it in soups and stews as a substitute for turnip roots.

Mâche Salad
with Marinated Cucumber and Red Onion

This summery first course is actually two salads in one. A brief soaking in fresh lemon juice, white wine vinegar, and olive oil softens and melds the cucumber and onion into a refreshing salad. Mounded on top of that is a leafy green salad of tender mâche, ripe tomatoes, and peppery radishes that have been tossed in the same vinaigrette, tying everything together in a sophisticated blend of textures, colors, and tastes. **SERVES 4 AS A SIDE SALAD**

2 teaspoons grated lemon zest

2 tablespoons fresh lemon juice

1 tablespoon white wine vinegar

Pinch of salt, or more to taste

Pinch of freshly ground black pepper,
   or more to taste

¹/₄ cup extra-virgin olive oil

1 small hothouse (seedless English)
   cucumber, peeled and thinly sliced

¹/₂ small red onion, thinly sliced

2 tablespoons coarsely chopped fresh
   flat-leaf parsley

1 teaspoon sesame seeds, toasted
   (see sidebar, page 273)

3¹/₂ ounces (about 5 cups) mâche

1 Roma (plum) tomato, cut into
   ¹/₄-inch dice

1 bunch (about 6) radishes, trimmed
   and thinly sliced

1. Combine the lemon zest and juice, vinegar, salt, and pepper in a bowl and slowly whisk in the olive oil. Taste for seasoning, adding more salt and/or pepper as needed. Add the cucumber, onion, parsley, and sesame seeds and let marinate in the vinaigrette at room temperature for 20 minutes.

FARM FRESH

mâche

Mâche, or lamb's lettuce, is a salad green with a mild, nutty flavor. It has long been popular in Europe and is now available across the United States. Mâche has small, rounded dark-green leaves, which grow in a tiny bunch, like a little rosette. In the supermarket, you may find mâche for sale with the leaves still clustered together or separated. Mâche is a delicious addition to salad blends or makes a special salad on its own.

2. Using a slotted spoon, remove the cucumber and red onion from the vinaigrette and divide them evenly among 4 salad plates. Do not discard the vinaigrette.

3. Place the mâche, tomato, and radishes in a large salad bowl. Add the vinaigrette you used as a marinade and toss to coat. Arrange the mâche mixture on top of the cucumber and onion salad. Serve immediately.

A tractor cultivates a field of broccoli in the Salinas Valley.

A New Leaf

Leaf lettuces and greens provide so much more flavor and nutrition than head lettuces. In fact, a mixed greens salad provides seven and a half times more vitamin C, ten times more iron, thirty-five times more vitamin A, as well as more calcium and fiber per serving than iceberg.

A Field Guide to Gourmet Greens

The most enticing salads balance sweet, peppery, and bitter tastes with frilly, flat, crisp, and soft textures. Mixing colors and shapes also contributes to a salad's visual appeal.

arugula *is a popular aromatic leaf, prized for its nutty flavor and peppery bite. Delicious in salads, it also adds a distinct flavor to a variety of dishes.*

belgian endive *is a chicory known for its succulent and velvety creamy-white leaves with a mildly bitter flavor.*

chard *comes in many colors, even rainbow. Baby chards can be a colorful addition to salads. Mature leaves taste similar to spinach when cooked.*

chervil, *a member of the parsley family, is a culinary herb with dark green leaves and a mild, anise-like flavor.*

cilantro, *a member of the parsley family, lends a strong and unique flavor to salads and is often used in Mexican, Caribbean, and Asian cooking.*

collard greens, *a cruciferous vegetable, is a member of the cabbage family with a fairly mild flavor similar to green kale. The leaves are sturdy and best when cooked.*

dill *is an herb with beautiful feathery leaves and a distinct flavor that's very strong when fresh, but more tame when it's cooked or dried.*

dino kale, *an Italian heirloom variety, has narrow, dark green, crumpled leaves that are smaller and more tender than other kales and are especially dense with antioxidants.*

friseé, *a chicory also known as curly endive, adds a fresh flavor and attractive texture to salads with its frilly leaves and white heart.*

green curly kale *has a cabbage-like flavor and frilly thick leaves that hold their shape better than other greens when cooked.*

green leaf lettuce, *as well as red leaf, are popular spring ingredients when picked small.*

green oak leaf lettuce *is very delicate with a mildly sweet, fresh flavor and a beautiful shape reminiscent of oak leaves.*

italian parsley, *also known as flat-leaf parsley, is an herb with a stronger flavor than its curly cousin. It is flavorful cooked or fresh.*

lollo rosa, *is a mildly flavored lettuce with intensely ruffled leaves that are green at the base and red at the edge.*

mâche *is a mild, tender, and buttery flavored green with delicate teardrop shaped leaves that are pretty and delicious in salads.*

mizuna *is a Japanese mustard green with a mildly tangy flavor. Its distinctively jagged baby leaves add architectural elegance to salads and its adult leaves are used in cooking.*

mustard leaves *can be red or green and have a pungent flavor that strengthens as they mature. Baby leaves give flavor to salads and sandwiches and adult leaves are used in cooking.*

nagoya kale *is a flowering kale with firm leaves and a cabbage-like flavor. Its firmness lends itself well to cooking.*

pea greens *are the leaves and shoots of young pea plants. They are sweet, tender, and have a strong pea taste— perfect in salads, stir fries, or wilted as a side dish.*

radicchio, *also known as Italian chicory, has a mildly bitter flavor. Its beautiful red leaves with white veins are a delicious and striking addition to salads.*

red oak leaf lettuce *is tender and delicate with a beautiful burgundy color that adds drama to any salad.*

red russian kale *has an unusual shape. Its mildly flavored leaves have reddish veins, and are lightly tinged with purple on the margins.*

romaine lettuce *is crisp and sweet when mature. Baby green and red romaine are common ingredients in spring mix.*

spinach *has a mild and delicate flavor and is packed with nutrients. Baby spinach is very tender and is commonly used in spring mix salads.*

tango, *a leaf lettuce, has distinctive curly, ruffled leaves which are tender and slightly tangier than other leaf lettuces.*

Summer Salad
with Butter Lettuce, Raspberries, and Hazelnuts

Delicate red berries and crunchy hazelnuts turn a simple green salad into an unusual first course for a warm summer evening meal. The raspberry vinaigrette accentuates the fruit and nut flavors. If you're pressed for time, skip the candied nuts and simply toast ¼ cup of raw nuts (see page 98). **SERVES 4 AS A SIDE SALAD**

1 large head butter lettuce, such as
   Bibb or Boston
About ¼ cup Raspberry-Hazelnut
   Vinaigrette (recipe follows)
1 half-pint (about 1¼ cups) fresh red or
   golden raspberries, or a combination
¼ cup Brown Sugar Glazed Hazelnuts
   (page 109)

1. Carefully pull the lettuce leaves from the core, tearing off and discarding any damaged parts. Rinse the leaves under gently running cold water, drain them well, and spin them dry. Wrap the lettuce in a clean kitchen towel or paper towels and refrigerate until serving time.

2. Just before you plan to serve the salad, gently tear the large lettuce leaves into smaller pieces. Keep smaller leaves whole. Place all of the lettuce in a large salad bowl and add 3 tablespoons of the Raspberry-Hazelnut Vinaigrette. Toss to lightly coat the leaves, then taste to see if more vinaigrette is needed.

3. Transfer the lettuce to individual salad plates. Top the lettuce with the raspberries and Brown Sugar Glazed Hazelnuts and serve immediately.

Raspberry-Hazelnut Vinaigrette

The flavors in this simple vinaigrette echo the fresh raspberries and candied hazelnuts in the Summer Salad with Butter Lettuce, Raspberries, and Hazelnuts, but it would be equally light and refreshing on a simple salad of mixed baby greens. You can substitute any flavorful nut oil to match the nuts you've used in the salad. **MAKES ABOUT ½ CUP**

2 tablespoons store-bought or
   homemade Raspberry Vinegar
   (page 380)
½ teaspoon Dijon mustard
3 tablespoons hazelnut oil
   (see sidebar, page 100)
3 tablespoons extra-virgin olive oil
Salt and freshly ground black pepper

Place the Raspberry Vinegar, mustard, hazelnut oil, and olive oil in a glass jar and seal the lid tightly. Shake the jar vigorously to combine. Season the vinaigrette with salt and pepper to taste. The vinaigrette can be refrigerated, covered, for up to 1 month. Let it return to room temperature before using.

Deliciously Edible Flowers

All flowers are beautiful, but not all are edible. A few Johnny-jump-ups or violas or some nasturtium, marigold, or bachelor's button petals sprinkled on a salad or cold soup are a delight.

Make sure the flowers have been specifically grown for eating. Decorative flowers from a nursery, garden shop, or florist may have been treated with chemicals that are not approved for foods.

While you sometimes find packages of edible flowers alongside fresh herbs in specialty food markets, many edible flowers can be grown organically at home. Don't forget that herb blossoms—such as chive, borage, hyssop, and thyme—are also delicious.

Nasturtium flowers, with their slightly peppery flavor, make a beautiful edible garnish, and are easy to grow, too.

Butter Lettuce Salad
with Passion Fruit Vinaigrette and Edible Flowers

Tender lettuce leaves and a buttery avocado decorated with delicate edible flowers make this a lovely starter for a summer luncheon. As if the flowers aren't delightful enough, the passion fruit dressing makes the salad irresistible. Fresh passion fruit can be hard to find, but it's worth seeking out because there's nothing quite like its remarkable flavor. However, if you can't find passion fruit or passion fruit juice in your local market, try the Sierra Mar Shallot Vinaigrette (see page 98) instead; it will be delicious, too. **SERVES 4 AS A SIDE SALAD**

1 head butter lettuce, such as Bibb or
   Boston
About $1/4$ cup Passion Fruit Vinaigrette
   (recipe follows)
1 ripe avocado, preferably Hass
$1/2$ cup assorted edible flowers, such as
   nasturtiums, pansies, and/or Johnny-
   jump-ups (see sidebar, this page)

1. Carefully pull the lettuce leaves from the core, tearing off and discarding any damaged parts. Rinse the leaves under gently running cold water, drain them well, and spin them dry. Wrap the lettuce in a clean kitchen towel or paper towels and refrigerate until serving time.

2. Just before you plan to serve the salad, gently tear the large lettuce leaves into smaller pieces. Keep smaller leaves whole; they'll add volume and texture to the salad. Place all of the lettuce in a large salad bowl and add 3 tablespoons of the Passion Fruit Vinaigrette. Toss to lightly coat the leaves, then taste to see if more vinaigrette is needed. Transfer the lettuce to individual salad plates.

3. Peel the avocado and discard the pit. Cut the avocado lengthwise into thin slices. Arrange 4 or 5 slices in a spoke pattern on top of each salad. Sprinkle the edible flowers on top of the avocado. Serve the salads immediately.

Passion Fruit Vinaigrette

Passion Fruit Vinaigrette even sounds deliciously exotic. This simple dressing shows off passion fruit's intense, sweet-tart flavor and intriguing aroma.

Tropical passion fruit is native to South America but is now being grown in California and Florida, so it's becoming more widely available. When buying passion fruit, look for yellow or purple egg-shaped ones with wrinkled skin, an indication of ripeness.

Be sure to bring home a few extra to eat over the kitchen sink. Scoop out the pulp with a spoon and enjoy it, seeds and all. If you have no choice but to buy smooth-skinned fruit, it will ripen in a few days on the kitchen counter. **MAKES ABOUT $1/3$ CUP**

Note: To remove the juice, cut the passion fruit in half and squeeze or spoon the juice and seeds into a strainer set over a small bowl. Push hard on the pulp to extract all the juice. If fresh fruit is not available, you may be able to find passion fruit juice in some specialty markets.

3 tablespoons seedless passion fruit juice
   (from about 3 fruits; see Note)
2 tablespoons extra-virgin olive oil
2 teaspoons fresh lime juice, or more
   to taste
1/2 teaspoon sugar, or more to taste
Pinch of salt, or more to taste

Place all of the ingredients in a glass jar and seal the lid tightly. Shake the jar vigorously to combine. The vinaigrette can be refrigerated, covered, for up to 3 days. Let it return to room temperature before using.

Baby Spinach Salad
with Creamy Herb Dressing

I love delicate tasting and exceptionally nutritious baby spinach paired with just about everything from the garden. Crunchy ribbons of carrot, juicy sweet tomatoes, creamy avocado, and a hint of salt from the sunflower seeds combine here to make a colorful, tasty salad. Radishes would be a nice addition, and you can't go wrong with croutons or wedges of hard-boiled egg. Use your imagination to create your own variations. **SERVES 4 AS A SIDE SALAD**

Hands make the best salad tossers. Even if it seems a little messy, it's quick and effective.

5 ounces (about 6 cups) baby spinach,
   carefully rinsed and dried, if needed
About 1/4 cup Creamy Herb Dressing
   (page 101)
1 ripe avocado, preferably Hass
12 ripe cherry tomatoes, cut in half

2 small carrots, peeled
1/4 cup store-bought roasted,
   salted sunflower seeds

1. Place the spinach in a large salad bowl. Add 3 tablespoons of the Creamy Herb Dressing. Toss to lightly coat the spinach, then taste to see if more dressing is needed. Transfer the spinach to individual salad plates.

2. Peel the avocado and discard the pit. Cut the avocado lengthwise into thin slices. Arrange the avocado slices and tomatoes on top of the spinach.

3. Using a vegetable peeler, shave the carrots into wide ribbons, allowing them to fall onto the spinach. Sprinkle the sunflower seeds over the salads and serve immediately.

California Waldorf Salad

The first Waldorf salad was created in the 1890s at the Waldorf-Astoria hotel in New York City. Originally, it was just apples and celery tossed with mayonnaise, but over the years, nuts, grapes, and raisins have become standard additions. In our Farm Stand's Organic Kitchen, we just couldn't resist giving the salad a West Coast spin by tossing the apple salad with tender baby spinach leaves and sparking up the dressing with curry and yogurt. **SERVES 4 AS A SIDE SALAD**

$^1/_3$ cup plain nonfat yogurt or sour cream

$^1/_3$ cup mayonnaise

1 teaspoon grated lime zest

2 tablespoons fresh lime juice

2 teaspoons curry powder

$^1/_2$ teaspoon honey or sugar

1 unpeeled apple, cut into $^1/_3$-inch dice
    (1 cup)

$^1/_2$ cup thinly sliced celery

$^1/_2$ cup raisins

$^3/_4$ cup seedless grapes, cut in half

$^1/_2$ cup pecans or walnuts, toasted
    (see box, page 98)

5 ounces (about 6 cups) baby spinach or
    mixed greens, carefully rinsed and
    dried, if needed

1. Place the yogurt, mayonnaise, lime zest and juice, curry powder, and honey in a small glass, ceramic, or wooden bowl and whisk to combine.

2. Place the apple, celery, raisins, grapes, and nuts in a large bowl. Add about half of the yogurt dressing and stir to combine. Just before serving, add the spinach and toss to combine. If the salad is too dry add more dressing. Any leftover dressing can be refrigerated, covered, for up to 1 week. It's good in chicken salad or as a dip for broccoli florets or apple slices.

Roasted Beet and Arugula Salad
with Walnuts and Feta Cheese

Baby beets are grown year-round at our Carmel Valley farm where the cool Pacific fog rolls in like nature's air conditioner. Our Organic Kitchen roasts a jewel-like assortment, and they always sell out quickly. The vibrant colors and sweetness of the beets and blood oranges in this salad are accentuated by the creamy-white feta and crunchy nuts. Feel free to substitute mixed baby greens, mâche, or frisée for the arugula. Fresh goat cheese works just as nicely as feta. If you can't find baby beets, larger ones will do fine. **SERVES 4 AS A SIDE SALAD**

1 pound Roasted Baby Beets (page 228),
    at room temperature

About $^1/_3$ cup Orange Walnut
    Vinaigrette (recipe follows) or
    Walnut Balsamic Vinaigrette
    (page 100)

5 ounces (about 6 cups) baby arugula,
    carefully rinsed and dried, if needed

2 blood oranges or naval oranges,
    segmented (optional; see sidebar,
    page 78)

$^1/_4$ cup (1 ounce) crumbled feta cheese

$^1/_2$ cup Spiced Candied Walnuts
    (page 108), or $^1/_2$ cup walnuts, toasted
    (see box, page 98)

How to Segment Citus Fruit

Citrus slices are tastier and easier to eat in a salad when you cut off the bitter white pith along with the peel and remove the tough membranes that hold the juicy segments together.

First, cut a thin slice off both ends of the fruit so that it can sit level on a cutting board. Using a sharp paring knife, cut downward following the contour of the fruit, removing wide strips of the peel and pith and leaving the flesh intact. Then, while holding the fruit over a bowl to catch the juice, slice between each white membrane to release the flesh in wedges, leaving behind the tough membrane casing.

1. Cut the beets in half or quarters so that they are bite size. If you are using larger beets, cut them into $^1/_2$-inch dice. Place the beets in a small bowl, add 1 to 2 tablespoons of the vinaigrette, and toss until the beets are coated. The salad can be prepared to this stage 1 day in advance, if desired.

2. Just before you plan to serve the salad, place the arugula in a large salad bowl. Add about 3 tablespoons of the vinaigrette. Toss to lightly coat the arugula, then taste to see if more vinaigrette is needed.

3. Transfer the arugula to a platter or individual salad plates. Arrange the beets and orange segments, if using, on top of the greens and sprinkle the feta and walnuts over them. Serve immediately.

Orange Walnut Vinaigrette

The candied walnuts and oranges in the roasted beet salad harmonize beautifully with the walnut oil and citrus in this dressing. Together, the flavors simply sing! The vinaigrette is also delicious drizzled over steamed green beans or grilled asparagus.

MAKES ABOUT 1 $^1/_4$ CUPS

$^1/_2$ cup good-quality roasted walnut oil
　　(see sidebar, page 100)
$^1/_4$ cup extra-virgin olive oil
1 tablespoon fresh orange juice or
　　blood orange juice
1 teaspoon finely grated orange zest
5 tablespoons sherry vinegar
2 teaspoons Dijon mustard
1 tablespoon finely minced shallots
$^1/_4$ teaspoon salt, or more to taste
$^1/_4$ teaspoon freshly ground black pepper,
　　or more to taste

Place all the ingredients in a glass jar and seal the lid tightly. Shake the jar vigorously to combine. Let the dressing sit at room temperature for 1 hour to allow the flavors to develop before serving. The vinaigrette can be refrigerated, tightly covered, for up to 1 month. Let it return to room temperature before using.

Red beets get cleaned up before their move from the field into boxes.

The Flying Fish Salad

Kenny and Tina Fukumoto, owners of the Flying Fish Grill in Carmel, have been successful restaurateurs on the Monterey Peninsula for more than three decades. My family enjoys their signature salad so much that each of us often orders it double-size, which the waitstaff jokingly refers to as the "Goodman size." This salad is delicious and simple: tender and crisp greens tossed with a sesame soy dressing and sprinkled with colorful vegetables. Toasted sesame seeds top off the salad. **SERVES 4 AS A SIDE SALAD**

1 romaine lettuce heart
3 ounces (about 4 cups) mixed baby
    greens
About $^1/_2$ cup Flying Fish Sesame
    Soy Dressing (recipe follows)
1 medium tomato, cut into $^1/_4$-inch dice
    (about 1 cup)
1 small carrot, peeled and cut
    into small matchsticks
    (julienne)
$^1/_2$ hothouse (seedless English)
    cucumber, peeled and cut into
    small matchsticks (julienne)
2 teaspoons sesame seeds, toasted
    (see sidebar, page 273)

1. Remove the core from the romaine heart. Carefully rinse the leaves under gently running cold water, drain them well, and spin them dry. Tear the leaves into bite-size pieces.

2. Just before you plan to serve the salad, place the romaine and mixed baby greens in a large salad bowl and toss to combine. Add $^1/_4$ cup of the salad dressing. Toss to lightly coat the leaves, then taste to see if more dressing is needed.

3. Transfer the greens to a platter or individual salad plates. Scatter the tomato, carrot, cucumber, and sesame seeds over the greens. Serve immediately.

The Flying Fish Sesame Soy Dressing

Kenny Fukumoto's sweet-tart, Japanese-style dressing is the secret to the success of the Flying Fish Grill's house salad. It can also double as a delicious marinade for chicken, pork, or beef. My family loves this dressing, so I've been known to leave the restaurant carrying wine bottles filled with it to enjoy at home. **MAKES ABOUT 1 $^1/_2$ CUPS**

$^1/_2$ **cup soy sauce**
$^1/_4$ **cup unseasoned rice vinegar**
$^1/_4$ **cup canola oil**
2 **tablespoons toasted sesame oil**
$^1/_2$ **cup sugar**

Place all of the ingredients and 2 tablespoons of water in a glass jar and seal the lid tightly. Shake the jar vigorously until the sugar dissolves. The dressing can be refrigerated, covered, for up to 1 month. Let it return to room temperature before using.

Inspecting the roots of a handful of just-picked baby spinach.

Baby Greens Salad
with Grilled Figs and Walnuts

I love these grilled figs—mouthfuls of heavenly sweetness wrapped in prosciutto. They are truly luscious, especially when perched on a bed of lively baby greens and surrounded by crunchy walnuts. Fresh figs are available in the early summer and again in the early fall. If your figs are not ripe, they will soften after a few days on the kitchen counter. **SERVES 4 AS A SIDE SALAD**

8 small ripe but firm figs
8 paper-thin slices prosciutto
2 tablespoons good-quality roasted
  walnut oil (see sidebar, page 100)
Freshly ground black pepper
4 ounces (5 to 6 cups) mixed baby
  greens, carefully rinsed and dried,
  if needed
About ¼ cup Walnut Balsamic
  Vinaigrette (page 100)
½ cup Candied Walnuts (page 108) or
  toasted walnuts (see box, page 98)

1. Cut each fig in half through the stem end. Cut each slice of prosciutto in half so each piece is just large enough to wrap around a fig half. Wrap each fig half with a piece of prosciutto so that the ends overlap on the fig's cut side.

Press the ends of the prosciutto together to seal them (the moisture from the fig and prosciutto will hold them together).

2. Set up a barbecue grill and preheat it to medium-high.

3. Brush each wrapped fig with some of the walnut oil and sprinkle pepper over it.

4. Place the figs on the grill and cook, turning occasionally with tongs, until the prosciutto is golden browned and slightly crisp, about 2 minutes on each side. Transfer the figs to a plate and set aside.

5. Just before you plan to serve the salad, place the greens in a large salad bowl. Add 3 tablespoons of the vinaigrette. Toss to lightly coat the greens, then taste to see if more vinaigrette is needed.

6. Transfer the greens to individual salad plates. Arrange 4 fig halves on each salad and top with the Candied Walnuts. Serve immediately.

California Salad
with Avocado, Apricots, Almonds, and Goat Cheese

Growing up in New York City, I really appreciate California's rich agricultural bounty that's available virtually year-round. This salad celebrates some of the Californian foods I love most—luscious avocados, chewy dried apricots, crunchy almonds, creamy goat cheese, and of course, beautiful baby greens! **SERVES 4 AS A SIDE SALAD**

4 ounces (5 to 6 cups) mixed baby greens, carefully rinsed and dried, if needed
$^1/_4$ cup fresh whole tarragon leaves
About $^1/_4$ cup Hazelnut Tarragon Vinaigrette (page 100) or Lemon Vinaigrette (page 97)
$^1/_4$ cup sliced almonds, toasted (see box, page 98)
$^1/_2$ cup (2 ounces) crumbled mild semisoft goat cheese or feta cheese
$^1/_2$ ripe avocado, preferably Hass
8 dried apricots, each cut into 3 or 4 strips

1. Just before you plan to serve the salad, place the greens and tarragon in a large salad bowl and toss to combine. Add 3 tablespoons of the vinaigrette. Toss to lightly coat the leaves, then taste to see if more vinaigrette is needed.

2. Transfer the greens to a platter or individual salad plates. Scatter the almonds and cheese on top of the greens.

3. Peel the avocado and discard the pit. Cut the avocado lengthwise into thin slices. Arrange the avocado slices around the edge of the platter or plates. Sprinkle the apricots over the salad. Serve immediately.

Dried Organic Apricots

When you buy dried organic apricots, you may be surprised to see that they are brown instead of bright orange. Organic apricots are not treated with sulfur preservatives. While they are not so pretty, they taste great.

FARM FRESH

avocados

Avocados contain a high percentage of healthy, monounsaturated oil. Perhaps the best-tasting avocado is the Hass variety, which has a very dark, pebbly skin and a buttery-rich, nutty tasting flesh. Smoother skinned avocados, such as the Fuerte and Reed, are also delicious and have a lower fat content.

Avocados are unusual because they don't start ripening until they are picked. You can tell an avocado is ripe if the flesh yields when gently pressed. Firm avocados will ripen on the kitchen counter within a week. You can speed up the process by placing the avocado in a paper bag with an apple or banana; these give off a gas that promotes ripening. Once ripe, avocados bruise easily, so handle them carefully. They can be stored for a few days in the refrigerator.

Avocado flesh quickly turns brown when exposed to air. Mixing lime or lemon juice with the avocado can slow down this process. You can also slow discoloration by storing dishes that include mashed avocado, such as guacamole, in a bowl covered with plastic wrap pressed directly against the surface of the food. Of course, any dish that contains avocado looks and tastes best on the day it's made.

a fridge full of greens

It'll probably come as no surprise to you that Drew and I eat salads all the time. And you can probably guess that we're always at the ready—our fridge is filled with packages of prewashed greens—just like when we first started out—only now our choices are more varied. Today it might be Earthbound's romaine heart leaves and mixed baby greens (spring mix). Tomorrow baby arugula and mâche.

While we sometimes enjoy more elaborate salads with lunch and dinner, if we're hungry in the mid afternoon or need a late night snack, we'll throw together a simple green salad to satisfy our particular cravings. Here are some favorite quick creations:

■ Equal amounts of spring mix and romaine leaves, torn into bite-size pieces, and tossed with vinaigrette, croutons, and grated Parmesan cheese. (Drew calls this the Goodman Mista Salad.)

■ Equal amounts of baby arugula and romaine leaves, torn into bite-size pieces, and tossed with vinaigrette and grated Parmesan cheese.

■ Equal amounts of mâche and baby arugula tossed with a drizzle of walnut oil, extra-virgin olive oil, balsamic vinegar, and a pinch of salt.

■ Baby arugula topped with diced ripe tomato and avocado and sprinkled with fresh lime juice, olive oil, and sea salt.

Autumn Salad
with Persimmons and Pomegranate Seeds

Persimmons and pomegranates are lovely fruits. They're harvested in California from October into December. Fuyu persimmons—a nonastringent variety that's good for salads—are round, sweet, and crisp, like an apple, but they have a golden-orange color, both inside and out. They taste great with pomegranates, which are nature's jewel boxes. When you cut through the pomegranate's leathery skin, you'll find it filled with juicy, ruby-red seeds loosely held together by a papery white membrane. Bite into a seed and you get an explosion of sweet-tart juice that's full of heart-healthy antioxidants. Persimmons and pomegranates teamed with tender baby greens, crunchy hazelnuts, and chewy dates make this colorful salad a crisp-weather favorite. **SERVES 4 AS A SIDE SALAD**

2 Fuyu persimmons, peeled
  (see box, this page)
1/2 pomegranate
4 ounces (5 to 6 cups) mixed baby
  greens or mâche, carefully rinsed
  and dried, if needed
About 1/4 cup Pomegranate Vinaigrette
  (recipe follows)
3 dried dates, each pitted and cut
  into 6 thin strips
2 tablespoons chopped hazelnuts,
  toasted (see box, page 98)

1. Cut the persimmons in half through
the stem end, then into very thin half-
moon slices, about 1/8-inch thick. Arrange
the slices so that they slightly overlap
around the edge of 4 salad plates.

2. Scrape the seeds from the pomegranate
and discard the leathery skin and white
membranes. Set the seeds aside.

3. Just before you plan to serve the salad,
place the baby greens in a large salad
bowl. Add 3 tablespoons of the
Pomegranate Vinaigrette. Toss to lightly
coat the greens, then taste to see if more
vinaigrette is needed.

4. Mound the greens on the salad plates
so the persimmons show around the
edge. Scatter some of the dates, hazelnuts,
and pomegranate seeds over each salad.
Serve immediately.

Pomegranate Vinaigrette

*Pomegranate juice, with its ruby-red color
and potent sweet-tart taste, makes a unique
vinaigrette, perfect for a festive salad.
Juicing fresh pomegranates is a messy task,*
*so look for bottled juice in the refrigerated
section of your grocery store.* **MAKES
ABOUT 1 CUP**

1 cup pomegranate juice
2 teaspoons finely minced shallot
2 tablespoons Champagne vinegar or
  white wine vinegar
1 tablespoon fresh lemon juice
2 tablespoons extra-virgin olive oil
5 tablespoons good-quality roasted
  walnut oil (see sidebar, page 100)
Coarse (kosher) salt

1. Place the pomegranate juice in a small
saucepan over medium-high heat and
bring it to a boil. Cook until the juice has
reduced to about 1/4 cup, about 12 minutes.
Let it cool to room temperature.

2. Transfer the pomegranate juice to a glass
jar with a lid. Add the shallot, vinegar,
lemon juice, olive oil, and walnut oil and
seal the lid tightly. Shake the jar vigorously
to combine. Season the vinaigrette with salt
to taste. The vinaigrette can be refrigerated,
covered, for up to 1 week. Let it return to
room temperature before using.

*Delicious, ruby-red
pomegranates are an
autumn favorite.*

FARM FRESH

persimmons

Persimmons, with their beautiful reddish-orange skin, are harvested
during the fall and early winter. There are two basic types of
persimmons, with very different uses.

■ *Hachiya* persimmons, with a tapered heart shape, have a mouth-
puckering astringency until they are very soft and ripe—then they are
excellent for baking.

■ *Fuyu* persimmons are not astringent at all and are delicious eaten
raw. They have a squat applelike shape, with a similarly crisp texture
that becomes somewhat softer as the persimmon ripens.

Strawberry-Tarragon Salad
with Aged Balsamic Vinegar

Some people raise their eyebrows when they see this unusual salad of strawberries, tarragon, blue cheese, and mixed baby greens. But when they taste it—wow! The secret to its success is a strawberry-infused balsamic vinegar that's easy to make. Just be sure to allow a couple of hours for the vinegar to absorb the berry flavor. Save this recipe for the lucky day when you find baskets of sugar-sweet, organic berries. The recipe makes more than enough dressing for the salad here, so you can enjoy an encore later in the week. **SERVES 4 AS A SIDE SALAD**

2 pints small ripe strawberries,
 rinsed and hulled

1/4 cup good-quality balsamic vinegar
 (see sidebar, this page)

2 tablespoons aged balsamic vinegar
 (optional), preferably at least
 6 years old

3/4 cup Herb-Flavored Oil
 (page 382; use tarragon) or
 extra-virgin olive oil

1/2 teaspoon Dijon mustard

Pinch of salt

4 ounces (5 to 6 cups) mixed baby
 greens, carefully rinsed and dried,
 if needed

1/2 cup fresh whole tarragon leaves

1/4 cup toasted pecans (see box, page 98),
 chopped

1/2 cup (2 ounces) crumbled
 blue cheese

1. Prepare the flavored vinegar by mashing three strawberries against the side of a small bowl with a fork. Add the 1/4 cup of good-quality balsamic vinegar and stir to combine. Let the vinegar stand at room temperature to absorb the strawberry flavor, 1 to 2 hours.

2. Meanwhile, cut the remaining strawberries in half lengthwise so they are bite size (if you have large berries, cut them into quarters). If using aged balsamic vinegar, place the cut berries in a small, shallow bowl, add the aged vinegar, and stir to coat. Let the berries marinate at room temperature for 1 to 2 hours, stirring occasionally. If not using aged balsamic vinegar, you do not need to marinate the strawberries.

Wild strawberries (frais du bois) *with their perfectly untamed strawberry flavor, are an extraordinary treat to savor.*

3. Strain the strawberry-flavored vinegar through a sieve, pressing down on the berries to extract all of the liquid from the fruit. Discard the solids. Place the flavored vinegar, Herb-Flavored Oil, mustard, and salt in a glass jar and seal the lid tightly. Shake the jar vigorously to combine.

4. Just before serving, place the mixed greens and tarragon in a large salad bowl and toss to combine. Add 3 tablespoons of the vinaigrette. Toss to lightly coat the leaves, then taste to see if more vinaigrette is needed. Any leftover vinaigrette can be stored, covered, in the refrigerator, for up to 3 days.

5. Divide the greens evenly among 4 salad plates. Arrange the strawberries on top and sprinkle with the pecans and blue cheese. Serve immediately.

Balsamic Vinegar

Balsamic vinegar comes in a wide range of prices, but a little of the good stuff goes a long way. Authentic balsamic vinegar comes only from Emilia-Romagna in Italy and is aged in wooden barrels, like wine. It becomes more smooth and syrupy as it ages, so the older the vinegar the better—and the more expensive—it will be.

When buying balsamic vinegar, examine the ingredient list. The highest quality ones will list only grape must, which is unfermented juice from wine grapes. Some will also indicate the number of years that the vinegar has been aged. More common are vinegars that list grape must and wine vinegar; these are fine for most salad dressings. However, avoid vinegars that include sweeteners, preservatives, or coloring.

The age of balsamic vinegar has a big impact on quality, and most organic ones are relatively young. This, of course, will change over time!

Grilled Caesar Salad
with Parmesan Crisps

Grilled lettuce? I know it sounds strange, but try this with romaine hearts the next time you have the grill heated up. The heart is the core of pale green inner leaves that's left when you strip the large mature leaves off a head of romaine lettuce. Before grilling whole hearts, brush them with the tangy Caesar Vinaigrette to add flavor and protect the tender leaves from the heat. A brief stint over the flames gives the romaine a smoky flavor and gently wilts the outside, leaving the innermost leaves crisp. Shavings of Parmesan cheese are the customary garnish for Caesar salad, but in this salad grated Parmesan bakes into crisp disks that can be served whole or crumbled over the salad. This, plus the Parmesan Croutons, give the salad a double hit of this delicious cheese. **SERVES 4 AS A SIDE SALAD**

$^1/_4$ **pound Parmesan cheese, finely grated (about 1$^1/_3$ cups)**
4 whole romaine lettuce hearts, carefully rinsed and dried
About $^1/_2$ cup Caesar Vinaigrette (page 97)
Parmesan Croutons (recipe follows)

1. Position a rack in the center of the oven and preheat the oven to 400°F. Line a baking sheet with parchment paper.

2. Spoon the grated cheese on the parchment paper, making four 3-inch rounds about $^1/_4$-inch thick, spaced 1 inch apart. Bake the cheese until it bubbles and turns golden, 8 to 10 minutes. Using a spatula, transfer the Parmesan crisps to paper towels to cool.

3. Set up a barbecue grill and preheat it to high.

4. Leaving the romaine hearts intact, liberally brush each with some of the Caesar Vinaigrette. Gently separate the leaves so that you can brush the inner leaves, too. Set the remaining Caesar Vinaigrette aside.

5. Place the whole romaine hearts on the grill and cook, turning frequently, until the outer leaves are wilted and charred slightly, about 4 minutes.

6. Transfer the romaine hearts to a cutting board and cut off the stem ends so that the leaves separate. Arrange the romaine on a large platter. Sprinkle the croutons over

Garlic braiding is a popular Farm Stand tradition every July.

the lettuce. Arrange the whole Parmesan crisps on the platter or break them into bite-size pieces and sprinkle them over the salad. Serve immediately with the remaining Caesar Vinaigrette on the side.

Parmesan Croutons

Crisp and flavor packed, these garlicky croutons are almost decadent thanks to the butter and Parmesan cheese. Making croutons is a yummy way to make good use of day-old bread. For a more rustic version, leave the crusts on, or if you prefer, cut them off. Either way, you'll enjoy these croutons sprinkled on salads and soups. **MAKES 3 CUPS**

Croutons give a flavorful crunch to salads and also to soups, especially purees.

4 tablespoons (¹/₂ stick) unsalted
    butter
¹/₄ cup extra-virgin olive oil
3 cloves garlic, peeled and crushed
3 cups bread cubes (¹/₂-inch cubes),
    cut from day-old bread, such as a
    baguette
¹/₂ cup (2 ounces) freshly grated
    Parmesan cheese

1. Cook the butter, olive oil, and garlic in a small saucepan over very low heat until hot, 5 to 10 minutes. Remove the butter mixture from the heat and let sit at room temperature to develop the flavor, about 1 hour.

2. Position a rack in the center of the oven and preheat the oven to 325°F.

3. Place the bread cubes in a large bowl. Remove and discard the garlic from the butter mixture, then pour it over the bread cubes and toss to coat. Spread the bread cubes on a large rimmed baking sheet in a single layer. Bake the croutons until they are golden, 15 to 20 minutes.

4. Remove the baking sheet from the oven and sprinkle the cheese evenly over the croutons while they are still warm. Spread out the croutons on paper towels to absorb any excess oil. If you are not planning on serving the croutons immediately, let them cool completely before storing in an airtight container. They will keep for up to 3 days refrigerated.

Farm Stand Greek Salad

Traditionally, a Greek salad is a mix of tomatoes, olives, cucumbers, onions, and feta cheese—but no lettuce. Of course, at our Farm Stand's Organic Kitchen, we just can't resist adding crisp hearts of romaine lettuce to our Greek salad. We also dress it up with strips of roasted red peppers or Roasted Balsamic Artichoke Bottoms (see page 225). **SERVES 6 AS A SIDE SALAD**

3 romaine hearts
1 small regular cucumber, peeled, seeded, and cut into ¹/₂-inch dice
¹/₂ small red onion, very thinly sliced
15 cherry tomatoes, cut in half, or 2 large tomatoes, cut into ¹/₂-inch dice
2 tablespoons capers, rinsed
30 kalamata olives, pitted
About ¹/₃ cup Classic Red Wine Vinaigrette (page 95)
3 ounces feta cheese, grated or crumbled (about ²/₃ cup)
1 red bell pepper, roasted (see page 384) and cut into 1-inch strips, for garnish

1. Remove the cores from the romaine hearts. Carefully rinse the leaves under gently running cold water, drain them well, and spin them dry. Cut the leaves crosswise into 1-inch strips.

2. Just before you plan to serve the salad, place the romaine in a large salad bowl. Add the cucumber, onion, tomatoes, capers, and olives and toss to combine. Add about one-half of the vinaigrette. Toss to lightly coat the leaves, then taste them to see if more vinaigrette is needed.

3. Transfer the salad to a platter or individual salad plates. Sprinkle the feta cheese on top and garnish with some of the bell pepper strips. Serve immediately.

Chopped Summer Vegetable Salad

It's fun to make this old-fashioned salad because there's no limit to the flavor combinations you can create. Almost any mix of vegetables will be good, as long as you include plenty of different colors, textures, and tastes to keep it lively. The secret to a great-looking chopped salad is to cut all the vegetables, except the lettuce, about the same size—¹/₄-inch dice would be ideal. If you're making it in advance, store all the diced vegetables in one container, separate from the lettuce. At serving time, mix the lettuce and the vegetables together and toss with the dressing. We love chopped salad with Buttermilk Blue Cheese Dressing (see page 101), but your own flavorful favorite will be great, too. **SERVES 6 TO 8 AS A SIDE SALAD**

Notes: You can use either a regular or hothouse (seedless English) cucumber here. Regular cucumbers will need to be seeded.

Fresh, very young corn kernels and sweet peas are delicious uncooked. But as they mature, both of these vegetables become starchy and tough. If you can't find really fresh ones, leave them out. For tips on cutting corn off the cob, see the box on page 29.

5 cups chopped romaine or iceberg lettuce, or a combination of both
1 large ripe tomato, seeded and diced (about 1 cup)
¹/₂ cup diced zucchini
¹/₂ cup diced yellow summer squash
¹/₂ cup diced carrots
¹/₂ cup diced radishes
¹/₂ cup peeled and diced cucumber (see Notes)
¹/₂ cup fresh, young corn kernels (from 1 ear; optional; see Notes), uncooked
¹/₂ cup fresh shelled young English peas (optional; see Note)
About ³/₄ cup Buttermilk Blue Cheese Dressing (page 101)
Salt and freshly ground black pepper

Just before you plan to serve the salad, place the lettuce in a large salad bowl and add the tomato, zucchini, summer squash, carrots, radishes, cucumber, and corn and peas, if using. Toss to combine. Add ¹/₂ cup of the Buttermilk

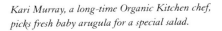

Kari Murray, a long-time Organic Kitchen chef, picks fresh baby arugula for a special salad.

Blue Cheese Dressing. Toss to lightly coat the salad, then taste to see if more dressing is needed. Season the salad with salt and pepper. Transfer the salad to a platter or individual salad plates. Serve immediately.

Classic Cucumber Salad

At our house, summer meals are often accompanied by a bowl of cucumber and onions steeped in a lightly seasoned vinegar. This salad is one of my mother's favorites, and I inherited her love for it. It's quick and easy to assemble when you use a vegetable slicer or mandoline to make very thin slices of cucumber and red onion (see sidebar, page 267). Or, for a more casual version, peel and cut small, young cucumbers in thick slices with a knife. A salad made from mature cucumbers with large seeds will taste best if, before slicing, the cucumbers are cut in half lengthwise and the large seeds are scraped out with a spoon. Slice the onion as thinly as you can, so it doesn't overwhelm the delicate cucumber flavor. For the best taste, serve the salad within four hours of making it, especially if your cucumbers are sliced very thin. **SERVES 4 AS A SIDE SALAD**

3 tablespoons white wine vinegar
$^1/_2$ teaspoon coarse (kosher) salt,
　　or more to taste
$^1/_4$ teaspoon sugar, or more to taste
1 hothouse (seedless English) cucumber,
　　unpeeled, cut into $^1/_8$-inch-thick slices
　　(about 2 cups)
$^1/_2$ red onion, cut in half through the
　　stem end and sliced very thinly
　　crosswise

1. Place the vinegar, salt, and sugar in a medium-size bowl and stir until the salt and sugar dissolve. Taste for seasoning, adding more salt and/or sugar as needed.

2. Add the cucumber and onion to the vinegar mixture and toss to coat. If you are not planning on serving the salad immediately, it can be refrigerated, covered, for up to 3 days.

Variation: For an Asian accent, substitute unseasoned rice wine vinegar for the white wine vinegar and stir in $^1/_2$ teaspoon of toasted sesame seed oil. Before serving, garnish the cucumbers with 2 teaspoons of toasted sesame seeds (see sidebar, page 273).

Caught at sunset, acres of fields present an almost surreal landscape.

Versatile Vinaigrettes, Dips, and Crunchy Nuts

Even the simplest green salad tastes sensational when lightly tossed with a flavorful dressing. But the dressings have even more uses. Try drizzling vinaigrettes on steamed vegetables or grilled fish as a lighter alternative to buttery sauces. Or serve a bowl of creamy dressing as a dip for crudités or steamed artichokes. You'll find that keeping a bottle or two of homemade dressing in your refrigerator makes it easy to experiment, adding a little extra flavor to everyday dishes. (The oil may solidify when cold, so let it come to room temperature before using.)

And as a counterpoint to tender greens, or to add some crunch, nothing tastes better than nuts, made sweet from a brown sugar glaze or savory from spices and a bit of honey. Keep extras around for nibbling.

A selection of nuts ready for nibbling plain, spiced up (page 108), or glazed (page 109).

Classic Red Wine Vinaigrette

It's worth keeping a bottle of this tasty salad dressing on hand. It enhances, without overwhelming, delicate greens and can also stand up to a robust salad overflowing with a garden of ingredients. **MAKES ABOUT 1 CUP**

1 small clove garlic, finely minced
1 teaspoon finely minced shallot
1 teaspoon dried oregano
$1/2$ teaspoon dried thyme
1 teaspoon salt
$1/4$ teaspoon freshly ground black pepper
Pinch of sugar
$1/4$ cup red wine vinegar
$2/3$ cup extra-virgin olive oil

Place all the ingredients in a glass jar and seal the lid tightly. Shake the jar vigorously to combine. The vinaigrette can be refrigerated, covered, for up to 1 month. Let it return to room temperature before using.

Fresh herbs from our Cut-Your-Own Herb Garden.

Sherry Vinaigrette

The best sherry vinegars come from southwest Spain and can be every bit as fine as balsamic vinegars from Italy, and much less expensive. Both kinds of vinegars benefit from long barrel aging, but sherry vinegar has a slightly nutty taste and a thinner consistency. The complex, yet mild, vinegar makes this dressing light enough for baby greens and delicate lettuces. **MAKES ABOUT 1 $1/3$ CUPS**

$1/4$ cup sherry vinegar
1 teaspoon finely minced shallot
    (optional)
$3/4$ teaspoon salt
$1 1/2$ teaspoon Dijon mustard
$3/4$ cup good-quality roasted walnut oil
    (see sidebar, page 100)
$1/3$ cup extra-virgin olive oil
Freshly ground black pepper

Place the vinegar, shallot (if using), salt, mustard, walnut oil, and olive oil in a glass jar and seal the lid tightly. Shake the jar vigorously to combine. The vinaigrette can be refrigerated, covered, for up to 1 month. Let it return to room temperature before using.

Choosing Olive Oils

There are so many olive oils on the supermarket shelf, how do you know which to buy? Your choice will depend on how you want to use the oil and the type of flavors you like best. You may want to keep a few different bottles on hand, but be sure to store them in a cool, dark place so they will stay fresh longer.

Olive oil for salads

All delicate baby greens really need is extra-virgin olive oil and a splash of vinegar to make a delicious salad. Extra-virgin is the highest grade of olive oil, made from the first pressing of olives. But even among extra-virgin oils, there's a wide range of quality and prices. For most salad dressings, a good-quality, medium-priced extra-virgin oil is fine, especially if your dressing has garlic, mustard, or another strongly flavored ingredient in it.

If you feel like splurging, try one of the more expensive extra-virgin oils from a single estate or particular variety of olive. A fancy bottle or high price tag doesn't always mean great quality, so if possible, taste the oil before you buy it. You'll discover that most oils made from Tuscan olives have a pleasant peppery taste, while French or Spanish oils are more mild. Save your special oils for the simplest salad dressings where their flavor will shine through. These oils are also good for drizzling over dishes like steamed vegetables or grilled fish just before serving for an extra touch of flavor.

Olive oil for cooking

A reasonably priced good-quality, extra-virgin oil can do double duty for salads and cooking. Virgin olive oil is another good choice for cooking, but not for salads, because it is less flavorful. Virgin oil comes from lower-quality olives or from a later pressing (after the extra-virgin oil has run off). Avoid bottles labeled olive oil, pure olive oil, or pomace oil. These lesser-quality oils that have been heated and/or chemically extracted from the olives.

Use the finest olive oil to marinate these olives (page 107).

Lemon Vinaigrette

*D*rew and I are lucky to have Meyer lemons growing in our backyard, so they are a main ingredient in our family's everyday "house dressing," which we enjoy on any type of salad green. Because Meyers are a little sweeter than regular lemons, they make an especially delicious dressing, but regular lemons will be good, too. The fresh-squeezed juice from either variety turns a basic vinaigrette into one that sparkles with bright flavors. (For more about Meyer lemons, see the sidebar on page 112). **MAKES ABOUT 1 CUP**

$\frac{1}{3}$ cup plus 2 tablespoons fresh lemon juice, preferably Meyer
$\frac{2}{3}$ cup high-quality extra-virgin olive oil
1 tablespoon Dijon mustard
3 large cloves garlic, peeled and crushed
$\frac{3}{4}$ teaspoon coarse (kosher) salt

Place all the ingredients in a glass jar and seal the lid tightly. Shake the jar vigorously to combine. The vinaigrette can be refrigerated, covered, for up to 1 week. Let it return to room temperature and remove the garlic cloves before using.

Meyer lemons on the branch.

Caesar Vinaigrette

*K*athy Goodman, Drew's stepmother, created this tangy vinaigrette, which has the flavor punch of Caesar dressing but without the egg. It's great with hearts of romaine and other sturdy lettuces, but it has a light consistency so it's also appropriate for more tender baby greens. Add some croutons and shaved Parmesan cheese for a quick version of the classic Caesar. **MAKES ABOUT $\frac{2}{3}$ CUP**

1 large clove garlic, minced
1 tablespoon Dijon mustard
1 teaspoon anchovy paste
$\frac{1}{4}$ teaspoon Worcestershire sauce
$\frac{1}{2}$ teaspoon Tabasco sauce
Juice of 1 lemon (about 3 tablespoons)
$\frac{1}{2}$ cup extra-virgin olive oil

1. Place the garlic, mustard, anchovy paste, Worcestershire sauce, and Tabasco sauce in a small bowl and, using a fork, mash them into a paste.

2. Add the lemon juice and stir to combine. Whisking constantly, slowly add the olive oil in a steady stream. Continue to whisk until the dressing thickens. The vinaigrette can be refrigerated, covered, for up to 1 week. Let it return to room temperature before using.

A quick toss of croutons and fresh grated Parmesan cheese complete a classic Caesar salad.

Sierra Mar Shallot Vinaigrette

When our family wants a special treat, we drive down the Big Sur coast to the Sierra Mar restaurant at the Post Ranch Inn. Chef Craig von Foerster works magic in his kitchen, creating adventurous combinations of ingredients unlike anything we've tasted before. I particularly adore his shallot vinaigrette, so I always ask for a little extra to take home. When he gave me the recipe, I was shocked to see how easy it is to re-create. While many of his dishes are intricate, Craig can also be a master of simplicity. **MAKES ABOUT 1 1/2 CUPS**

1/3 cup Champagne vinegar
2 tablespoons minced shallots
1 teaspoon chopped fresh tarragon
    leaves (optional)
1 teaspoon coarse (kosher) salt, or
    more to taste
1/2 teaspoon freshly ground black
    pepper, or more to taste
1 cup canola oil

Place all the ingredients in a glass jar and seal the lid tightly. Shake the jar vigorously to combine. The vinaigrette can be refrigerated, covered, for up to 1 month. Let it return to room temperature before using.

Our tractor heads back to its shed after a long day's work.

toasting nuts & seeds

Toasting brings out the wonderful aroma and flavor of nuts and seeds and makes them crisp. It takes only a few minutes, but watch nuts and seeds carefully, as they can burn easily. To reduce the risk of burning, toast nuts whole or in large pieces.

On the stove top: Place the nuts or seeds in a single layer in a skillet over medium heat. Slowly toast the nuts, stirring occasionally, until they are warm to the touch, lightly colored, and fragrant, 5 to 10 minutes.

In the microwave: Spread the nuts or seeds in a single layer on a microwave-safe plate. Microwave on high power for 1 to 3 minutes, checking and stirring every 30 seconds to 1 minute, until the nuts are warm, lightly colored, and fragrant. The cooking time will depend on the variety of nut, the amount you're toasting, and the wattage of your microwave oven.

In the oven: Position a rack in the center of the oven and preheat the oven to 350°F. Spread the nuts or seeds in a single layer on a rimmed baking sheet. Bake them for 5 minutes, then stir them. Continue baking the nuts until they are warm to the touch, lightly colored, and fragrant, 3 to 5 minutes longer, 8 to 10 minutes total.

Pesto Vinaigrette

You'll get an explosion of fresh basil flavor with this brilliant, emerald-green dressing. It is intense and lively and tastes best with a hearty lettuce, like romaine or iceberg, but it's also great on baby greens. If you add some red radicchio to the lettuces, you will find the pleasant bitterness and bright color blends nicely with the flavorful dressing. It's also good on blanched zucchini, carrots, and other vegetables.

MAKES ABOUT 1 CUP

1 small shallot, peeled and coarsely
    chopped
1 small clove garlic, peeled
$^2/_3$ cup packed fresh basil leaves
2 tablespoons pine nuts, toasted
    (see box, facing page)
2 tablespoons freshly grated
    Parmesan cheese
$^3/_4$ teaspoon salt, or more to taste
$^1/_4$ teaspoon freshly ground black pepper,
    or more to taste
$^1/_2$ teaspoon sugar
2 tablespoons unseasoned rice wine
    vinegar
$^2/_3$ cup extra-virgin olive oil

1. Place the shallot, garlic, basil, pine nuts, Parmesan cheese, salt, pepper, sugar, and vinegar in a food processor. Pulse the machine until the mixture becomes a finely chopped paste, stopping once or twice to scrape the side of the bowl with a rubber spatula.

2. With the machine running constantly, add the oil in a slow, steady stream to fully emulsify it. The vinaigrette can be refrigerated, covered, for up to 1 week. Let it return to room temperature before using.

Fresh green and opal basil.

Nut Oils

Nut oils, such as hazelnut and walnut, are a delicious addition to salad dressings. When buying nut oils, the most flavorful ones come from toasted or roasted nuts that have been cold pressed or expeller pressed. This means that the oil has been extracted by pressure, without using heat or solvents.

Unfortunately, nut oils go rancid quickly. To slow down the process, store them in a dark bottle in the refrigerator and use them within a few months. Smell the oil before using it to make sure it's still good. If the odor is unpleasant, the oil is rancid and should be thrown away.

Hazelnut Tarragon Vinaigrette

Tarragon, a tender herb with an aniselike flavor, blends beautifully with the nuttiness of the hazelnut oil in this dressing. The combination is delicious with mâche, mixed baby greens, or Bibb lettuce, especially if you garnish the salad with some toasted hazelnuts. **MAKES ABOUT 1 CUP**

1/4 cup plus 1 tablespoon Tarragon Vinegar (page 381)
1 tablespoon fresh lemon juice
2 teaspoons Dijon mustard
1/2 teaspoon salt
1 teaspoon dried tarragon
1/3 cup hazelnut oil (see sidebar, this page)
1/3 cup extra-virgin olive oil
Freshly ground black pepper

Place the Tarragon Vinegar, lemon juice, mustard, salt, tarragon, hazelnut oil, and olive oil in a glass jar and seal the lid tightly. Shake the jar vigorously to combine. Taste the vinaigrette and season it with pepper to taste. The vinaigrette can be refrigerated, covered, for up to 1 month. Let it return to room temperature before using.

Walnut Balsamic Vinaigrette

The quality of the oil and vinegar makes all the difference in this dressing. If you find a roasted walnut oil, the nutty flavor will not be lost in the rich balsamic vinegar. This is an intensely flavored dressing that also makes a nice basting sauce for grilled figs. **MAKES ABOUT 1 CUP**

3/4 cup roasted walnut oil (see sidebar, this page)
1/4 cup good-quality balsamic vinegar (see sidebar, page 87)
2 teaspoons Dijon mustard
Salt and freshly ground black pepper

Place the walnut oil, vinegar, and mustard in a glass jar and seal the lid tightly. Shake the jar vigorously to combine. Season the vinaigrette with salt and pepper to taste. The vinaigrette can be refrigerated, covered, for up to 1 month. Let it return to room temperature before using.

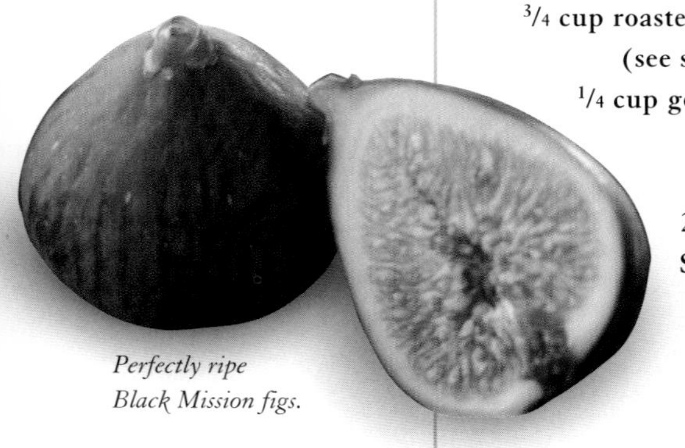

Perfectly ripe Black Mission figs.

Creamy Herb Dressing

A touch of cream adds a mellow richness that calms the vibrant flavors of the garden-fresh herbs and garlic in this dressing. It has a medium body and creamy color that is a feast for the eyes when drizzled on romaine and iceberg.

MAKES ABOUT 1 CUP

3 tablespoons Tarragon Vinegar
   (page 381) or white wine vinegar
2 tablespoons heavy (whipping) cream
1 teaspoon Dijon mustard
2 tablespoons mayonnaise
1/2 teaspoon minced garlic
1/2 cup canola oil
1 tablespoon minced fresh flat-leaf
   parsley
1 tablespoon finely minced fresh chives
1 teaspoon minced fresh tarragon
Salt and freshly ground black pepper

Place the vinegar, cream, mustard, mayonnaise, garlic, oil, parsley, chives, and tarragon in a glass jar and seal the lid tightly. Shake the jar vigorously to combine. Season the dressing with salt and pepper to taste. The dressing can be refrigerated covered, for up to 1 week. Let it return to room temperature before using.

A beautiful assortment of just-snipped herbs.

Buttermilk Blue Cheese Dressing

Tangy and herby, this blue cheese dressing is perfect for iceberg, romaine, or spinach salads. It's especially delicious in our Chopped Summer Vegetable Salad (see page 92) and would make a great dip for grilled chicken wings. Leave out the blue cheese, and you'll have a fresh-tasting ranch dressing that's better than anything you'll ever get from a bottle. **MAKES ABOUT 1 1/2 CUPS**

1/4 cup fresh flat-leaf parsley
   leaves
2 tablespoons fresh snipped chives
1 small clove garlic, peeled
1/2 cup (2 ounces) blue cheese,
   chopped or crumbled
1/2 cup mayonaise
3/4 cup buttermilk
Salt and freshly ground
   black pepper

1. Place the parsley, chives, and garlic in a food processor or blender. Pulse the machine until the herb mixture is finely chopped, stopping once or twice to scrape the side of the bowl with a rubber spatula.

2. Add the blue cheese, mayonnaise, and buttermilk and blend until the dressing is smooth, then season with salt and pepper to taste. The dressing can be refrigerated, covered, for up to 1 week.

Farm Stand Green Goddess Dip or Dressing

Green Goddess dressing was created in the 1920s by the chef at San Francisco's Palace Hotel. We've created our own version of this classic for our Farm Stand customers; they love its delicate green color and thick, creamy consistency. Loaded with a mix of herbs freshly clipped from our garden, it's great as a dip for fresh vegetables and can be thinned to use as a dressing for sturdy full-grown lettuces, such as romaine, iceberg, red leaf, and oak leaf. **MAKES ABOUT 1 CUP**

2 anchovy fillets, or 2 teaspoons
   anchovy paste
2 small cloves garlic, peeled
2 scallions, including white and
   3 inches of green, trimmed and
   cut into 1/2-inch pieces
2 tablespoons packed fresh flat-leaf parsley
1 tablespoon packed fresh cilantro,
   or 1 teaspoon dried cilantro
1 tablespoon packed fresh dill,
   or 1 teaspoon dried dill
1 tablespoon packed fresh tarragon,
   or 1 teaspoon dried tarragon
1 teaspoon sugar
1 teaspoon salt
2 tablespoons Tarragon Vinegar
   (page 381) or white wine vinegar
3/4 cup sour cream
1/2 cup mayonnaise
Freshly ground black pepper

1. Place the anchovies, garlic, scallions, parsley, cilantro, dill, tarragon, sugar, salt, and vinegar in a food processor or blender. Pulse the machine until the herb mixture is finely chopped, stopping once or twice to scrape the side of the bowl with a rubber spatula.

2. Add the sour cream and mayonnaise and run the machine until the dressing is smooth. Season with pepper to taste, running the machine to combine.

3. Transfer the dip to a clean container and refrigerate it, covered, until the flavors meld, at least 6 hours. The dressing can be refrigerated for up to 1 week.

Note: To make this a dressing, increase the vinegar to 3 tablespoons, and decrease the sour cream to 1/2 cup, the mayonnaise to 1/4 cup, and the refrigeration time to 3 hours.

Visitors to our Farm Stand get to venture past this point on their tours or field walks.

Ideas for Crudités

With so many wonderful vegetables showing up in the markets, it's fun to create a bountiful display to be eaten raw or lightly cooked with a dipping sauce or two. Be sure to thoroughly rinse the vegetables and peel any that have thick or bitter skins. Here are some ideas:

- Grilled asparagus spears (see sidebar, page 227)
- Blanched green string and yellow wax beans
- Red, yellow, and orange bell pepper sticks
- Broccoli and cauliflower florets
- Tiny, whole baby carrots, with a bit of their leafy tops
- Celery sticks
- Cucumber spears
- Jicama sticks
- Kohlrabi slices
- Radishes, sliced in half lengthwise, with a bit of their leafy tops
- Cherry tomatoes, in a variety of shapes and colors
- Zucchini and yellow summer squash spears

Sesame Miso Dressing

There's no lack of interesting flavors and textures in this rich and thick dressing, thanks to the toasted sesame oil, ginger, garlic, and a surprising crunch of sesame seeds. Plus, the silky tofu and flavorful miso add health benefits of their own. The dressing is thick enough to use as a vegetable dip, or thinned with a bit of water, it becomes light enough to dress delicate baby spinach or mixed baby greens.

MAKES ABOUT 1 CUP

Delicate cosmos grow in abundance in the Carmel Valley sunshine.

½ cup (about 4 ounces) coarsely chopped silken tofu

2 tablespoons white miso (see sidebar, page 48)

1 small clove garlic, peeled

2 tablespoons toasted sesame oil

1 tablespoon soy sauce

1 tablespoon Ginger Vinegar (page 380) or unseasoned rice vinegar or 1 teaspoon grated peeled fresh ginger, if not using Ginger Vinegar

2 tablespoons sesame seeds, toasted (see sidebar, page 273)

1. Place the tofu, miso, garlic, sesame oil, soy sauce, vinegar, or ginger, in a food processor or blender. Run the machine until the dressing is smooth. Add 1 tablespoon of water, or more, to reach the desired consistency, stirring or blending to combine.

2. Transfer the dressing to a clean container, add the sesame seeds, and stir to combine. The dressing can be refrigerated, covered, for up to 1 week.

Creamy Avocado Dip

Thick and rich, this dip is perfect for artichokes, crudités, and chips, and also makes a flavorful sandwich spread. Avocado dip can be transformed into a salad dressing for such crunchy lettuces as romaine and iceberg by thinning it with water or canola oil to form the consistency you like. If you don't care for anchovies, leave them out, but you'll probably want to add some more salt, about a quarter teaspoon.

MAKES ABOUT 1 CUP

2 anchovies, or 2 teaspoons
    anchovy paste
2 scallions, including white and
    3 inches green, trimmed and coarsely
    chopped
1 small clove garlic, peeled
1 tablespoon fresh tarragon leaves
2 tablespoons coarsely chopped fresh
    chives
2 tablespoons fresh flat-leaf parsley
    leaves
$^1/_2$ teaspoon grated lemon zest
1 tablespoon fresh lemon juice
1 tablespoon Tarragon Vinegar
    (page 381) or white wine vinegar
1 small ripe avocado, preferably
    Hass, peeled, pitted, and
    coarsely chopped
$^1/_4$ cup mayonnaise
$^1/_4$ cup sour cream or plain yogurt
Coarse (kosher) salt and freshly
    ground black pepper

1. Place the anchovies, scallions, garlic, tarragon, chives, and parsley in a food processor or blender. Pulse the machine until the herb mixture is finely chopped, stopping once or twice to scrape the side of the bowl with a rubber spatula.

2. Add the lemon zest, lemon juice, vinegar, and avocado and blend until the dip is smooth.

3. Add the mayonnaise and sour cream and pulse briefly to combine. Season the dip with salt and pepper to taste. It can be refrigerated, covered, for up to 3 days.

Marea and I are unable to resist tasting just a few more raspberries on the way in from picking a bowl full in our backyard raspberry patch.

Edamame Hummus

Edamame—fresh soybeans—give this unusual hummus its lovely green color. They blend beautifully with chickpeas to create a delicious spread that's a powerhouse of vegetable protein, fiber, and nutrients. The flavors stay lively thanks to a healthy dose of fresh garlic, parsley, cumin, and a splash of lemon juice. Feel free to experiment with the herb—we often substitute fresh cilantro for half of the parsley. This is a Farm Stand favorite that we love as a dip for raw vegetables and pita toasts or as a sandwich spread. **MAKES ABOUT 2 CUPS**

Edamame

Edamame are fresh soybeans, and when eaten straight from the pod, makes a healthy snack or hors d'oeuvre. You can find whole edamame in their pods in the freezer section of specialty stores or well-stocked grocery stores. The beans are delicious served warm, chilled, or at room temperature.

To prepare whole edamame as a snack, place one pound of edamame pods in a bowl, sprinkle them with one to two tablespoons of salt, and toss until the pods are evenly coated. Allow the edamame to rest at room temperature to absorb the salt, about 15 minutes.

Meanwhile, bring a medium-size saucepan of water to a boil over high heat. Add the salted edamame pods and cook until tender, three to five minutes. Drain the pods in a colander and spread them on a clean dish towel to absorb the remaining water. For the best flavor, shell and eat the edamame the same day they are cooked.

About 1 cup shelled, fresh or
   frozen (unthawed) edamame
   (soybeans; from 1 pound unshelled)
2 large cloves garlic, peeled
1/2 teaspoon salt
1/2 cup fresh flat-leaf parsley leaves
3/4 cup canned chickpeas
   (garbanzo beans), drained
1/4 cup plain yogurt
2 tablespoons tahini (sesame paste)
3 tablespoons fresh lemon juice
Pinch of cayenne pepper
1 teaspoon ground cumin, or
   1 teaspoon whole cumin seeds,
   toasted (see sidebar, page 273),
   and ground

1. Bring a large pot of salted water to a boil over high heat. Add the edamame and cook until tender, 4 to 5 minutes. Drain the edamame into a colander and set aside to cool.

2. Place the garlic, salt, and parsley in a food processor and pulse the machine until they are finely chopped.

3. Add the edamame and chickpeas and pulse 5 or 6 times until they are coarsely chopped.

4. Add the yogurt, tahini, lemon juice, cayenne pepper, cumin, and 1/2 cup of water and process until the hummus is smooth. The hummus can be refrigerated, covered, for up to 1 week. It can be served chilled or at room temperature.

Tapenade on Crostini

Tapenade is an olive spread that originated along the Mediterranean, where olive trees mingle with grapevines. There's nothing shy about this tapenade's intense flavors, punctuated with garlic, capers, and anchovies. Black olives are traditional, but tapenade is also delicious made with green olives. It's often spread on crostini— *Italian for "little crusts"—toasts made from day-old bread. Tapenade crostini are great with cocktails and as an accompaniment to a simple green salad. The olive spread is also tasty on its own, paired with grilled chicken or tuna, or as an addition to pasta sauce.* **MAKES ABOUT 1 CUP OF TAPENADE, ENOUGH FOR ABOUT 16 CROSTINI**

1 cup black olives, such as kalamata
   or niçoise, pitted and rinsed
2 anchovy fillets
1 clove garlic, peeled
1 tablespoon capers, drained
1 tablespoon fresh lemon juice
Pinch of dried red pepper flakes

3 tablespoons olive oil
1 tablespoon packed fresh thyme
   or oregano leaves
1 loaf of crusty, day-old bread,
   such as a baguette, cut into 1/4-inch
   slices and toasted

1. Place the olives, anchovies, garlic, and capers in a food processor or blender and pulse the machine until they are coarsely chopped, stopping once or twice to scrape the side of the bowl with a rubber spatula.

2. Add the lemon juice, red pepper flakes, olive oil, and thyme and run the machine until the mixture is smooth. Serve the tapenade on the toasted bread. The tapenade can be refrigerated, covered, for up to 1 month. Let it return to room temperature before using.

Mediterranean Marinated Olives

Infused with citrus and herbs, these marinated olives absolutely burst with flavor. They keep for months in the refrigerator, so I always make a large batch to have on hand for a quick appetizer, salad garnish, or snack. Create your own blend from olive varieties of different sizes, such as tiny purple niçoise, slender green picholine, and plump black kalamata olives. If you prefer, you can use pitted olives. They taste just as good, although they don't hold their shape during cooking as well as the ones with pits. For the best flavor, allow enough time for the olives to warm to room temperature before serving. **MAKES ABOUT 4 CUPS**

4 cups assorted green and black olives,
    pitted or unpitted
1 cup extra-virgin olive oil
8 cloves garlic, peeled and crushed
1 teaspoon dried red pepper flakes
1 teaspoon whole fennel seeds
2 bay leaves
1 teaspoon freshly ground black pepper
2 sprigs (each 3 inches long) fresh
    rosemary
Grated zest and juice of 1 orange
Grated zest and juice of 1 lemon

1. Position a rack in the lower third of the oven and preheat the oven to 200°F.

2. Place all the ingredients in a baking dish or casserole and toss to combine. Tightly cover the baking dish with aluminum foil. Bake the olives until they are warmed through, about 1 hour.

3. Remove the baking dish from the oven, uncover it, and let the olives cool to room temperature. Discard the rosemary.

4. The olives can be served immediately or refrigerated, covered, for up to 3 months. Cold makes the olive oil congeal, so allow time for the olives to come to room temperature before serving.

From the bowl to my plate—it's hard to get enough of these intensely flavorful olives.

Spicy Pecans

Laced with the exotic aroma of cardamom and coriander, spicy pecans are delicious on salads. My kids love them as a healthy snack, and guests enjoy them by the bowlful as an appetizer with cocktails or beer. Substituting other nuts, such as walnuts or almonds, would be delicious, too. **MAKES 2 1/2 CUPS**

2 tablespoons sugar
1/2 teaspoon salt
1/2 teaspoon ground cardamom
   (see sidebar, page 368)
1/2 teaspoon ground cayenne pepper
1/2 teaspoon ground coriander
1 tablespoon canola oil
1 large egg white
2 1/2 cups (about 10 ounces) pecan halves

1. Position a rack in the center of the oven and preheat the oven to 300°F. Line a rimmed baking sheet with parchment paper (for the easiest cleanup) or grease the baking sheet. Set it aside.

2. Place the sugar, salt, cardamom, cayenne, and coriander in a large bowl and stir to combine. Add the oil and egg white and whisk until smooth. Add the pecans and stir to coat all over with the spice mixture.

3. Transfer the pecans to the prepared baking sheet and spread them out in a single layer. Bake the pecans until they are crisp and lightly browned, 20 to 30 minutes.

4. Let the pecans cool completely. Stored in an airtight container they will keep for up to 2 weeks.

Spiced Candied Walnuts

Sweet and spicy walnuts make memorable a simple salad or dessert. The unusual flavor of these candied nuts comes from the Chinese five-spice powder and they are especially good on salads that have roasted walnut oil in the dressing. Hazelnuts, almonds, or pecans are also good prepared this way. **MAKES 2 1/2 CUPS**

Walnuts—delicious and healthy right out of the shell.

1/4 cup sugar
1/2 teaspoon Chinese five-spice powder
2 tablespoons honey
2 1/2 cups (8 ounces) walnut halves
   or pieces
Salt

1. Position a rack in the center of the oven and preheat the oven to 350°F. Line a rimmed baking sheet with parchment paper (for the easiest cleanup) or grease the baking sheet. Set it aside.

2. Place the sugar, five-spice powder, honey, and 2 tablespoons of water in a medium-size saucepan and stir to combine. Bring the mixture to a boil over high heat and add the walnuts. Reduce the heat to medium-high and cook, stirring constantly, until the liquid evaporates, 3 to 5 minutes.

3. Transfer the walnuts to the prepared baking sheet and spread them out in a single layer. Bake the walnuts until they are golden brown, 10 to 12 minutes. Stir the nuts after 4 minutes, and keep a close eye on them during the final minutes of baking because they can burn very quickly.

4. Season the walnuts with salt to taste, then let them cool to room temperature.

5. Break apart any nuts that are stuck together. Store the walnuts in an airtight container, placing pieces of waxed paper between the layers to separate them. The nuts can be kept at room temperature for up to 1 month. If the walnuts become too moist or sticky, recrisp them by spreading them on a parchment paper–lined baking sheet and heating them in a 325°F oven for 10 minutes. Cool the nuts before serving.

Brown Sugar Glazed Hazelnuts

You'll probably catch your kids—or even yourself—sneaking a taste of these sweet nuts before serving time, so you may want to double the recipe. Depending on the humidity, the hazelnuts may be sticky even after they cool. But don't worry, they will still taste great. Try this basic recipe with almonds, pecans, or walnuts, too. **MAKES 1 1/2 CUPS**

1 1/2 cups whole raw hazelnuts,
   with or without skins
1/4 cup light brown sugar
Pinch of salt
1 large egg white

1. Position a rack in the center of the oven and preheat the oven to 350°F. Line a rimmed baking sheet with parchment paper (for the easiest cleanup) or grease the baking sheet. Set it aside.

2. Combine the hazelnuts with the brown sugar and salt in a small bowl. Add the egg white and stir to combine. Using a slotted spoon or a fork, transfer the nuts to the prepared baking sheet and spread them out in a single layer.

3. Bake the hazelnuts until they are golden brown, 10 to 12 minutes. Turn off the oven, leaving the baking sheet inside with the oven door closed for 10 minutes to dry the nuts.

4. Transfer the baking sheet to a wire rack and let the hazelnuts cool completely. Store the nuts in an airtight container, placing pieces of waxed paper between the layers to separate them. The nuts can be kept at room temperature for up to 3 weeks. If the nuts become moist or sticky, recrisp them by spreading them on a parchment paper–lined baking sheet and heating them in a 325°F oven for 10 minutes. Let the nuts cool before serving.

The distinct flavor of hazelnuts is a wonderful addition to salads.

Chapter 4

Meat and Poultry Main Dishes

Because Drew and I grow organic produce, some people assume we're vegetarians. Nothing could be farther from the truth! Steak and olive sauce, roast chicken, and beef stew are a few of my family's favorite dishes; we enjoy them again and again. I expect most home cooks have a similar repertoire of surefire winners that make up their regular main-dish rotation. But while working on this cookbook, I've discovered new favorites to add to my list.

Cleome, also known as spider flower, is an unusual beauty.

With our busy lives, it makes sense to select main dishes that will provide leftovers. It's easy to cook two rosemary-roasted chickens at once. Eat one for dinner and save the other for Curried Chicken Salad the next day. Flank Steak with Lemon Shallot Marinade is delicious sliced for dinner and makes great sandwiches later.

Some main dishes also get better with time. Short ribs braised in merlot and Braised Lamb Shanks with Rosemary both take a while to prepare, but the next day's leftovers seem to taste even better than the first night's serving. They are well worth the effort.

Cooking extra to freeze is another way to make the most of your cooking time. One-Pot Beef Stew makes enough for eight servings; enjoy a family dinner and freeze the leftovers for a day when you're too busy to cook. Farm Stand Meatballs also freezes well. Thaw just the number of meatballs you need, warm them in marinara sauce while the pasta boils, and you'll have an easy meal of spaghetti and meatballs.

Everyone needs recipes that require little preparation, but never boring. Quick Grilled Lemon Chicken can soak overnight in a simple marinade and cooks up in less than ten minutes. For a celebration, try the luxurious, but no-fuss, beef kebabs wrapped in prosciutto. If your family members are meat lovers, you'll find plenty here to satisfy them. I'll be delighted if some of these main dishes make the cut for your own dinner rotation!

Facing Page:
Grilled Lamb Chops with Mongolian Sauce (page 130).

Note: If Meyer lemons are not available, you can sweeten regular lemon juice to simulate their taste. For this marinade, substitute 1¼ cups of fresh lemon juice and ¼ cup of fresh orange juice for the Meyer lemon juice. Or, add 1 tablespoon of sugar to 1½ cups of lemon juice.

Flank Steak
with Lemon Shallot Marinade

This flank steak is one of our all-time family favorites. A Meyer lemon and soy sauce marinade, which doubles as a sauce, tenderizes the meat. I serve the flank steak thinly sliced with roasted potatoes and a seasonal vegetable. The next day, leftovers make great sandwiches coupled with a crusty baguette, baby arugula, and Jalapeño Arugula Aioli (see page 224). **SERVES 6 TO 8**

3 pounds flank steak
1½ cups fresh Meyer lemon juice (see Note)
½ cup soy sauce
6 medium-size shallots, coarsely chopped
2 tablespoons toasted sesame oil or peanut oil (optional)

1. Pierce both sides of the flank steak all over with a fork. Place the meat in a 1-gallon resealable plastic bag.

2. Pour the lemon juice in a small bowl and whisk in the soy sauce. Add the shallots and whisk in the sesame oil, if using. Pour about ⅔ cup of the marinade into a covered microwave-safe container and refrigerate it until it's time to use as a sauce.

3. Pour the remaining marinade into the bag with the flank steak and seal it, pressing out any excess air. Refrigerate the steak overnight, or up to 24 hours, turning the bag once or twice to distribute the marinade evenly.

4. When ready to cook, set up a barbecue grill and preheat it to high or preheat the broiler.

5. Remove the flank steak from the marinade and discard the used marinade. Grill or broil the steak about 3 inches from the heat source, until cooked to taste, 3 to 4 minutes per side for rare, or 4 to 6 minutes per side for medium-rare. When done, an instant-read meat thermometer inserted at an angle into the center of the steak will register 125°F for rare or 135°F for medium-rare.

6. Let the flank steak rest for about 5 minutes.

7. Meanwhile, warm the reserved ⅔ cup of marinade in the microwave and place it in a serving bowl. Cut the steak against the grain into very thin slices, holding the knife almost parallel to the surface of the steak and slicing it at a shallow angle. Serve the flank steak with the warm or room temperature marinade on the side for spooning over the steak.

Meyer lemons.

Sizzling Steak
with the Goodman Family Olive Sauce

My family always looks forward to a perfectly cooked steak served with an amazing olive sauce. But when guests join us, I feel the need to reassure them that what the sauce lacks in visual appeal, it makes up for in flavor. One taste and they agree that the tangy bold sauce brings out the best in a juicy, sizzling steak. Any leftover sauce makes a delicious spread for flank steak sandwiches or dip for crudités or toasted pita bread wedges. Good quality black olives make a big difference, but for the green olives, average quality is fine. When you are making the sauce, don't over process it, because it's best a little chunky. Serve it with any type of tender beef steak sizzled in a cast-iron skillet or grilled outdoors. **SERVES 2**

1 or 2 beef steaks (1¼- to 1¾-inches
thick; about 1½ pounds total),
such as porterhouse, rib eye, or
New York strip, at room temperature
Olive oil
Coarse (kosher) salt and freshly ground
black pepper
Goodman Family Olive Sauce
(recipe follows)

1. Position a rack in the lower third of the oven and preheat the oven to 500°F. Place a large cast-iron skillet on the oven rack and let it heat for at least 15 minutes.

2. Rub the steak all over with olive oil and season both sides with salt and pepper.

3. Place the steak in the hot skillet and cook until the bottom of the steak is browned, about 5 minutes. (If your steak is thicker than 1¼ inches, increase the time by 1 minute for each additional ¼-inch.) Turn the steak over and continue cooking to the desired degree of doneness, 5 to 6 minutes for medium-rare. When done, an instant-read meat thermometer inserted into the center of the steak, but not touching the bone, if any, will register 130°F for medium-rare.

4. Remove the skillet from the oven and transfer the steak to a cutting board. Let the steak rest for 10 minutes.

5. Cut the meat off the bone, if any, and carve it into ¼-inch slices, if desired. Serve immediately with plenty of olive sauce on the side.

Marea, beloved dog Jack, me, Drew, and Jeffrey at home in Carmel Valley.

Goodman Family Olive Sauce

There's nothing quite like a sizzling steak served with a big spoonful of our family's olive sauce on the side. Our guests always rave about it so we keep plenty on hand, but the recipe can be easily halved. **MAKES ABOUT 3 CUPS**

2 large cloves garlic, peeled
1/4 teaspoon salt
2 tablespoons Dijon mustard
1/2 cup fresh lemon juice
1/2 cup extra-virgin olive oil
3 cups good-quality pitted black olives, drained
2 cups pitted green salad olives (without pimientos), drained

1. Place all of the ingredients in a food processor or blender and pulse until the olives are coarsely chopped. Scrape the side of the processor bowl with a rubber spatula, then run the machine continuously for 30 seconds. Scrape the side again, then run the machine until the olive sauce is coarsely pureed, 30 to 45 seconds longer.

2. Serve the sauce at room temperature or chilled. It can be refrigerated, covered, for up to 2 weeks.

Merle's Beef Brisket

Drew's family moved to New York City from Buffalo when he was seven years old. Fortunately, his sister Jill has kept alive the hearty Goodman family recipes from their Buffalo years. Our kids have warm memories of their Aunt Jill's dinners, which often feature a big platter of fork-tender brisket—a recipe that Drew and Jill's late mother, Merle, prized and that Jill continues to prepare. Long, slow cooking is her secret, but you'd never guess that this brisket is so easy to prepare. The onions melt into the tomato and meat juices, making a flavorful sauce that's soaked up by the potatoes as they cook. This is the ultimate comfort food; it can bring warmth to even the most bitter cold Buffalo winter. **SERVES 6**

3 tablespoons onion powder
3 tablespoons garlic powder
1 tablespoon salt
1 teaspoon freshly ground black pepper
2 1/2 pounds first-cut beef brisket
3 cups canned tomato sauce
4 large yellow onions, sliced into thin rings
8 medium-size (about 3 pounds) Yukon Gold or waxy potatoes (such as White Rose), peeled and cut into quarters

1. Position a rack in the lower third of the oven and preheat the oven to 350°F.

What Is Organic Meat?

When you buy beef, pork, or lamb that is certified organic by the USDA, you can be sure that the animals were:

■ Raised without antibiotics.

■ Raised without growth hormones. (Federal regulations prohibit the use of growth hormones to produce any pork, whether or not it is organic.)

■ Fed 100 percent organic feed or allowed to graze on pastures that are certified organic.

Note: It is unnecessary to brown the brisket for this recipe, but if you wish to, place it in the pot fat-side down and brown it over medium heat for 5 minutes. Turn the meat and brown the other side for 5 minutes. Turn the meat again so the fat side is up and continue with the recipe.

2. Combine the onion powder, garlic powder, salt, and pepper in a small bowl, then rub the seasoning mixture all over the brisket.

3. Place the brisket, fat-side up, in a heavy ovenproof pot with a tight-fitting lid (see Note). Pour the tomato sauce over the meat and scatter the onion rings on top. Cover the pot.

4. Bake the brisket for 3 hours, then check it and add ¼ cup of water if the sauce is too dry. Arrange the potatoes around the brisket, replace the cover, and cook until the potatoes are tender when pierced with a fork, 60 to 70 minutes longer.

5. Transfer the brisket to a cutting board and let it cool for 5 minutes, then thinly slice it across the grain. Arrange the meat on a warm serving platter and spoon the potatoes and sauce on top.

Prosciutto-Wrapped Beef Kebabs

Decadent is the best description for these kebabs. The meltingly tender chunks of marinated fillet are wrapped in prosciutto and nestled up against sweet onions. They are my first choice for a special occasion; Drew makes them for my birthday and Mother's Day. The kebabs are simple to prepare, even at the last minute. The marinating time is brief and, once the skewers are assembled, the grilling is fast.

SERVES 4; 2 SKEWERS PER PERSON

2 tablespoons Worcestershire sauce
¹/₂ teaspoon garlic powder
Pinch of salt
1¹/₄ pounds beef tenderloin, trimmed and cut into 1¹/₂-inch cubes
1 sweet yellow onion, such as Walla Walla or Vidalia
8 ounces prosciutto, thinly sliced

1. Place the Worcestershire sauce, garlic powder, and salt in a medium-size bowl and stir to blend. Add the beef cubes and stir until well coated. Let the meat marinate at room temperature, stirring occasionally, for 20 to 30 minutes.

2. Meanwhile, set up a barbecue grill and preheat it to medium.

3. Cut the onion into quarters lengthwise through the root end. Then slice each onion wedge in half crosswise to make eight chunks.

4. Cut the slices of prosciutto in half, lengthwise. Wrap each beef cube with a half slice of prosciutto.

5. Assemble the kebabs by alternating pieces of onion (3 or 4 layers) with cubes of prosciutto-wrapped beef on 8 skewers.

6. Grill the kebabs, turning occasionally, until cooked to taste, a total of 6 to 8 minutes for medium-rare.

7. Transfer the kebabs to a platter and serve hot.

Merlot-Braised Short Ribs
with Cipollini Onions

A lengthy braising magically transforms humble short ribs into fork-tender morsels smothered in a robust sauce enriched with red wine, earthy mushrooms, and balsamic vinegar. The good thing about cooking short ribs this way is that once you brown the ribs and start them simmering with the wine and vegetables, you can relax for most of the afternoon. Boneless short ribs have less waste and are easier to work with, but bone-in ribs have more flavor. If you use boneless ribs, you'll want to use a rich, full-bodied, homemade stock. If you opt for store-bought broth, go for the bone-in ribs. Sweet cipollini onions, about an inch and a half in diameter, are a delicious alternative to the old standby, pearl onions. This is one dish that only gets better with reheating. Your family won't complain about these leftovers!

SERVES 8 TO 10

1 ounce dried porcini mushrooms
5 pounds boneless beef short ribs,
   or 7 pounds bone-in beef short ribs
Salt and freshly ground black pepper
4 tablespoons olive oil
2 ounces pancetta, cut in ¼-inch dice
   (about ½ cup)
2 carrots, coarsely chopped
2 ribs celery, coarsely chopped
2 small yellow onions, coarsely
   chopped
3 cloves garlic, peeled and thinly sliced
1 bay leaf
3 tablespoons fresh thyme leaves
¼ cup tomato paste
1 bottle (750 milliliters) merlot
4 cups Slow Simmering Beef Stock
   (page 376) or store-bought low-
   sodium beef broth
12 ounces cipollini or pearl onions
   (12 to 16 onions)
¼ cup good-quality balsamic vinegar

1. Soak the dried mushrooms in 1 cup of warm water until soft, at least 5 minutes. Drain the mushrooms in a sieve set over a small bowl. Set the mushrooms aside. Strain the soaking liquid through a paper coffee filter, then set aside the soaking liquid.

2. Position a rack in the lower third of the oven and preheat the oven to 350°F.

3. Dry the ribs with paper towels, then liberally season them with salt and pepper.

4. Heat 2 tablespoons of the olive oil in a large, heavy ovenproof pot or roasting pan over medium-high heat. Working in batches if needed to avoid crowding the pot, add the ribs and brown well on all sides, 8 to 10 minutes per batch. Using tongs or a slotted spoon, transfer the ribs to a platter and set aside.

Note: You can make the short ribs and prepare the cipollini onions through Step 10 (page 120) up to a day in advance. Remove the ribs from the sauce and refrigerate them, covered. Refrigerate the onions, covered, after peeling them. Let the sauce cool to room temperature, then refrigerate it, covered, until a layer of fat solidifies on the surface, at least 4 hours or overnight. Remove the layer of fat from the sauce and discard it before proceeding with Step 13. Letting the sauce rest overnight helps the flavor to develop and lets you eliminate more fat than degreasing the sauce while still warm.

5. Reduce the heat to medium and add the remaining 2 tablespoons of olive oil to the pot. Add the pancetta and cook, stirring occasionally, until it starts to soften, 1 to 2 minutes. Add the carrots, celery, yellow onions, and garlic and cook, stirring occasionally, until the vegetables begin to caramelize, 15 to 20 minutes.

6. Add the bay leaf, thyme, and tomato paste to the pot and cook, stirring frequently, for 5 minutes.

7. Return the ribs and any accumulated juice to the pot, stacking them to fit, if necessary. Add the soaked mushrooms, mushroom soaking liquid, and merlot. Add 3 to 4 cups of the stock, enough that the ribs are covered. Heat the ribs over medium-high heat until the liquid begins to simmer.

8. Cover the pot tightly with a lid or aluminum foil. Bake the ribs until they are tender when pierced with a fork, about 3 hours. Check the pot about every 30 minutes to make sure the sauce is gently simmering but not boiling. If needed, adjust the oven temperature to maintain a slow simmer.

9. Meanwhile, fill a large bowl of water with ice cubes and set aside.

10. Bring a medium-size saucepan of water to a boil over medium-high heat. Add the onions and cook until their skins loosen, about 2 minutes. Drain the onions, then plunge them into the bowl of ice water. When cool enough to handle, peel the onions, cutting a small sliver off the root end and pulling the skin off. Set the onions aside (see Note, page 119).

11. Remove the ribs from the sauce, place them on a platter, and loosely cover them with aluminum foil to keep warm.

12. Let the sauce rest for a few minutes until the fat rises to the surface. Degrease the sauce by skimming off the fat with a metal spoon or ladle.

13. Pour the sauce through a strainer and discard the solids, including the bay leaf. Wash the pot and return the sauce to it. Bring the sauce to a simmer over medium heat.

14. Add the vinegar and onions to the sauce, then let it simmer gently until it is concentrated and the onions are tender, 20 to 30 minutes. Add the ribs and let simmer until they are warmed through, then serve.

Children on a school tour at our Farm Stand spend a tranquil moment in our chamomile-carpeted walking labyrinth.

One-Pot Beef Stew

I'm always on the lookout for easy meals with minimal cleanup. This one-pot stew suits me perfectly. The meat slowly simmers with the mushrooms and onions until it is meltingly tender. Simply stirring in a little bit of tomato paste and sour cream at the end creates a creamy sauce, perfect for spooning over white rice or egg noodles.

SERVES 8 TO 10

4 pounds boneless beef chuck roast,
    trimmed and cut into
    $1^1/_2$-inch cubes
Salt and freshly ground black pepper
$^1/_4$ cup olive oil
3 large yellow onions (about 2 pounds),
    sliced $^1/_4$-inch thick (about 6 cups)
1 pound white mushrooms, sliced
    $^1/_4$-inch thick
1 tablespoon Worcestershire sauce
$^1/_4$ cup tomato paste
$^1/_2$ cup sour cream

1. Season the meat with salt and pepper.

2. Heat the olive oil in a large, heavy pot or Dutch oven over medium-high heat. Working in batches, add the meat and brown well on all sides, 5 to 8 minutes per batch. Add the onions to the meat and cook, stirring frequently, until they soften and turn golden, about 10 minutes. Add the mushrooms, cover the pot, and cook, stirring occasionally, until they soften, 5 to 10 minutes.

3. Add the Worcestershire sauce and $^1/_4$ cup of water. Cover the pot and bring the stew to a simmer. Decrease the heat to low and let simmer gently, covered, for 1 hour. Add the tomato paste and continue to cook until the meat is fork-tender, about 30 minutes longer. Check the stew occasionally and add more water if needed. Adjust the heat, if necessary, to maintain a gentle simmer.

4. Just before serving, add the sour cream and stir to blend. Serve the stew hot. If you are not planning on serving the stew at this time, don't add the sour cream. Let the stew cool to room temperature. It can be refrigerated, covered, for up to 3 days or frozen for up to 3 months. Thaw the stew overnight in the refrigerator, then reheat it over low heat and add the sour cream.

The hills provide a dramatic backdrop to the growing fields.

Farm Stand Meatballs

*M*oist meatballs, filled with herbs and Parmesan cheese, are a Farm Stand staple. *They are delicious sliced on sandwiches, simmered in pasta sauce, or tossed into soups. The recipe calls for a mixture of beef and pork, but you can play around with combinations of meat to suit your taste. All-beef meatballs are delicious, or for a spicier meatball, substitute a half pound of Italian sausage meat for an equal amount of the beef or pork. Add the meatballs to our Farm Stand Marinara Sauce (see page 191) and spoon it over spaghetti—a perfect partnership.*

MAKES ABOUT 20 MEATBALLS

Olive oil for greasing the foil
3 large eggs
$1/2$ cup whole milk
1 tablespoon minced garlic
1 tablespoon dried oregano
2 tablespoons chopped fresh basil,
    or 2 teaspoons dried basil
1 teaspoon dried thyme
2 teaspoons salt
1 teaspoon freshly ground black pepper
$1/2$ teaspoon dried red pepper flakes
$1^1/2$ cups freshly grated Parmesan or
    Asiago cheese
1 cup unseasoned dry bread crumbs
1 pound lean ground beef
1 pound ground pork

1. Position a rack in the center of the oven and preheat the oven to 400°F. Line a rimmed baking sheet with aluminum foil or parchment paper for easier cleanup. Lightly oil the foil or paper liner. Set the baking sheet aside.

2. Place the eggs, milk, garlic, oregano, basil, thyme, salt, black pepper, and red pepper flakes in a large bowl and whisk to combine. Add the cheese and bread crumbs and stir to mix.

3. Using your hands, break the beef and pork into small chunks and add them to the bowl. Blend the mixture with your hands until just combined, working the mixture as little as possible.

4. Gently form the meat mixture into 2-inch meatballs and arrange them on the prepared baking sheet so they do not touch each other.

5. Bake the meatballs until an instant-read meat thermometer inserted into the center of one reads 160°F, 25 to 30 minutes.

6. If you are not planning on serving the meatballs at this time, let them cool to room temperature. They can be refrigerated, covered, for up to 3 days or frozen for up to 3 months. To freeze the cooked meatballs, place them on a tray in a single layer in the freezer. Once they are frozen solid, transfer the meatballs to an airtight container or freezer bag. Because they are individually frozen, you can take out just the number you need. Let the meatballs thaw in the refrigerator overnight before using.

Meatball Sandwiches

Our meatballs make a deliciously messy sandwich for a casual lunch. To make meatball sandwiches, cut a baguette in half lengthwise and toast one half. Slice the meatballs and place them on the baguette half. Top the meatballs with a little Farm Stand Marinara Sauce (see page 191) and some grated mozzarella. Melt the cheese under the broiler or in a microwave, then sprinkle it with Parmesan cheese. Enjoy the sandwich open-faced with a knife and fork or toast the other half of the baguette to top it.

Grilled Pork Tenderloin
with Spiced Orange Sauce

An unusual marinade adds a juicy flavor boost to lean pork tenderloins, and will stimulate your senses with its aroma of oranges mingled with freshly ground spices. The marinade does double duty as a sauce, making this dish special enough for guests but easy enough for a weeknight dinner. It's great with Moroccan-Spiced Bulgur Pilaf (see page 271) and Sautéed Broccoli Rabe (see page 233). **SERVES 6 TO 8**

Zest of 3 oranges, finely grated
2 cups fresh orange juice
$\frac{1}{2}$ cup Dijon mustard
$\frac{1}{3}$ cup honey
$4\frac{1}{2}$ teaspoons balsamic vinegar
3 tablespoons whole fennel seeds
  (see Note)
2 sticks cinnamon (each 3 inches),
  broken into small pieces
1 teaspoon whole black peppercorns
1 teaspoon whole cumin seeds
3 pork tenderloins (about 1 pound
  each)
2 tablespoons apricot jam
Salt and freshly ground black pepper
1 tablespoon unsalted butter
  (optional)

1. Place the orange zest, $1\frac{1}{2}$ cups of the orange juice, and the mustard, honey, and vinegar in a small bowl and whisk to combine.

2. Grind the fennel seeds, cinnamon sticks, peppercorns, and cumin seeds to a fine powder in a spice mill (see sidebar, page 124).

3. Add the ground spices to the orange juice mixture and whisk to combine. Set aside $\frac{3}{4}$ cup of the marinade for the sauce.

4. Trim any fat off the tenderloins and remove the tough silver-skin membranes, if any. Place the tenderloins in a 1-gallon resealable plastic bag and add the remaining marinade. Seal the bag, pressing out any excess air, and refrigerate the pork for at least 6 hours or up to 2 days, turning the bag occasionally to distribute the marinade evenly.

5. Set up a barbecue grill and preheat it to medium.

6. Remove the tenderloins from the bag and discard the marinade. Grill the tenderloins, turning once, until they are slightly pink but still moist, and an instant-read meat thermometer inserted

Note: If you don't have a spice mill, you can use ground spices. You'll need 3 tablespoons of ground fennel seeds, $2\frac{1}{2}$ teaspoons of ground cinnamon, $1\frac{1}{2}$ teaspoons of ground black pepper, and $1\frac{1}{4}$ teaspoons of ground cumin.

Autumn rudebeckia is an elegant fall favorite at our Farm Stand.

Grind Your Own Spices

Whole spices have the big advantage of staying fresh much longer than ground ones. When stored in a glass container away from direct light and heat, whole spices retain their fragrance for a year, but the aroma of ground spices can become dull in just a few months.

It's easy to grind spices at home using an inexpensive coffee grinder. But it's a good idea to buy a spice mill or a separate grinder just for spices. To ensure that your spices will be as fresh as possible, buy small quantities of them from a busy store with a fast turnover.

Note: Center-cut rib chops are great, but loin chops, with their morsels of flavorful tenderloin attached to the bone, are even better. Look for chops with solid pink flesh, without white streaks running through it. The white streaks are connective tissues that become tough when cooked.

in the center registers 145°F, 15 to 20 minutes.

7. Transfer the tenderloins to a cutting board, cover them loosely with aluminum foil, and let rest for 5 to 10 minutes.

8. Meanwhile, place the remaining ¹/₂ cup of orange juice, the reserved ³/₄ cup of marinade, and the apricot jam in a small saucepan and stir to combine. Cook over medium heat until the sauce reduces and thickens, about 8 minutes. Remove the sauce from the heat and season it with salt and pepper to taste. For a thicker sauce, add the butter, if desired, and stir to blend.

9. To serve, slice the tenderloins into 1-inch thick pieces. Drizzle each slice with the warm sauce or serve the sauce on the side.

Maple-Brined Pork Chops

Brining is the secret to making lean pork flavorful and juicy. Soaking pork chops in salty water infused with spices and sugar tenderizes and seasons the meat throughout (see sidebar, page 126). These chops cook up fast, but plan ahead to allow time for them to soak in the brine. A brush of maple syrup just before cooking enhances the deep caramel color and brings out the natural sweetness of the pork. Unlike a marinade, the flavor the brine adds to the meat is subtle. Your guests will not be able to put their finger on exactly why these are the most juicy, flavorful pork chops they've ever tasted. They'll just think you're a culinary genius. **SERVES 4 AND CAN BE DOUBLED**

FOR THE BRINE
¹/₂ **cup pure maple syrup**
¹/₂ **cup firmly packed light brown sugar**
¹/₄ **cup coarse (kosher) salt**
1 tablespoon mustard seeds
1 tablespoon black peppercorns
1 bay leaf
10 sprigs fresh thyme, coarsely chopped

FOR THE CHOPS
**4 bone-in, center-cut pork chops,
   cut 1¹/₄ inches thick (about 3 pounds
   total; see Note)**
3 tablespoons pure maple syrup
Olive oil

1. Make the brine: Combine the maple syrup, brown sugar, salt, mustard seeds, peppercorns, bay leaf, and thyme with 4 cups of water in a large saucepan. Heat the brine over high heat and stir until the brown sugar and salt dissolve. Remove the pan from the heat. Add 1 cup of ice water. Pour the brine into a glass or ceramic dish just large enough to hold the pork chops and refrigerate it until chilled. (The brine should be chilled so that it doesn't raise the temperature of the chops when they are added.)

Brining Pork or Poultry

When you soak poultry or pork in a brine, the results are almost magical. The most basic brine is simply a solution of salt and water, but other flavorings are often added, such as spices, sugar, stock, or juice. The meat absorbs the salty liquid, making it more juicy and tender and lightly seasoned all the way through. Sugar adds sweetness to meat and turns a nice caramelized color during cooking. If that isn't reason enough to try brining, the added moisture makes it harder to overcook the meats. Imagine, no more dry pork chops or turkey breast! You'll find a recipe for brined turkey on page 154.

2. Prepare the pork chops: Place the chops in the brine, making sure the meat is completely submerged. Cover the dish and refrigerate the chops for at least 24 hours or up to 48 hours.

3. Remove the pork chops from the brine and discard the brine. Rinse the chops under cold water and dry them thoroughly with paper towels. Brush both sides of the chops with the maple syrup. Let the chops sit at room temperature for 1 hour.

4. Position a rack in the lower third of the oven and preheat the oven to 425°F.

5. Brush the chops with olive oil. Heat 1 tablespoon of olive oil in a large, oven-proof skillet over medium-high heat. Cook the chops until browned, about 3 minutes per side.

6. Transfer the skillet to the oven and bake the chops until they are firm to the touch and an instant-read meat thermometer inserted through the side into the center of one registers 145°F, 8 to 15 minutes. (Don't let the thermometer touch the bone.)

7. Let the chops rest for 5 minutes, then serve warm.

Baby Back Ribs
with Mango Sauce

Smoky ribs so tender the meat nearly falls off the bone are well worth their weight in napkins. Like most barbecued ribs, these are slathered in a sweet and spicy hot sauce. The toasted spices are the ones you'd expect—chili powder, red pepper flakes, and cumin. But instead of sugar, we've used a juicy ripe mango for sweetness. Balsamic vinegar and a squeeze of lime provide the perfect balance. On another night, this sauce would be great for marinating chicken for the grill. **SERVES 4**

2 teaspoons ground cumin
1 teaspoon dried red pepper flakes
1 teaspoon chili powder
1 teaspoon garlic powder
$1/2$ teaspoon dried thyme
$1/4$ teaspoon ground cayenne pepper
1 teaspoon salt
$1/4$ cup olive oil
2 tablespoons balsamic vinegar

1 tablespoon fresh lime juice
2 tablespoons apricot jam
$1/2$ small ripe mango, pureed until
   smooth (about $1/2$ cup)
2 racks pork baby-back ribs
   (about 3 pounds total)
Lime wedges (optional),
   for serving

1. Place the cumin, red pepper flakes, chili powder, garlic powder, thyme, cayenne, and salt in a small skillet. Cook, stirring frequently, over medium-low heat until the spices are hot and fragrant, about 3 minutes.

2. Turn off the heat and add the olive oil to the skillet, stirring to blend. Let the spice mixture sit so the olive oil absorbs the flavors, about 15 minutes. Strain the oil through a fine-mesh sieve and discard the solids.

3. Transfer the flavored oil to a medium-size glass jar. Add the vinegar, lime juice, apricot jam, and mango puree to the flavored oil and seal the lid tightly. Shake the jar vigorously to combine. The sauce can be refrigerated for up to 3 days.

4. Place the ribs in a shallow baking pan and coat them with the sauce. Let the ribs marinate in the refrigerator, covered, for at least 1 hour or as long as overnight, turning the racks occasionally so that they marinate evenly.

5. Set up a barbecue grill for indirect grilling (see Note) and preheat it to medium.

6. Remove the ribs from the sauce, setting aside the sauce. Place the ribs, meat side down, on the hot grill away from the heat. Cover the grill and cook the ribs for 10 minutes. Turn the ribs and baste them with the sauce. Cover the grill and continue cooking, basting every 15 minutes, until the meat is tender and shrinks away slightly from the bone, 1¼ to 1½ hours. Don't baste in the last 10 minutes of grilling.

7. Let the ribs rest for a few minutes, then slice the racks into individual ribs and serve hot, with lime wedges, if desired.

Note: To set up a charcoal grill for indirect grilling, mound the coals on opposite sides of the grill, leaving a space in the middle for a drip pan. Place the food being cooked on the grate over the drip pan, away from the direct heat. To indirect grill on a gas grill, you'll need at least two burners. Light one to the temperature suggested and place the food being cooked over the unlit burner. For both charcoal and gas grills, you'll need to cover the grill as the food cooks.

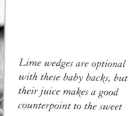

Lime wedges are optional with these baby backs, but their juice makes a good counterpoint to the sweet mango sauce.

Pork Chili Colorado

Colorado *means red in Spanish, which describes the deep color of this Tex-Mex pork stew. It's all about spice—hot chili powder, fragrant coriander, and sweet paprika. While the combination of flavors is complex, the heat is tame. If you like a fiery chili, just add more cayenne pepper. At our Farm Stand, we make our Chili Colorado with lean pork tenderloin, but less expensive cuts of pork, as well as beef or chicken, would be good substitutes. When cut into half-inch cubes, these will cook in the same length of time as the tenderloin. Serve the red chili in a bowl over rice with fresh tortillas on the side.* **SERVES 4 TO 6**

A field of red lettuce awaits harvest.

2 tablespoons sweet paprika
¼ cup chili powder
½ teaspoon cayenne pepper
½ teaspoon ground coriander
¼ teaspoon ground cumin
1½ teaspoons sugar
2 tablespoons whole raw almonds
2 tablespoons unseasoned dry bread
    crumbs
1½ pounds pork tenderloin, cut into
    ½-inch dice
Coarse (kosher) salt and freshly ground
    black pepper
2 tablespoons canola oil
1 small yellow onion, coarsely chopped
2 teaspoons minced garlic
2 Roma (plum) tomatoes, coarsely
    chopped
2 cups Blond Chicken Stock
    (page 372), Dark Chicken Stock
    (page 373), or store-bought
    low-sodium chicken broth
½ cup sour cream, for garnish
¼ cup chopped fresh cilantro,
    for garnish

1. Position a rack in the center of the oven and preheat the oven to 350°F.

2. Place the paprika, chili powder, cayenne, coriander, cumin, sugar, almonds, and bread crumbs in a small bowl and stir to blend. Transfer the spice mixture to a small baking dish and toast in the oven until hot and fragrant, about 10 minutes. Set aside the spice mixture.

3. Season the pork with salt and black pepper.

4. Heat a large skillet over medium heat. When the skillet is hot, add the oil. Working in batches if needed to avoid overcrowding the skillet, add the pork and brown well on all sides, 6 to 10 minutes per batch. Using a slotted spoon, transfer the pork to a platter and set aside.

5. Reduce the heat to medium-low. Add the onion and garlic to the skillet and cook, stirring frequently, until soft and golden, 5 to 10 minutes.

6. Add the tomatoes to the onion mixture and cook, stirring occasionally, until they soften, 3 to 5 minutes.

7. Add the toasted spices to the skillet and stir to combine. Add the chicken stock, increase the heat to high, and bring to a boil. Reduce the heat to low and let the sauce simmer until the flavor is concentrated, about 15 minutes.

8. Let the sauce cool a bit, then transfer it to a blender or food processor and puree until smooth.

9. Return the sauce to the skillet and add the browned pork and any accumulated juice. Bring the chili to a boil over high heat, then reduce the heat to low and let it simmer gently until the meat is tender, 20 to 30 minutes.

10. Serve the chili hot in bowls, garnished with the sour cream and cilantro.

A beautiful head of radicchio.

Herb-Crusted Rack of Lamb
with Roasted Vegetables

*D*on't wait for your anniversary or a promotion to enjoy rack of lamb. Any day will be a celebration when you slice these racks into delicate rib chops, with morsels of juicy meat rimmed with an elegant and flavorful mustard-herb crust. The lamb is first roasted on a bed of aromatic vegetables and herbs, which then serve as a side dish. Then, the lamb cooks directly in the hot roasting pan, developing a crisp crust, while the vegetables finish baking on their own. Racks of lamb look most impressive when you ask your butcher to french them by trimming the meat from the ends of the rib bones. **SERVES 4**

2 racks of lamb chops (8 chops each; 4 to 5 pounds total), bones frenched
Coarse (kosher) salt and freshly ground black pepper
3 tablespoons olive oil
2 medium-size carrots, cut into matchsticks ¹/₃ inch wide and 2 inches long
2 medium-size parsnips, cut into matchsticks ¹/₃ inch wide and 2 inches long
2 ribs celery, cut into matchsticks ¹/₃ inch wide and 2 inches long

1 small yellow onion, cut in half, each half cut into ¹/₂-inch-thick slices
4 cloves garlic, peeled and crushed
4 sprigs fresh thyme, plus 2 tablespoons fresh thyme leaves (see Note)
1 bay leaf
1 cup fresh bread crumbs
3 tablespoons minced fresh flat-leaf parsley
¹/₂ cup Dijon mustard

Note: If you don't have fresh thyme, substitute 1 tablespoon dried thyme for the sprigs, plus 2 teaspoons dried thyme for the leaves.

1. Position a rack in the lower third of the oven and preheat the oven to 450°F.

2. Season the lamb all over with salt and pepper. Heat the olive oil in a heavy, shallow roasting pan or large ovenproof skillet over medium-high heat. Add the racks of lamb, fat side down, and cook until browned, about 3 minutes. Turn the racks over and cook to brown the second side, about 3 minutes longer, about 6 minutes total. Transfer the lamb racks to a platter.

3. Pour off and discard any fat accumulated in the roasting pan. Add the carrots, parsnips, celery, onion, garlic, thyme sprigs, and bay leaf to the pan and stir to combine. Place the lamb, bone side down, on top of the vegetables and bake for 15 minutes.

4. Meanwhile, place the bread crumbs, parsley, and the 2 tablespoons of thyme leaves in a small bowl and stir to blend.

5. Transfer the lamb to a platter or cutting board. Transfer the vegetables to a second roasting pan.

6. Peel or trim the thick outer layer of fat off the lamb, if desired. Spread the mustard all over the lamb meat, not the bones. Pat the bread crumb mixture over the meat, pressing on it lightly, so that the crumbs stick to the mustard coating.

7. Return the lamb racks to the still-warm roasting pan, placing them meat side up. Place the lamb and the roasting pan with the vegetables in the oven and bake until the vegetables are tender and the lamb is cooked to taste, 10 to 15 minutes for medium-rare. To test for doneness, insert an instant-read meat thermometer in the end of a rack of lamb, without touching a bone. It will register 135°F when the rack is done to medium-rare.

8. Remove and discard the bay leaf and thyme sprigs, if any, from the vegetables. Transfer the vegetables and lamb to a platter, cover them loosely with aluminum foil, and let the lamb rest for 10 minutes. Slice the lamb into chops and serve with the vegetables.

Grilled Lamb Chops
with Mongolian Sauce

Thick and rich but not too sweet, with a subtle bite of spicy heat, the Asian-flavored sauce here is terrific with tender, juicy lamb chops. Once boiled, the marinade becomes a delicious sauce. Keep an eye on the lamb chops as they cook because the brown sugar in the Mongolian marinade can burn easily. **SERVES 4**

2 tablespoons grated peeled fresh ginger

2 tablespoons minced garlic

2 medium-size shallots, thinly sliced

1/2 cup Ginger Vinegar (page 380) or balsamic vinegar

2 tablespoons firmly packed light brown sugar

1/4 cup toasted sesame oil

1/3 cup tamari or soy sauce (see Note)

1/3 cup teriyaki sauce, homemade (page 378) or store-bought

1/4 cup hoisin sauce, homemade (page 379) or store-bought

1 tablespoon Asian chile garlic sauce (see Note)

8 loin or rib lamb chops (1 to 1 1/2 inches thick; each 6 to 8 ounces)

1. To make the marinade, place the ginger, garlic, shallots, vinegar, brown sugar, sesame oil, tamari, teriyaki sauce, hoisin sauce, and chile sauce in a medium-size bowl and whisk to combine.

2. Place the lamb chops in a large resealable plastic bag and add the marinade. Let the chops marinate in the refrigerator for at least 8 hours or up to 48 hours, turning the bag occasionally to distribute the marinade evenly.

3. Set up a barbecue grill and preheat it to medium.

4. Remove the chops from the marinade and transfer them to a platter. Strain the marinade through a fine-mesh sieve into a small saucepan. Discard the solids. Bring the marinade to a boil over high heat and cook until it thickens into a sauce, 3 to 5 minutes.

5. Place the lamb chops on the hot grill and cook them for about 2 minutes on each side. Baste the chops with some of the boiled marinade. Cover the grill and cook the chops, turning once, until cooked to taste, about 6 minutes longer for medium-rare. To test for doneness, insert an instant-read meat thermometer through the side into the center of a chop without touching the bone. It will register 145°F when the chop is done to medium-rare.

6. Let the chops rest for 5 minutes, then serve them with the boiled marinade on the side.

Note: Tamari is similar to soy sauce, only it is usually thicker with a smoother taste. Chile garlic sauce—a spicy-hot condiment made from red chile peppers, garlic, and vinegar—is used in Vietnamese and Thai cooking. Look for tamari and chile garlic sauce in Asian markets or on the Asian food aisle of the supermarket.

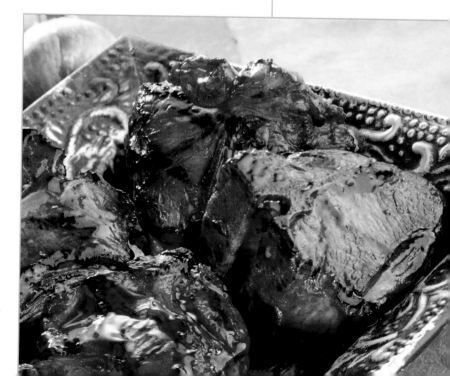

Grilled Lamb Chops with Mongolian Sauce— one of our favorite indulgences.

Braised Lamb Shanks
with Rosemary

The secret to this hearty, rustic dish is a long, slow braising until the meat nearly falls off the bone. As the lamb simmers in a combination of robust red wine and homemade stock, it makes its own rich sauce, infused with rosemary and garlic. The shanks may be even better cooked a day or two in advance and gently reheated in their sauce on the stove top or in the oven. This is classic Italian comfort food, delicious paired with Creamy Polenta (see page 211) or Tuscan White Bean Stew with Rosemary (see page 54). **SERVES 4**

Note: You can make the lamb shanks through Step 7 up to a day in advance. Let the shanks and sauce cool to room temperature, then remove the shanks from the sauce. Refrigerate the shanks and sauce, covered, separately, until a layer of fat solidifies on the surface of the sauce, at least four hours or overnight. Remove the layer of fat from the sauce and discard it before proceeding with Step 10. Letting the sauce rest overnight helps to develop its flavor and lets you eliminate more fat than degreasing the sauce while still warm.

$1/4$ cup unbleached all-purpose flour
1 teaspoon coarse (kosher) salt
$1/2$ teaspoon freshly ground black pepper
4 lamb shanks (about 12 ounces each)
3 tablespoons olive oil
1 large yellow onion, thinly sliced
    (about 2 cups)
2 tablespoons chopped fresh rosemary,
    or 2 teaspoons dried rosemary
2 tablespoons minced garlic
$1^{1}/2$ cups dry red wine
2 tablespoons good-quality balsamic
    vinegar (optional; see box, page 87)
4 cups Slow Simmering Beef Stock
    (page 376)
2 cups Dark Chicken Stock (page 373),
    Blond Chicken Stock (page 372),
    or water
1 tablespoon tomato paste

1. Position a rack in the lower third of the oven and preheat the oven to 350°F.

2. Place the flour, salt, and pepper on a plate and stir to combine. Roll the lamb shanks in the flour mixture to coat and shake off the excess flour.

3. Heat 2 tablespoons of the olive oil in a large, heavy ovenproof pot or Dutch oven over medium-high heat. Working in batches if needed to avoid overcrowding the pot, add the lamb shanks and brown well all over, about 10 minutes total. Transfer the shanks to a platter and set aside.

4. Reduce the heat to medium-low and add the remaining 1 tablespoon of olive oil to the pot. Add the onion and rosemary and cook, stirring occasionally, until the onion is soft and golden, about 5 minutes. Add the garlic and cook until soft and fragrant, 3 to 5 minutes.

5. Add the wine and vinegar, if using, increase the heat to medium-high and bring to a boil. Add the beef stock, chicken stock, and tomato paste.

6. Return the lamb shanks and any accumulated juice to the pot, stacking them to fit, if necessary. If they are not completely submerged in the cooking liquid, add enough water to cover them. Cook the shanks over medium-high heat until the sauce begins to simmer.

7. Cover the pot tightly with a lid or aluminum foil. Transfer the shanks to the oven until they are tender when pierced with a fork and the meat easily slides off the bone, about 2 hours. Check the pot about every 30 minutes to make sure the sauce is simmering gently, not boiling. If needed, adjust the oven temperature to maintain a gentle simmer.

8. Remove the lamb shanks from the sauce and place them on a platter. Loosely cover the shanks with aluminum foil and let them rest while you finish making the sauce.

9. Let the sauce rest for a few minutes until the fat rises to the surface. Degrease the sauce by skimming off the fat with a metal spoon or ladle (see Note, facing page).

10. Pour the sauce through a strainer pressing on the solids to extract all of the liquid. Discard the solids. Return the sauce to the pot. Bring the sauce to a simmer over medium-low heat and let simmer gently until concentrated, about 10 minutes. Return the lamb shanks to the pot and let simmer until they are warmed through.

Lamb Curry
with Saffron Couscous

*T*he aroma of this mild Indian curry sauce with chunks of tender lamb, potatoes, and peas will whet your appetite as it simmers on the stove. And the finished dish doesn't disappoint. It's simple to prepare, and you may be tempted to make it even easier by reaching for a jar of premixed curry spices, but try to resist. By adding the spices individually, you can tweak the flavors to suit your own taste. For more heat, increase the cayenne. Or go easy on the cloves if it's not your favorite spice. For the freshest, most aromatic spices, take a few minutes to grind your own. The lamb curry is delicious served over Saffron Scallion Couscous or basmati rice, with a spoonful of Cucumber Raita and Mango Chutney on the side.

SERVES 4

Lamb Curry with Saffron Couscous combines an exciting taste of India with a touch of the Middle East.

Note: If you want to grind whole spices for the curry, you'll need 1 cinnamon stick, about 2½ inches long, ½ teaspoon each of cardamom, cumin, and coriander seeds, and 3 cloves. It's not practical to freshly grind turmeric. For more about grinding your own spices, see the sidebar on page 124.

1 pound boneless lamb stew meat, such as shoulder or sirloin, cut into 1-inch cubes

Coarse (kosher) salt and freshly ground black pepper

¼ cup canola oil or olive oil

1 medium-size yellow onion, cut into ¼-inch dice (about 1 cup)

½ teaspoon turmeric

1 teaspoon ground cinnamon (see Note; see sidebar, page 368)

½ teaspoon ground cardamom (see Note)

½ teaspoon ground cumin (see Note)

½ teaspoon ground coriander (see Note)

¼ teaspoon ground cloves (see Note)

½ teaspoon ground cayenne pepper

2 tablespoons minced peeled fresh ginger

1 tablespoon minced garlic

1 can (15 ounces) diced tomatoes with their juice

3 medium-size (about 1 pound) Yukon Gold or waxy potatoes (such as White Rose), peeled and cut into ½-inch dice (about 2 cups)

1 cup fresh or frozen (unthawed) green peas

Saffron Scallion Couscous (page 274)

Cucumber Raita (recipe follows)

Mango Chutney (optional; recipe follows)

1. Season the lamb with salt and pepper. Heat the oil in a heavy, large pot over medium-high heat. Working in batches if needed to avoid overcrowding the pot, add the lamb and brown well on all sides, 5 to 8 minutes per batch. Using a slotted spoon, transfer the lamb to a bowl and set aside.

2. Reduce the heat to medium-low and add the onion and turmeric and stir. Then add the cinnamon, cardamom, cumin, coriander, cloves, cayenne pepper, and 1 teaspoon of salt to the pot. Cook, stirring frequently, until the onion softens, about 5 minutes. Add the ginger and garlic and cook, stirring constantly, until fragrant, about 2 minutes.

3. Return the lamb to the pot. Add 2 cups of water and the tomatoes with their juice, increase the heat to medium-high, and bring to a boil. Reduce the heat to low, cover the pot, and let simmer for 30 minutes.

4. Add the potatoes and cook, covered, until the lamb and potatoes are tender, 20 to 30 minutes. Add the peas and cook until the peas are heated through, about 5 minutes. Taste for seasoning, adding more cayenne if needed.

5. Serve the lamb curry hot with the Saffron Scallion Couscous, Cucumber Raita, and Mango Chutney, if using, on the side.

Cucumber Raita

I enjoy a curry dish even more with a cucumber raita served on the side. This yogurt sauce is a traditional accompaniment to Indian dishes; its cooling flavor helps offset the spicy heat. Even better, it's quick and easy to make. **MAKES ABOUT 3 CUPS**

2 cups nonfat or low-fat plain yogurt

1 medium-size cucumber, peeled, seeded, and coarsely grated

¾ teaspoon salt

¾ teaspoon ground cumin

Dash of ground cayenne pepper

Place all the ingredients in a medium-size bowl and stir to combine. Refrigerate the raita, covered, until the flavors meld, at least 15 minutes. The raita can be refrigerated, covered, for up to 3 days.

Mango Chutney

Sweet mangoes and raisins, tart lime, and warm spices come together in a condiment that perks up simple dishes, like roast pork, and complements complex ones, like curried stews. This chutney is medium-hot, so tone it up or down to suit your taste by adjusting the amount of red pepper flakes.

MAKES ABOUT 2 CUPS

$1/2$ teaspoon ground ginger
1 teaspoon curry powder
$1/2$ teaspoon ground cardamom
   (see sidebar, page 368)
$1/4$ teaspoon red pepper flakes
$1/2$ cup distilled white vinegar or
   cider vinegar
$1/2$ cup firmly packed light
   brown sugar
Grated zest of 1 lime
Juice of 1 lime
2 tablespoons grated peeled fresh
   ginger
1 medium-size yellow onion,
   cut in $1/3$-inch dice (about $1/2$ cup)
$1/2$ red bell pepper stemmed, seeded,
   and cut in $1/3$-inch dice
2 slightly underripe mangoes,
   peeled, pitted, and cut in
   $1/2$-inch cubes (see sidebar, page 170)
$1/4$ cup raisins (optional)

1. Place the ground ginger, curry powder, cardamom, and red pepper flakes in a medium-size saucepan and cook, stirring constantly, over low heat until the spices are fragrant, about 3 minutes.

2. Add the vinegar, brown sugar, lime zest and juice, fresh ginger, onion, and bell pepper and increase the heat to high. Bring the onion mixture to a boil, then reduce the heat to medium and let simmer for 10 minutes.

3. Add the mango and raisins, if using, and cook until the chutney softens and thickens, 10 to 15 minutes.

4. Let the chutney cool at room temperature. It can be refrigerated, covered, for up to 3 months.

Delicious and tangy Mango Chutney makes a lively accompaniment to spicy meat dishes.

Poultry

Whether you are roasting rosemary chicken or a holiday turkey, your meal will be even more delicious if you choose organic poultry, which cooks up moist, tender, and loaded with flavor that typical supermarket poultry just can't match. Perhaps there's a difference because organic poultry is raised in a less crowded environment (see box, page 138) and fed an all-organic diet. Whatever the reason, it makes sense that a healthier chicken is a tastier one—and well worth the extra cost.

Kathy's Rosemary-Roasted Chicken

Fresh herbs bring out the flavors of great food, and this roast chicken is no exception. Drew's stepmother, Kathy Goodman, tucks sprigs of rosemary under the chicken breasts and rubs the skin with garlic and more rosemary. Lemons keep the taste bright and fresh, and a sprinkling of cayenne adds just a little hint of heat and a nice color to the skin. Kathy often serves her roast chicken with Roasted Garnet Yams (see page 265) and something simple and fresh, like the Garlicky String Beans (see page 261). At our house, we always roast two chickens so everyone can enjoy a breast, a crisp wing, and a leg. You may want to try this, too; even if your family members are less hearty eaters, you'll have great leftovers. Try adding slices of the chicken to the Grilled Caesar Salad (see page 88) to turn a salad into a meal. **SERVES 4**

1 small roasting chicken (5 pounds)
Olive oil
3 cloves garlic, minced
2 lemons, preferably Meyer
    (see sidebar, page 112), cut in half
1/2 cup coarsely chopped fresh rosemary
    leaves, plus 8 rosemary sprigs
1/4 teaspoon cayenne pepper
Coarse (kosher) salt

1. Position a rack in the center of the oven and preheat the oven to 375°F.

2. Rinse the chicken with cold water and pat it dry, inside and out, with paper towels. Remove and discard any excess fat.

3. Place the chicken breast side down in a roasting pan. Rub the back of the chicken

with some olive oil and half of the garlic. Squeeze the juice of 2 of the lemon halves over the chicken back; set the juiced lemon halves aside. Sprinkle ¼ cup of the chopped rosemary and ⅛ teaspoon of the cayenne over the chicken back.

4. Turn the chicken breast side up. Using your fingers, gently separate the skin from the breast meat and tuck 2 rosemary sprigs in the pocket, 1 over each breast half.

5. Rub the chicken breast with olive oil and the remaining garlic. Squeeze the juice of the remaining lemon halves over the chicken breast; set aside the juiced lemon halves. Sprinkle salt to taste and the remaining ¼ cup of chopped rosemary and ⅛ teaspoon of cayenne over the chicken breast.

6. Tuck the wings behind the back of the chicken and place 1 rosemary sprig under each wing. Place the juiced lemon halves and the remaining 4 sprigs of rosemary in the chicken cavity.

7. Bake the chicken, breast side up, basting it once or twice with the pan juices, until an instant-read meat thermometer inserted into the thickest part of the thigh, but not touching a bone, registers 170°F, 1 to 1½ hours.

8. Let the chicken rest, loosely covered with aluminum foil, for 20 minutes before carving and serving it.

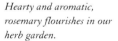

Hearty and aromatic, rosemary flourishes in our herb garden.

what is organic poultry?

When you buy poultry that is certified organic by the USDA, you can be sure that the birds were:

■ **Raised without antibiotics.**

■ **Raised without growth hormones (Federal regulations prohibit administering growth hormones to all poultry, whether or not it is organic).**

■ **Allowed access to the outdoors.**

■ **Fed a 100 percent organic diet.**

Poultry that is labeled free-range is not organic unless it also meets all the organic standards. According to the USDA standards, poultry can be called free range if the birds were allowed access to the outdoors for as little as five minutes a day. In some areas, you may find small poultry producers who offer "pasture-raised" organic chickens that are allowed to freely forage for food on pastures that are organic certified.

Chicken Paprikash

My mother grew up in Hungary, and this is one of the recipes she makes from her home country. The chicken simmers in a velvety sauce flavored with mild Hungarian paprika and is especially delicious served over thick egg noodles. If you want a little heat, add a dash of hot paprika and, for extra color, garnish the dish with a handful of chopped parsley. **SERVES 6 TO 8**

4 skinless, boneless chicken thighs
    (8 to 10 ounces total), cut into
    $^1/_2$-inch strips
4 skinless, boneless chicken breast halves
    (about $1^1/_2$ pounds, total), cut into
    $^1/_2$-inch strips
Salt and freshly ground black pepper
2 tablespoons sweet Hungarian paprika
2 tablespoons ($^1/_4$ stick) unsalted butter
2 tablespoons olive oil
1 medium-size yellow onion, cut into
    $^1/_4$-inch dice (about 1 cup)
1 tablespoon minced fresh garlic
2 tablespoons tomato paste
2 cups Blond Chicken Stock (page 372)
1 cup sour cream
2 tablespoons unbleached all-purpose
    flour
$^1/_4$ teaspoon hot Hungarian paprika
    (optional)
Coarsely chopped flat-leaf parsley
    (optional), for garnish

1. Keeping the thigh and breast meat separate, season the chicken pieces with salt, pepper, and the sweet paprika.

2. Heat the butter and olive oil in a large, nonstick skillet over medium heat. Add the thigh meat and cook, stirring frequently, about 5 minutes. Add the breast meat to the thighs and cook, stirring frequently, until cooked through, 3 to 5 minutes longer. Using a slotted spoon, transfer the chicken to a bowl and set aside.

3. Add the onion to the skillet and cook, stirring occasionally, until it begins to soften, 5 to 8 minutes. Add the garlic and tomato paste and cook, stirring constantly, for 1 minute.

4. Add the chicken stock, increase the heat to high, and let come to a boil. Reduce the heat to low and add the chicken strips and any accumulated juice. Cover the skillet and let simmer until the chicken is warmed through, about 5 minutes.

5. Place the sour cream in a small bowl and whisk in the flour. Add the sour cream mixture to the chicken and stir to blend. Cook over low heat until the sauce thickens slightly, 3 to 5 minutes. Do not let the sauce boil or the sour cream will separate.

6. Add the hot paprika, if using, to the paprikash and season with more salt and pepper to taste. Transfer the paprikash to a serving platter and garnish it with the parsley, if desired.

A retired irrigation pipe tractor welcomes guests to our Farm Stand.

Curried Chicken Salad

Curry makes this chicken salad lightly spicy, giving it a lovely golden hue. But it's the grapes that make it special. Their sweet, succulent texture creates the perfect counterpoint to the crunchy celery and nuts. I enjoy this chicken salad with a salad of mixed baby greens, and find it irresistible in a croissant sandwich. A scoopful is also pretty served on an avocado half or cupped in a lettuce leaf. If you are pressed for time, using breasts from take-out rotisserie chickens speeds things up. **SERVES 4**

4 skin-on, bone-in chicken breasts
    halves (10 to 12 ounces each;
    see Note)
4 cups Blond Chicken Stock
    (page 372) or store-bought
    low-sodium chicken broth
1 cup mayonnaise
1 teaspoon ground ginger
2 teaspoons curry powder
4 celery ribs, cut into ¼-inch dice
    (about 1 cup)
½ cup toasted pecans (see box,
    page 98), coarsely chopped
1 cup seedless grapes, preferably red,
    cut in half
3 tablespoons minced fresh flat-leaf
    parsley
Coarse (kosher) salt and freshly
    ground white pepper

1. Cut a piece of parchment paper or waxed paper in the shape of the Dutch oven or large saucepan that you will use to cook the chicken. Set the paper aside.

2. Place the chicken breasts in the Dutch oven. Add the broth and just enough water to cover the breasts. Bring the liquid to a boil over medium-high heat. Reduce the heat to low and place the parchment paper directly on the cooking liquid. (The paper holds in the heat and keeps the chicken moist in case the level of liquid drops.) Let the breasts simmer gently until they are cooked through, 35 to 45 minutes.

3. Remove the chicken breasts from the liquid and let them cool enough to handle. The broth from cooking the chicken can be set aside for another use. Remove and discard the chicken skin and bones. Cut the breast meat into approximately ¾-inch cubes.

4. Place the mayonnaise, ginger, and curry powder in a medium-size bowl and stir to combine. Add the cubed chicken, celery, pecans, and grapes to the mayonnaise mixture and stir to combine. Add the parsley and stir. Season the chicken salad with salt and pepper to taste. The chicken salad can be refrigerated, covered, for up to 3 days.

Note: You can substitute cooked chicken; you'll need 4 cups of ¾-inch cubes. If you're using precooked chicken, skip Steps 1 through 3.

There are so many varieties of juicy and delicious grapes. These beauties are Red Flame, Thompson Seedless, Concord (far right), and the smallest and most delectable of all, Champagne grapes (in the middle).

Grilled Tahini Chicken
with Eggplant and Mushrooms over Soba Noodles

*S*tir-fried eggplant and shiitakes are delicious tossed with thin soba noodles flavored with soy sauce and sesame oil. You don't need anything more for a delicious vegetarian meal, but adding grilled chicken breasts drizzled with tahini sauce makes it one of my Farm Stand favorites. The satisfying one-dish meal is as good at room temperature as it is piping hot. **SERVES 6**

The foundation of a garlic braid that will soon be hanging in my kitchen.

6 skinless, boneless chicken breast halves (6 to 8 ounces each)
About 3^1/$_2$ cups Ginger Garlic Tahini Sauce (recipe follows)
3 tablespoons canola oil
1 medium-size Italian eggplant (about 1^1/$_4$ pounds), unpeeled and cut into ^{1}/$_2$-inch dice (about 4 cups)
2 cups sliced (^{1}/$_4$ inch thick) shiitake mushroom caps (about 4 ounces)
8 ounces soba (buckwheat) noodles
2 tablespoons soy sauce or tamari
1 tablespoon toasted sesame oil
1 cup thinly sliced scallions, for garnish
^{1}/$_2$ cup chopped fresh basil, for garnish

1. Place the chicken breasts in a 1-gallon resealable plastic bag and add 2^1/$_2$ cups of the Ginger Garlic Tahini Sauce. Let the chicken marinate in the refrigerator for 2 to 6 hours.

2. Set up a barbecue grill and preheat it to medium-high.

3. Remove the chicken from the marinade and discard the marinade. Grill the chicken for 5 minutes. Turn the breasts over and cook until an instant-read meat thermometer inserted through the side into the thickest part of a breast registers 160°F, 3 to 5 minutes longer. Transfer the chicken breasts to a platter and loosely tent them with aluminum foil.

4. Bring a large pot of water to a boil over high heat.

5. Meanwhile place a wok or large skillet over medium-high heat and add the canola oil. When the oil is hot but not smoking, add the eggplant and cook, stirring constantly, for 2 minutes. Add the mushrooms and cook, stirring constantly, until tender, 5 minutes longer.

6. Add the soba noodles to the boiling water and cook according to the package directions, about 8 minutes. Drain the noodles in a colander, then return them to the pot. Add the soy sauce and sesame oil and toss to combine. Add the eggplant mixture and stir to combine. Transfer the noodle mixture to a large platter.

7. Cut the chicken breasts diagonally into ^{1}/$_4$-inch-wide strips. Arrange the chicken strips over the noodles and sprinkle the

Perfect rows of romaine

scallions and basil on top. Drizzle some of the remaining Ginger Garlic Tahini Sauce over the chicken or serve the sauce on the side.

Ginger Garlic Tahini Sauce

You'll want to make this versatile Asian sauce again and again. Use it as a flavorful marinade for poultry, beef, or shrimp or add it to stir-fries. I love it drizzled over steamed vegetables or tofu, and it even makes a deliciously different salad dressing. The Asian flavors are ones you'd expect—soy sauce and sesame oil spiked with ginger, garlic, and red pepper—but the tahini gives it a unique nutty flavor. Tahini is a paste made from ground sesame seeds; it has a texture similar to peanut butter or almond butter. You can use either raw or roasted tahini for the sauce, but the roasted (or toasted) version has more flavor. If your supermarket doesn't carry tahini, you'll find it at health food or Middle Eastern stores. Or, you can substitute almond or peanut butter. The taste will be a little different, but just as good. **MAKES ABOUT 3¹/₂ CUPS**

1 cup soy sauce or tamari
¹/₂ cup unseasoned rice vinegar
2 tablespoons tahini, preferably roasted
2 tablespoons minced or grated peeled fresh ginger
1 tablespoon minced garlic
¹/₃ cup firmly packed light brown sugar
1¹/₂ teaspoons dried red pepper flakes
³/₄ cup toasted sesame oil
³/₄ cup canola oil

Place all of the ingredients in a medium-size bowl and whisk to combine. The Ginger Garlic Tahini Sauce can sit at room temperature for up to 4 hours or can be refrigerated, covered, for up to 2 weeks.

Perfect rows of romaine lettuce.

Quick Grilled Lemon Chicken

A lemon, garlic, and basil marinade adds a fresh flavor spark to these grilled chicken breasts. The breasts easily absorb the marinade, and they cook up quickly and evenly when you pound them until they are thin. Nothing beats the flavor a grill provides, but you can also cook the chicken breasts on the stove top using a ridged grill pan, or you can broil them. These chicken breasts are great served with an assortment of grilled summer vegetables (see page 271). The leftovers will keep for up to three days, so cook extra—grilled chicken and vegetables make an extraordinary sandwich on focaccia bread spread with Jalapeño Arugula Aioli (see page 224). **SERVES 6**

6 skinless, boneless chicken breast halves
   (6 to 8 ounces each)
¹/₄ cup fresh lemon juice
¹/₃ cup olive oil
¹/₃ cup Herb-Flavored Oil (page 382;
   use basil) or more olive oil
1 tablespoon minced garlic
2 tablespoons minced fresh basil,
   or 2 teaspoons dried basil
¹/₂ teaspoon salt
¹/₄ teaspoon freshly ground pepper
Garlic Basil Butter (optional, recipe
   follows)

Butter, made more flavorful with the addition of fresh garlic and basil, melts invitingly atop Quick Grilled Lemon Chicken.

1. Remove the tenders from the chicken breast halves and set them aside for another use. Place a chicken breast half between 2 pieces of plastic wrap or waxed paper. Gently pound the breast with the smooth side of a meat mallet, a rolling pin, or a heavy skillet, until it is ¹/₄ to ¹/₂ inch thick. Repeat with the remaining chicken breast halves.

2. Place the lemon juice, olive oil, herb oil, garlic, basil, salt, and pepper in a small bowl and whisk to combine.

3. Place the chicken in a 1-gallon resealable plastic bag and add the marinade. Seal the bag and turn it so that the chicken is evenly coated with the marinade. Let the chicken marinate for at least 3 hours or overnight, turning the bag once or twice to distribute the marinade evenly.

4. Set up a barbecue grill and preheat it to medium-high.

5. Remove the chicken breasts from the marinade and discard the marinade. Grill the breasts, turning them once, until they are cooked through, 2 to 4 minutes on each side. Watch the chicken carefully. Because the breasts are thin, they will cook quickly.

6. Serve the chicken immediately, topped with a slice of Garlic Basil Butter, if desired.

Garlic Basil Butter

Chicken, corn on the cob, fish, grilled veggies, bread—the list of foods that taste great with a slice of herb butter is endless. Almost any herb can be substituted for the basil, including thyme, chives, sage, or parsley. If you like pungent herbs, such as minced rosemary, use a smaller amount so it isn't overwhelming. Grated citrus zest is a nice addition. Herb butters freeze well, so you can make a large batch and slice off just the amount you need. **MAKES ABOUT ³/₄ CUP**

8 tablespoons (1 stick) unsalted
   butter, softened
¹/₃ cup minced fresh basil
1 clove garlic, minced
1 teaspoon fresh lemon juice

1. Using a fork, blend the butter, basil, garlic, and lemon juice in a small bowl. Transfer the butter mixture to a piece of plastic wrap that is about 12 inches long.

2. Form the butter into a cylinder and roll it in the plastic wrap to seal tightly. Refrigerate the butter until firm, at least 2 hours or up to 3 days. For longer storage, wrap the butter in a second layer of plastic wrap or in aluminum foil. It can be frozen for up to 3 months.

3. To serve the butter, unwrap it and, using a sharp knife that has been held under hot running water, cut the butter into as many slices as you need. Return any leftover butter to the refrigerator or freezer.

Garlic, waiting to be trimmed.

Chicken Piccata

Classic Italian flavor combinations—like this buttery sauce with lemon, capers, and garlic—are inviting and perfect for family or company. This version of chicken piccata may be a little lighter than ones you've tried before because it uses chicken stock in place of some of the butter, but there's no loss of flavor. Pork, veal, or turkey cutlets are good cooked this way, too. Pounded thin, the chicken cooks quickly and the sauce is easy, so have all your ingredients ready to go before you heat up the skillet. Roasted Asparagus (see page 227) or Sautéed Broccoli Rabe (see page 233) would each be tasty served with the chicken. **SERVES 4**

¹/₄ cup unbleached all-purpose flour
4 skinless, boneless chicken breast halves
   (6 to 8 ounces each), rinsed and dried
Coarse (kosher) salt and freshly ground
   black pepper
About 3 tablespoons unsalted butter
About 1 tablespoon olive oil

¹/₄ cup dry white wine
2 tablespoons fresh lemon juice
²/₃ cup Blond Chicken Stock (page 372)
2 tablespoons capers, drained
1 tablespoon coarsely chopped fresh
   flat-leaf parsley
1 lemon, thinly sliced and seeded

1. Position a rack in the center of the oven and preheat the oven to 250°F. Spread the flour on a plate and set it aside.

2. Remove the tenders from the chicken breast halves and set them aside for another use. Place a chicken breast half between 2 pieces of plastic wrap or waxed paper. Gently pound the breast with the smooth side of a meat mallet, a rolling pin, or a heavy skillet until it is 1/4 to 1/2 inch thick. Repeat with the remaining chicken breast halves.

3. Season the breasts with salt and pepper. Lightly dip both sides of the breasts in the flour and shake off the excess.

4. Heat 1 tablespoon of the butter and the olive oil in a large skillet over medium-high heat. Add the chicken and cook until it is golden brown on the bottom, 2 to 3 minutes. Turn the breasts over, cover the skillet, and cook until they are cooked through, 1 to 2 minutes. If all the breasts will not fit comfortably in the skillet, cook the chicken in 2 batches, adding more butter and olive oil, if needed.

5. Transfer the breasts to an oven-safe platter, tent them loosely with aluminum foil, and place them in the oven to stay warm.

6. Add the wine to the skillet and, using a spoon or spatula, scrape up the brown bits from the bottom. Let simmer until all but about 1 tablespoon of the wine is evaporated, 1 to 2 minutes. Add the lemon juice, stock, and capers and let simmer until the flavors are concentrated, about 1 minute.

7. Add the remaining 2 tablespoons of butter and the lemon slices and parsley to the sauce and stir until the butter melts, about 1 minute. Remove the chicken breasts from the oven, pour the sauce and lemon slices over them, and serve immediately.

Harvesting green curly kale in Carmel Valley.

Stir-Fried Chicken
with Broccoli, Yellow Bell Pepper, and Zucchini

Brilliant green broccoli, yellow bell pepper, and zucchini turn ordinary chicken breasts into a colorful one-dish meal. The trick is to cook every ingredient quickly on its own, adjusting the cooking time so each comes out tender but still a bit crisp. Once you learn this basic technique, you can adapt it to take advantage of whatever small amounts of fresh vegetables, meat, or tofu are left over in the refrigerator. You can also save prep time by buying precut vegetables, like broccoli florets, making this an even faster everyday meal. Serve the stir-fry with rice or soba noodles. **SERVES 4**

$^1/_2$ cup soy sauce

2 tablespoons firmly packed light brown
   sugar

2 tablespoons unseasoned rice vinegar

1 teaspoon Asian chile garlic sauce,
   or $^1/_4$ teaspoon dried red pepper flakes

1 tablespoon cornstarch

2 tablespoons toasted sesame oil

4 tablespoons peanut oil

2 medium-size zucchini or summer
   squash, cut into $^1/_2$-inch dice
   (about $1^1/_2$ cups)

1 tablespoon minced garlic

2 tablespoons grated peeled fresh ginger

4 cups bite-size broccoli florets
   (about 8 ounces)

1 yellow bell pepper, stemmed, seeded,
   and cut into $^1/_4$-inch strips

$1^1/_2$ pounds skinless, boneless chicken
   breasts, cut into $^1/_2$-inch cubes
   or $^1/_4$-inch strips

$^1/_2$ cup thinly sliced scallions, including
   whites and 3 inches of green

About 3 cups cooked rice or soba
   noodles, for serving

$^1/_2$ cup cashews, for garnish

1. Place the soy sauce, brown sugar, vinegar, chile sauce, cornstarch, and $^3/_4$ cup of water in a small bowl and whisk to combine. Set the soy sauce mixture aside.

2. Place a wok or large skillet over medium-high heat and add 1 tablespoon of the sesame oil and 1 tablespoon of the peanut oil. Add the zucchini and cook, stirring constantly, until it is tender and golden, 4 to 6 minutes. Using a slotted spoon, transfer the zucchini to a large bowl.

3. Add 1 tablespoon of the peanut oil to the wok. Add the garlic and ginger and cook for 30 seconds, stirring constantly. Add the broccoli and $^1/_2$ cup of water and cook, stirring constantly, until the broccoli is crisp-tender, 3 to 4 minutes. Using a slotted spoon, transfer the broccoli to the bowl with the zucchini.

4. Add 1 tablespoon of the peanut oil to the wok. Add the bell pepper and cook, stirring constantly, until it is crisp-tender, about 3 minutes. Using a slotted spoon, transfer the bell pepper to the bowl with the zucchini.

5. Add the remaining 1 tablespoon each of the sesame oil and peanut oil to the wok. Add the chicken and cook, stirring constantly, until cooked through, about 4 minutes. Add the soy sauce mixture and stir until the sauce thickens, 1 to 2 minutes.

6. Add the reserved zucchini, broccoli, and bell pepper and the scallions to the chicken. Cook until the vegetables are just heated through, about 3 minutes.

7. Serve the stir-fried mixture immediately with the rice and sprinkle the cashews on top.

Yellow Sebring zucchini flowering in the field.

Chicken Satays
with Peanut Sauce

Southeast Asia is the birthplace of these grilled chicken skewers, which are infused with a spicy coconut milk marinade and served with a nutty sauce on the side. They make great party hors d'oeuvres or a light main course for lunch or dinner. Inexpensive bamboo skewers, usually available in supermarkets, are perfect for making individual portions. You'll need twelve skewers that are roughly 10 inches long. To prevent the bamboo from burning, soak the skewers in water for about half an hour before using them. If you don't feel like firing up the grill, the chicken can be cooked under the broiler instead. **SERVES 6 AS AN APPETIZER OR 4 AS A MAIN DISH**

2 tablespoons curry powder
1 tablespoon ground coriander
1 teaspoon ground cumin
1 tablespoon sugar
$1/2$ teaspoon salt
1 pound skinless, boneless chicken breasts, cut into $3/4$-inch wide diagonal strips
$1^1/2$ cups unsweetened coconut milk
$1^1/2$ tablespoons unseasoned rice vinegar
$3/4$ cup peanut oil or canola oil
Peanut Sauce (recipe follows)

1. Place the curry, coriander, cumin, sugar, and salt in a small bowl and whisk to blend. Spread the spice blend on a plate and set it aside.

2. Thread 2 or 3 chicken strips on each skewer, completely covering the bamboo, except at the handle end. Don't crowd the meat on the skewer; it will not cook evenly.

3. Dip each skewer into the spice mixture, coating the chicken all over. Place the skewers in a baking pan just large enough to hold them comfortably. Let the satays rest at room temperature to absorb the spices, about 15 minutes.

4. Whisk together the coconut milk, rice vinegar, and oil in a small bowl. Pour this mixture over the satays and let them marinate, covered, in the refrigerator for at least 2 hours or overnight.

5. Set up a barbecue grill and preheat it to medium-high.

6. Remove the chicken skewers from the marinade, discarding the marinade. Grill the satays, turning them once, until the chicken is cooked through, 5 to 8 minutes total.

7. Arrange the skewers on a platter and serve with the Peanut Sauce on the side.

Peanut Sauce

Coconut milk adds richness to this nutty sauce, and you can control the spicy heat by adding just enough curry powder or pepper sauce to suit your taste. If you like a bit of crunchy texture, use chunky peanut butter.
MAKES ABOUT 1 CUP

1 cup unsweetened coconut milk
3 tablespoons chunky or smooth
    peanut butter
1 tablespoon curry powder

2 tablespoons sugar, or more to taste
Red pepper sauce, such as Tabasco

Combine the coconut milk, peanut butter, curry powder, and sugar in a small saucepan and bring to a simmer over low heat. Cook, stirring frequently, until the sauce thickens, about 5 minutes. Season with red pepper sauce to taste and more sugar as needed. The sauce can be refrigerated, covered, for up to 1 week.

Spicy Chicken Lettuce Wraps

These Asian-inspired lettuce wraps are one of my favorite meals. They're filled with a mixture of finely diced chicken, tender baby bok choy, and crunchy water chestnuts, enlivened with ginger, garlic, and jalapeño. The wraps are also good made with diced or ground beef, pork, or turkey. **SERVES 8 AS AN APPETIZER OR 4 AS A MAIN DISH**

1½ pounds skinless, boneless chicken
    breasts, cut into ½-inch dice
3 tablespoons cornstarch
2 tablespoons toasted sesame oil
2 tablespoons peanut oil
¾ cup finely sliced scallions, including
    white and 3 inches of green
    (about 1 bunch)
3 tablespoons grated peeled fresh ginger
2 tablespoons very finely diced jalapeño
    pepper
2 tablespoons minced fresh lemongrass
    (optional; see sidebar, page 46)
1 tablespoon minced garlic
1 can (8 ounces) water chestnuts,
    rinsed, drained, and cut into
    ¼-inch dice

3 baby bok choy (about 8 ounces),
    including white ribs, very
    thinly sliced
2 tablespoons soy sauce
¼ cup teriyaki sauce, homemade
    (page 378) or store-bought
¼ cup mirin (sweet rice wine)
1 tablespoon Thai or Vietnamese fish
    sauce (optional; see Note)
3 tablespoons thinly sliced fresh cilantro
    or mint leaves
2 heads Boston lettuce or
    1 head iceberg lettuce, leaves
    individually separated, rinsed,
    and dried
Asian Dipping Sauce
    (optional; recipe follows)

Note: Asian fish sauce is made from fermented anchovies, salt, and water. The sauce has an intense, salty flavor, much appreciated in Vietnam and Thailand as a condiment or flavoring for cooking. Fish sauce is sold in bottles in Asian markets or specialty food stores.

1. Spread the chicken on a plate. Place 2 tablespoons of the cornstarch in a sieve and sprinkle it evenly over the chicken.

2. Heat 1 tablespoon each of the sesame oil and the peanut oil in a large skillet, preferably nonstick, over medium heat. Add the chicken and cook, stirring frequently, until it is cooked through, about 5 minutes. Using a slotted spoon, transfer the chicken to a medium-size bowl, leaving the pan juices in the skillet. Set the chicken aside.

3. Add the remaining 1 tablespoon each of sesame oil and peanut oil to the skillet. Add the scallions, ginger, jalapeño, lemongrass, if using, and garlic and cook over medium heat, stirring constantly, until fragrant, 1 to 2 minutes.

4. Add the water chestnuts, bok choy, soy sauce, teriyaki sauce, mirin, and fish sauce, if using. Cook, stirring frequently, until the bok choy wilts and the sauce is hot, 3 to 5 minutes.

5. Return the chicken and any accumulated juices to the skillet and cook until heated through, about 5 minutes.

6. Using a slotted spoon, transfer the chicken mixture to the center of a large platter and cover it loosely with aluminum foil to keep warm. Whisk the remaining 1 tablespoon of cornstarch into the liquid remaining in the skillet and cook, stirring constantly, until it thickens. Pour the sauce over the chicken.

7. Sprinkle the cilantro over the chicken mixture and arrange the lettuce leaves around the edge of the platter. Divide the Asian Dipping Sauce, if using, among individual small sauce bowls. To assemble the wraps, spoon a few tablespoons of the chicken mixture into a lettuce leaf. Loosely roll the lettuce around the chicken and dip the lettuce roll into the dipping sauce, if desired, before eating.

Asian Dipping Sauce

A balanced blend of sweet and tart flavors, this simple sauce is perfect as a dip for Asian lettuce wraps or dumplings. It's also delicious lightly drizzled over white rice or fish.

MAKES ABOUT 1 1/2 CUPS

1/4 cup toasted sesame seeds (see sidebar, page 273)
3/4 cup soy sauce
1/4 cup unseasoned rice vinegar
2 tablespoons mirin (sweet rice wine)
Grated zest and juice of 1 lime
2 tablespoons toasted sesame oil

Place all the ingredients in a glass jar and seal the lid tightly. Shake the jar vigorously to combine. The dipping sauce can be refrigerated, covered, for up to 7 days. Let it return to room temperature before using.

Herbed Turkey Loaf
with Honey Mustard Glaze

There's a pleasant surprise in this turkey loaf. When you slice through the honey-mustard glaze into the moist loaf, you'll find a vibrant layer of baby arugula, spinach, basil, and parsley hidden in the middle, adding yet another dimension of flavor. Using ground turkey makes a lighter alternative to the classic beef meat loaf. You can substitute mature greens for the baby arugula and spinach if you wash and blanch them first. This recipe makes enough for one large loaf or two smaller ones— one loaf to eat right away and another to freeze for later. But since leftover turkey loaf makes great sandwiches, your second loaf may never make it to the freezer!

SERVES 8 TO 10

2 tablespoons olive oil

3 medium-size yellow onions, finely chopped (about 2¹/₂ cups)

1 teaspoon salt

¹/₂ teaspoon freshly ground black pepper

8 ounces baby spinach (about 6 cups; see Note)

5 ounces baby arugula (about 6 cups; see Note)

¹/₄ cup minced fresh basil

¹/₄ cup minced fresh flat-leaf parsley

3 large eggs, beaten

2 tablespoons ketchup

1 tablespoon Dijon mustard

¹/₃ cup Worcestershire sauce

¹/₂ cup **Blond Chicken Stock** (page 372) or store-bought low-sodium chicken broth

2¹/₂ pounds ground turkey breast

1 cup bread crumbs (fresh or dry)

2 tablespoons honey mustard, or 4¹/₂ teaspoons Dijon mustard mixed with 1¹/₂ teaspoons honey

1. Position a rack in the center of the oven and preheat the oven to 375°F.

2. Heat the olive oil in a large, nonstick skillet over medium heat. Add the onions and cook, stirring frequently, until soft, about 5 minutes. Add the salt and pepper and, using a slotted spoon, transfer the onions to a small bowl to cool.

3. Add the baby spinach and arugula and 1 teaspoon of water to the skillet (if all the greens don't fit in the skillet at first, add more greens by the handful as they wilt). Cook the greens until all of them wilt, 2 to 3 minutes. Remove the skillet from the heat and let the greens cool for 5 minutes, then add the basil and parsley and stir to combine.

Note: If you substitute mature spinach and arugula for the baby greens, in Step 3 thoroughly wash them and remove the stems. Fill a large bowl of water with ice cubes and set aside. Bring a large saucepan of salted water to a boil over high heat. Add the greens and cook until just wilted, about 1 minute. Immediately drain the greens in a colander, then plunge them into the bowl of ice water to stop the cooking. Drain the greens again and squeeze out any excess water with your hands. Coarsely chop the greens and add the basil and parsley, stirring to combine.

Smelling, touching, and learning . . . a school tour at our Carmel Valley farm.

4. Place the eggs, ketchup, Dijon mustard, Worcestershire sauce, and stock in a large bowl and whisk to combine. Add the ground turkey, bread crumbs, and cooked onions and blend thoroughly using your hands.

5. Place half of the turkey mixture in a 10-inch loaf pan or in two 8-inch loaf pans. Spread the wilted greens evenly on

top. Spread the remaining turkey mixture over the greens. Smooth the surface of the turkey loaf and brush it with the honey mustard.

6. Bake the turkey loaf until an instant-read meat thermometer inserted in the center registers 160°F, about 1½ hours for a 10-cup pan or about 50 minutes for the 2 smaller pans.

7. Let the turkey loaf rest in the pan for about 15 minutes. To serve, turn the turkey loaf out of the pan, slice it, and arrange the slices on a serving platter. If you are not planning on serving the turkey loaf at this time, let it cool in the pan and then wrap the pan tightly in plastic wrap. It can be refrigerated for up to 5 days. For longer storage, wrap a layer of aluminum foil over the plastic wrap and freeze the turkey loaf in the pan; it will keep for up to 2 months. Let the loaf thaw overnight in the refrigerator and unwrap it before reheating in a 375°F oven for 20 to 30 minutes.

A majestic sunflower reaches up to the blue summer sky.

Note: Some turkeys have been injected with a salt solution, so brining will make them overly salty. Double check the wrapping (if wrapped) before buying.

Brined Roast Turkey

Thanksgiving dinner is served twice a year at our house. We feast in November with the rest of the country, then again in February on our daughter's birthday. Marea's favorite meal is roast turkey with all the fixings. Of course, everyone loves roast turkey that is moist, tender, and flavorful, but sometimes this ideal is hard to attain. In our Organic Kitchen, we've learned that brining is the answer for cooking consistently moist turkeys. This technique does require advance planning, though. You'll need a stock pot, ice cooler, or clean plastic bucket just large enough to hold the turkey in the salt and sugar solution, and room in your refrigerator to store it for twenty-four hours. Look for an organic or "natural" turkey, one that doesn't have any additives (see Note, facing page). While the turkey is soaking up the brine, you can get a head start on your meal by preparing Make-Ahead Turkey Gravy using the turkey's giblets. And, of course, Easy Cranberry Sauce is almost obligatory with roast turkey. **SERVES 12**

1¹/₂ cups coarse (kosher) salt

1¹/₂ cups firmly packed light brown
    sugar

¹/₄ cup whole black peppercorns

4 bay leaves

1 small bunch fresh thyme

1 gallon of ice cubes

14- to 16-pound , organic or "natural"
    turkey, giblets and neck reserved for
    Make-Ahead Turkey Gravy

8 tablespoons (1 stick) unsalted butter,
    melted, or ¹/₂ cup olive oil

1 cup dry white wine (optional)

Make-Ahead Turkey Gravy
    (optional; recipe follows),
    for serving

Easy Cranberry Sauce (page 157),
    for serving

1. Combine the salt, brown sugar, peppercorns, bay leaves, and thyme with 2 quarts of water in a large stockpot. Heat the brine over high heat and stir until the salt and brown sugar dissolve. Remove the pot from the heat. Add 2 more quarts of water and the ice cubes to cool the brine quickly to room temperature or colder.

2. Place the turkey in a container that is just large enough to hold it comfortably. Pour the cooled brine over the turkey until it is covered. If the turkey is not totally submerged in the brine, add just enough cold water to cover it (do not dilute the brine more than necessary).

Refrigerate the turkey in the brine, covered, for 24 hours.

3. Position a rack in the lower third of the oven and preheat the oven to 375°F.

4. Remove the turkey from the brine and discard the brine. Dry the turkey, inside and out, with paper towels. Cut off the wing tips, which burn easily, and truss the bird, if desired.

5. Place the turkey, breast side up, on a rack set inside a large burner-proof roasting pan. Brush the turkey with some of the butter. Add 2 cups of warm water to the roasting pan.

6. Roast the turkey, uncovered, for 30 minutes. Reduce the oven temperature to 325°F and continue roasting the turkey, basting it occasionally with the remaining butter. If the turkey starts to brown too quickly, loosely cover it with aluminum foil. After 2 hours, add the wine to the pan, if desired (the wine will add flavor to the pan drippings). Continue to roast the turkey until an instant-read meat thermometer inserted into the thickest part of the thigh, but not touching a bone, registers 180°F, 3¹/₄ to 4 hours total cooking time.

7. Transfer the turkey to a large platter and let it rest, loosely covered with foil, for

Reducing Turkey Pan Drippings for Gravy

When you roast a turkey, there's a lot of flavor left in the juices in the bottom of the pan that's great for making gravy. After transferring the turkey to a serving platter, place the roasting pan (make sure it is burner-proof—glass isn't) with the drippings over two stove-top burners. Heat the pan juices over medium heat, scraping and loosening the brown bits from the bottom of the pan. Bring the liquid to a boil and let simmer until there is only ¹/₄-inch of liquid left in the pan, about 10 minutes. The liquid will be thick, like a glaze. Pour the reduced pan juices into a heatproof measuring cup and let sit until the clear liquid fat rises to the top. Skim off the fat and discard it. Add the remaining brown drippings to enhance the flavor of Make-Ahead Turkey Gravy (page 156), or simply spoon the reduced drippings over the turkey slices.

20 to 30 minutes. If desired, use the pan drippings for gravy (see sidebar, page 155).

8. Carve the turkey and serve warm or at room temperature with the Make-Ahead Turkey Gravy, if desired, and Easy Cranberry Sauce on the side.

Make-Ahead Turkey Gravy

Getting a turkey dinner on the table can be stressful enough without having to make gravy at the last minute. Even though this gravy can be prepared in advance, it's deeply colored and full of flavor, thanks to the roasted vegetables and stock that form the gravy base. For even more flavor, reduce the pan drippings from the turkey and add them to the gravy just before serving.

MAKES ABOUT 4 CUPS

2 medium-size carrots, sliced
 $1/4$-inch thick (about 1 cup)
3 ribs celery, sliced $1/4$-inch thick
 (about 1 cup)
1 large yellow onion, cut into
 $1/2$-inch dice (about 2 cups)
6 cloves garlic, peeled and crushed
Salt and freshly ground black pepper
5 cups Dark Chicken Stock
 (page 373), Blond Chicken
 Stock (page 372), or store-bought
 low-sodium chicken broth
2 bay leaves
Giblets and neck from 1 turkey
 (do not use the liver)
About $1/2$ cup half-and-half or
 whole milk
$1/3$ cup unbleached all-purpose flour
Reduced and defatted turkey pan
 drippings (optional; see sidebar,
 page 155)

Note: If serving the gravy on the day it is made, add the reduced turkey pan drippings, if using, in Step 6 before you add the flour mixture. If you're making it in advance, continue with the recipe, adding in the drippings once the turkey is made and the reserved gravy is reheated in Step 7.

1. Position a rack in the lower third of the oven and preheat the oven to 375°F.

2. Place the carrots, celery, onion, and garlic in a large Dutch oven and season with salt and pepper. Bake the vegetables, uncovered, stirring them once or twice, until they are tender and browned, about 1 hour.

3. Transfer the Dutch oven to the stove top. Add the stock and 3 cups of warm water and bring to a boil over high heat. Add the bay leaves and turkey giblets and neck. Reduce the heat to low and let simmer until the liquid is reduced to about 3 cups, 1 to $1^{1}/2$ hours.

4. Strain the stock through a sieve into a medium-size saucepan, pressing hard on the solids to extract all the liquid. Discard the solids. If you are planning on adding the turkey pan drippings, refrigerate the reduced stock, covered, until you are ready to proceed.

5. Place 1 cup of the strained stock in a medium-size bowl and add the half-and-half and flour. Whisk until smooth.

6. Place the saucepan with the remaining stock over high heat and bring to a boil (see Note). Stir in the flour mixture. Reduce the heat to low and let simmer, whisking frequently, until the gravy thickens and the raw taste of the flour cooks off, about 15 minutes. If the gravy is too thick, add more half-and-half or water. If it is not thick enough, add $1/2$ to 1 tablespoon more flour and let the gravy cook for 3 to 5 minutes longer. Taste for seasoning, adding more salt and/or pepper, as needed.

7. If you are not planning on serving the gravy immediately, transfer it to a clean container and let it cool. The gravy may be refrigerated, covered, for up to 2 days. Reheat over medium-low heat.

Easy Cranberry Sauce

Homemade cranberry sauce is great any time of year with roast chicken, pork, or turkey. The tartness of the soft cranberries in this sauce is balanced by sweet orange juice. When the dinner is for adults only, a splash of port adds a special treat. Since fresh cranberries are not available year-round, buy an extra bag or two in the fall and stick them in the freezer. This recipe is easily doubled or even tripled. **MAKES ABOUT 2 CUPS**

1 cup sugar
Grated zest of 1 orange
$1/4$ cup fresh orange juice
12 ounces (1 bag) fresh or frozen (unthawed) cranberries
2 tablespoons port (optional)

1. Place the sugar and 1 cup of water in a small saucepan and bring to a boil over high heat, stirring until the sugar dissolves.

2. Add the orange zest, orange juice, and cranberries and let return to a boil. Reduce the heat to low and let simmer until the berries burst and soften and the sauce thickens, about 15 minutes.

3. Remove the cranberries from the heat and stir in the port, if using. Let the cranberry sauce cool to room temperature. The cranberry sauce can be served at room temperature or chilled. It can be refrigerated, covered, for up to 1 month.

Tart and flavorful cranberries are featured in many special holiday dishes.

Chapter 5

Fish and Shellfish

My family is lucky to live near Monterey Bay, where we can watch the fishermen tie their boats to the wharf and unload their bounty. Our fishmongers display the day's catch of fresh creamy-white halibut, huge Dungeness crabs, and glistening spot prawns, alongside fish that are available nationwide, like wild salmon and mild tilapia. No matter which I choose to take home, with a side dish of steamed vegetables and leafy green salad, I can have dinner on the table in minutes.

While the USDA has not established standards for organic seafood, there are many reasons—and ways—to enjoy the deliciously healthful benefits of fish. One of my favorites is wild Alaskan salmon; it's rich in omega-3 fatty acids, a good fat that promotes a healthy heart and circulatory system. Serve it up as Ginger Lime Salmon dressed in lively Asian flavors or broil the fish glazed in a flavorful barbecue sauce.

Or try Alaskan halibut, roasted and served with a Mediterranean-inspired sauce of capers, anchovies, and lots of deep green parsley. For an easy preparation with minimal clean-up, bake tilapia in parchment (or aluminum foil) with a medley of spring vegetables and fresh herbs.

If your taste runs to shellfish, don't miss the recipe for Seared Sea Scallops. Quickly sautéed in olive oil, they have a light crust that keeps them sweet and juicy on the inside. When nestled in a bed of steamed spinach, or served with fresh green beans, the scallops make a lovely presentation. If you're a shrimp lover, serve them grilled with a sassy tropical salsa of pineapple, mango, and kiwi. And don't miss the absolutely delicious Monterey Cioppino.

Obviously, I love fresh, well-prepared fish. But, unfortunately, there are many types of seafood that are being over fished, farmed unsustainably, or that pose health risks because of contaminants in our waters. These issues highlight the importance of maintaining the health of our environment. With that in mind, this chapter includes information and resources to help you make the best seafood choices, along with appealing recipes to help you enjoy the wide variety of sustainable fish available today.

The red flower is a clue to identifying these as Scarlett Runner beans.

Facing Page:
Grilled Shrimp with Tropical Salsa (page 170).

Herbed Fish and Spring Vegetables
in Parchment

Wonderfully versatile, fish baked in parchment paper is impressive for special dinner parties and a quick option for family meals. Everyone loves the drama of opening the wrapping to release the aromatic steam and to discover a moist fish fillet perched on a bed of spring vegetables and herbs. If you prefer, use aluminum foil instead of parchment paper. Foil isn't fancy, but it's so easy to use that even kids can create a tight seal to hold in the steam. They'll love making their own personalized packets, since almost any mix of vegetables and herbs will be delicious. Just be sure that the vegetables are cut into small pieces so they cook quickly. **SERVES 4**

Young visitors are captivated by the sights, sounds, and smells of the farm.

4 tablespoons (¹/₂ stick) unsalted butter, softened
Grated zest of 1 lemon
2 tablespoons minced fresh tarragon
1 tablespoon minced fresh flat-leaf parsley
4 thin white fish fillets (about ¹/₂ inch thick and 6 ounces each), such as tilapia, rainbow trout, or sole
Olive oil
Salt and freshly ground black pepper
16 pencil-thin asparagus spears, woody ends trimmed
¹/₄ cup thinly sliced leek or scallions, both white and light green parts
1 packed cup baby spinach or arugula, or a combination
¹/₂ cup radicchio, torn into bite-size pieces
4 tablespoons dry white vermouth or white wine, or 4 tablespoons water

1. Position a rack in the lower third of the oven and place a rimmed baking sheet on it. Preheat the oven to 400°F.

2. Cut 4 pieces of parchment paper or aluminum foil, each about 12 by 16 inches. Fold each piece in half, folding the short ends together, and make a distinct crease. Unfold the pieces of parchment paper and set them aside.

3. Place the butter, lemon zest, tarragon, and parsley in a small bowl and blend them together, using a fork. Set this aside.

4. Rub both sides of the fish fillets with olive oil and season them with salt and pepper. Set aside.

5. Cut the asparagus spears, if necessary, so that they are about the same length as the fish fillets. Place 4 asparagus spears on each piece of parchment paper, arranging them on one side of the crease. Scatter about 1 tablespoon of leek over each portion of asparagus and place about ¹/₄ cup of the spinach and about 2 tablespoons of radicchio on top of each. Arrange a fish fillet on top of each mound of greens and top each with about 1 tablespoon of the

making good fish & shellfish choices

Decades of poor environmental stewardship have affected the quality of our rivers, lakes, and oceans—and the fish that swim in them. Fish provide many health benefits, but some of these benefits are offset when the fish become contaminated by heavy metals (like mercury or lead), industrial chemicals (like PCBs), or pesticides. Years of overfishing popular varieties along with poor fishing methods also have endangered some wild species.

The USDA has not set standards for organic fish and seafood, so there's no USDA organic seal to vouch for the purity of the fish you buy. However, the Monterey Bay Aquarium has partnered with Environmental Defense—both are nonprofit organizations—to provide shopping guides for selecting seafood that's environmentally sustainable. They also provide guidelines for avoiding certain fish that may be contaminated by pollutants. Visit these Web sites for current information and regional pocket guides for buying fish and shellfish that's good for you and our environment.

Monterey Bay Aquarium:
www.mbayaq.org
Environmental Defense:
www.oceansalive.org

You also help clean up our waters when you support organic farmers because they don't use harmful agricultural pesticides that can make their way into streams, rivers, and oceans. Together, we can help protect our waters.

---

herb butter. Sprinkle 1 tablespoon of vermouth over each fillet.

6. Fold the parchment paper over the fish so that the edges meet. Starting at one end of the crease, seal the packet by folding the edge in a series of small, tight, overlapping pleats to create a half-moon shaped package. Make sure the packets are sealed tightly enough to hold in the liquid and steam.

7. Carefully transfer the packets to the preheated baking sheet. Bake the packets until they puff up, 8 to 12 minutes. To check for doneness, open the packet you are serving yourself, being careful to avoid the escaping steam. The fish should be opaque and easily flaked with a fork. If it isn't, close the packet and bake for another 1 to 2 minutes. Serve immediately, again being careful to avoid the steam when the packets are opened.

Variation: Cooking fish in parchment can also be used for fillets between ½- and 1-inch thick, such as wild salmon, sablefish (black cod), and Pacific halibut. Instead of quick-cooking asparagus, leeks, and greens, substitute vegetables that can withstand a longer cooking time, like whole sugar snap peas, carrots cut into matchsticks, and thinly sliced fennel bulb. Bake the packets at 400°F for 12 to 15 minutes.

You can almost see the flavor of these fresh carrots.

Roasted Halibut
with Mediterranean Green Sauce

The Mediterranean seaside, where garlic, lemon, and anchovies reign, is the inspiration for this lusty green sauce that makes the perfect counterpoint to mild and creamy-white halibut fillets. The sauce is a puree of fresh parsley and scallions with the adventuresome flavors of capers, lemon zest, garlic, and anchovies. The halibut soaks up the flavors as it marinates and cooks in the sauce, which is also drizzled on top before serving. The green sauce livens the subtle flavor of halibut but will work equally well with shrimp, scallops, and other white fish. **SERVES 4**

Edible borage flowers are sweet and delicate, but grow on a spiny plant.

$1/3$ cup olive oil

3 cloves garlic, peeled

$3/4$ cup chopped scallions, including
   white and 3 inches of green

1 cup fresh flat-leaf parsley leaves

$1/4$ cup celery leaves (optional)

2 tablespoons capers, rinsed

2 anchovy fillets, or 2 teaspoons
   anchovy paste

Grated zest of 1 lemon

$1/4$ cup fresh lemon juice

Freshly ground black pepper

4 skinless halibut fillets
   (about 6 ounces each)

Salt

12 very thin seeded lemon slices
   (from 2 lemons)

$1/2$ cup dry white wine

1. Place the olive oil and garlic in the bowl of a food processor and pulse the machine until the garlic is coarsely chopped. Add the scallions, parsley, celery leaves, if using, capers, and anchovies and pulse until finely minced. Transfer the scallion mixture to a small bowl and add the lemon zest and juice and stir to combine. Season the green sauce with pepper to taste.

2. Rub the halibut fillets with some of the green sauce and season them with salt and pepper. Spread the remaining green sauce on the bottom of a shallow baking pan that is large enough to hold the fillets in one layer. Place the fillets on top of the sauce and arrange 3 overlapping lemon slices on top of each fillet. Cover the fillets with plastic wrap and let them marinate in the refrigerator for 1 hour.

3. Position a rack in the center of the oven and preheat the oven to 500°F.

4. Remove the baking pan with the fillets from the refrigerator and discard the plastic wrap. Pour the wine over the fish. Bake the fillets until they are just opaque and can be flaked with a fork, 8 to 15 minutes, depending on the thickness of the fish.

5. Serve the fillets warm, drizzling the cooked green sauce from the pan over them.

Broiled Salmon
with Barbecue Sauce

If your goal is to get kids to eat fish, this one's a slam dunk. Marea's former basketball coach, Ron Powell, gave us this recipe for barbecued salmon and it's become a family favorite. The salmon makes a quick and delicious weeknight dinner because all you have to do is add brown sugar and lots of lemon juice to your favorite store-bought barbecue sauce. The lemon cuts the sweetness and thins out the sauce, so the fresh salmon flavor shines through the caramelized barbecue glaze. And cleanup is quick when you line the pan with aluminum foil to catch any sauce that may burn around the edges. **SERVES 4**

1 cup store-bought barbecue sauce,
   mild or spicy
$^1/_2$ cup firmly packed light brown sugar
$^1/_2$ cup fresh lemon juice
4 salmon fillets (6 to 8 ounces each),
   with or without skin, pin bones
   removed (see sidebar, this page)
1 lemon (optional), thinly sliced and
   seeded, for garnish

1. Position a rack 3 or 4 inches from the broiler and preheat the broiler on high.

2. Combine the barbecue sauce, brown sugar, and lemon juice in a small bowl and whisk until blended.

3. Pour half of the barbecue sauce mixture into a shallow baking pan just large enough to comfortably hold the fillets in a single layer. Arrange the fish fillets, skin side up, if any, in the pan and cover them with the remaining sauce mixture.

4. Broil the salmon fillets 4 minutes, then using a spatula, carefully turn them over. Continue broiling the fillets until the sauce glazes the salmon and the interior of the fish is nearly opaque but still moist, 5 to 10 minutes, depending on the thickness of the fish. If the fillets are 1 inch thick or more, they are done when an instant-read meat thermometer inserted in the thickest part registers 130°F.

5. Using a spatula, transfer the fillets to a warm platter. Spoon some of the sauce from the pan over the fish and garnish with the lemon slices, if using.

How to Remove Pin Bones

Pin bones are the tiny bones you feel as you run your finger over a salmon fillet. If you don't have a fancy pair of fish tweezers, use needle-nose pliers, tweezers, or even your fingers to pull them straight out.

An irrigator resets pipe in a field of broccoli, creating a beautiful geometry.

Ginger Lime Salmon

When Drew's stepmother, Kathy Goodman, is in town, Ginger Lime Salmon is often on our menu. Kathy knows how to bring out the best in salmon, using tamari sauce and toasted sesame oil spiked with tangy lime and the heat of ginger. For extra flavor, marinate the fish for up to ten minutes, but no longer, because the lime juice will begin to "cook" the salmon. The fish's natural color is gorgeous, but if you like a caramelized surface, brush on a little more tamari during the final minutes of cooking. For a healthy, light meal serve the salmon with Sautéed Ginger Baby Bok Choy (see page 230) and steamed brown rice. **SERVES 4**

Grated zest of 1 lime
$^1/_4$ cup fresh lime juice
   (from about 2 limes)
1 tablespoon finely minced shallots
1 tablespoon finely grated peeled
   fresh ginger (see box, page 231)
$4^1/_2$ teaspoons tamari or soy sauce

2 tablespoons canola oil
2 tablespoons toasted sesame oil
$^1/_4$ cup minced fresh cilantro
   (optional)
4 salmon fillets (6 to 8 ounces each),
   with or without skin, pin bones
   removed (see sidebar, page 163)

FRESH AND WILD

salmon

The most tasty and environmentally safe salmon is wild—caught from the pristine waters off Alaska. California, Washington, and Oregon have great tasting wild salmon too, but it is less abundant as a result of urban development and historic overfishing. The good news is that the fishing industry is working hard to ensure that we have wild Pacific salmon to enjoy for years to come.

There are five types of wild Pacific salmon at the market: chinook (or king), chum, coho, pink, and sockeye, all are delicious. You'll find fresh wild salmon at fishmongers from May through October. It is also available frozen or previously frozen during the rest of the year.

Wild Atlantic salmon is an endangered species and cannot be legally caught by American commercial fisheries. Most Atlantic salmon found in stores and restaurants is farmed fish from Chile or Canada. Salmon farms have a reputation for creating environmental problems. Salmon is typically farmed in open-water net pens, which can have a negative impact on the wild fish population and the quality of ocean water. Because the fish are raised in close quarters, pesticides and antibiotics are often administered to control disease. Some salmon farms are more environmentally friendly, but there are no USDA organic standards for salmon or other seafood.

Although all retail stores are required to provide a label identifying the country of origin for fish and shellfish and whether it is wild or farmed, it's best to shop for seafood in stores you know and trust. While farmed salmon may be less expensive, wild salmon is tastier and healthier for both people and the environment.

1. Position a rack in the lower third of the oven and preheat the oven to 500°F.

2. Combine the lime zest and juice, shallots, ginger, tamari sauce, canola oil, sesame oil, and 2 tablespoons of the cilantro, if using, in a shallow baking dish just large enough to comfortably hold the salmon fillets in a single layer. Add the fillets and turn them to coat all over, then arrange them skin side down, if any.

3. Bake the salmon fillets, without turning, until the fish is just firm to the touch and the interior is nearly opaque but still moist, 6 to 12 minutes, depending on the thickness of the fish. You can use an instant-read meat thermometer to test for doneness in thicker fillets. When the fish is done, the thermometer will register 130°F when inserted in the thickest part of a fillet.

4. Transfer the salmon fillets to plates, drizzle some of the sauce from the pan over them, and garnish with the remaining 2 tablespoons of cilantro, if using. Serve immediately.

Grilled Salmon
with Artichoke, Olive, and Caper Sauce

*G*rilled wild salmon is the perfect showcase for a rustic Mediterranean-inspired sauce featuring tender artichoke hearts, glistening black olives, summer-ripe tomatoes, and salty capers. Everything is coarsely chopped, so the sauce is a cinch to prepare and can be made up to a day ahead. The flavors are vibrant because the sauce isn't cooked through, just warmed while the fish grills. If you have time, soak the salmon in brine for an hour before you cook it (see the box on page 166). You'll find that brining makes the salmon more moist, so there's less chance of overcooking it, and it's less likely to stick to the grill. **SERVES 6**

A perfect artichoke, ready for harvest.

1 tablespoon minced garlic
¹/₄ cup coarsely chopped fresh flat-leaf
    parsley
¹/₂ cup coarsely chopped fresh basil
Grated zest of 1 orange
Grated zest of 1 lemon
²/₃ cup Kalamata olives, drained, pitted,
    and cut in half
¹/₄ cup capers, drained
¹/₃ cup extra-virgin olive oil, plus more
    for brushing the salmon
3 medium-size (about 1 pound)
    tomatoes, seeded and cut into ¹/₂-inch
    dice (about 3 cups)
1 can (about 13 ounces) water-packed
    artichoke hearts, drained and
    quartered
1 teaspoon salt
Freshly ground black pepper
Sugar (optional)
6 salmon fillets (6 to 8 ounces each),
    with or without skin, pin bones
    removed (see sidebar, page 163)
¹/₂ cup dry white wine
2 tablespoons (¹/₄ stick) unsalted butter
1 tablespoon good-quality balsamic
    vinegar (see sidebar, page 87)

1. Combine the garlic, parsley, basil, orange zest, lemon zest, olives, capers, and olive oil in a large bowl and stir to blend.

Coastal Monterey County is the ideal environment for growing artichokes— 70 percent of the country's artichokes are grown here.

Add the tomatoes, artichokes, and salt and season with pepper to taste. If the tomatoes taste bland or too acidic, add 1 to 2 teaspoons of sugar to balance the flavors. Stir gently to combine. If you are not planning on using the sauce within 1 hour, cover and refrigerate it for up to 24 hours.

2. Set up a barbecue grill and preheat it to high.

3. Brush the salmon fillets on both sides with olive oil. Grill the fillets for 4 minutes, then turn and cook until the fish is just firm to the touch and the interior is nearly opaque, about 4 minutes. You can use an instant-read meat thermometer to test for doneness in thicker fillets. When the fish is done, the thermometer will register 130°F when inserted in the thickest part of a fillet. Transfer the salmon fillets to a platter and cover with aluminum foil to keep warm.

4. Place the sauce in a large skillet. Add the wine and stir. Bring the sauce just to a simmer over medium heat. Remove the sauce from the heat and add the butter and balsamic vinegar. Stir to combine. Serve the salmon with the sauce spooned over it or on the side.

brining salmon

Soaking salmon in brine makes the fish more flavorful and moist. The added moisture makes the fish easier to remove from the cooking surface. Plus, the flesh is less likely to dry out from overcooking, giving you more flexibility when estimating your cooking time.

To make 1¹/₂ quarts of salmon brine—enough for 3 pounds of salmon fillets—add 2 cups of salt and 1 cup of sugar to 5 cups of water. Heat the brine just enough that the salt and sugar dissolve. Let the brine cool thoroughly in the refrigerator before using it. Submerge the salmon fillets in the chilled brine and let them soak, covered, in the

refrigerator for one to two hours, depending on the thickness of the fillets. Fillets that are 1-inch thick will take 1 hour to brine; 1¹/₂-inch-thick fillets will be brined in an hour and a half; and 2-inch-thick fillets will need to soak the full two hours. Rinse and pat the salmon dry before cooking.

Buying Fresh Tuna

When selecting tuna it's important to pay attention to which kinds are environmentally sustainable. The best choices for fresh tuna are albacore, bigeye, and yellowfin (also called ahi) that have been caught by pole-fishing or trolling (pulling fishing lines behind the boat). Avoid bluefin because it is in such high demand that its population is declining.

Tuna is a good source of heart-healthy omega-3 fatty acids but is likely to have a higher level of mercury than smaller fish. So as delicious as tuna is, it's best to enjoy eating it only a few times a month; children under six and pregnant women would do best avoiding it altogether.

Seared Tuna
with a Fennel-Coriander Crust

A lively combination of freshly ground spices makes a perfect crust for pan-seared tuna. It takes only a few minutes to sear the fish so that it is medium-rare and rosy red at the center. If you like your tuna cooked throughout, add a minute or two more to the cooking time, but to ensure that it stays moist and delicious, don't let it overcook. **SERVES 4**

1/4 cup fennel seeds
3 tablespoons coriander seeds
2 tablespoons whole white or black peppercorns
Coarse (kosher) salt
4 tuna steaks (each about 3/4 inch thick and 6 ounces; see sidebar, this page)
2 tablespoons olive oil

1. Place the fennel, coriander, and peppercorns in a spice mill or clean coffee grinder and grind to a fine powder. Spread the spice mixture on a plate.

2. Sprinkle salt on both sides of the tuna steaks. Dip each tuna steak in the spice mixture, lightly coating it all over.

3. Heat the olive oil in a large nonstick skillet over medium-high heat. Add the tuna and cook, turning once, until cooked to taste, about 2 minutes per side for medium-rare. Serve warm.

Seared Tuna with a Fennel-Coriander Crust, cooked rare and tender.

Linguine
with Shrimp, Tomatoes, and Capers

All the flavors of summer-ripe tomatoes and plump, sweet shrimp are captured in this pasta sauce. There's no need to peel or seed the tomatoes, and since you use the tails and shells from the shrimp to make a quick shrimp stock, nothing is wasted. It's the stock that gives the sauce its bold flavor, accentuated with garlic, capers, lemon, and basil. This dish comes together fast, making it appropriate for a weeknight dinner. **SERVES 4 TO 6**

A handful of summer: heirloom tomatoes and pattypan squash.

1 pound large (16 to 20 count) raw, unpeeled shrimp
1 pound dried linguine
3 tablespoons unsalted butter
2 large cloves garlic, minced
1/2 cup dry white wine
1 tablespoon capers (see box, page 175), drained
1 medium-size ripe tomato, seeded and cut in 1/2-inch dice (about 1 cup)
2 tablespoons coarsely chopped fresh basil leaves, plus additional leaves for garnish
Juice of 1 lemon
Salt and freshly ground black pepper

1. Rinse and peel the shrimp, setting aside the shells and tails. If desired, devein the shrimp: Using a paring knife and working under cool running water, cut down the back of the shrimp and remove the vein. Drain the shrimp in a colander.

2. Place the shrimp shells and tails in a small pot, add 1 cup of water, and bring to a boil over high heat. Reduce the heat to medium-low and let simmer until the shrimp stock is flavored, about 15 minutes. Strain the shrimp stock through a sieve and discard the shells.

3. Meanwhile, bring a large pot of salted water to a boil over high heat. Add the linguine and cook according to the package directions.

4. Melt 2 tablespoons of the butter in a large skillet over low heat. Add the garlic and cook, stirring frequently, until soft and fragrant, about 2 minutes. Add the wine and increase the heat to medium. Bring the wine to a simmer, add the shrimp in one layer, and let simmer gently for 4 minutes. Turn the shrimp and continue cooking until completely pink and just cooked through, about 2 minutes longer.

5. Add the capers, tomato, and 1/2 cup of the shrimp stock. Bring the liquid to a simmer and cook for 2 minutes. Add the remaining 1 tablespoon of butter and the chopped basil and lemon juice and cook until heated through, about 1 minute. Season with salt and pepper, to taste.

6. Drain the linguine in a colander and transfer it to a warm serving bowl. Pour the shrimp with its pan juices over the pasta. Garnish with the whole basil leaves and serve.

How to Peel and Cube a Mango

Mangoes have an oblong pit that makes slicing them tricky. Start by cutting a thin slice off the top and bottom of the mango so that you can stand it on end. Then, using a paring knife, cut the mango flesh from the pit, from top to bottom, keeping the knife as close to the pit as you can. Repeat on the opposite side so that you have two mango "cheeks."

Place each cheek on a counter, skin-side down. Using the paring knife, and being careful not to pierce the skin, make a crosshatch of cuts through the mango flesh to create 1/2-inch squares. Turn the mango inside-out so that the cubes of mango fan out from the skin. Using the knife, carefully detach the cubed mango from the skin.

Grilled Shrimp
with Tropical Salsa

*B*efore they hit the grill, these jumbo shrimp soak up a marinade inspired by the flavors of Southeast Asia—tangy lemongrass and lime, warmed with chiles and ginger. The subtle heat is married with a colorful salsa bursting with tropical fruits: pineapple, mango, and kiwi. You'll find it's easy to grill jumbo shrimp, but they are pricey. If you use smaller shrimp, they will be just as tasty. Just remember to decrease the cooking time and thread them on skewers to make turning easier. Some stores sell shrimp that are peeled and deveined, which reduces preparation time. But if you cook the shrimp in their shells, they will have better flavor and are less likely to overcook if your timing isn't perfect. **SERVES 4**

3 cloves garlic, minced
Grated zest of 1 lime
2 tablespoons fresh lime juice
1 tablespoon grated peeled fresh ginger
1/4 teaspoon Asian chile garlic sauce, or
    1/4 teaspoon dried red pepper flakes
1 stalk lemongrass, finely chopped
    (see sidebar, page 46)
2 tablespoons soy sauce
1/2 cup olive oil
2 tablespoons mirin (Asian sweet rice
    wine) or honey
20 jumbo (8 to 12 count per pound)
    shrimp, unpeeled
Tropical Salsa (recipe follows)

1. To make the marinade, combine the garlic, lime zest and juice, ginger, chile sauce, lemongrass, soy sauce, olive oil, and mirin in a large bowl and whisk well to combine.

2. Devein the shrimp by cutting down the back of each shell with kitchen shears or a paring knife. Remove the vein, then rinse the shrimp under cool water and drain them thoroughly in a colander.

3. Add the shrimp to the marinade and toss to mix. Cover and refrigerate for 4 to 8 hours.

4. Set up a barbecue grill and preheat it to medium.

5. Remove the shrimp from the marinade and drain them in a strainer, discarding the marinade. Arrange the shrimp on the grill in a single layer and grill until just cooked through, 2 to 3 minutes per side, turning with tongs. To check for doneness, remove a shrimp from the grill and peel off the shell to see if the flesh is firm and opaque. Be careful not to overcook the shrimp or they will be dry.

6. Serve the warm shrimp with the Tropical Salsa.

Note: If you don't have time to prepare an entire pineapple, look for precut fresh pineapple in the produce section of the grocery store. Unsweetened canned pineapple is surprisingly good and can be substituted if fresh is not available.

Tropical Salsa

While this sweet-hot salsa is great with grilled shrimp, it's equally fabulous with chicken, halibut, catfish, or tortilla chips. The salsa's golden orange color and fresh fruit flavors are a fun change from the typical tomato salsa. **MAKES ABOUT 2 CUPS**

1 ripe mango, peeled and cut into
    1/2-inch dice (see sidebar, page 170)
1 cup fresh pineapple chunks, cut into
    1/2-inch dice (see Note)
1 kiwi, peeled and cut into 1/2-inch dice
1/4 cup thinly sliced scallions, including
    white and 3 inches of green
1/2 red bell pepper, stemmed, seeded, and
    cut into 1/4-inch dice (about 1/4 cup)
2 teaspoons diced jalapeño pepper
    (1/8-inch dice), seeds and ribs
    removed
Grated zest of 1 lime

2 tablespoons finely chopped crystallized
    ginger (see box, page 231)
1 tablespoon minced fresh cilantro or
    basil
Juice of 1 lime
2 tablespoons pineapple juice or water
1 tablespoon honey

1. Place the mango, pineapple, kiwi, scallions, bell pepper, jalapeño, lime zest, ginger, and cilantro in a medium-size nonreactive bowl and stir to combine.

2. Place the lime juice, pineapple juice, and honey in a small bowl and whisk to combine. Pour the juice mixture over the fruit mixture and stir to combine.

3. Refrigerate the salsa, covered, until the flavors develop, at least 2 hours. The salsa can be refrigerated, covered, for up to 2 days.

Cheerful nasturtiums brighten any garden with the highly-saturated colors of their blossoms and rich green lily pad-like leaves.

Shrimp Cakes
with Lemon-Caper Aioli

When she owned a restaurant on the island of Nantucket, chef Pam McKinstry was famous for her crab cakes. This shrimp variation is incredibly moist, thanks to a mix of pureed shrimp, egg white, and cream, which holds together small chunks of shrimp and sautéed vegetables. The light, crunchy bread crumb crust provides the perfect contrast. Because the shrimp isn't served whole, you can use smaller, less expensive ones. Be sure to allow time for the pureed shrimp mixture to refrigerate overnight. This lets the flavors develop, and the delicate mixture is easier to handle when it's very cold. Don't worry if the cakes seem too soft when you form them, they will firm up as they cook. The shrimp cakes are delicious, and when served with Lemon-Caper Aioli on the side, they make an elegant first course or a main dish. (For a crab cake variation, see page 175.) **MAKES 12 SMALL CAKES**

¼ cup olive oil

½ cup minced scallions, including
    white and 3 inches of green

3 tablespoons minced shallots

1 small red or orange bell pepper,
    stemmed, seeded, and cut into
    ⅛-inch dice (about ½ cup)

1½ pounds small raw shrimp,
    peeled and deveined

1 large egg white

½ cup plus 2 tablespoons heavy
    (whipping) cream

2 teaspoons Worcestershire sauce

1 tablespoon fresh lemon juice

¼ cup mayonnaise

½ teaspoon cayenne pepper

½ teaspoon salt

1 tablespoon unsalted butter

2 tablespoons dry white wine

½ cup minced fresh flat-leaf parsley

⅓ cup minced fresh dill

1 cup fine, dried bread crumbs,
    store-bought or homemade

Lemon-Caper Aioli (optional; recipe
    follows)

1 lemon, cut into wedges, for serving

1. Heat 2 tablespoons of the olive oil
in a medium-size skillet over low heat.
Add the scallions, shallots, and bell pepper
and cook, stirring occasionally, until the
vegetables are soft, about 5 minutes.
Let the mixture cool.

2. Place a third (½ pound) of the shrimp
in a food processor. Add the egg white
and run the machine continuously until
the shrimp is pureed. Add the cream and
pulse to blend. Add the Worcestershire
sauce, lemon juice, mayonnaise, cayenne,
and salt and pulse briefly to blend.

3. Transfer the shrimp mixture to a
medium-size bowl, add the scallion

mixture, and stir to combine. Cover the
bowl with plastic wrap and refrigerate it.

4. Heat the butter in a large nonstick
skillet over medium heat. Add the
remaining 1 pound of shrimp and cook
for 1 minute. Add the wine and cook,
turning the shrimp occasionally, until
they are completely pink and just cooked
through, 2 to 3 minutes. The cooking
time will depend on the size of the
shrimp. Drain the shrimp in a colander,
and let them cool enough to handle.

5. Cut the shrimp into small pieces,
about ⅓-inch dice. The shrimp cakes
should have chunks of shrimp, but if
they are too large the cakes will not
hold together well.

6. Add the diced shrimp, parsley, and
dill to the pureed shrimp mixture and
stir to combine. Cover the bowl again
and refrigerate the shrimp mixture until
it is firm, at least 6 hours or preferably
overnight.

7. Spread the bread crumbs on a plate.
Form the shrimp mixture into cakes
about 2½ inches in diameter and 1 inch
thick. Dip the cakes in the bread crumbs
and coat them all over.

8. Heat the remaining 2 tablespoons of
olive oil in a large nonstick skillet over
medium heat. Working in batches so that
they do not touch, cook the shrimp cakes
until the bottom is golden brown, about
3 minutes. Turn the cakes over and cook
until golden brown and cooked through,
3 to 4 minutes. Serve hot with the
Lemon-Caper Aioli, if using, and lemon
wedges on the side.

Buying Shrimp

When buying shrimp, look for ones caught or farmed in the United States and avoid ones that have been imported. Because of poor foreign regulation, farming and catching shrimp have damaged tropical coastal environments.

In the United States, wild shrimp are caught using traps (preferably) or bottom trawl nets that allow sea turtles and fish to escape. Also, U.S. shrimp farms are regulated to reduce their environmental impact.

Some farms are raising the bar on shrimp farming by using environmentally friendly feed and building the farms in inland areas so that marine life will not be affected.

Since shrimp is so perishable, most shrimp sold in stores has been frozen and thawed before you buy them. Smell fresh or thawed shrimp to make sure they don't have an off odor and cook them the same day you purchase them.

Variation: Crab Cakes

It's easy to turn the Shrimp Cakes into crab cakes, using the pureed shrimp to bind the crab together. Substitute 1 pound of best-quality cooked lump crab meat plus ½ pound of shrimp, for the puree, in place of the 1½ pounds of shrimp. Pick over the crab meat and, using your hands, gently squeeze out the excess liquid so the final mixture will not be too runny to form into cakes.

Make the shrimp puree as described in Steps 1 through 3. Then make the crab cakes following Steps 6 through 8 using the crab meat in place of the chunks of shrimp. The cooking time will be the same. Parsley is good in crab cakes, but leave out the dill because it can overwhelm the delicate crab flavor.

Lemon-Caper Aioli

Homemade aioli is easy to make, and this version, with its lemon, garlic, and caper flavors, is especially robust. The aioli is a delicious complement to artichokes, shrimp or crab cakes, seafood salads, or roasted vegetables. **MAKES 1¼ CUPS**

2 cloves garlic, peeled
2 teaspoons Dijon mustard
2 large egg yolks, at room temperature (see Note)
1 teaspoon fresh lemon juice
¼ teaspoon salt
½ cup extra-virgin olive oil
½ cup canola or grapeseed oil
2 tablespoons minced drained capers
Grated zest of 1 lemon

1. Place the garlic, mustard, egg yolks, lemon juice, and salt in a food processor and process until the garlic is minced, about 15 seconds.

2. With the machine running, add the olive and canola oils in very slow, steady streams, stopping when needed to scrape the side of the bowl with a rubber spatula. Run the machine until the aioli is smooth and thick.

3. Transfer the aioli to a small bowl and add 1 tablespoon of hot water. Whisk to blend (if the aioli has started to separate, this will recombine it). Add the capers and lemon zest and stir to blend.

4. Refrigerate the aioli, covered, until the flavors develop, at least 6 hours. Stored in an airtight container, the aioli can be refrigerated for up to 5 days.

Note: This recipe uses uncooked egg yolks. If you make it, you want to be sure to use the best farm-fresh eggs that have been kept refrigerated.

FARM FRESH

capers

Capers are the pickled buds of a shrub that grow wild around the Mediterranean. Even today, capers are not cultivated, they are foraged from those wild bushes. The buds are graded according to size. You usually find the smallest size, called nonpareils, bottled in vinegar on supermarket shelves, and these are delicious. Some specialty food stores also sell capers packed in salt. Salt-packed capers tend to be larger buds that need to be soaked in warm water for five minutes to remove the salt before you use them. However, their flavor is pure and even more robust than that of vinegar-packed capers.

Seared Sea Scallops
on a Bed of Sautéed Spinach

When you have very fresh sea scallops, their sweet, succulent taste doesn't need the adornment of rich sauces. The trick to keeping scallops moist is to quickly sauté them over high heat. Cooking them with arrowroot helps form a delectable crisp, brown crust. Remove the scallops from the heat just before they are done, because once off the heat they continue cooking for a minute or two. For a memorable dinner nestle the scallops in garlicky spinach. Or try them as a starter course with a garnish of string beans and lemon slices (as shown). **SERVES 4**

Note: Arrowroot is a starchy powder, similar to cornstarch, made from the root of a West Indian plant. You can find it in the spice section of most grocery stores.

1 pound fresh sea scallops (see box, this page)
$^1/_4$ cup arrowroot (preferred; see Note), cornstarch, or flour

$^1/_2$ teaspoon coarse (kosher) salt
Freshly ground black pepper
Garlicky Sautéed Spinach (optional; recipe follows)
Olive oil
Lemon slices, for serving

F A R M   F R E S H

buying sea scallops

Most wild sea scallops are caught by dragging heavy nets that rake across the ocean bottom. This fishing method, called dredging, often captures sea turtles and other sea life and damages the seafloor habitat. Because scallops deteriorate quickly and most commercial boats are at sea for days at a time, the scallops are shucked soon after being caught and are usually frozen or dipped in a phosphate solution. While scallops treated with phosphates look beautiful—plump and pure white—when cooked, they are more watery and less flavorful than untreated scallops.

The most environmentally friendly scallops are farmed or caught by professional divers. Wild scallops caught from commercial day boats, which go on short trips of twenty-four hours or less, arrive on shore the freshest. For the best taste, look for scallops that are dry-packed and untreated, with a dull ivory, pink, or orange color. Ask fishmongers questions about how the seafood was caught and handled. All the answers may not be available, but your questions may encourage them to provide more detailed information in the future.

1. If there is a tough, white muscle on the side of any of the scallops, using a paring knife, trim it off and discard it. Pat the scallops dry with paper towels.

2. Place the arrowroot, salt, and some pepper in a shallow bowl and whisk to blend. Dredge the scallops in the arrowroot mixture, shaking off the excess.

3. If serving with the sautéed spinach, spoon the spinach into the center of a serving platter and cover it with aluminum foil to keep warm.

4. Pour just enough olive oil in a large, nonstick skillet to thinly coat the bottom. Heat the oil over medium heat until it is hot but not smoking. Add the scallops in a single layer, working in batches if needed.

5. Cook the scallops until a brown crust forms on the bottom, 1 to 2 minutes. Turn the scallops with tongs and cook until lightly seared on the other side, about 30 seconds. Immediately transfer the scallops to the platter of spinach, arranging them with their crusty sides up, and serve immediately with lemon slices alongside.

Garlicky Sautéed Spinach

Tender, mild baby spinach paired with fragrant garlic makes a simple but delicious bed for quickly pan-seared sea scallops. **SERVES 4**

    2 pounds prewashed baby spinach
    2 tablespoons olive oil
    1 tablespoon minced garlic
    Salt and freshly ground black pepper

1. Heat the olive oil in a large skillet over medium heat. Add the garlic and cook, stirring constantly, until fragrant, about 2 minutes.

2. Add the baby spinach (if all the leaves don't fit in the skillet at first, add more by the handful as they wilt) and sprinkle with 1 tablespoon water. Turn the spinach with tongs until all the leaves are wilted and the garlic is evenly distributed. Season the spinach with salt and pepper to taste and serve.

An early morning harvest.

Monterey Cioppino

Cioppino is a rich, tomato-based fisherman's stew. Its popularization is usually credited to Italian immigrants in the San Francisco area. But Monterey's Italian fishing heritage is just as strong, and you'll find bowls of cioppino sold all along our Fisherman's Wharf. The seafood used is based on what's fresh from the ocean, so there's no set recipe. The version here overflows with shellfish—shrimp, clams, mussels, scallops, and crab legs—in a tomato broth enriched with clam juice, chicken stock, and wine. The broth can be made a couple of days ahead and the seafood added just before serving. Locals use legs from the huge, dinner-plate-size Dungeness crabs pulled from Monterey Bay. But in other parts of the country, king crab is a good substitute. If you want to add a firm white fish, mahimahi or halibut would be delicious. **SERVES 4**

3 tablespoons olive oil

2 to 3 celery ribs, thinly sliced
(about 1 cup)

1 large leek, both white and green parts,
rinsed well and thinly sliced
(about 1 cup)

1 small fennel bulb, cut into $^{1}/_{4}$-inch
dice (about 1 cup)

1 tablespoon minced garlic

1 cup dry white wine

2 cups bottled clam juice

1 cup Blond Chicken Stock
(page 372) or 1 cup store-bought
low-sodium chicken broth

2 medium-size ripe tomatoes, cut into
$^{1}/_{4}$-inch dice (about 2 cups)

1 bay leaf

1 tablespoon fresh thyme or coarsely
chopped tarragon leaves

4 cooked large Dungeness crab legs,
cracked, or 2 king crab legs, split and
cut into 2-inch lengths

12 littleneck clams, scrubbed

12 mussels, scrubbed and debearded

$^{1}/_{2}$ pound large (about 8) raw shrimp,
peeled and deveined

$^{1}/_{2}$ pound sea scallops, trimmed if
necessary (see Note)

1 teaspoon ground fennel seeds

Coarse (kosher) salt and freshly
ground black pepper

$^{1}/_{3}$ cup coarsely chopped fresh flat-leaf
parsley

Note: If there is a tough, white muscle on the side of any of the scallops, trim it off with a paring knife and discard it.

Fennel's mild licorice flavor is a wonderful addition to classic Monterey Cioppino.

1. Heat the olive oil in a large stockpot over low heat. Add the celery, leek, fennel bulb, and garlic and cook, stirring frequently, until the vegetables are soft and fragrant, 8 to 10 minutes.

2. Add the wine, increase the heat to high, and bring to a boil. Reduce the heat to medium and let simmer until the wine is reduced by about half, about 5 minutes.

3. Add the clam juice, chicken stock, tomatoes, bay leaf, and thyme and bring to a simmer. Reduce the heat to low and let simmer gently, covered, for 20 minutes. If you are not planning on serving the cioppino at this time, the broth can be cooled and refrigerated, covered, for up to 2 days.

4. Increase the heat to medium and add the crab, clams, and mussels. Cover the pot and let simmer for 2 minutes.

5. Add the shrimp and scallops, cover the pot, and let simmer until the clams and mussels have opened and the shrimp and scallops are just cooked through, 3 to 5 minutes. Discard the bay leaf and any unopened clams or mussels. Stir in the fennel seed and season with salt and pepper to taste.

6. Serve the cioppino immediately in deep bowls, sprinkling the parsley on top.

Chapter 6

Pasta and Vegetarian Main Dishes

My whole family loves pasta. A plate of pasta with a big green salad and hot, crusty bread makes for a simple, yet perfect, meal. The smell of tomatoes simmering with garlic and herbs quickly lures everyone to the dinner table. In my house, we eat pasta frequently, and to keep it interesting, I often experiment by adding different ingredients to marinara sauce. Some of my favorite add-ins include anchovy paste, capers, kalamata olives, grilled Italian sausage, chicken, onions, garlic, and a variety of fresh vegetables and herbs. If the pasta is cooked just right, and you splurge on good olive oil and good Parmesan cheese, it's almost impossible for your creation not to be appreciated.

Freshly grated Parmesan cheese completes our Caesar salad, as well as many of our pasta dishes.

A few times a year I make big batches of several pasta sauces and freeze them in ready-to-serve portions, and I suggest you do the same. They'll come in handy on days when you want a quick, easy meal. If you've got a bumper crop of basil in your summer garden or if it's especially bountiful at the market, turn it into Emerald Green Pesto. Pesto makes a wonderful addition to many different dishes, but it's particularly yummy when tossed with any type of pasta.

Farm Stand Marinara is great to make in the summer when fresh tomatoes and herbs are bountiful. Use it in two of our most popular Farm Stand pasta dishes: Farm Stand Spinach Cannelloni and Grilled Vegetable Lasagna with Pesto. We also offer a slowly simmered marinara sauce made with canned tomatoes and flavored with pancetta that is just right for the rest of the year.

I've been pleasantly surprised by how much my family has come to like

Facing Page:
Farm Stand Spinach Cannelloni (page 194).

the chewy texture and flavor of healthy whole wheat pasta. Edamame and portobello mushrooms mixed with whole wheat shells are now a family favorite. The streamlined version is ready in less than thirty minutes, but when time isn't an issue, try making the longer version, which features intensely flavored roasted tomatoes.

Tofu is also a great stand-in for meat. Instead of chicken or beef, toss tofu cubes into vegetable stir-fries. Or try a batch of Hoisin Tofu Snacks. My kids love the robust flavor. Paired with brown rice and steamed vegetables, you have a complete dinner. "Wild" Mushroom Ragout with Polenta is another great choice when you're looking for something hearty, but want to take a break from meat.

Our pizza nights bring the whole family together. Although I usually pick up pizza dough from our Farm Stand, it's easy and fun to make from scratch if you have the time. My husband, Drew, is the pizza artist at our house. He rolls a perfectly thin crust and makes an assortment of delectable masterpieces. We usually bake them one at a time, and gather around the counter to eat the slices as soon as they're cut. You'll find our favorite topping combinations here to help get your own creative juices flowing. Pizza toppings are limitless.

Summer means plenty of fresh basil for pesto, refreshing salads, and of course, pasta dishes.

Spaghetti
with Fresh Tomatoes, Zucchini, and Basil

The garden-fresh taste and vibrant color of juicy, vine-ripened tomatoes make this light pasta dish stellar. The tomatoes are not cooked, so be sure to select the most intensely flavorful ones you can find. A bright blend of diced red and gold tomatoes, or sweet cherry tomato halves, will be especially lovely. You'll need to allow an hour for the tomatoes to reach their full flavor as they marinate with basil and parsley in your best extra-virgin olive oil and some truffle oil, if available. Gently mixed with warm pasta and garlicky zucchini, the tomato dish makes a first course or light main dish that's impossible to resist. Adding thin slices of silky fresh mozzarella just before serving will take this over the top. **SERVES 8 AS A FIRST COURSE OR 4 AS A MAIN COURSE**

2 medium-size ripe tomatoes (about
   2 cups cut into ¹/₂-inch dice) or
   2 cups cherry tomatoes, cut in half
3 tablespoons extra-virgin olive oil
1 tablespoon truffle oil, or 1 additional
   tablespoon extra-virgin olive oil
¹/₄ cup chopped fresh basil
¹/₄ cup chopped fresh flat-leaf parsley
Pinch of dried red pepper flakes
Salt
1 pound dried spaghetti
2 medium-size zucchini (about
   8 ounces), cut into ¹/₄-inch dice
   (about 1¹/₂ cups)
1 large clove garlic, minced
Freshly ground black pepper

1. Place the tomatoes, 2 tablespoons of the olive oil, the truffle oil, basil, parsley, and pepper flakes in a medium-size bowl and stir to combine. Season with salt to taste. Let the tomato mixture sit at room temperature until the flavor develops, about 1 hour.

2. Bring a large pot of salted water to a boil over high heat. Add the spaghetti and cook according to the package directions.

3. Meanwhile, heat the remaining 1 tablespoon of olive oil in a medium-size skillet over medium-low heat. Add the zucchini and garlic and cook, stirring occasionally, until the zucchini is crisp-tender, 4 to 5 minutes. Season the zucchini with black pepper to taste.

4. Drain the spaghetti into a colander and transfer it to a large bowl. Add the tomato and zucchini mixtures to the spaghetti and toss to combine. Taste for seasoning, adding more salt and/or pepper, if needed. Serve the spaghetti warm or at room temperature.

Spaghetti with a lively mix of fresh ripe tomatoes and sauteed zucchini.

Peeling and Seeding Tomatoes

Tomatoes are easy to peel if you briefly blanch them in boiling water first. The hot water loosens the skin so it slips off easily. (Blanching also works well for peeling soft-skinned fruits, like peaches.)

Fill a large bowl with ice water and set it close to the stove. Bring a large pot of water to a boil. Using a slotted spoon, lower the tomatoes into the boiling water and let them cook until the skin splits, about 1 minute. Remove the tomatoes and plunge them into the ice water, letting them soak until cool enough to handle. Using a paring knife, cut out the tomato cores and slip off the peels. To remove the seeds, cut the tomatoes in half crosswise and gently squeeze the seeds out into the sink or pry them loose with your fingers.

Ziti
with Ratatouille

Chunks of purple eggplant and green zucchini harmonize beautifully with red and yellow peppers in this summery ratatouille from the south of France. Cooking each vegetable separately before warming them together with a sauce of tomatoes, garlic, and herbs takes a little extra time but ensures that each vegetable is perfectly tender and not overcooked. If you want to save a few minutes—with no loss of flavor— use good-quality canned tomatoes and you won't have to peel fresh ones. This is a dish that's just as delicious at room temperature as it is warm, so make enough for leftovers. While ratatouille is great over pasta, it's usually served on its own as a side dish. It also makes a fine appetizer served with thin slices of toasted baguette.

SERVES 4 TO 6

1/2 cup olive oil
1 small yellow onion, cut into 1/2-inch
  dice (about 1 cup)
8 large cloves garlic, thinly sliced
1 medium-size eggplant, cut into 3/4-inch
  cubes (about 3 cups)
Salt and freshly ground black pepper
1 small yellow bell pepper, stemmed,
  seeded, and cut into 3/4-inch dice
1 small red bell pepper, stemmed, seeded,
  and cut into 3/4-inch dice
1 pound dried ziti
3 medium-size zucchini
  (about 12 ounces), cut into 1/2-inch-
  thick quarter-moon pieces
6 large ripe tomatoes, peeled, seeded,
  and coarsely chopped (see sidebar,
  this page), or 2 cans (28 ounces each)
    diced tomatoes, drained
3/4 cup coarsely chopped fresh
    flat-leaf parsley
1/2 cup coarsely chopped fresh basil
1 wedge of Parmesan cheese
  (at least 2 ounces), for garnish

1. Heat 2 tablespoons of the olive oil in a large skillet over medium-low heat. Add the onion and cook, stirring frequently, until soft, about 10 minutes. Add the garlic and cook until the onion is golden and the garlic fragrant, about 3 minutes longer. Transfer the onion mixture to a large bowl, being careful to remove all the garlic.

2. Add 4 tablespoons of the olive oil to the skillet and heat over medium heat. When hot, add the eggplant. Season it with salt and pepper. Cook the eggplant until just soft, about 10 minutes.

3. Using a slotted spoon, transfer the eggplant to the bowl with the onion. Add 1 more tablespoon of olive oil to the skillet and, when hot, add the yellow and red bell peppers. Season them with salt. Cook the bell peppers, stirring frequently, until they are soft, about 8 minutes. Using a slotted spoon, transfer

the bell peppers to the bowl with the onion and eggplant.

4. Meanwhile, bring a large pot of salted water to a boil over high heat. Add the ziti and cook according to the package directions.

5. Add the remaining 1 tablespoon of olive oil to the skillet and, when hot, add the zucchini. Season it with salt and pepper. Cook the zucchini until crisp-tender, 5 to 7 minutes. Using a slotted spoon, transfer the zucchini to the bowl with the other vegetables.

6. Add the tomatoes, parsley, basil, and ½ teaspoon each of salt and pepper to the skillet. Increase the heat to medium-high and cook until hot, about 4 minutes.

7. Add the vegetables and any liquid in the bowl to the tomato mixture and cook until warmed through, about 2 minutes. There should be quite a bit of liquid in the skillet with the ratatouille.

8. Drain the ziti in a colander, setting aside ½ cup of the pasta cooking water.

9. Transfer the ziti to the large bowl and add the ratatouille. Stir gently to combine. If the pasta seems too dry, add some of the pasta cooking water.

10. Transfer the ratatouille and pasta mixture to a serving platter or pasta bowls. Using a vegetable peeler, shave curls of the Parmesan cheese over the pasta and serve immediately.

A young farmer proudly displays her bounty—an armload of fresh chard.

Grilled Vegetable Lasagna
with Emerald Green Pesto

When the crispness of autumn begins to chase away the summer heat, it's the perfect time to make vegetable lasagna. While warm-weather vegetables are still around, the cooler air seems to call for heftier fare. At our Farm Stand, we make this dish every day when the fields are still overflowing with heirloom tomatoes, zucchini, eggplant, summer squash, red peppers, and basil. Hot from the oven, this looks like a typical lasagna. But when you slice it, you'll discover layers of colorful vegetables forming brilliant red, green, and yellow stripes between the layers of pasta and cheese.

This can be a time-consuming recipe, but you can skip a few steps by substituting a good-quality marinara sauce and pesto from a jar. Using a mandoline or vegetable slicer makes quick work of thinly slicing the vegetables (see the sidebar on page 267).

You can also cook the vegetables under the broiler instead of lighting the grill. If your family is small, consider dividing the recipe between two 9-inch-square baking pans. Bake one to eat right away; the other can be frozen for up to a month. Before baking, let the frozen lasagna thaw in the refrigerator for a day. The baking time will be about 15 minutes longer if the lasagna is cold. **SERVES 10**

3 medium-size eggplants, peeled and cut lengthwise into 1/4-inch-thick slices

3 medium-size yellow summer squash, cut lengthwise into 1/8-inch-thick slices

3 medium-size zucchini, cut lengthwise into 1/8-inch-thick slices

1 cup olive oil

Salt and freshly ground black pepper

2 large red bell peppers

8 ounces lasagna noodles

1 1/4 cups freshly grated Parmesan cheese

3 cups (24 ounces) ricotta cheese

2 large eggs

1/4 cup minced fresh basil

1/3 cup minced fresh flat-leaf parsley

4 cups Farm Stand Marinara Sauce (recipe follows) or good-quality store-bought marinara sauce

12 ounces mozzarella cheese, coarsely grated (about 3 cups)

2/3 cup Emerald Green Pesto (page 192) or store-bought pesto

1. Place the eggplant, squash, and zucchini on a baking tray and brush them on both sides with some of the olive oil. Lightly season them with salt and pepper.

2. Set up a barbecue grill and preheat it to medium.

3. Grill the eggplant until just soft, 2 1/2 to 4 minutes per side. Transfer the grilled eggplant to a wire rack to cool. Leave the grill burning.

4. Grill the squash and zucchini until just soft, about 2 minutes per side. Transfer the grilled squash and zucchini to the wire rack with the eggplant to cool. Leave the grill burning.

5. Place the bell peppers on the grill and cook, turning frequently, until the skin is just charred black, about 10 minutes. Transfer the bell peppers to a paper bag, close it tightly, and let the peppers steam for about 5 minutes. Remove the peppers from the bag and, when they are cool enough to handle, pull off the charred skin. Discard the skin, seeds, and stems and cut the roasted peppers into long, 1-inch-wide strips.

6. Bring a large pot of salted water to a boil over high heat. Add the lasagna noodles and cook according to the package directions until just tender. Do not undercook the lasagna noodles because they will not continue to cook in the oven. Drain the noodles well and lay them out flat on a clean dish towel (not terry cloth) so they do not stick together.

7. Place 3/4 cup of the Parmesan cheese and the ricotta cheese, eggs, basil, and parsley in a small bowl. Add 1/2 teaspoon each of salt and pepper and stir well to combine.

8. Position a rack in the center of the oven and preheat the oven to 375°F.

9. Brush a 9 by 13–inch baking pan lightly with $1/4$ to $1/2$ cup of the marinara sauce. Arrange one fourth of the lasagna noodles in a single layer over the marinara sauce, trimming them to fit if necessary. Arrange half of the eggplant slices over the noodles. Spread half of the ricotta mixture evenly over the eggplant and sprinkle a third of the mozzarella on top.

10. Arrange a third of the remaining lasagna noodles over the mozzarella. Spread about $1/2$ to $3/4$ cup of the marinara sauce over the pasta (the lasagna will hold together better and be easier to serve if you use thin layers of marinara sauce). Cover the sauce with a layer each of the squash, zucchini, and red peppers, using them all up. Spread the remaining ricotta mixture over the vegetables and top this with half of the remaining mozzarella.

11. Arrange half of the remaining lasagna noodles over the mozzarella and cover them with the remaining eggplant. Brush the eggplant with the pesto and sprinkle the remaining mozzarella on top.

12. Arrange the remaining lasagna noodles over the mozzarella. Spread about 1 cup of the marinara sauce over the noodles so they are completely covered and sprinkle the remaining $1/2$ cup of Parmesan cheese on top.

13. Bake the lasagna until it is hot and bubbly, about 1 hour. Remove the pan from the oven and let the lasagna rest for at least 15 minutes before cutting it. Heat the remaining marinara sauce (about 2 cups) in a small saucepan over medium heat. Slice the lasagna and serve it while still hot, with the remaining marinara sauce on the side.

Farm Stand Marinara Sauce

When tomatoes are at their peak and prices are low, it's time to make a big batch of marinara sauce for the freezer. Having a supply of marinara sauce on hand can be a great help on a busy day. In less time than it takes to have a pizza delivered, you can boil a pot of pasta water and warm up the sauce. To please the vegetarians in your life, add sautéed mushrooms or eggplant to the pasta or, for meat lovers, Italian sausage, ground beef, or pancetta. The recipe can be easily multiplied, so stock up! **MAKES ABOUT 5 CUPS**

2 cloves garlic, peeled
1 small carrot, coarsely chopped
1 small yellow onion, coarsely chopped
3 tablespoons olive oil
$1/3$ cup dry red wine
5 pounds ripe tomatoes, peeled (see sidebar, page 186) and coarsely chopped, juices reserved, or 2 cans (28 ounces each) diced or crushed tomatoes, with their juice
$1/4$ cup chopped fresh basil, or 2 teaspoons dried basil
1 tablespoon fresh oregano, or 2 teaspoons dried oregano
1 tablespoon fresh thyme leaves, or 1 teaspoon dried thyme
1 teaspoon coarse (kosher) salt
$1/2$ teaspoon freshly ground black pepper, or $1/2$ teaspoon dried red pepper flakes
1 to 2 teaspoons sugar (optional)

1. Place the garlic and carrot in a food processor and pulse until finely chopped. Add the onion and continue to pulse until minced, scraping the side of the bowl with a rubber spatula occasionally.

Cherokee purple heirloom tomatoes.

Storing and Freezing Pesto

Freshly made pesto will keep for a month in the refrigerator. Preserve its vivid green color by pouring a thin film of olive oil over the pesto to seal out the air. Pesto can be frozen for up to three months; place it in small containers with tight fitting lids so you can thaw just the amount you need. For even smaller portions, freeze the pesto in ice cube trays and transfer the cubes to a resealable plastic freezer bag to add to dressings or garnish soups.

A bumper crop of basil means it's time to make pesto.

2. Heat the olive oil in a large, heavy pot over medium-low heat. Add the onion mixture and cook, stirring frequently, until soft but not browned, about 11 minutes. Add the wine and stir well, loosening any bits stuck to the bottom of the pot. Bring to a simmer and cook until reduced slightly, about 3 minutes.

3. Add the tomatoes and their juices to the pot. Add the basil, oregano, and thyme and let simmer gently until the flavors are concentrated, 35 to 45 minutes. Add the salt and pepper. Taste for sweetness and, if the sauce tastes too acidic, add 1 to 2 teaspoons of sugar. If you are not planning on using the sauce immediately, let it cool to room temperature. It can be refrigerated, covered, for up to 1 week or frozen for up to 3 months.

Emerald Green Pesto

Every summer my family makes huge batches of pesto that we freeze to enjoy later in the year. With a supply always on hand, it's easy on a busy night to make a fuss-free dish of pasta with pesto sauce. It also adds a fresh flavor burst when stirred into vegetable soups, drizzled over pizzas, or spooned over grilled fish or chicken. We often add a heaping spoonful of pesto to our Lemon Vinaigrette (see page 97) and toss it with a salad of mixed baby greens

sprinkled with toasted pine nuts and grated Parmesan cheese. Our Farm Stand pesto recipe adds parsley to the traditional ingredients to help keep the basil's bright green color vibrant. If you prefer, you can also substitute an equal amount of baby spinach with excellent results. For a traditional pesto, use only basil. **MAKES ABOUT 2 CUPS**

4 cloves garlic, peeled
6 packed cups fresh basil leaves
¹/₂ packed cup fresh flat-leaf parsley leaves, baby spinach, or more basil
¹/₄ cup pine nuts
1 cup olive oil, plus (optional) more for storing the pesto
¹/₂ teaspoon salt
1 cup (3 ounces) finely and freshly grated Parmesan cheese

1. Place the garlic, basil, parsley, and pine nuts in a food processor and pulse until coarsely chopped.

2. With the machine running constantly, add the olive oil in a slow, steady stream, until the pesto is smooth, stopping when needed to scrape the side with a rubber spatula.

3. Transfer the pesto to a medium-size bowl. Add the salt and Parmesan cheese and stir to combine. For storing and freezing instructions see the sidebar, this page.

A Field Guide to Great-Tasting Tomatoes

Bite into one of these heirloom or specialty vine-ripened beauties and discover the makings of a real tomato: vibrant color, intense flavor, and dripping with juice. These are just a few of the wonderful warm-weather tomatoes well worth trying.

aunt ruby's german green *have a pale yellow-green color with a pink blush that extends into the flesh when fully ripe. They are sweet and slightly spicy, and their large size makes them great for slicing and for salads.*

banana legs *are bright yellow, thin, and long—like their namesake. They have a meaty texture with few seeds, making them good for cooking.*

black from tula *are Russian heirlooms with reddish-brown or purple skin and deep green shoulders. They have a sweet flavor with a slightly salty, smoky taste; their medium to large size makes them good for slicing or salads.*

brandywines *have a deep pink-red colored skin and are, perhaps, the most popular heirlooms. They are intensely flavorful with low acidity; one big slice can cover a whole slice of bread.*

green zebras *have spectacular yellow-gold skin with dark green stripes. Their bright green flesh has a lemon-lime taste that is very tasty and showy in salads.*

lemon boys *are hybrids, not heirlooms, and were the first bright yellow tomatoes ever grown. These medium-size fruits are great for a sunshine-colored salsa, adding plenty of mild, sweet flavor with a bit of tang.*

tigerellas *are small red tomatoes—about the size of silver dollars—with jagged golden stripes. Their slightly tart taste and pretty appearance make them a nice addition to a mixed tomato salad.*

yellow oxhearts *have a distinctive heart shape with bright yellow skin. They are meaty yet juicy with a rich taste, and their medium to large size makes them good for salads or slicing.*

Farm Stand Spinach Cannelloni

Tender baby spinach, creamy ricotta, and fresh basil and thyme rolled into plump pasta tubes and blanketed with a fresh tomato sauce make a satisfying lunch or dinner. At the Farm Stand, we roll the filling in organic lasagna noodles, which is just as easy as stuffing cannelloni tubes. We also use prewashed, organic baby spinach because it's easy to prepare. You can use bunches of mature leaf spinach instead, but be sure to wash them well and remove the tough stems. The cannelloni can be made up to two days ahead of time, and it also freezes well. **MAKES 16 CANNELLONI; SERVES 4**

8 lasagna noodles (10 inches in length)
1 tablespoon olive oil
1/2 cup minced shallots or yellow onion
1 tablespoon minced garlic
1 tablespoon fresh thyme leaves
1 tablespoon chopped fresh basil
1 1/4 teaspoons salt
1 pound (about 12 cups) fresh baby spinach, coarsely chopped
1 3/4 cups (15 ounces) ricotta cheese

1 large egg
Pinch of ground nutmeg
1/2 teaspoon freshly ground black pepper
1 1/2 cups freshly grated Parmesan cheese
1/4 cup minced fresh flat-leaf parsley, plus coarsely chopped parsley, for garnish
3 cups Farm Stand Marinara Sauce (page 191)

Lasagna noodles give a nice ruffled edge to these cannelloni.

1. Bring a large pot of salted water to a boil over high heat. Add the lasagna noodles and cook according to the package directions until just tender. Do not undercook the lasagna noodles because they will not continue to cook in the oven. Drain the noodles well and lay them out flat on a clean dish towel (not terry cloth) so they do not stick together.

2. Heat the olive oil in a large, preferably nonstick, skillet over medium-low heat. Add the shallots and cook until soft, about 5 minutes. Add the garlic, thyme, basil, and 1/4 teaspoon of the salt and cook, stirring frequently, 1 minute.

3. Add about a quarter of the spinach to the skillet and cook, turning frequently with tongs, until it wilts, 2 to 5 minutes. Continue adding spinach until all of it has wilted. Drain the spinach mixture in a strainer, pressing down on it to extract the liquid. Transfer the spinach mixture to a medium-size bowl and let it cool.

4. Place the ricotta cheese, egg, nutmeg, pepper, and the remaining 1 teaspoon of salt in a bowl. Add ½ cup of the Parmesan cheese and the minced parsley. Stir to combine. Add the cheese mixture to the cooled spinach and stir to combine.

5. Position a rack in the center of the oven and preheat the oven to 350°F.

6. Spread 1 cup of the marinara sauce on the bottom of a 9 by 13–inch baking pan.

7. Cut each lasagna noodle in half crosswise to make 16 pieces, each 4 to 5 inches long. Place a piece of lasagna noodle on a work surface. Spoon ¼ cup of the spinach filling along the short edge of the noodle and roll it up to enclose the filling. Repeat with the remaining pieces of noodle and filling. Arrange the cannelloni in the baking pan, side by side, seam side down, fitted closely together.

8. Cover the cannelloni with the remaining 2 cups of marinara sauce and sprinkle the remaining 1 cup of Parmesan cheese on top. Prepared up to this point, the cannelloni can be covered with plastic wrap and refrigerated for up to 2 days. They can be frozen for up to a month; wrap the baking pan tightly in several layers of plastic wrap before freezing (there's no need to thaw the cannelloni before baking, but you will need to increase the baking time by 30 minutes).

9. Bake the cannelloni until they are hot, the sauce bubbles, and the Parmesan cheese melts, 25 to 35 minutes. Sprinkle the chopped parsley on top of the cannelloni and serve hot.

My Spaghetti Bolognese

My family loves my home-style spaghetti with a thick, rich meat sauce. There's nothing fancy about the ingredients I use—olive oil, onions, garlic, ground beef, oregano, and basil. This recipe tastes great using a high-quality store-bought sauce, but to make it extra special, use our Marinara Sauce with Pancetta, if you have some in the freezer. It gently clings to the pasta, bringing all the other ingredients together. Served with garlic bread and a Caesar salad, the spaghetti makes a perfect cool weather meal. **SERVES 4 TO 6**

1 pound dried spaghetti

2 tablespoons olive oil

1 medium-size yellow onion,
    cut into $1/4$-inch dice
    (about 1 cup)

1 tablespoon minced garlic

1 tablespoon dried oregano

2 teaspoons dried basil

$1/2$ teaspoon salt

1 pound lean ground beef

4 cups Marinara Sauce with Pancetta
    (recipe follows) or good-quality
    store-bought marinara sauce

$1/4$ cup chopped freshly flat-leaf
    parsley

$1/2$ cup freshly grated Parmesan
    cheese

1. Place a large pot of salted water over high heat and let it come to a boil.

2. Meanwhile, heat the olive oil in a large saucepan over medium-low heat. Add the onion and cook, stirring frequently, until soft, about 5 minutes. Add the garlic, oregano, basil, and salt and cook, stirring occasionally, until the garlic softens, about 1 minute.

3. Add the ground beef and stir to combine and break up the meat. Increase the heat to medium and cook until the meat browns, 5 to 8 minutes.

4. Add the spaghetti to the boiling water and cook according to the package directions.

5. Add the marinara sauce to the saucepan with the beef mixture, reduce the heat to low, and let simmer gently until the flavors are concentrated, about 15 minutes.

6. Drain the spaghetti into a colander. Just before serving, add the parsley to the sauce and stir to combine. Place the spaghetti on a serving platter or in pasta bowls. Pour the sauce over the spaghetti and serve hot, topped with the Parmesan cheese.

Marinara Sauce with Pancetta

Rao's restaurant in New York City is famous for Italian dishes that have been handed down through the Rao family for generations. Their fabulous marina sauce was the springboard for this flavorful homemade version. Most marinara sauces are vegetarian, but the diced pancetta adds even more flavor. Of course, you can leave out the pancetta if you want a more traditional taste. **MAKES ABOUT 4 CUPS**

2 cans (28 ounces each) whole,
    imported Italian plum tomatoes,
    with their juice

$1/4$ cup olive oil

$1/3$ cup finely diced pancetta or bacon
    (about 2 ounces)

$1/4$ cup minced yellow onion

3 large cloves garlic, minced

Salt

1 tablespoon chopped fresh oregano,
    or 1 teaspoon dried oregano

Freshly ground black pepper

Sugar (optional)

1. Place a strainer over a medium-size bowl. Pour the tomatoes and their juice into the strainer, reserving the juice. Working over the bowl, break the tomatoes apart with your hands and discard any seeds, skin, or woody cores.

The tipi in the Kids' Garden at our Farm Stand is a favorite hangout for young visitors.

Finely chop the tomatoes and add them to the juice in the bowl. Set aside the tomatoes.

2. Heat the olive oil in a large saucepan over medium heat and add the pancetta. Cook the pancetta until it just begins to color, about 2 minutes. Add the onion and cook until it softens and begins to color, about 4 minutes. Stir in the garlic and cook for 1 minute.

3. Add the tomatoes and their juice and season with salt to taste. Bring the sauce to the start of a boil. Reduce the heat to low and let the sauce simmer gently until it has thickened and the flavor has intensified, about 1 hour.

4. Just before serving, stir in the oregano and taste for seasoning, adding more salt as needed and pepper to taste. If the sauce is too acidic, add ¹/₂ teaspoon of sugar, or more to taste. If not using immediately, let the sauce cool to room temperature. It can be refrigerated, covered, for up to 1 week or frozen for up to 3 months.

Armloads of statice will fill the flower buckets in front of our Farm Stand.

Creamy Macaroni and Three Cheeses

Who doesn't love mac and cheese? It's one of those nostalgic foods that takes us back to our childhood. The one here may be even better than you remember because it has three types of cheese. There's no hard-and-fast rule about the varieties of cheese, so feel free to use your favorites. I like to mix in a cupful of diced, lightly browned sausage or ham and some blanched, fresh green peas or lightly steamed broccoli to turn this into an even more interesting, hardy main dish. **SERVES 4**

1¹/₂ cups (6 ounces) dried macaroni
2 tablespoons (¹/₄ stick) unsalted butter
2 tablespoons unbleached all-purpose flour
1¹/₂ cups whole milk
2 cups (8 ounces) lightly packed, coarsely grated extra-sharp Cheddar cheese
Salt and freshly ground white pepper

1 cup (4 ounces) lightly packed, coarsely grated Gruyère or Swiss cheese
¹/₂ cup half-and-half
²/₃ cup fresh (soft) bread crumbs
¹/₃ cup freshly and finely grated Parmesan cheese or Dry Jack

1. Position a rack in the lower third of the oven and preheat the oven to 375°F.

2. Bring a large pot of salted water to a boil over high heat. Add the macaroni and cook according to the package directions. Drain the macaroni in a colander, transfer it to a large bowl, and set aside.

3. Melt the butter in a medium-size saucepan over medium heat. Add the flour and whisk constantly until smooth and thick, about 2 minutes. Slowly add the milk while whisking constantly to prevent lumps from forming. Cook, stirring frequently, until the white sauce begins to simmer and thicken, 3 to 4 minutes.

4. Add the cheddar cheese to the white sauce and stir constantly until the cheese melts. Add the cheese sauce to the macaroni and stir to combine. Season the macaroni and cheese with salt and pepper to taste.

5. Transfer the macaroni to a 2-quart shallow baking dish. Evenly sprinkle the Gruyère cheese on top of the macaroni and drizzle the half-and-half over it. The macaroni and cheese can be prepared up to this point and refrigerated, covered, for up to 2 days.

6. Combine the bread crumbs and Parmesan cheese in a small bowl and sprinkle this mixture over the macaroni and cheese.

7. Bake the macaroni and cheese until it is hot and the top is golden brown, 25 to 30 minutes (15 minutes longer if it's been refrigerated). Serve hot.

Using Pasta Water in Sauces

As pasta cooks, it releases some of its starch into the water. Before you drain the pasta, save a cupful of the cooking water in case you need to add it to the sauce. Pasta cooking water is often useful for lightly binding ingredients together, thickening a sauce slightly, or adding flavorful moisture.

Whole Wheat Penne
with Edamame, Portobellos, and Slow-Roasted Tomatoes

If prizes were awarded for great tasting and healthy pasta dishes, this would be a strong contender. Edamame is in the spotlight here. These soybeans look like little green gemstones hidden among the strips of intensely flavored tomatoes and hearty portobellos. Edamame also make an appearance in the pesto-like puree that coats the pasta. Admittedly, this dish has a lot of components, but all the elements add up to layers of incredible flavor. You'll find a streamlined version on page 202. **SERVES 4**

About 1 cup shelled, fresh or frozen
   (unthawed) edamame (soy beans,
   from 1 pound unshelled)
2 cups (8 ounces) dried whole wheat
   penne
$^{1}/_{4}$ cup olive oil
2 large portobello mushroom caps
   (about 8 ounces total), sliced
   $^{1}/_{4}$-inch thick
1 clove garlic, peeled and crushed
2 tablespoons dry white wine or water
$^{2}/_{3}$ cup sliced Slow-Roasted Tomatoes
   (page 383), or $^{2}/_{3}$ cup sliced sun-dried
   tomatoes (see sidebar, page 242)
$^{1}/_{2}$ cup minced fresh basil
1 tablespoon fresh thyme leaves
Pinch of dried red pepper flakes
Salt and freshly ground black pepper
$^{3}/_{4}$ cup Edamame "Pesto"
   (recipe follows)
$^{1}/_{2}$ cup freshly grated Parmesan cheese
Basil sprigs (optional), for garnish

1. Bring a large pot of salted water to a boil over high heat. Add the edamame and cook until tender, 4 to 5 minutes. Drain the edamame in a strainer, transfer them to a bowl, and set aside.

2. Let the water return to a boil, add the penne, and cook according to the package directions.

3. Meanwhile, heat the olive oil in a large skillet over medium heat and add the mushrooms. Cook, stirring occasionally, until they begin to soften, about 2 minutes. Add the garlic and wine and stir to combine. Cover the skillet, reduce the heat to medium low, and cook until the mushrooms are tender, about 5 minutes.

4. Add the edamame and the tomatoes, basil, thyme, and pepper flakes. Season with salt and pepper to taste. Cook until the tomatoes are warmed through, about 3 minutes.

5. Drain the penne in a colander, setting aside 1 cup of the pasta cooking water. Return the penne to the pot. Add $^{1}/_{2}$ cup of the Edamame "Pesto" and stir to combine. If the pasta is too dry, add $^{1}/_{3}$ cup or more of the reserved pasta cooking water.

6. Add the mushroom mixture to the pot with the pasta and stir to combine. Taste for seasoning, adding more Edamame "Pesto," salt, pepper, or pasta cooking water, if needed.

7. Transfer the pasta to a serving platter or pasta bowls, and sprinkle the Parmesan cheese on top. Serve immediately, garnished with basil, if desired.

Edamame "Pesto"

Edamame are fresh soybeans, pale green and oval, about the size of a fingernail. Look for them in the grocer's freezer section, although sometimes you can find them fresh. They are very nutritious, and when pureed like a pesto, with garlic, lemon, parsley, and pine nuts, their usually mild taste comes alive. Serve this unusual "pesto" on pasta, or spread it on thin baguette slices or crackers for a quick appetizer. It's great spread on sandwiches instead of mayonnaise, too.

MAKES ABOUT $^{3}/_{4}$ CUP

3/4 cup shelled, fresh or frozen
  (unthawed) edamame (soybeans,
  from 3/4 pound unshelled)
1 clove garlic
3 tablespoons pine nuts
1/2 cup (packed) flat-leaf parsley leaves
1/3 cup extra-virgin olive oil
1 tablespoon fresh lemon juice
1/4 teaspoon salt

1. Bring a large pot of salted water to a boil over high heat. Add the edamame and cook until tender, 4 to 5 minutes. Drain the edamame in a strainer and set aside to cool completely.

2. Place the edamame in a food processor or blender and add the garlic, pine nuts, and parsley. Process until coarsely pureed, stopping to scrape down the side of the bowl once or twice.

3. Add the olive oil, lemon juice, and salt and process to combine, about 30 seconds. The "pesto" will not be completely smooth. The pesto can be refrigerated, covered, for up to 5 days, or frozen for up to 3 months.

Quick Whole Wheat Shells
with Edamame and Portobellos

With my busy life, I like to streamline my cooking so there's no extra pot or bowl to wash. But even when a dish is fast, easy, and nutritious, it must also taste great. This pasta dish fits the bill. It's a quick and easy adaptation of the more complex Whole Wheat Penne with Edamame, Portobellos, and Slow-Roasted Tomatoes (see page 199). I've found that browning the mushrooms intensifies their flavor, and the garlic and red pepper flakes awaken the taste buds. Edamame (soybeans) are incredibly nutritious, and leftover green beans, when I have them, make a nice addition, too. The entire dish comes together in the time it takes to cook the pasta.

SERVES 4

3 cups whole wheat pasta shells
  (12 ounces)
About 2 cups shelled, fresh or frozen
  (unthawed) edamame (soybeans,
  from 2 pounds unshelled)
1/4 cup olive oil
2 large portobello mushroom caps
  (about 8 ounces total), sliced
  1/4-inch thick

1/2 teaspoon salt
4 large cloves garlic, thinly sliced or
  minced
Pinch of dried red pepper flakes
1 cup lightly cooked green beans,
  cut into 1-inch pieces (optional)
2 tablespoons minced fresh flat-leaf
  parsley
1/2 cup freshly grated Parmesan cheese

1. Bring a large pot of salted water to a boil over high heat. Add the pasta shells and cook according to the package directions.

2. Meanwhile, if the edamame is frozen or refrigerated, place it in a colander and rinse it under hot running water to warm it, about 1 minute. Set the edamame aside.

3. Heat the olive oil in a large skillet over medium-high heat. Add the mushrooms and cook, without stirring, until they begin to brown deeply on the bottom, 3 to 4 minutes. Add the salt and cook, stirring frequently, until the mushrooms release their liquid, 2 to 3 minutes.

4. Add the garlic and pepper flakes to the mushrooms, reduce the heat to medium-low, and cook until the garlic is soft and fragrant, about 2 minutes. Add the green beans, if using, and the parsley. Cook, stirring occasionally, until the green beans are heated through and the mushrooms are tender, 2 to 5 minutes.

5. When the pasta shells have 2 minutes of cooking time remaining, add the edamame to the pasta.

6. After the pasta shells are cooked, drain them and the edamame in a colander, then return them to the pot. Add the mushroom mixture to the pasta and edamame and stir to combine. Transfer the pasta to a serving platter or pasta bowls and sprinkle the Parmesan cheese on top. Serve immediately.

Hefty delicious portobello mushrooms are actually mature cremini mushrooms.

Sweet Pea Risotto
with Prosciutto

Spring always brings to mind tender sweet peas, and one of the perfect ways to take advantage of them is in a creamy pea risotto. Whole tender peas and a fresh pea puree add a delicate green color and flavor to the rice. I enjoy the bits of prosciutto, but for a vegetarian version, leave it out and use vegetable stock instead of chicken. The risotto makes a light main course or an elegant side dish, especially with lamb. Or, if you want to follow the Italian tradition of serving a soupy risotto as a first course, add some more stock at the end and serve the risotto in shallow bowls with soup spoons. **SERVES 4 AS A FIRST COURSE OR SIDE DISH, 2 AS A MAIN COURSE, OR CAN BE DOUBLED**

$4^{1}/_{4}$ cups Blond Chicken Stock
   (page 372)
2 cups fresh shelled English peas
3 tablespoons olive oil
1 large leek, both white and light
   green parts, rinsed well and
   thinly sliced (about 1 cup)
1 large fennel bulb, trimmed and
   thinly sliced
1 teaspoon minced garlic
1 cup arborio or carnaroli rice
$^{3}/_{4}$ cup dry white wine
2 ounces thinly sliced prosciutto,
   cut into $^{1}/_{2}$-inch squares
   (about $^{1}/_{2}$ cup)
1 cup freshly grated Parmesan cheese
2 tablespoons minced fresh tarragon
Salt and freshly ground black pepper
$^{1}/_{4}$ cup chopped fennel fronds, if any,
   for garnish

1. Pour $1^{1}/_{4}$ cups of chicken stock in a medium-size saucepan and bring to a boil over medium-high heat. Add the peas and cook until barely tender, about 5 minutes. Using a slotted spoon, remove about half of the peas from the pan and rinse them under cold water so they retain their color. Set these peas aside.

2. Let the remaining peas cook until they are very tender, 5 minutes longer. Using an immersion blender, puree the peas in the stock in the saucepan. Or let the peas and stock cool slightly, then puree them in a blender or food processor. Set the pea puree aside.

3. Place the remaining 3 cups of stock in a medium-size saucepan and bring to a gentle simmer over medium heat.

4. Meanwhile, heat the olive oil in a large skillet over medium-low heat. Add the leeks and fennel and cook, stirring occasionally, until they are soft and translucent, about 5 minutes. Add the garlic and cook until it is fragrant, about 2 minutes. Add the rice, stir to coat the grains with the olive oil, and cook until the rice is hot to the touch, about 2 minutes. Add the wine and cook until it is absorbed by the rice, about 10 minutes.

5. Add 1/2 cup of the simmering stock to the rice and cook, stirring frequently, until the liquid is absorbed. Cook the rice, adding stock 1/2 cup at a time as it is absorbed, until the rice is almost cooked through but still firm in the center when you bite into it. The total cooking time will be 20 to 30 minutes and the rice will absorb about 2 1/2 cups of the stock.

6. Add the whole peas, pea puree, and prosciutto to the risotto. Cook, stirring

constantly until heated through, 1 to 2 minutes. If you want the risotto to be soupier, add more stock.

7. Remove the skillet from the heat and add the Parmesan cheese and tarragon. Taste for seasoning and add salt, as needed, and pepper to taste. Serve the risotto with the fennel fronds, if any, sprinkled on top.

Tricolor Spaghetti Squash

Moist, pale-yellow strands of spaghetti squash make a delicious, nutritious, low calorie substitute for pasta. If you've never tried this squash, you'll be amazed at how the cooked flesh easily pulls apart in spaghettilike strands. At our Farm Stand, we serve it in a colorful casserole with wide stripes of toppings—green pesto, creamy white mozzarella cheese, and red marinara sauce—resembling the Italian flag. Of course, you can use as many or as few toppings as you'd like or bake it in individual casserole dishes. If you don't have time to make your own sauces, and if you've baked the squash in advance, a good store-bought pesto or marinara will make this quick to prepare. **SERVES 4 TO 6**

Spaghetti squash is a favorite autumn dish at our house. We love it cooked and mixed with butter, Parmesan cheese, and salt.

1 large spaghetti squash
   (about 4 pounds)
1 tablespoon olive oil, plus more for
   oiling the baking dish
Coarse (kosher) salt and freshly
   ground black pepper

1/4 cup (about 3/4 ounce) freshly
   grated Parmesan cheese
1/4 cup (about 1 ounce) shredded
   mozzarella
1/2 cup Emerald Green Pesto
   (page 193) or good-quality
   store-bought pesto
1/2 cup Farm Stand Marinara Sauce
   (page 191) or good-quality
   store-bought marinara sauce

1. Position a rack in the lower third of the oven and preheat the oven to 350°F.

2. Pierce the skin of the spaghetti squash with the tip of a knife in several places. Place the squash on a rimmed baking sheet and add water to a depth of about ¹/₈ inch. Bake the squash until a fork easily pierces its flesh, 70 to 90 minutes. Let the squash cool. Leave the oven turned on.

3. Oil an 8-inch-square baking dish, then set it aside.

4. When the squash is cool enough to handle, cut off and discard the stem end. Cut the squash in half lengthwise. Remove and discard the seeds and their stringy fibers. Scrape the squash flesh with a fork so that it pulls apart in spaghetti-like strands. Transfer the strands of squash to a large bowl and fluff them with a fork to separate them. The squash can be prepared up to this point and refrigerated, covered, for up to 3 days.

5. Add the olive oil to the squash and toss so that all the strands are coated, then season it with salt and pepper to taste. Place the squash in the prepared baking dish, pressing on it with the back of a wooden spoon to flatten it into a single layer.

6. Mix the Parmesan and mozzarella cheeses in a small bowl.

7. Starting at one edge of the baking dish and working from left to right, spread the pesto over the squash so that it covers a third of it. Spread the cheese mixture over the middle third of the squash. Finally, spread the marinara sauce over the remaining third. The idea is to form 3 vertical stripes, duplicating the green, white, and red bands on the Italian flag. Cover the baking dish tightly with aluminum foil and bake the squash for 15 minutes.

8. Uncover the baking dish and continue to bake the squash until the cheese has melted and the marinara sauce is bubbling, 10 to 15 minutes longer. Serve the squash hot.

Portobello Mushrooms
Stuffed with Spinach, Parmesan, and Fennel

My family loves meat, but I make it a point regularly to tempt them with tasty vegetarian meals. Portobello mushrooms, with their hefty size and meaty texture, are nearly as satisfying as a tender beef fillet, especially when the mushrooms are stuffed with spinach, cheese, fennel, and fresh tarragon and parsley. As an added bonus, the flavor-packed stuffing also includes shiitake mushrooms, which enhance the portobellos' earthy taste. If your guest list includes a vegan—a strict vegetarian who avoids dairy products—substitute bread crumbs for the cheese, adding just enough to lightly bind the stuffing. I like to serve these healthy mushrooms for lunch with sliced heirloom tomatoes over baby arugula to brighten up the plate. **SERVES 4**

4 large portobello mushroom caps
(about 1½ pounds total)
¼ cup olive oil, plus more for oiling
the baking dish
½ cup finely minced shallots
(from 3 medium-size shallots)
1½ cups finely minced fennel
(2 small bulbs)
4 cloves garlic, finely minced
6 ounces shiitake mushrooms, stems
discarded, caps minced (about 1 cup)
12 ounces baby spinach, cut into
ribbons (about 8 cups)
¼ cup minced fresh flat-leaf parsley
3 tablespoons minced fresh tarragon
1¼ cups freshly grated Parmesan cheese
Salt and freshly ground black pepper

1. Wipe the portobello mushroom caps clean with a damp paper towel. Using a small paring knife or teaspoon, remove the gills to create a shallow depression for the stuffing. Place the portobellos on a lightly oiled baking dish and set aside.

2. Position a rack in the center of the oven and preheat the oven to 400°F.

3. Heat the olive oil in a large skillet over medium-low heat. Add the shallots and fennel and cook until soft, 8 to 10 minutes.

4. Add the garlic and shiitake mushrooms and cook until the moisture has evaporated, about 10 minutes. Stir in the spinach and cook until it wilts, about 5 minutes, working in batches, if necessary.

5. Add the parsley, tarragon, and ½ cup of the Parmesan cheese and stir to combine. Cook until the cheese melts, about 1 minute. Season the filling with salt and pepper to taste.

6. Spoon the filling into the portobellos, mounding it slightly. Sprinkle 3 tablespoons of the remaining Parmesan cheese over each mushroom. (The mushrooms can be prepared up to this stage 4 hours ahead. Refrigerate them, covered until ready to bake.)

7. Bake the mushrooms until they are tender but not soggy and the cheese on top has browned, 20 to 25 minutes. Serve immediately.

Tilling cover crops of rye, vetch, and peas helps to enrich our soil.

"Wild" Mushroom Ragout with Polenta

The late autumn rains invite wild mushrooms to emerge from their summer hideouts and cluster under the Monterey pine and oak trees. Picking them is very risky, a task that must be left to the experts. But fortunately, mushroom farmers are learning to tame many wild varieties that were once only available from the forest. Hearty shiitakes, frilly oysters, and densely layered maitakes (hens of the woods) are only a few of these cultivated "wild" mushrooms popping up in the markets, many of them available organically. This luscious ragout provides the perfect showcase for their earthy tastes and textures, especially when served over soft polenta with a side of Sautéed Broccoli Rabe (see page 233). **SERVES 6**

Note: Chanterelles, morels, and cèpes are harder to come by, as they are not commonly cultivated, but all would be delicious in the ragout.

1¹/₂ pounds assorted mushrooms, such as shiitake, oyster, and maitake (see Note)
2 tablespoons (¹/₄ stick) unsalted butter
1 tablespoon olive oil
2 tablespoons minced shallots
1 tablespoon minced garlic
¹/₄ cup Cognac or brandy
³/₄ cup Slow Simmering Beef Stock (page 376) or store-bought low-sodium beef broth
2 tablespoons fresh thyme leaves
1 tablespoon minced fresh tarragon
1 cup heavy (whipping) cream (optional)
Salt and freshly ground black pepper
Creamy Polenta (recipe follows)

1. If using shiitake mushrooms, remove and discard the stems. For other types of mushrooms, trim the stem ends. Wipe the mushrooms clean with a damp paper towel. Cut large mushrooms into ¹/₂-inch-thick slices, leaving small mushrooms whole.

2. Heat the butter and olive oil in a large skillet over medium heat. Add the mushrooms and cook, stirring occasionally, until they begin to brown and release their juices, about 5 minutes. If the mushrooms will not all fit in one skillet, cook them in two batches until they have reduced enough to fit in a single skillet.

3. Add the shallots and garlic and continue cooking, stirring constantly, until the shallots and garlic are soft, about 2 minutes.

4. Add the Cognac, increase the heat to high, and cook until the liquid is almost all evaporated, about 1 minute.

5. Add the stock, thyme, and tarragon and bring to a boil. Reduce the heat to low and let simmer until the stock is reduced by about half, 5 to 10 minutes.

6. Stir in the cream, if using. Cook until the mushrooms are tender and the cream sauce, if any, is thick enough to coat the back of a spoon, about 10 minutes.

7. Season the mushrooms with the salt and pepper to taste and serve hot over the Creamy Polenta.

Creamy Polenta

Warm golden polenta is as soothing as mashed potatoes and just as delicious served with hearty stews or roasted meats. The half-and-half makes this polenta especially creamy, but an additional cup of stock or water can be substituted for a lighter version. **SERVES 6**

> About 3 cups Blond Chicken Stock (page 372), store-bought low-sodium chicken broth, or water
> 1 cup polenta (medium or coarse stone-ground yellow cornmeal)
> 1 cup half-and-half, or 1 additional cup chicken stock, chicken broth, or water
> Salt and freshly ground black pepper

1. Bring the stock to a simmer in a medium-size, heavy-bottomed saucepan over medium-high heat.

2. Slowly add the polenta, whisking constantly. Reduce the heat to medium-low and cook, stirring occasionally, until the cornmeal begins to absorb the liquid, about 5 minutes.

3. Add the half-and-half and let simmer gently, stirring frequently, until the polenta thickens to the consistency of soft mashed potatoes, 20 to 30 minutes.

4. Season the polenta with salt and pepper to taste. If the polenta is too thick, add additional stock or water to thin the polenta to a creamy consistency. If not serving the polenta now, transfer it to the top of a double boiler set over simmering water. Place a piece of plastic wrap or buttered waxed paper directly on the surface of the polenta to prevent a "skin" from forming. The polenta can be kept warm for up to 30 minutes.

Tangerine Tofu
with Broccoli and Red Peppers

When tofu is fried, it develops a crunchy crust yet the center remains soft. Toss these crisp cubes in an Asian citrus sauce along with sautéed red bell pepper triangles and broccoli florets and you have a memorable dish that's a bestseller at our Farm Stand's Organic Kitchen. Enjoy this on the day it's made for optimal flavor and crunch.

SERVES 4

Broccoli, a member of the cabbage family, is full of nutrients—especially vitamin C, folate (folic acid), and potassium.

3 cups canola oil

1 cup plus 1 tablespoon cornstarch

Coarse (kosher) salt and freshly
    ground black pepper

1/4 cup plus 1 tablespoon sugar

14 ounces extra-firm tofu,
    pressed and drained
    (see sidebar, this page),
    cut into 1-inch cubes

3 tablespoons toasted sesame oil

1 red bell pepper, stemmed, seeded, and
    cut into bite-size triangles

1 tablespoon minced garlic

1 tablespoon grated peeled fresh
    ginger

1/2 cup fresh tangerine or orange
    juice

1/2 cup soy sauce

4 cups bite-size broccoli florets
    (about 3 ounces), steamed until
    crisp-tender

2 teaspoons grated tangerine or
    orange zest

1. Heat the canola oil in a deep frying pan
or large, deep saucepan over medium heat
until it registers 375°F on a candy
thermometer.

2. Place 1 cup of the cornstarch in a small
bowl. Add 1/2 teaspoon of salt, 1/4 teaspoon
of pepper, and 1 tablespoon of the sugar.
Whisk to combine.

3. Place the tofu in a large bowl and add
the cornstarch mixture. Toss to combine.

4. Working in small batches, shake off
any excess cornstarch, then use a slotted
spoon or strainer to lower the tofu into the
oil and fry until lightly golden and crisp,
about 5 minutes. Drain the tofu on paper
towels. (Once cool, the canola oil can be
strained and set aside for another use.)

5. Heat the sesame oil in a small skillet
over medium heat. Add the bell pepper
and cook, stirring constantly, until crisp-
tender, about 2 minutes. Using a slotted
spoon, transfer the peppers to a large
bowl.

6. Decrease the heat to low and add the
garlic and ginger to the skillet. Cook,
stirring frequently, until fragrant, 1 to 2
minutes. Add the tangerine juice, soy
sauce, and the remaining 1/4 cup of sugar.
Increase the heat to high and bring to
a boil.

7. Place the remaining 1 tablespoon of
cornstarch in a small bowl and add 1
tablespoon of water. Stir to blend. Add
this mixture to the skillet and cook until
the sauce thickens, 3 to 5 minutes.

8. Add the broccoli and fried tofu to the
bowl with the red pepper triangles and
toss to combine. Add the tangerine sauce
and stir gently to coat. Add the tangerine
zest and season the tofu with salt and
pepper to taste. The tofu can be served
warm or at room temperature.

How to Press and Drain Tofu

If your tofu is
packed in water,
you need to press out
the excess liquid to
get a crisp exterior
when it's fried. To
make it possible for
the liquid to drain
into the sink, lean a
cutting board on a
small object so that
the board tilts slightly
over the sink edge.
Cover the board with
a clean dish towel and
place the block
of tofu on top. Cover
the tofu with a second
dish towel and place
another cutting board
on top. Placing several
heavy cans on the
cutting board will
weigh it down and
force the water out
of the tofu, into the
towels and sink.
Let the tofu drain
for about 30 minutes,
then pat it dry with
paper towels.

Stir-Fried Tofu
with Green Beans and Shiitake Mushrooms

*F*lashes of color from carrot, sweet red bell pepper, and green and wax beans brighten this stir-fry that features tender shiitakes and teriyaki-marinated tofu. While you can use bottled teriyaki sauce, it can't touch our easy homemade version. All stir-fry dishes require a fair amount of cutting and chopping, but the cooking goes very quickly. You can prepare the vegetables a day in advance and refrigerate them separately until it's time to heat up the wok. This stir-fry is delicious over Asian soba (buckwheat) noodles or steamed rice. **SERVES 4 TO 6**

7 ounces extra-firm tofu, cut into
  $3/4$-inch cubes
$1/4$ cup Teriyaki Sauce, homemade
  (page 378) or store-bought
4 ounces green beans and/or
  yellow wax beans, trimmed and
  cut into 1-inch lengths
  (about 2 cups)
1 tablespoon peanut oil
2 tablespoons toasted sesame oil
4 ounces shiitake mushrooms,
  stems discarded, caps cut into
  $1/3$-inch slices (about 2 cups)
1 medium-size carrot, cut in half
  lengthwise, then in $1/8$-inch
  half-moon slices
$1/2$ red bell pepper, stemmed, seeded,
  and cut into $1/4$-inch thick strips
1 jalapeño pepper, thinly sliced
  crosswise with seeds, or
  $1/4$ teaspoon dried red pepper
  flakes
2 tablespoons soy sauce or tamari
1 tablespoon grated peeled fresh
  ginger
1 teaspoon minced garlic
4 scallions, including whites and
  3 inches of green, cut in
  $1/2$-inch pieces

$1/4$ cup toasted sesame seeds
  (see box, page 273), for garnish
2 fresh or frozen Kaffir lime leaves
  (optional; see sidebar, page 47),
  minced, for garnish

1. Combine the tofu cubes and teriyaki sauce in a small bowl and let them marinate at room temperature for at least 1 hour or up to 24 hours.

2. Meanwhile, fill a large bowl of water with ice cubes and set aside.

3. Bring a large pot of salted water to a boil over high heat. Add the beans and cook for 2 minutes to set the color. Immediately drain the beans in a colander, then plunge them into the bowl of ice water to stop the cooking. Drain the beans again in the colander and set aside.

4. When the tofu has finished marinating, heat the peanut oil and 1 tablespoon of the sesame oil in a large skillet or wok over medium-high heat. Add the mushrooms and cook, stirring constantly, until just tender, about 3 minutes. Transfer the mushrooms to a bowl and set them aside.

5. Add the remaining 1 tablespoon of sesame oil to the skillet. Add the carrot, bell pepper, jalapeño, soy sauce, ginger, and garlic and cook, stirring constantly, until the bell pepper is crisp-tender, about 2 minutes.

6. Add the scallions, beans, and tofu with its teriyaki marinade and cook, stirring constantly, for 2 minutes. Add the mushrooms and cook, stirring constantly, until the vegetables are heated through, about 2 minutes.

7. Sprinkle the sesame seeds and lime leaves, if using, on top of the stir-fry, and serve immediately.

Hoisin Tofu Snacks

*P*acked with protein, warm, crisp, baked tofu is a great snack, or served over rice with steamed veggies, it makes a healthy meal. Cold tofu snacks are wonderful in sandwiches—we like them on multi-grain bread spread with hummus or mustard, along with avocados, lettuce, and ripe tomatoes. It's also great cut into bite-size "croutons" and served on salad. If you're making croutons in advance, allow them to cool completely, then cut them before you refrigerate them.

14 to 16 ounces extra-firm tofu
1/2 cup Hoisin Sauce from Scratch
    (page 379)
2 tablespoons tamari or soy sauce
1 tablespoon hulled sesame seeds
    (optional)

1. Preheat the oven to 350°F.

2. Cut the tofu into rectangles, approximately 1 inch wide by 2 inches long by 1/3-inch thick. Arrange the pieces in a baking pan just large enough to hold them in a single layer. To make sure the tofu get crispy all over, the slices should be slightly separated.

3. Combine the Hoisin Sauce, tamari, and sesame seeds, if using, in a small bowl and pour the mixture over the tofu. Turn the tofu so that both sides are evenly coated.

4. Bake for 30 minutes. Remove the pan from the oven and use a spatula and large spoon to flip the tofu pieces. Return the pan to the oven and bake for 20 minutes longer. Then turn the tofu over again, and bake until deep golden brown, 10 minutes more. Remove the pan from the oven and allow the tofu to cool for at least 5 minutes. The longer it sits out, the firmer the tofu will become. Serve warm. The tofu snacks will keep, covered, in the refrigerator for up to 3 days (although they will lose their crispness).

Fresh Tomato Pizza
with Pesto, Goat Cheese, and Arugula

This summertime favorite begins with a light layer of pesto that's embellished with slices of ripe tomato and dots of creamy goat cheese. It's a beautiful pizza, especially if you mix slices of red and yellow tomatoes. The peppery arugula, tossed with olive oil, goes on just before serving. The heat from the pizza wilts the greens by the time it reaches your lips! **MAKES 1 PIZZA, 10 TO 12 INCHES IN DIAMETER**

Dough for 1 pizza (recipe follows), freshly made or frozen (thawed at room temperature)

Unbleached all-purpose flour, for dusting the work surface

Cornmeal, for dusting the pizza paddle

$1/4$ cup Emerald Green Pesto (page 192)

1 medium-size, ripe red or yellow tomato, thinly sliced

$1^1/2$ ounces (about $1/3$ cup) goat cheese, crumbled

1 ounce (about $1^1/2$ cups) baby arugula

2 teaspoons olive oil

1. If you're using dough that was frozen, once it has thawed, let it sit, covered with a damp towel, at room temperature until it has almost doubled in size, 30 minutes to 1 hour. If the room is cool, it may take longer for the dough to rise. Freshly made dough doesn't need this second rise.

2. Meanwhile, position a rack at the lowest position in the oven and place a pizza stone or baking tiles, if using, on the rack. Preheat the oven to 500°F for at least 30 minutes so that the stone will be hot.

3. Lightly flour the work surface and a rolling pin, if using. Generously dust a pizza paddle (see box, page 218) with cornmeal. Or, turn a baking sheet upside down and dust it with cornmeal.

4. Shape the dough by patting it into a flat, round disk, then roll it out on the work surface into a 10- to 12-inch circle, $1/8$- to $1/4$-inch thick. Or use your hands to gently stretch the dough into shape. Transfer the dough to the prepared pizza paddle or baking sheet.

5. Working quickly, spread a light coat of the pesto over the dough, leaving 1 inch around the edge bare. Arrange the tomato slices and goat cheese on top of the pesto.

6. Slide the pizza off the paddle or baking sheet onto the preheated stone, using a jerking motion to release it. Bake the pizza until the crust is golden brown on the bottom and the toppings are sizzling hot, 5 to 10 minutes.

7. Meanwhile, place the arugula in a small bowl and toss it with the olive oil.

Pizza Creations

Kids love making their own individual-size pizzas using their favorite ingredients. It's hard to resist loading up a pizza, but encourage everyone to use a light hand with the sauces and toppings. The pizzas will be easier to cook and the crust will be crisper. You'll find a recipe for pizza dough on page 218.

These are two Goodman family favorites:

■ **Prosciutto and Black Olive Pizza:** Spread a thin layer of marinara sauce on the dough and top it with grated mozzarella cheese, fresh tomato slices, sliced prosciutto, and kalamata olives.

■ **Sausage and Mushroom Pizza:** Spread a thin layer of marinara sauce on the dough and top it with grated mozzarella cheese, slices of smoked, cooked sausage, and thinly sliced mushrooms and yellow onions.

Handy Pizza Tools

If you like to make pizzas at home, here are two tools worth investing in.

Pizza stone

A ceramic pizza stone (or a set of baking tiles) absorbs the oven's heat, turning pizza crust golden brown and crisp. If you don't have a pizza stone, you can bake the pizza in a pizza pan or on a large baking sheet, but your crust will be softer and lighter in color. If you use a baking sheet, you can turn it upside down so the rim doesn't get in the way. If you are shopping for a pizza stone, look for one with handles—it will be easier to put in and take out of the oven.

Pizza paddle

The best tool for transporting a pizza to and from the oven is a large pizza paddle, also called a pizza peel. The handle keeps you well away from the oven heat as you slide the pizza in and out.

8. Remove the pizza from the oven by sliding the paddle or baking sheet under it or, if your pizza stone has handles, by removing the entire stone with the pizza on it. Slide the pizza onto a cutting board. Sprinkle the arugula over the pizza, then cut it into wedges and serve hot.

Pizza Dough

This dough is easy to make and freezes well. If you prefer, you can knead the dough by hand until it is smooth and elastic instead of using a stand mixer. **MAKES ENOUGH DOUGH FOR 4 PIZZAS, 10 TO 12 INCHES IN DIAMETER**

2 packages active dry yeast
    ($1/4$ ounce each)
2 tablespoons sugar
3 tablespoons olive oil, plus more for
    oiling the bowl
$3^1/2$ cups unbleached all-purpose flour,
    plus more for dusting the dough
$1/2$ cup white bread flour, or more as
    needed
1 tablespoon coarse (kosher) salt

1. Place the yeast and sugar in a small bowl. Add $1^1/2$ cups of lukewarm water (105° to 115°F on an instant-read thermometer) and whisk to blend. Let the yeast mixture sit until it begins to foam, about 5 minutes. Add the olive oil to the yeast mixture and stir to combine.

2. Place the all-purpose flour, $1/2$ cup of bread flour, and the salt in the bowl of a heavy-duty stand mixer fitted with a hook attachment. Add the yeast mixture and mix on low speed until the dough is smooth, elastic, and only slightly sticky, 10 to 15 minutes. (Stop the mixer and push the dough back into the bowl if it climbs up the hook.) If the dough seems too sticky, add 2 more tablespoons of bread flour and mix 2 minutes longer.

3. Transfer the dough to a large, lightly oiled bowl. Turn the dough over in the bowl so that it is lightly coated in oil. Cover the bowl with a clean, damp dish towel or with plastic wrap. Let the dough sit in a warm (90° to 110°F), draft-free spot until it has doubled in size, $1^1/2$ to 2 hours (an oven heated only by the pilot light is a good place).

4. Punch down the dough. If you want to make 10- to 12-inch pizzas, divide the dough into 4 equal pieces. For smaller, individual pizzas, divide the dough into 8 equal pieces. Keep the pieces you're not working with covered with the damp towel.

5. Form a piece of dough into a ball: Flour your hands, then pull the opposite edges of a piece of dough toward the center and pinch them together to form a seal. Working around the circumference, continue pulling and pinching the dough until a smooth, tight ball forms. Repeat with the remaining pieces of dough. The dough is now ready to be used to make a pizza, following the instructions in the recipe on page 217. Or, wrap the balls of dough individually in plastic wrap. They can be refrigerated for up to 24 hours or frozen for up to 2 months. Let the dough thaw in the refrigerator overnight before using. The baking time will be the same whether you make large or small pizzas.

Chapter 7

Side Dishes

I still feel a sense of awe every time I walk through a field of beautiful baby spinach. It's so green and radiant . . . just so alive! How different this spinach tastes from the canned version many of us grew up eating. As a parent, I've learned that kids will love practically any vegetable if their first taste of it is fresh and delicious. When children are given perfectly roasted asparagus spears they can eat with their fingers, chances are they will grow up loving asparagus. And sweet peas nibbled straight from the pod awaken kids' taste buds in a way that canned peas never will.

Scarlet runner beans.

Fresh vegetables are the answer when I'm looking for delicious ways to satisfy my family's appetite while feeding them the healthiest food possible. My daughter, Marea, recently discovered that she loves the sweet, delicate taste of sautéed baby bok choy. Fresh beet greens are also delectable when stir-fried, and the same cooking method works well for Swiss chard, collards, or kale. For a quick side dish, a skillet of crisp-tender zucchini topped with melted cheese is one my family's favorites. When I have more time and fava beans are in season, a salad combining the beans with orzo pasta and sun-dried tomatoes makes a memorable dish.

It's worth seeking out a variety of potatoes. Thinly sliced yellow-fleshed potatoes, like Yukon Golds, turn brown and crisp in Sarah's Potato-Thyme Tart. Thin-skinned fingerling potatoes don't need to be peeled for yummy Blue Cheese Smashed Potatoes. And there's always room on our plate for russets, which are the best choice for Twice-Baked Potatoes.

An interesting selection of side dishes always enlivens the table with a variety of colors, tastes, and textures. These recipes invite you to taste the cornucopia of organic vegetables and grains that are starting to appear at farmers' markets, produce stands, and grocery stores across the nation. We hope to awaken you to the vibrant flavors and colors of the farm.

Facing Page:
Twice-Baked Potatoes
(page 250).

Artichokes left to mature transform into beautiful purple flowers.

Whole Artichokes
with Dipping Sauces

It must have been a very hungry person who first figured out how to eat this prickly thistle! But aren't we glad that person did? There's no other vegetable quite like it. Artichokes are a favorite at our house. We love to break off the thick leaves, dip them in a flavorful sauce, and scrape off the flesh with our teeth. When all the tough leaves are gone, there's a hidden treasure—the tasty, tender heart with its meaty bottom. Practically any salad dressing can double as a dip, but artichokes have a special affinity for my lemony vinaigrette spiked with mustard and garlic. For a thicker dip with an unusual peppery note, try a creamy aioli with arugula and jalapeño. **SERVES 4**

4 medium-size artichokes
(see box, this page)
1 lemon, cut in half
Lemon Vinaigrette (page 97)
or Jalapeño Arugula Aioli
(recipe follows)

1. Bring a large-size pot of salted water to a boil over high heat.

2. Meanwhile, using a very sharp, stainless steel knife, cut off the top third of each artichoke. Discard this and the small tough outer leaves at the stem end. Using kitchen scissors, snip the prickly tips off the remaining leaves. Cut the stems off so the artichokes will stand upright (if you want to eat the stems, leave about an inch and peel it with a vegetable peeler). Rub the cut

FARM FRESH

artichokes

Artichokes are grown year-round, but they're at their best in the spring and again in the fall. They come in a wide range of sizes, from tiny babies to huge ones the size of softballs. Regardless of how big they are, the tastiest artichokes are the freshest ones. Look for an artichoke that feels heavy for its size, with tightly closed, vibrant-colored leaves. Most artichokes in the supermarket are green, but some specialty farmers are introducing a European variety that's deep purple. The gorgeous color fades when cooked, but the artichokes are still delicious. During the colder months, you may find artichokes with dark spots. These chokes are called frost kissed and some say that artichokes with a little bite of frost have a nuttier flavor. However, avoid artichokes that have extensive damage or a brownish color.

Generally, artichokes with a round, rather than conical, shape will have a larger heart—the tender leaves and meaty bottom at the artichoke's base. Green Globe artichokes are especially prized for their big hearts. Sometimes they have prickly thorns, especially in the summer and fall, but these are easy to snip off with kitchen shears. Other varieties, such as the Imperial Star, can be thornless but not as meaty.

surfaces of the artichoke with the cut side of the lemon to prevent them from discoloring.

3. Squeeze the juice from the lemon halves and add it to the boiling water. Add the artichokes to the pot and place a plate on top of them to keep them submerged.

4. Cover the pot, reduce the heat to low or medium-low, and let the artichokes simmer until the base of each (or the stem if using), can be easily pierced with a small knife, 15 to 35 minutes, depending on the size of the artichoke.

5. Place the artichokes upside down on a wire rack to drain. When cool enough to handle, gently spread the leaves open with your fingers and scrape out the fuzzy choke with a small serrated grapefruit spoon. Serve slightly warm or at room temperature with the aioli or vinaigrette on the side.

Jalapeño Arugula Aioli

The customers at our Farm Stand's Organic Kitchen crave this creamy green sauce that, despite its spicy name, has just a slight bite. Arugula gives the aioli its peppery freshness, and baby spinach provides the delicate green color. While some jalapeño peppers are fairly mild, others are quite hot. If the jalapeños are too hot for your taste, use less and leave out the ribs and seeds. Fresh and piquant, arugula aioli makes a great dip for raw vegetables, *steamed artichokes, and chips. Its devotees also love it spread on flank steak sandwiches or drizzled over beef kebabs.* **MAKES ABOUT 1 1/2 CUPS**

1 or 2 fresh jalapeño peppers, to taste
2 small cloves garlic
1 large egg (see Note)
1 tablespoon Dijon mustard
Grated zest of 1 lemon
1 tablespoon fresh lemon juice
1 packed cup baby arugula
1 packed cup baby spinach
1/4 teaspoon salt, or more to taste
1/2 cup olive oil
1/2 cup canola oil

1. Cut off and discard the stem end of the jalapeño(s). Cut the jalapeño(s) into quarters and place in a food processor (do not remove the seeds and ribs). Add the garlic and pulse until finely minced. Add the egg, mustard, lemon zest and juice, arugula, spinach, and salt to the food processor and process until smooth.

2. With the machine running, add the olive and canola oils in a slow, steady stream. Taste for seasoning, adding more salt, if needed. Transfer the aioli to a clean container and cover it. Refrigerate the aioli for at least 3 hours before serving to allow the flavors to develop. The aioli can be refrigerated, covered, for up to 3 days.

Note: The egg in this aioli remains uncooked, so if you decide to make it, be sure to use only a very fresh egg that has been kept refrigerated.

artichoke hearts and bottoms

The artichoke heart is what remains when the tough leaves and fuzzy choke are removed, leaving only the tender greenish-yellow leaves attached to the meaty bottom. Trimmed and cooked, the entire artichoke heart is edible.

Roasted Balsamic Artichoke Bottoms (see this page) calls for trimming off the tender leaves of the heart and using only the fleshy artichoke bottom and the edible stem.

To trim an artichoke down to its bottom, remove the outer leaves, starting at the base, by bending back a leaf until it snaps, then pulling down on it to remove the leaf and some of the tough outer flesh. Continue working around the artichoke until only the pale inner leaves remain.

Using a sharp knife, cut off the inner leaves, leaving behind the fuzzy choke, artichoke bottom, and stem. Trim off the tip of the stem and discard it, leaving the rest of the stem attached. Using a vegetable peeler or paring knife, trim away the remaining tough, outer layer of the artichoke bottom and stem. While you work, place trimmed artichokes in water mixed with lemon juice to help prevent them from turning brown.

Once trimmed, the artichoke bottom should be pale, with none of the darker green remaining. Scrape out the fuzzy choke with the tip of a spoon and discard the choke. A serrated grapefruit spoon works well for this, if you have one.

Roasted Balsamic Artichoke Bottoms

It's not surprising that artichokes are a local favorite, especially since Castroville, the "Artichoke Capital of the World," is right up the coast. Unadorned, artichokes are high in fiber and vitamin C and low in calories. The edible part of a large one can have as few as twenty-five calories. The balsamic vinegar marinade here, using only a bit of olive oil and honey, helps keep the calorie count low, and roasting transforms the marinade into a flavorful glaze. Artichokes thrive year-round, but are bountiful from March to May, making this a perfect spring appetizer or side dish. **SERVES 4**

1/2 cup balsamic vinegar
2 cloves garlic, minced
1 tablespoon minced shallot
1 tablespoon fresh thyme leaves
4 medium-size artichokes
   (see box, page 222)
2 tablespoons honey
2 tablespoons extra-virgin olive oil
Coarse (kosher) salt and freshly
   ground black pepper

During a spring farm tour, kids discover crowning treasures: beautiful, ripe artichokes.

1. Combine the vinegar, garlic, shallot, and thyme in a medium-size bowl and set aside.

2. Trim an artichoke down to its bottom (see box, page 225), leaving most of the stem attached. Slice the trimmed artichoke in half through the stem and place it in the vinegar marinade. Repeat with the remaining artichokes.

3. Toss the artichokes in the vinegar marinade to coat. Cover the bowl and let the artichokes marinate at room temperature for 2 to 3 hours, tossing occasionally.

4. Position a rack in the center of the oven and preheat the oven to 375°F.

5. Using tongs, remove the artichoke halves from the marinade and place them, cut side down, in a roasting pan. Add the honey to the marinade and whisk to blend. Pour this mixture over the artichokes.

6. Cover the roasting pan with aluminum foil. Bake the artichokes for 20 minutes. Remove the foil and bake the artichokes, uncovered, until they are tender when pierced with the tip of a knife and the marinade has reduced to a glaze, 10 to 15 minutes longer.

7. Place each on a serving plate. Drizzle the olive oil over the artichokes and season them with salt and pepper to taste. Serve hot or at room temperature.

Green globe artichokes are prized for their tender hearts and large, meaty bottoms.

Roasted Asparagus

We get excited when the first asparagus of spring starts to emerge. Beginning in early March, we search the asparagus beds, looking for tender shoots breaking through the moist soil after lying dormant all winter. Fresh, local asparagus is so tender and delicious that little work is needed to bring out its flavor. Simply steamed, it makes a delicious side dish. But roasting concentrates the flavor even more, and it's just as easy, especially if your oven is already warm. A drizzling of truffle oil just before serving will add an intriguing aroma to the asparagus. Asparagus is delicious with Kathy's Rosemary-Roasted Chicken (see page 136), and you can bake it while the chicken rests. **SERVES 4**

1 pound asparagus, woody ends
    trimmed (see box, this page)
2 tablespoons olive oil
Salt and freshly ground black pepper
Truffle oil (optional)

1. Position a rack in the center of the oven and preheat the oven to 450°F.

2. Rinse the asparagus and dry it with paper towels. Arrange the asparagus in a shallow baking dish in a single layer with the tips all facing in the same direction for easier serving.

3. Drizzle the olive oil over the asparagus spears and roll them in the pan until they are coated. Sprinkle salt and pepper over the asparagus.

4. Bake the asparagus until the spears are lightly browned, just tender, and easily pierced with the tip of a knife, 5 to 10 minutes (thicker spears will take longer than thin ones). Serve the asparagus hot or at room temperature, with a little truffle oil, if desired, drizzled on top.

Grilling Asparagus

Grilling concentrates the flavor of asparagus while adding a smoky flavor that's irresistible. Handling individual spears on the grill can be tricky, though, because they are hard to turn and can fall between the grates. To make the job easier, create an asparagus "raft" by running two thin bamboo skewers, spaced two or three inches apart, through the bottom ends of about six asparagus spears. Brush both sides of the spears with olive oil and sprinkle them with salt and pepper. Grill the asparagus over medium heat for 3 minutes. Turn the asparagus "raft" over and cook the spears until they are lightly browned, just tender, 3 to 6 minutes longer.

FARM FRESH

asparagus

Some people insist that thick asparagus is best, while others argue for thin. Both are delicious, but choose asparagus spears of equal thickness so they will cook evenly.

Avoid buying asparagus that looks dried out or slimy, or with tips that are starting to yellow or flower. Asparagus spears break easily where the tender stem turns woody, so the simplest way to trim asparagus is to bend a spear until it snaps in two.

Thin asparagus spears and very fresh thick ones don't need to be peeled. If you have thick spears that aren't just-picked fresh, peel the stems with a vegetable peeler before cooking so they will be tender from tip to end.

Farm Stand Beet Salad

Carmel Valley's weather is so mild that we can grow beets year round, giving us a steady supply for our roasted beet salad. Lightly dressed in a tasty vinaigrette, beets take on a jewel-like glow, making this a lovely side dish on its own or as a topping for an arugula or mixed baby green salad. I love the way red and gold beets look together, so I make two separate batches, and combine them just before serving so the colors stay vibrant. **SERVES 4**

Note: Look for baby beets that are about the size of golf balls. If you use larger beets, increase the cooking time by 15 to 30 minutes.

1 pound Roasted Baby Beets (recipe follows), room temperature, quartered

$1/2$ cup thinly sliced red onion

1 teaspoon fresh thyme leaves or chopped fresh tarragon leaves

2 tablespoons Classic Red Wine Vinaigrette (page 95) or Hazelnut Tarragon Vinaigrette (page 100), or more to taste

Salt and freshly ground black pepper

Place the beets, onion, and thyme in a medium-size bowl and add the vinaigrette. Season with salt and pepper, and stir to combine. Add more vinaigrette if needed. The salad tastes best at room temperature, but can be served chilled. The beets can be refrigerated, covered, for up to 3 days.

Roasted Baby Beets

Freshly roasted beets are a far cry from the canned beets I remember from my childhood. Baby golden or ruby red beets are sweet and lovely, but larger beets are quicker to peel, and both large and small beets taste equally delicious. In any case, try to select beets that are similar in size so they will cook at the same rate. Since they will keep for several

FARM FRESH

beets

When you go to a farm stand or specialty market, you may find red beets, golden beets, even red-and-white striped Chioggia beets that look like a bull's eye when sliced. Usually beets are cooked, but for a change, try grating raw gold or striped beets over a salad. Beet roots have the highest sugar content of any vegetable, but they are high in fiber and vitamin C. The greens are even better for you, offering just as much fiber and even higher levels of vitamins A and C.

When buying beets, select ones with firm, unblemished skins. You can store them in the refrigerator for up to three weeks. If you buy beets with their greens attached, you'll know they were recently picked. Because the greens draw moisture from the beets, cut them off before you store the beets, leaving about an inch of stem attached. But don't automatically toss the greens. Tiny, tender leaves can be added raw to mixed baby salad greens. If the leaves are a bit bitter but are still young and fresh, they will be delicious braised or stir-fried by themselves or with a mix of other sturdy greens, such as kale, chard, or collards (see the recipe on page 230).

days, roast extra beets to add to salads at the last minute or to warm as a quick side dish, drizzled with extra-virgin olive oil and balsamic vinegar. Or, quarter roasted baby beets and use them to garnish Stir-Fried Sesame Beet Greens (see page 230).

SERVES 4

1 pound baby beets, preferably
    an assortment of varieties
    (see Note, facing page)
1 tablespoon olive oil
Salt and freshly ground black pepper

1. Position a rack in the center of the oven and preheat the oven to 400°F.

2. Trim off the beet greens, leaving the stringy root end and about 1/2 inch of the stem attached. Set the beet greens aside for another use (see box, facing page). Rinse the beets under cool water and gently scrub them with a vegetable brush to remove any dirt. Dry the beets with paper towels.

3. Place the beets in a shallow baking dish and coat them with the olive oil. Sprinkle salt and pepper over the beets. Tightly cover the baking dish with aluminum foil.

4. Bake the beets until they are tender when pierced with the tip of a knife, 35 to 45 minutes (larger beets will take longer).

5. Let the beets cool enough to handle, then, using a paring knife, remove the stems and stringy roots and slip off the skins. If you are using different colored beets, cook and keep each variety separate until serving so that the colors do not bleed together. The beets can rest for up to 2 hours at room temperature. They can be refrigerated, covered, for up to 3 days.

Slice into a Chioggia beet and discover a delightful surprise—a red and white bull's-eye!

Stir-Fried Sesame Beet Greens

When you buy beets with their greens still attached, you know you are getting them freshly picked. Most people cook only the ruby or golden beet roots, but it's a shame to waste the greens since they are mild, tender, and surprisingly delicious when stir-fried with garlic and ginger. The baby beet greens of spring cook up fast, but if you can find only mature, but unblemished, greens, they will work as well. Just allow a little longer for them to cook. If you don't have beet greens, try this with kale, chard, or mustard greens. **SERVES 4**

Just-picked Earthbound Farm beets, ready for sale.

1 tablespoon toasted sesame oil
1 tablespoon peanut oil
2 cloves garlic, peeled and cut in half
8 slices (¹/₈-inch thick) fresh unpeeled ginger
12 ounces stemmed baby beet greens, rinsed, drained, and cut into 1-inch slices (about 8 cups)
1 tablespoon soy sauce
Pinch of sugar
1 tablespoon toasted sesame seeds (see box, page 273)

1. Heat the sesame oil and peanut oil in a large skillet over medium heat. Add the garlic and ginger and cook, stirring constantly, until fragrant, about 2 minutes.

2. Add the beet greens and ¹/₄ cup of water. Increase the heat to medium-high and cook, stirring frequently, until the water evaporates and the greens wilt and become tender, 3 to 5 minutes. Add the soy sauce and sugar and stir to combine.

3. Remove and discard the garlic and ginger slices. Transfer the greens to a platter and sprinkle the sesame seeds on top. Serve hot.

Sautéed Ginger Baby Bok Choy

Baby bok choy is as tasty as it is pretty. Its light green leaves are small enough to fit in the palm of your hand, and the creamy white stems turn tender and sweet when cooked. Bok choy is as nutritious as cabbage and broccoli, with the added bonus of being a good source of calcium. Briefly blanching the bok choy in boiling water makes it tender and juicy and neutralizes any bitterness. Bok choy's mild taste goes great with Ginger Lime Salmon (see page 164) or Grilled Pork Tenderloin with Spiced Orange Sauce (see page 123). **SERVES 4**

ginger

Ginger adds a distinctive spicy heat and aroma to foods and beverages as wide-ranging as gingerbread cookies, ginger ale, and stir-fries. It benefits extend beyond great taste because it contains health-promoting anti-oxidants and helps relieve inflammation. You can buy ginger in three different forms: as a fresh root, crystallized, and ground. Each has its own specific uses for cooking; you cannot substitute one for another.

Fresh ginger: Fresh ginger is most often used as an aromatic spice in stir-fries and other savory dishes. Frequently, grocery stores sell it loose in the produce section so you can break off just the amount you want to buy. Look for roots with tan, smooth skin, without wrinkles or cracks, and store them in a cool, dark place. When preparing fresh ginger, cut off any knobby or dry parts and remove the skin before grating or chopping the fibrous flesh. Instead of a vegetable peeler or paring knife, try using the edge of a spoon to scrape away the skin, leaving the flesh intact. A small ceramic ginger grater, available in Asian markets and kitchen stores, does a fine job of grating the root, and it helps you capture the spicy juice. However, if you don't have a ceramic grater, a hand-held or metal box grater works also. Cut off and discard the stringy fibers that remain behind when you grate the flesh.

Crystallized ginger: Crystallized, or candied ginger, is fresh ginger that has been cooked in syrup and coated with sugar. Its spicy-sweet taste is delicious in baked goods, desserts, or simply eaten like candy. It's usually available in the bulk section of health food stores or in bags near the dried fruits. Sometimes small bottles of crystallized ginger are sold in the spice section, but this form is usually more expensive. Store crystallized ginger at room temperature in a tightly sealed jar or plastic bag.

Ground ginger: Ground dried ginger is used in baked goods and as an ingredient in curry spice blends. Look for it in the spice section of the supermarket. Buy from a store with a brisk turnover, so you'll know your spice is fresh.

Coarse (kosher) salt

6 heads baby bok choy, cut in half lengthwise

2 tablespoons toasted sesame oil

1 tablespoon grated peeled fresh ginger

1/8 teaspoon red pepper flakes

Teriyaki sauce, homemade (page 378) or store-bought (optional)

1. Bring 2 quarts of water to a boil in a large pot over high heat. Add 1 tablespoon of salt and the bok choy and cook for 1 minute. Drain the bok choy well in a colander, then pat it dry with paper towels.

2. Heat the sesame oil in a large, nonstick skillet over medium heat. Add the bok choy, ginger, and red pepper flakes and cook, turning occasionally, until the bok choy is crisp-tender and lightly browned on both sides, 5 to 8 minutes. Brush the bok choy with teriyaki sauce, if desired, and serve immediately.

Bacon and Broccoli Salad

You'll get rave reviews with this salad. Maybe it's the crisp crunch of the raw broccoli. Or maybe it's the unexpected accents of sweet raisins and salty sunflower seeds. Either way, this is a great picnic or potluck salad that can be made a day ahead. If you're traveling a distance, be sure to pack the salad with ice to keep the mayonnaise cool. You can save time by buying a package of precut broccoli florets. Experiment with substituting dried cranberries for the raisins or adding a quarter cup of walnuts or pine nuts—whatever catches your fancy. **SERVES 6**

8 ounces (5 to 6 slices) lean, thick-cut
    bacon, cut in $^1/_3$-inch dice
$^2/_3$ cup mayonnaise
2 tablespoons distilled white vinegar or
    cider vinegar
$^1/_4$ cup honey or sugar
6 cups uncooked bite-size broccoli florets
    (from about 3 pounds of broccoli)
$^1/_3$ cup finely minced red onion
    (from 1 small onion)
$^1/_4$ cup raisins
2 tablespoons salted sunflower seeds

1. Cook the bacon in a large skillet over medium heat, turning occasionally, until brown and crisp, about 4 minutes. Transfer the bacon to paper towels to drain and discard the fat.

2. Place the mayonnaise, vinegar, and honey in a large bowl and whisk until the dressing is smooth.

3. Add the broccoli and stir until the florets are uniformly coated.

4. Add the onion, raisins, sunflower seeds, and bacon to the broccoli and stir to combine. Refrigerate the salad, covered, for at least 2 hours before serving to allow the flavors to develop. The salad tastes best the day it's made; it can be refrigerated, covered, for up to 24 hours, however the bacon will lose its crispness.

Light from the winter sun glows through a broccoli leaf.

Sautéed Broccoli Rabe

Broccoli rabe—also known as broccoli raab or rapini—is quite different from broccoli. Common broccoli is a big showy bunch of florets and a chunky stem; its leaves are throwaways. Broccoli rabe lush saw-toothed leaves are as tasty as its tiny florets. Broccoli rabe's slightly bitter flavor is highly prized in Italy and China alike and is becoming increasingly popular here in the United States. When shopping, look for thin stems, abundant dark-green leaves, and tightly closed florets. If you are lucky enough to find very young, fresh broccoli rabe, you won't need to blanch it in boiling water, just sauté the tender stems whole or chopped into bite-size pieces. For extra flavor, serve the sautéed broccoli rabe drizzled with your best olive oil and/or splashed with a little balsamic or red wine vinegar. **SERVES 4**

1 pound broccoli rabe, tough stems and
    damaged leaves discarded
Coarse (kosher) salt
3 tablespoons olive oil
2 cloves garlic, peeled and crushed
1 small dried red pepper, such as cayenne

1. Fill a large bowl of water with ice cubes and set it aside.

2. Bring 2 quarts of water to a boil in a large pot over high heat. Add the broccoli rabe and some salt and cook for 1 minute. Drain the broccoli rabe in a colander, then plunge the greens into the bowl of ice water to stop the cooking and preserve the bright green color. Thoroughly drain the broccoli rabe again in the colander, then pat it dry with paper towels.

3. Heat the olive oil in a large skillet over medium heat. Add the garlic and red pepper. Cook, stirring constantly, until the oil is flavored, about 3 minutes. Remove and discard the garlic and pepper.

4. Increase the heat to medium-high, add the drained broccoli rabe, and cook it until tender but still slightly crisp, 5 to 8 minutes. Season the broccoli rabe with salt to taste and serve immediately.

Broccoli rabe's slightly bitter flavor matches up well to a mild pasta or grilled fish main dish.

Fusion Coleslaw

Vibrant bits of green and red cabbage blended with orange carrots make this tasty coleslaw as colorful as a bowl of confetti. The dressing has Asian roots, with ginger, jalapeño pepper, and red chile sauce giving it a pleasant bite. The surprise is the sweet raisins and honey-roasted peanuts that counterbalance the mild spiciness. A handful of thinly sliced pineapple chunks, or even mango, is another nice addition. This slaw tastes best the day it's made and is delicious with Quick Grilled Lemon Chicken (see page 143) or Ginger Lime Salmon (see page 164). **SERVES 6**

Carrots don't get fresher than this!

2 cups shredded red cabbage
    ($^{1}/_{4}$-inch shreds)
1 cup shredded of Napa cabbage
    ($^{1}/_{4}$-inch shreds)
2 large carrots, coarsely grated
$^{1}/_{3}$ cup thin strips of scallion greens
    (from about 6 scallions)
1 jalapeño pepper, cut into slivers
3 tablespoons toasted sesame oil
3 tablespoons unseasoned rice
    vinegar
1 tablespoon sugar
$^{1}/_{2}$ teaspoon Asian chile garlic sauce,
    or more to taste
1 tablespoon finely grated peeled
    fresh ginger
Salt (optional)
$^{1}/_{2}$ cup honey-roasted peanuts
$^{1}/_{2}$ cup raisins
2 tablespoons sesame seeds, toasted
    (see sidebar, page 273)

1. Place the red cabbage, Napa cabbage, carrots, scallion greens, and jalapeño in a large bowl. Stir to combine.

2. Place the sesame oil, vinegar, sugar, chile sauce, and ginger in a glass jar and seal the lid tightly. Shake the jar vigorously to combine. Taste for seasoning, adding salt and/or more chile garlic sauce as needed.

3. Pour the dressing over the cabbage mixture and toss to combine. Add the peanuts and raisins and toss again. Refrigerate the coleslaw, covered, to allow the flavors to develop, 2 to 4 hours. Serve the coleslaw chilled, garnished with the sesame seeds.

Corn and Black Bean Salad

Perfect for a picnic or a summer barbecue, this salad is easy to throw together at the last minute. Ripe tomatoes, onions, parsley, and spices provide a fresh flavor perk that makes convenience foods like canned beans and frozen corn taste delicious. If you want to prepare the salad a day or two in advance, don't add the dressing until it's almost time to serve. If the salad sits overnight, the vinegar in the dressing may dim the bright parsley and tomato colors. **SERVES 4 TO 6**

1 can (15 ounces) black beans, rinsed and drained

1 cup uncooked fresh or frozen (thawed) corn kernels (see box, page 29)

1 large ripe tomato, cut into 1/4-inch dice (about 1 cup)

1 small red onion, cut into 1/4-inch dice (about 1/2 cup)

2 tablespoons finely chopped fresh flat-leaf parsley

2 teaspoons minced garlic

2 tablespoons white wine vinegar or distilled white vinegar

1/4 cup extra-virgin olive oil

1 teaspoon chili powder

1/4 teaspoon ground cumin

1 teaspoon sugar

1/2 teaspoon salt

1/4 teaspoon freshly ground black pepper

1. Place the black beans, corn, tomato, onion, and parsley in a large bowl and stir gently to combine.

2. Place the garlic, vinegar, olive oil, chili powder, cumin, sugar, salt, and pepper in a small bowl and whisk to combine.

3. Pour the dressing over the bean mixture and toss to coat. The salad can be kept at room temperature for up to 6 hours.

We plant flower borders alongside our fields to provide a home for beneficial insects like ladybugs and lacewings.

Grilled Corn on the Cob
with Herb Butter

Who doesn't love corn on the cob? It is delicious, fun to eat, and easy to throw on the grill while burgers or steaks sizzle. My family likes to spread the ears with an herb butter that accents the corn's sweet taste. Almost any combination of herbs tastes great. Or, perk up the butter with smoky paprika or ground cayenne pepper for a spicy accent. **SERVES 4**

4 tablespoons ($^1/_2$ stick) unsalted butter, softened
1 tablespoon minced fresh dill
1 tablespoon fresh thyme leaves
1 teaspoon fresh lemon juice
Salt and freshly ground black pepper
4 ears fresh corn, shucked and silk removed

1. Set up a barbecue grill and preheat it to medium. Cut 4 pieces of heavy-duty aluminum foil, about 12 by 18 inches or you can use double layers of regular aluminum foil. Set the aluminum foil aside.

2. Using a fork, blend the butter, dill, thyme, and lemon juice in a small bowl. Season the butter with salt and pepper to taste.

3. Smear about 1 tablespoon of the butter mixture on an ear of corn. Place the buttered ear on top of a piece of aluminum foil, tightly roll the foil around it, and seal the edges. Repeat with the remaining butter mixture, corn, and aluminum foil.

4. Grill the corn, turning frequently, until it is hot and tender, 8 to 12 minutes.

5. To serve, unwrap the corn, being careful to avoid the escaping steam and keep the melted herb butter in the foil. Place the corn on a serving platter and pour the melted butter over the ears. Serve hot.

Sweet white corn is a midsummer treat well worth the long winter wait.

Sweet Creamed Corn
with Thyme

When corn is sweet, young, and fresh from the farm, gently warming the kernels in butter turns them into an ethereal dish, perfect for an elegant or casual meal. The milky liquid from the kernels gives the corn a creamy texture. For a decadently memorable first course, stir in about one cup of picked-over crab or lobster meat just before serving the corn in flat-bottomed soup bowls. **SERVES 4**

8 ears fresh corn, shucked and silk
    removed
4 tablespoons ($^1/_2$ stick) unsalted butter
1 teaspoon fresh thyme leaves
Salt and freshly ground black pepper

1. Cut the kernels off the corn cobs (see box, page 29). You should have at least 4 cups of kernels and their milky liquid. Discard the cobs.

2. Melt the butter in a medium-size skillet over low heat. Add the corn and its milky liquid. Cook very gently, stirring constantly, until the liquid is reduced and the corn becomes very creamy, 10 to 15 minutes. Do not let the corn to come to a simmer.

3. Stir the thyme into the corn, season it with salt and pepper to taste, and serve immediately.

My niece Nina wouldn't give up her basket of little heirloom tomatoes—not even for a walk in the corn maze!

Summer Corn Pudding

Corn pudding is the comfort food of summer. Make this dish only when you can find fresh local corn. It won't be the same made with frozen or canned corn. Yes, it's rich, so team it up with lighter fare like Quick Grilled Lemon Chicken (see page 143) and a fresh salad of mixed salad greens. This is a vegetable dish worth skipping dessert for.

SERVES 6

Shucking fresh-picked corn for dinner. Always choose nice, tight ears.

4 tablespoons (¹/₂ stick) unsalted butter, melted, plus butter for greasing the baking dish
8 ears fresh corn, shucked and silk removed
1 cup reduced-fat buttermilk
¹/₂ cup heavy (whipping) cream
4 large eggs
2 tablespoons unbleached all-purpose flour
2 teaspoons baking powder
1 teaspoon sugar
¹/₂ teaspoon salt
2 tablespoons minced fresh flat-leaf parsley
1 tablespoon minced fresh chives
Generous pinch of ground cayenne pepper

1. Position a rack in the center of the oven and preheat the oven to 350°F. Generously butter a two-quart baking dish.

2. Cut the kernels off the corn cobs (see box, page 29). You should have at least 4 cups of kernels and their milky liquid. Discard the cobs.

3. Place 2 cups of the corn kernels in a blender or food processor. Add the buttermilk and cream and process to a coarse puree. Transfer the buttermilk mixture to a large bowl.

4. Add the remaining corn kernels and the eggs, melted butter, flour, baking powder, sugar, salt, parsley, chives, and cayenne to the buttermilk mixture and whisk to blend. Pour the mixture into the prepared baking dish.

5. Make a water bath by placing the baking dish in a roasting pan. Pour hot water into the roasting pan so that it comes halfway up the side of the baking dish.

6. Bake the pudding in the water bath until it is just set and slightly golden, 50 minutes to 1 hour. Carefully remove the roasting pan from the oven and let the pudding rest in the water bath for 10 minutes before serving.

Fava Bean and Orzo Salad

*L*ong, *plump pods of fava beans appear in farmers' markets in the early spring. Once peeled, you may mistake them for butter beans or lima beans, only they are more sweet and tender. Admittedly, it takes a little extra work to peel favas, but don't let that dissuade you from trying this distinctive springtime pasta salad. It's a lovely pale green, tinted by the fava bean "pesto" that coats the rice-shaped orzo pasta. The whole baby fava beans and crisp, corn kernels (from fresh corn, if you can find it in fava season) are delectable, peeking out among bits of feta cheese, pine nuts, and sun-dried tomatoes. With a taste that's even better the next day, it's a great make-ahead pasta salad.* **SERVES 6**

Softening Sun-Dried Tomatoes

Sun-dried tomatoes packed in oil are already soft and ready to use. To rehydrate sun-dried tomatoes that are not packed in oil, place the tomatoes in a small bowl and add a third of a cup of hot water. Let the tomatoes soak until softened, at least 5 minutes. The soaking liquid is full of flavor, so add it to the dish with the tomatoes when you can.

Salt
1 cup shelled fresh, young fava beans
   (from 1 pound of pods)
8 ounces orzo pasta
1/2 cup Fava Bean "Pesto"
   (recipe follows)
2 tablespoons olive oil (optional)
1 cup uncooked fresh corn kernels
   (from 2 ears; see box, page 29)
1/2 cup pine nuts, toasted
   (see box, page 98)
1/3 cup coarsely chopped fresh basil
   leaves
4 ounces feta cheese, cut into 1/4-inch
   dice or crumbled (about 1 cup)
8 sun-dried tomatoes, softened and
   thinly sliced (see sidebar, this page)
Juice of 1 lemon
Freshly ground black pepper

1. Fill a large bowl of water with ice cubes and set it aside.

2. Bring a large pot of salted water to a boil over high heat. Add the fava beans and cook until the skins loosen, about 1 minute. Immediately drain the beans in a colander, then plunge them into the bowl of ice water to stop the cooking. Drain the beans again in the colander.

3. When the fava beans are cool enough to handle, peel them by pinching a small hole in the tough outside skin of a bean with your fingernail. Gently squeeze the bean to release the 2 tender inner bean halves. Repeat with the remaining beans, then set them aside.

4. Bring a large pot of salted water to a boil over high heat. Add the orzo and cook according to the package directions.

5. Drain the orzo thoroughly in a colander, then transfer it to a large nonreactive bowl. Add the Fava Bean "Pesto" and stir to combine. Add the olive oil if the orzo mixture is too dry.

6. Add the fava beans, corn, pine nuts, basil, and feta cheese to the orzo. Add the sun-dried tomatoes and their soaking liquid, if any, and the lemon juice; stir to combine. Season the salad with salt and pepper to taste. The orzo salad can be kept at room temperature for up to 2 hours or refrigerated, covered, for up to 2 days. Let the salad return to room temperature before serving.

Fava Bean "Pesto"

Pale green fava beans replace the traditional basil in this unusual version of pesto. Like classic basil pesto, it's good tossed with pasta, but Fava Bean "Pesto" has a thicker consistency that makes it a delicious appetizer spread on toasted baguette slices. **MAKES ABOUT 1 CUP**

1 cup shelled fresh fava beans
   (from 1 pound of pods)
2 small cloves garlic
1 tablespoon fresh lemon juice
About 1/2 cup extra-virgin olive oil
1/2 cup freshly grated Parmesan or
   Pecorino Romano cheese
1/2 teaspoon salt
1/4 teaspoon freshly ground black pepper

1. Fill a large bowl of water with ice cubes and set aside.

2. Bring a large pot of salted water to a boil over high heat. Add the fava beans and cook until the skins loosen, about 1 minute. Immediately drain the beans in a colander, then plunge them into the bowl of ice water to stop the cooking. Drain the beans again in the colander.

3. When the fava beans are cool enough to handle, peel them by pinching a small hole in the tough outside skin of a bean with your fingernail. Gently squeeze the bean to release the 2 tender inner bean halves. Repeat with the remaining beans.

4. Place the fava beans and garlic in a blender or food processor and pulse until coarsely pureed. Add the lemon juice and 1/3 cup of the olive oil and puree until smooth, stopping to scrape the side of the bowl, as necessary.

5. Add the Parmesan cheese, salt, and pepper. Process briefly to combine. If the mixture seems too dry, add the remaining olive oil and process to blend. The "pesto" can be kept at room temperature for up to 4 hours, or refrigerated, covered, for up to 5 days.

Fava beans require a little extra work to peel, but their delicate taste is worth it.

Grilled Portobello Mushrooms

Bathed in a simple balsamic vinaigrette, grilled portobello mushrooms have a meaty texture that is very satisfying. When friends visit, these portobellos provide an easy vegetarian option for a barbecue menu that features hamburgers or steak. If there are any leftovers, the mushrooms are delicious sliced and added to sandwiches or pasta dishes. **SERVES 4**

4 large portobello mushroom caps
2 tablespoons olive oil
2 tablespoons balsamic vinegar
1 tablespoon fresh thyme leaves
Salt and freshly ground black pepper

1. Wipe the mushroom caps clean with a damp paper towel. If desired, scrape out the gills with a small paring knife or spoon.

2. Place the olive oil, vinegar, and thyme in a small bowl and whisk to combine. Brush both sides of the mushrooms with the oil mixture and sprinkle salt and pepper on them. Let the mushrooms sit at room temperature to absorb the flavors, about 30 minutes.

3. Set up a barbecue grill and preheat it to medium.

4. Grill the mushrooms for 5 minutes. Turn the mushrooms over and grill them until they are just tender and easily pierced with the tip of a knife, 5 to 8 minutes longer. Serve hot or at room temperature.

Marea shows off her basketful of Ruby Crescent and Yellow Finn potatoes.

Picnic Potato Salad

You'll find this potato salad is a bit different from traditional ones but just as delicious. It's creamy, yet piquant, and features tender fingerling potatoes that don't need to be peeled. The potatoes are steamed, rather than boiled, so they retain their shape and vitamins. The still-warm fingerlings quickly soak up the Dijon vinaigrette. There's a little mayonnaise added later for creaminess along with some scallions and celery for crunch. Make this salad your own by stirring in your favorite ingredients like capers, salad pickles, diced hard-boiled egg, or bacon bits—whatever suits you best. **SERVES 8**

potatoes

Yellow Finn, Red Bliss, Peruvian purple, and French fingerlings are just a few of the types of potatoes that are becoming common choices in markets across the country. Even with so many potatoes to choose from, knowing which type is best for a recipe is not difficult when you become familiar with the three basic categories: low starch (or waxy), high starch (or starchy), and medium starch.

Low starch (or waxy) potatoes: The typical round white- or red-skinned creamer potatoes found in supermarkets stay moist and hold their shape when cooked. Their texture is good for potato salads, soups, and gratins because the slices or cubes will remain intact as they cook.

High starch (or starchy) potatoes: Russet (also called Idaho) potatoes are the most common starchy potato. When cooked, the flesh is dry, flaky, and fluffy and easily absorbs other ingredients, such as butter and milk. Starchy potatoes have a texture that lends itself well to baking, frying, and mashing.

Unusual varieties in this category include mature blue- or purple-fleshed potatoes (like Russian Blue) and fingerling potatoes, which have a long, oblong shape similar to a finger.

Medium starch potatoes: Yellow-fleshed Yukon Gold and Yellow Finn varieties combine the best of the other two types. They have enough starch to make them great for mashing, yet they stay moist and intact when used in potato salads.

New potatoes: True new potatoes are young potatoes that are harvested while the potato plant's leaves are still green. Any type of potato, waxy or starchy, that's harvested very young is a new potato. The skin is thin and delicate, so new potatoes often look a little scruffy after harvesting and are very perishable. Because they are immature, the flesh is moist and flavorful.

Most potatoes are harvested after the plant has died down and the potatoes have been allowed to "cure" in the ground for several weeks so their skin toughens. Sometimes small red potatoes harvested at maturity are marketed as "new" potatoes, even though they are not truly new.

Buying potatoes: Look for firm, sprout-free potatoes with no cuts or hints of green on the skin. Store potatoes in a cool, dark place, ideally at about 50°F. New potatoes should be used within a week, but properly stored mature potatoes last for weeks, or even months. Green-tinged skin indicates that the potato has been overexposed to light, allowing an alkaloid to develop, which can be toxic if eaten in large quantities. If your potatoes turn green after you buy them, cut off and discard any green parts before cooking.

2 pounds thin-skinned potatoes, preferably fingerlings, cut in 1/2-inch chunks
1 teaspoon Dijon mustard
2 tablespoons red wine vinegar
1/3 cup extra-virgin olive oil
Salt and freshly ground black pepper
1/2 cup mayonnaise, or more to taste
2 tablespoons minced fresh dill
3 tablespoons minced fresh flat-leaf parsley
3/4 cup sliced celery
1 bunch scallions, including white and about 3 inches of green, trimmed and thinly sliced (about 3/4 cup)

1. Place the potatoes in a steamer basket set over a large saucepan filled with boiling water to a depth of about 1/2 inch. Steam the potatoes over medium-high heat, covered, until they are tender when pierced with the tip of a knife, 10 to 15 minutes.

2. Meanwhile, place the mustard, vinegar, olive oil, and ¹/₂ teaspoon of salt in a glass jar and seal the lid tightly. Shake the jar vigorously to combine. Taste the vinaigrette for seasonings, adding pepper to taste and more salt as needed.

3. Drain the potatoes in a colander and transfer them to a large bowl. Add ¹/₄ cup of the vinaigrette and toss to coat the warm potatoes. Let the potatoes cool and set the remaining vinaigrette aside.

4. When the potatoes cool to room temperature, add the mayonnaise and stir to combine. If the salad seems too dry, stir in some of the remaining vinaigrette. Add the dill, parsley, celery, and scallions and stir to combine.

5. Refrigerate the salad, covered, for at least 2 hours before serving for the flavors to develop. It can be refrigerated for up to 3 days. Serve the potato salad chilled.

Blue Cheese Smashed Potatoes

New potatoes, fresh from the earth with delicate skins and creamy flesh, are perfect for this rustic version of mashed potatoes. You coarsely smash the potatoes, peels and all, to a chunky consistency, rather than the usual smooth one. Add garlic and blue cheese for an intense flavor and texture that's almost impossible to resist. Keep in mind that some blue cheeses, such as French Roquefort, are more strongly flavored than others, so adjust the amount according to your taste. For a different flavor, substitute Asiago or Gruyère for the blue cheese. **SERVES 6**

2 pounds unpeeled thin-skinned
    potatoes, such as new potatoes or
    fingerlings, cut into ¹/₂-inch chunks
4 cloves garlic, peeled
¹/₄ cup whole or low-fat milk
2 tablespoons (¹/₄ stick) unsalted
    butter
3 to 4 ounces crumbled blue cheese
    (about 1 cup), at room temperature
Salt and freshly ground black pepper

1. Place the potatoes, garlic, and 5 cups of water in a large saucepan and bring to a boil over high heat. Reduce the heat to medium-low and let the potatoes simmer, covered, until tender, about 15 minutes.

2. Meanwhile, heat the milk and butter in a small saucepan over low heat. Keep warm.

3. Drain the potatoes and garlic in a colander, then transfer them to a large bowl. Using a potato masher or large fork, coarsely mash the potatoes and garlic. Add the warm milk and butter mixture and the blue cheese and mash to combine.

4. Season the potatoes with salt and pepper to taste. If they have cooled, reheat them slowly in a medium-size saucepan over low heat, stirring frequently, until warmed through, then serve. The smashed potatoes can be kept warm for up to 1 hour in the top of a double boiler set over simmering water.

Garlic Buttermilk Mashed Potatoes

Yellow-fleshed potatoes, such as Yukon Gold or Yellow Finn, moistened with tangy buttermilk, make deliciously creamy mashed potatoes, especially when they are studded with nuggets of golden roasted garlic. Don't be put off by the amount of garlic in this recipe—when roasted, the garlic is transformed, becoming mild and sweet. Everyone will beg for seconds when the potatoes are served alongside marinated Flank Steak (see page 112) or Brined Roast Turkey (see page 154). **SERVES 6**

A garlic braid decorated with straw flowers.

6 medium-size Yukon Gold or Yellow
   Finn potatoes (about 2 pounds),
   peeled and cut into $1/2$-inch chunks
5 cups Blond Chicken Stock (page 372),
   store-bought low-sodium chicken
   broth, or water
2 medium-size heads Roasted Garlic
   (recipe follows)
$3/4$ cup reduced-fat buttermilk
4 tablespoons ($1/2$ stick) unsalted butter
Salt and freshly ground black pepper

1. Place the potatoes and stock in a large saucepan and bring to a boil over high heat. Reduce the heat to medium-low and let the potatoes simmer, covered, until tender, about 15 minutes.

2. Meanwhile, squeeze the soft garlic pulp from the garlic cloves into a small bowl and discard the garlic skins. Set the garlic aside.

3. Heat the buttermilk and butter in a small saucepan over low heat. Keep warm.

4. Drain the potatoes, setting the stock aside for another use (such as soup), and transfer the hot potatoes to a medium-size bowl.

5. Using a potato masher or large fork, coarsely mash the potatoes. Add the warm buttermilk and butter mixture and mash until smooth. Add the roasted garlic to the potatoes and stir to combine.

garlic

When shopping for garlic, look for large, firm heads with no signs of sprouting. Most supermarket garlic has a white, papery skin, but purple-skinned garlic is wonderful, too. Huge, mild flavored elephant garlic is not really garlic at all, but a member of the leek family. It can be used as a substitute for regular garlic in recipes where you want a less assertive garlic flavor. One clove of elephant garlic can be as large as three regular garlic cloves, but it's much more mild. Garlic should not be refrigerated but stored in a cool area with good air circulation.

The flavor and texture of garlic changes over time. When first harvested in the summer, the garlic cloves are moist and mild. As it is stored over the winter, garlic gradually becomes drier, its flavor intensifies, and green sprouts appear in the cloves. The sprouts sometimes have a bitter taste, especially when eaten raw. You may want to cut the cloves in half and remove the spouts, especially if you will not be cooking the garlic.

When garlic cloves are pureed or minced, more of their oil is released, resulting in more intense garlic flavor. For milder flavor, slice or coarsely chop the cloves. Cook garlic gently so that it doesn't burn and become bitter tasting.

---

6. Season the potatoes with salt and pepper to taste. If they have cooled, reheat them slowly in a medium-size saucepan over low heat, stirring frequently, until warmed through, then serve. The mashed potatoes can be kept warm for up to 1 hour in the top of a double boiler set over simmering water.

Roasted Garlic

Whenever our October wedding anniversary rolls around, I think of garlic. Drew and I had a tiny marriage ceremony, but the next day we threw a party for all of our friends. While garlic should be in the ground by early October, in the wedding rush, we didn't have time to plant our crop. Before we left for our honeymoon, everyone gave us a great send-off gift: They solved our farming crisis by pitching in and helping us get the cloves in the ground. Our honeymoon was worry-free. The garlic cloves grew into mature bulbs over the winter, and in the summer, we harvested them as usual, leaving the stalks attached. I use the stalks to make long garlic braids and hang them on the kitchen wall so they are always available.

Roasted garlic has a buttery-soft texture and mellow taste that's totally different from raw garlic. It's easy to throw a couple heads of garlic in the oven when roasting chicken or meats. The soft, baked cloves are delicious in Garlic Buttermilk Mashed Potatoes (see recipe, facing page) or simply spread on fresh, crusty bread. **MAKES 2 HEADS OF GARLIC**

2 medium-size garlic heads
2 teaspoons olive oil

1. Position a rack in the center of the oven and preheat the oven to 375°F.

2. Cut off and discard the top ½ inch of each garlic head. Remove the loose, outer layers of paperlike skin, leaving the heads intact. Rub the garlic heads with the olive oil and tightly seal both of them together in heavy-duty aluminum foil or a double layer of regular aluminum foil.

My signature touch for a garlic braid is to top it with a small garlic head with its roots standing up straight, like a little, rustic tiara!

3. Place the foil package directly on the oven rack and bake the garlic until the cloves are very soft, 40 to 50 minutes (larger heads will take longer).

4. Open the foil package and let the garlic heads cool. To use, squeeze the soft, golden garlic pulp out of the papery skins. The garlic can be refrigerated, covered, for up to 1 week.

Twice-Baked Potatoes

Our Farm Stand's Organic Kitchen bakes up these hearty potatoes for customers to enjoy as a luncheon dish with a green salad or as a side dish for dinner. We often use a blend of cheeses for the filling, such as cheddar and Swiss, or provolone and Asiago—there's no hard-and-fast rule. While they're good as a hearty side dish, twice-baked potatoes become a meal when you add sautéed vegetables, bacon, or tofu. The creamy sour cream and buttermilk tie all the ingredients together beautifully. **SERVES 4**

Digging for potatoes—
a Farm Stand treasure hunt.

4 medium-size russet (baking) potatoes
   (about 8 ounces each), scrubbed
   and patted dry
2 tablespoons olive oil
Coarse (kosher) salt
2 tablespoons ($^1/_4$ stick) unsalted
   butter, softened
$^1/_2$ cup sour cream or crème fraîche,
   homemade (page 389) or store-
   bought
2 to 3 tablespoons buttermilk
$^1/_2$ cup thinly sliced scallions, including
   white and 3 inches of green
1 cup freshly grated (4 ounces)
   cheddar or Swiss cheese
Freshly ground black pepper
$^1/_4$ cup (1 ounce) freshly grated
   Parmesan cheese
Paprika, for garnish

1. Position a rack in the lower third of the oven and preheat the oven to 425°F.

2. Rub the potatoes with the olive oil and sprinkle salt over them. Place the potatoes on a baking sheet and bake until tender and easily pierced with the tip of a knife, 45 to 55 minutes. Let the potatoes cool.

3. Reduce the oven temperature to 375°F.

4. Lay a potato down flat and slice off the top $^1/_2$ inch (if desired, set aside the potato slice for another use). Using a small spoon, carefully scoop out the flesh from inside the potato and transfer it to a medium-size bowl, leaving a $^1/_4$-inch-thick shell of potato skin. Repeat with the remaining potatoes.

A cheese-topped mound of creamy mashed potatoes acts as a filling in Twice-Baked Potatoes.

5. Add the butter, sour cream, buttermilk, scallions, and cheddar cheese to the bowl with the potato. Using a potato masher or a large fork, mash and combine the filling ingredients until smooth. Season the potato filling with salt and pepper to taste.

6. Spoon the filling into the potato shells, mounding it up. Place the stuffed potatoes on a baking sheet and sprinkle 1 tablespoon of the Parmesan cheese on each potato. Sprinkle each potato with paprika. (The potatoes can be prepared up to this point and refrigerated, covered, for up to 2 days.)

7. Bake the potatoes until the filling is heated through and the cheese is golden brown, 15 to 20 minutes (allow about 10 minutes of additional baking time if the potatoes are not room temperature). Serve hot.

Sarah's Potato-Thyme Tart

We have our friend Sarah LaCasse, owner of Catering-by-the-Sea in Carmel, to thank for this potato side dish that rivals gratins for comforting satisfaction but has fewer calories. The potatoes cook up crisp, thin, and light, making this dish one of my favorites. Brown the bottom of the tart on the stovetop to ensure that it will be crusty and golden. Then bake the tart gently until the layer of thyme-scented potatoes is tender. Once baked, flip the tart out of the skillet so that the bottom becomes the top. Use a mandoline or vegetable slicer to make quick work of slicing the potatoes. Don't forget to select the prettiest slices for the bottom layer because they will form the showy top when the dish is served. **SERVES 4 TO 6**

A medley of heirloom potatoes—Candy Cane, Alby's Gold, and Austrian Crescent.

3 medium-size russet (baking) or Yukon Gold potatoes (about 1¹/₂ pounds total), peeled and sliced ¹/₈-inch thick (see sidebar, page 267)
3 tablespoons unsalted butter, melted
2 tablespoons olive oil
2 teaspoons fresh thyme leaves
Salt and freshly ground black pepper

1. Position a rack in the center of the oven and preheat the oven to 375°F.

2. Place the potatoes in a large bowl. Add 1 tablespoon of the butter and the olive oil and thyme. Toss to mix, then season with salt and pepper to taste.

3. Generously brush the sides and bottom of an ovenproof 7-inch skillet with the remaining butter (you may have a little butter left over). Arrange the potato slices in the skillet, starting at the side and working around the edge and toward the center, overlapping the slices until the bottom of the skillet is covered. Continue, making 2 to 3 layers, until all the potato slices are used.

Spicy, edible nasturtium flowers surrounded by fragrant rosemary.

4. Tightly cover the skillet with aluminum foil. Place the skillet over medium heat and cook until the potatoes begin to brown on the bottom, 12 to 20 minutes. (Slip a heat-resistant rubber spatula under the potatoes and lift them up a bit to check the color.)

5. Transfer the covered skillet to the oven and bake the potatoes until they are tender and easily pierced with the tip of a paring knife, 15 to 25 minutes.

6. Carefully remove the foil and loosen the potato tart from the pan with a spatula or knife. Place a large plate on top of the skillet and, holding the plate securely against the skillet, carefully turn the pan over to release the tart. Cut it into 4 or 6 wedges and serve hot.

Creamy Potato Gratin

Creamy potato slices scented with nutmeg and garlic make an indulgent side dish that's elegant and comforting at the same time. Using starchy russet potatoes creates a tender gratin that thickens nicely, but waxier potatoes, such as Yukon Gold, can be substituted if you like a firmer texture. Either will be delicious. Blanching the garlic before adding the cream removes some of the bite from strongly flavored cloves. Potato gratin is a good choice to serve alongside a hearty meat dish like Merlot-Braised Short Ribs (see page 119) or Herb-crusted Rack of Lamb (see page 129) and a simple low-fat vegetable, like Sautéed Broccoli Rabe (see page 233). **SERVES 8 TO 10**

Butter, for greasing the baking dish
8 cloves garlic, peeled
2^1/$_2$ cups heavy (whipping) cream
1 cup whole or low-fat milk
Pinch of freshly grated nutmeg
(about 8 gratings)
3^1/$_2$ pounds russet (baking) potatoes
(about 8 large)
Salt and freshly ground black pepper
^{1}/$_2$ cup freshly grated Parmesan or
Gruyère cheese

1. Position a rack in the lower third of the oven and preheat the oven to 350°F. Generously butter a 9 by 13-inch baking dish or a gratin dish.

2. Place the garlic cloves in a medium-size saucepan. Add enough cold water to barely cover the garlic and bring to a boil over high heat. Pour the water out, leaving the garlic in the saucepan.

3. Add the cream, milk, and nutmeg to the garlic and cook over low heat until the cream begins to simmer. Turn off the heat and let the cream mixture sit at room temperature until the flavors are absorbed, about 30 minutes. Discard the garlic.

4. Meanwhile, peel the potatoes, then rinse and pat them dry with paper towels. Using a mandoline (see sidebar, page 267) or the slicing blade of a food processor, cut the potatoes into ^{1}/$_8$-inch-thick slices. Do not rinse or soak the potato slices, as this would wash out the potato starch.

5. Arrange a layer of potatoes in the prepared baking dish, overlapping the slices by about a third. Sprinkle salt and pepper over the potatoes. Pour about ^{2}/$_3$ cup of the cream mixture over the potatoes. Make 1 or 2 more layers using all of the remaining potatoes and cream. Sprinkle the cheese over the top of the gratin.

6. Cover the baking dish tightly with aluminum foil and bake the gratin for 45 minutes. Uncover the baking dish and continue baking the gratin until the potatoes are browned and tender and the liquid has been absorbed, 45 to 55 minutes longer. If the top browns too quickly, loosely recover the pan with the foil. Let the gratin rest for 10 minutes before serving.

Yukon Gold "Risotto"
with Winter Greens

Risotto is a creamy rice dish, right? Not necessarily! One of our renowned local chefs, Cal Stamenov from the Bernardus Lodge in Carmel Valley, took this northern Italian classic in a new direction by replacing the rice with finely diced golden potatoes. His creation is a tasty surprise, combining the sophisticated look of the traditional dish with the comfort of mashed potatoes. But Cal doesn't stop there; he adds wilted greens, which provide the perfect counterpoint for the decadent "risotto." Cal made this dish for one of the Chef Walks that we host each summer at our Farm Stand. Our guests were wowed, and yours will be, too. **SERVES 6 TO 8**

Note: A mandoline or vegetable slicer makes preparing these potatoes surprisingly easy, especially if it has a julienne blade for slicing matchstick-size strips (see sidebar, page 267). After cutting the potatoes into tiny strips, use a knife to slice them crosswise at about ¹⁄₈-inch intervals for tiny dice. If you don't have a julienne blade, slice the potatoes into ¹⁄₈-inch-thick slices. Stack the slices, cut them into ¹⁄₈-inch strips, then cut the strips into ¹⁄₈-inch dice.

A basket of just-cut Swiss chard.

2 cups heavy (whipping) cream
4 large Yukon Gold potatoes
    (about 2 pounds total), peeled
1¹⁄₂ teaspoons minced garlic
3 ounces goat cheese, crumbled
    (about ¹⁄₃ cup)
²⁄₃ cup (about 2 ounces) freshly grated
    Parmesan cheese
Salt and freshly ground black pepper
2 bunches (about 2 pounds total)
    Swiss chard
2 tablespoons olive oil
5 ounces baby spinach (about 6 cups)
Extra-virgin olive oil, for garnish

1. Pour the cream into a large, nonstick skillet and set it aside.

2. Cut the potatoes in very small dice, about ¹⁄₈-inch (see Note). Add the potatoes to the cream as you dice them to prevent discoloration.

3. Add the garlic, goat cheese, and ¹⁄₃ cup of water to the potatoes and bring to a simmer over medium heat. Reduce the heat to low and let simmer gently, stirring frequently, until the potatoes have absorbed the liquid and become tender, about 25 minutes. If all the liquid is absorbed before the potatoes are tender, add an additional ¹⁄₄ cup of water and continue cooking.

4. Add ¹⁄₃ cup of the Parmesan cheese to the potatoes and season them with salt and pepper to taste. Keep the potatoes warm over very low heat, stirring occasionally.

5. Meanwhile, rinse the chard and cut out and discard the stems. Cut the leaves crosswise into 1-inch-wide strips.

6. Heat the olive oil in another large skillet over medium-high heat. Add the chard and cook, stirring occasionally, until crisp-tender, about 4 minutes (if the pan does not hold all the greens, cook them in batches). Add a splash of water if the chard becomes too dry. Add the spinach and continue cooking until it wilts, 3 to 5 minutes.

7. To serve, spoon the warm potatoes onto plates and top with some of the greens. Sprinkle the remaining 1/3 cup of Parmesan cheese on top and drizzle with the olive oil.

Creamed Parmesan Spinach

If you know people who claim not to like spinach, this rich and creamy side dish blended with Parmesan cheese and a hint of nutmeg may change their mind. Try creamed spinach with unadorned roasted meats like beef tenderloin or a standing rib roast for a special occasion dinner. You may be surprised by who asks for seconds.

SERVES 4 TO 6

2 pounds baby spinach, or 2 bunches mature spinach, thick stems removed and large leaves coarsely chopped (see Note)
2 tablespoons (1/4 stick) unsalted butter
2 tablespoons unbleached all-purpose flour
1 1/2 cups whole or low-fat milk
1/2 cup heavy (whipping) cream
1/4 cup freshly grated Parmesan cheese
1/4 teaspoon freshly ground nutmeg
Coarse (kosher) salt and freshly ground black pepper

Note: You can substitute frozen spinach with good results. Thaw two packages (10 ounces each) of frozen, chopped spinach. Squeeze the spinach with your hands or in a clean dishcloth to remove any water. Start the recipe with Step 2; the thawed spinach doesn't need to be steamed.

1. Steam the spinach in a steamer basket over boiling water until it wilts, about 1 minute. Transfer the spinach to a colander to drain. Wrap the spinach in a clean dishcloth and squeeze out any remaining water. (If you don't want a green-tinted dishcloth, you can squeeze out the water with your hands after the spinach cools slightly.)

2. Melt the butter in a large skillet over medium-low heat. Add the flour and cook for 2 minutes, whisking constantly. Add the milk and the cream in a steady stream, continuing to whisk, and cook until the cream thickens, about 2 minutes.

3. Add the spinach to the cream sauce and stir to combine. Add the Parmesan cheese and nutmeg, stir to combine, and cook until the spinach is heated through, about 1 minute. Season the spinach with salt and pepper to taste and serve hot.

FARM FRESH

spinach

Spinach is highly nutritious, an excellent source of vitamin A and health-promoting antioxidants. It is also naturally rich in folate, a B vitamin with many health benefits, including providing protection against heart disease. (Synthetic folate is called folic acid.) Raw spinach, especially baby spinach, is a healthy and delicious addition to salads, but try cooked spinach occasionally, too. Cooking makes it possible for the body to absorb the antioxidants in spinach more easily.

Buying spinach: Most baby spinach is sold prewashed in packages. The leaves are tender and mild, so baby spinach is delicious raw or cooked. Even the stems are small and tender, so there's no need to remove them. Mature spinach, usually sold in bunches, may have flat or curly leaves. It tastes best cooked with any large stems removed. A pound of spinach looks like a lot when raw, but it cooks down to about one cup, which will serve two people. Whether you choose baby or mature spinach, look for bright green leaves that are not dried out, wilted, or bruised. Since spinach is one of the vegetables most likely to have residual pesticides, select spinach that's organically grown.

Washing spinach: Unless you buy it packaged and prewashed, rinse spinach thoroughly. If the leaves are grit free and clean, rinsing them with a spray of fresh water may be all they need. However, most mature spinach, especially the curly leafed varieties, needs a more thorough rinsing to remove the dirt or grit trapped in its leaves. First, discard any large stems. Then place the spinach leaves in a sink or large bowl filled with cool water. Give the leaves a gentle swish and let them sit a minute to allow the grit to settle to the bottom. Lift the leaves out a handful at a time and place them into a colander to drain. Rinse the spinach again in fresh water. It will probably take two or three rinsings before the spinach is free of any grit.

A field of blue-green broccoli seems to stretch on for miles against the California hills.

Garlicky String Beans

Green and yellow string beans mingled with red pepper strips make a side dish that's pretty on the plate and delicious served warm, cold, or at room temperature. This is our Organic Kitchen's most popular vegetable salad during the summer months, when tender string beans are in season. My kids love these string beans so much they can each eat a container-full on the way home from the Farm Stand! **SERVES 4**

1 pound tender green beans or yellow (wax) beans, or a combination of both, trimmed
Salt
1 tablespoon olive oil
1 tablespoon minced fresh garlic
$^1/_2$ red bell pepper (optional) stemmed, seeded, and sliced into thin strips
Freshly ground black pepper

1. Fill a large bowl of water with ice cubes and set aside.

2. Bring a large pot of water to a boil over high heat. Add the beans and 1 teaspoon of salt and cook until the beans are just crisp-tender, about 5 minutes. Immediately drain the beans in a colander, then plunge them into the bowl of ice water to stop the cooking. Drain the beans again in the colander.

3. Heat the olive oil in a large skillet over medium heat. Add the garlic and bell pepper, if using. Cook, stirring constantly, until the garlic is fragrant, about 2 minutes. Add the drained beans and cook until heated through, about 2 minutes. Season the beans with salt and pepper to taste and serve hot or at room temperature.

A Quick Way to Peel Garlic

Lay the garlic clove on a cutting board and place the flat side of a broad knife blade (such as a chef's knife) on top of the clove. Hold the knife handle steady while you press down on the blade with the heel of your other hand (don't press too hard or you'll crush the garlic). This loosens the papery skin so you can easily pull it off the clove.

Bite-Size Bloody Marys

Here's a fun and tasty "cocktail" that will get a grown-up barbecue or party going. Fill a large bowl with sweet cherry tomatoes, perhaps a mix of brilliant orange Sungolds and bright red Sweet 100s. Surround the bowl with a shot glass filled with toothpicks, two small bowls—one filled with ice-cold vodka, one with gin—and shallow dishes of fine sea salt and freshly ground pepper. If you want to go all-out, you can also set out pepper-flavored vodka and a bowl of celery salt.

Stab a tomato with a toothpick, dunk it in the liquor, followed by a light dip in the salt and pepper, and pop the miniature Bloody Mary in your mouth. Share one with a friend and soon the party will roll.

Bite-size Bloody Marys are a great conversation starter.

Swiss Chard
with Raisins and Pine Nuts

Swiss chard is one of the loveliest greens we grow at Earthbound Farm. The most common variety has crinkly green leaves accented with milky white or ruby red ribs. But rainbow chard, with its bright green leaves displaying showy ribs of yellow, orange, pink, and even fuchsia, is our favorite. Large and small chard leaves are equally tasty—and don't toss out those colorful ribs. When thinly sliced, they can be cooked along with the leaves. In the Mediterranean, the slight, pleasant bitterness of chard is often combined with sweet raisins, lemon zest, and pine nuts. If you prefer, omit these ingredients and follow the steps for gently braising the chard with olive oil and shallots until the chard is meltingly tender. Either way, it's healthy and delicious.

SERVES 4 TO 6

1 bunch (about 1 pound) Swiss chard, any variety
2 tablespoons olive oil
3 tablespoons minced shallots
Grated zest of 1 lemon
1/4 cup raisins
1/2 cup toasted pine nuts (see box, page 98)
Coarse (kosher) salt and freshly ground black pepper

1. Rinse the chard and cut the ribs off the leaves. Cut the ribs into 1/2-inch dice and set aside. Stack the leaves and cut them into 1/2-inch strips. Set the leaves aside separately.

2. Heat the olive oil over medium heat in a large, heavy pot or large, deep skillet (preferably nonstick) with a tight-fitting lid. Add the shallots and chard ribs and cook, uncovered, until soft, about 5 minutes.

3. Add the chard leaves and cook, stirring frequently, about 1 minute. Add 2 tablespoons of water, most of the lemon zest, and the raisins. Cover the pot and cook, stirring occasionally, until the chard is tender and the water has almost evaporated, 4 to 8 minutes. If the water evaporates before the chard is tender, add an additional splash of water.

4. Remove the pot from the heat. Stir in the pine nuts, and season the chard with salt and pepper to taste. Serve immediately garnished with the remaining lemon zest.

Roasted Garnet Yams

When cubed yams are roasted, they turn crisp on the outside and soft in the center, and look as gorgeous as deep-orange candies. This easy cooking method makes a healthy and satisfying alternative to French fries. They are great served with Kathy's Rosemary-Roasted Chicken (see page 136) and a green vegetable, like steamed broccoli or Garlicky String Beans (see page 261). Most yams sold in this country are actually sweet potatoes. But no matter what you call them, they are loaded with nutrients. The orange-fleshed varieties, such as garnet and jewel, are especially rich in the health-promoting antioxidant, beta-carotene. **SERVES 6**

3 medium-size (about 1 pound total)
   garnet or jewel yams, peeled and
   cut into $1/2$-inch dice
2 tablespoons olive oil
Coarse (kosher) salt

1. Position a rack in the center of the oven and preheat the oven to 425°F.

2. Place the yams in a large bowl, add the olive oil, and season with salt. Toss the yams to coat them with the oil. Spread the yams in a single layer on a rimmed baking sheet.

3. Bake the yams until they are crisp outside and soft inside, 25 to 30 minutes. As they bake, shake the baking sheet or stir the yams occasionally so that each piece develops a crisp crust on all sides.

4. Transfer the yams to a serving bowl and serve immediately.

Fairylike cosmos grow in abundance at our Farm Stand.

Marinated Zucchini Salad

In a sophisticated spin on old-fashioned cucumber salad, zucchini creates a light and refreshing summer side dish, perfect for a picnic or luncheon. It's quick and simple to prepare with a mandoline or vegetable slicer (see the sidebar on page 267). The key to success is to slice the zucchini paper-thin and allow it to marinate for at least an hour before serving. **SERVES 4**

1 pound (about 4) small zucchini,
     ends trimmed
$^1/_3$ cup high-quality extra-virgin
     olive oil
2 tablespoons fresh lemon juice,
     preferably Meyer (see sidebar,
     page 112)
3 tablespoons finely sliced fresh basil,
     plus 1 sprig of basil (optional),
     for garnish
Coarse (kosher) salt and freshly
     ground black pepper
Wedge of Parmesan cheese,
     for garnish

1. Using a mandoline or vegetable slicer, cut the zucchini into paper-thin rounds.

2. Pour the olive oil and lemon juice into a medium-size bowl and whisk to combine. Add the zucchini and toss until it is thoroughly coated.

3. Add the sliced basil and toss to mix evenly. Season with salt and pepper to taste. Cover the bowl and let the zucchini marinate in the refrigerator for at least 1 hour but no more than 6 hours.

4. Just before serving, stir the zucchini salad to redistribute any liquids that may have accumulated on the bottom. Using a vegetable peeler, shave very thin slices of cheese on the top of the salad, $^1/_2$ to $^3/_4$ cup, or to taste. Garnish with a basil sprig, if desired.

Cheesy Zucchini

*M*y daughter, Marea, says that my Cheesy Zucchini is more delicious than chocolate. *What a statement from a teenager with a sweet tooth! My family loves this dish so much I make it at least once a week in season. They are happy with just zucchini, but mixing a variety of summer squashes—scallop-edged pattypans, golden straightnecks, green-striped globes, yellow crooknecks—is especially pretty. What gives the dish special appeal is the Parmesan and mozzarella cheeses. No one seems to mind that I serve the squash straight from the skillet.* **SERVES 4**

2 tablespoons extra-virgin olive oil
4 large cloves garlic, thinly sliced
1$^1/_2$ pounds medium-size zucchini or
     other summer squash, cut in $^1/_2$-inch-
     thick slices (about 4 cups; see Note)
2 tablespoons coarsely chopped fresh
     flat-leaf parsley
$^1/_4$ teaspoon salt
$^1/_3$ cup freshly grated Parmesan cheese
$^1/_2$ cup freshly grated mozzarella cheese

1. Heat the olive oil in a large nonstick skillet over medium heat. Add the garlic and cook, stirring frequently until softened, 1 to 2 minutes.

2. Add the squash and stir to coat it with the garlic-oil mixture. Cover the skillet and cook the squash, stirring occasionally, until it is glossy and crisp-tender, 4 to 6 minutes.

Note: If your zucchini, or other long summer squash, is larger than 1 inch in diameter, slice the squash in half lengthwise, then cut it into $^1/_2$-inch-thick half-moon pieces. Cut pattypan or other round summer squashes in half through the stem end and cut them crosswise into about $^1/_2$-inch-thick pieces.

3. Sprinkle the parsley and salt evenly over the squash and cook, stirring frequently, until the parsley wilts, about 1 minute longer. Stir in the Parmesan cheese and stir constantly until it melts, about 1 minute.

4. Sprinkle the mozzarella cheese evenly over the squash, cover the skillet again, and remove it from the heat. Let the squash sit until the mozzarella cheese melts, 1 to 2 minutes. Serve immediately.

Provençal Tomato, Eggplant, and Zucchini Tian

Overlapping layers of purple eggplant, red tomatoes, and green zucchini brushed with fragrant basil oil make this tian—*a vegetable casserole from the south of France—as beautiful as it is delicious. For the prettiest presentation, select vegetables that are about the same diameter. Slicing the vegetables almost paper-thin brings out their flavors, making this dish a real standout. While it sounds like a lot of trouble, you'll find it's easy to create superthin slices using a vegetable slicer or mandoline (see the sidebar on this page). You can adapt the recipe to serve more people by adding additional vegetables and a little more flavored oil; just use a larger pan so that all the vegetables fit comfortably in one overlapping layer. The cooking time remains the same.* **SERVES 4**

1 small eggplant (about ¹/₂ pound)
1 medium-size zucchini (about 6 ounces)
3 to 4 ripe medium-size tomatoes (about 1¹/₄ pounds)
¹/₃ cup Herb-Flavored Oil (page 382; use basil) or extra-virgin olive oil
Salt and freshly ground black pepper

1. Position a rack in the bottom third of the oven and preheat the oven to 425°F.

2. Using a vegetable slicer or mandoline, cut the eggplant and zucchini crosswise into ¹/₁₆-inch-thick slices (see Note, page 268). If the eggplant is much larger in diameter than the zucchini and tomatoes,

cut the eggplant in half lengthwise before slicing. Brush both sides of the eggplant and zucchini slices with some of the Herb-Flavored Oil. Cut the tomatoes into ¹/₄-inch-thick slices.

3. Brush a shallow 7 by 11–inch or 9 by 13-inch baking dish with oil. Starting at a short end of the baking dish, arrange a slice of eggplant in the dish so that it rests at an angle against the side of the dish. Working down the length of the baking dish, arrange 1 or 2 slices of zucchini over the eggplant so that they partially overlap it, then place a slice of tomato on top of the zucchini. Continue to alternate the vegetables, overlapping them in rows,

Quick and Easy Slicing

A mandoline, or vegetable slicer, is a kitchen tool that allows you to cut thin, even slices quickly. For home use, the inexpensive plastic models work just as well as the expensive stainless steel versions. You can find a good-quality plastic Japanese vegetable slicer or German "V-slicer" that costs $50 or less in kitchen stores or houseware departments. Look for a model with interchangeable slicing blades, usually ranging from ¹/₁₆ inch to ¹/₄ inch, as well as a julienne blade for cutting vegetables into matchstick-size strips, and a baton blade for creating french fry–size strips. Also make sure the mandoline has a safety guard that keeps your hand away from the blade while you work.

Note: If you don't have a vegetable slicer or mandoline, slice the vegetables about ¼-inch thick with a knife and increase the cooking time by ten minutes.

until they fill the baking dish in a single layer; you will have at least two rows of vegetables.

4. Lightly brush the top of the vegetables with the remaining Herb-Flavored Oil and sprinkle salt and pepper on top.

5. Bake the vegetables until they are just tender, about 20 minutes. Remove the *tian* from the oven and let it cool for 5 minutes. Carefully pour off and discard any accumulated liquid. Serve the *tian* while still warm or at room temperature.

Roasted Root Vegetable Medley

*R*oasting root vegetables at a high temperature brings out their inherent sweetness. This recipe is a great jumping-off point for creating your own medley of favorite vegetables and herbs. Fennel, turnips, or shallots would be great additions (if you want to add beets, see Note). If rutabaga isn't your favorite, leave it out. In the dead of winter, when fresh herbs are harder to find, dried herb blends, such as herbes de Provençe, will work just fine. **SERVES 6 TO 8**

Note: Roasted beets are delicious, but when roasted with other vegetables, they turn everything red. If you're adding beets to your medley, roast them separately.

3 medium-size parsnips
   (about 12 ounces total), peeled
3 medium-size carrots
   (about 8 ounces total), peeled
1 medium-size (about 4 ounces)
   Yukon Gold or waxy potato
   (such as White Rose), peeled
8 small (about 8 ounces) cipollini
   onions, peeled, or 2 small yellow
   onions, peeled
1 small (about 12 ounces) rutabaga,
   peeled
2 to 3 tablespoons olive oil
1 tablespoon fresh thyme leaves
1 teaspoon chopped fresh rosemary
Salt and freshly ground black pepper,
   to taste

1. Position a rack in the center of the oven and preheat the oven to 450°F. Line a

rimmed baking sheet with parchment paper for easy clean-up and set it aside.

2. Cut the parsnips, carrots, potato, onions, and rutabaga into ¾-inch cubes or wedges so that they will all cook in the same amount of time.

3. Place all of the vegetables in a large bowl. Add the olive oil, thyme, rosemary, salt, and pepper, and toss to coat the vegetables. Spread them in a single layer on the prepared baking sheet.

4. Bake the vegetables until they are tender and caramelized, 35 to 45 minutes. As they bake, shake the baking sheet or stir the vegetables occasionally so that each piece develops a crisp crust on all sides. Serve immediately.

Grilled Summer Vegetables
with Basil Oil

Ah, summer! Time to fire up the barbecue and grill some of the season's farm-fresh, organic vegetables. Brushing them with herb-flavored oil brings out the flavor even more. When grilling vegetables, always make extras—the leftovers make a great addition to sandwiches or pasta sauces. **SERVES 6 TO 8**

4 small zucchini (about 1 pound total), ends trimmed

4 small yellow summer squash (about 1 pound total), ends trimmed

2 small eggplants (about 1 pound total), ends trimmed

2 medium-size onions (about 1 pound total), trimmed and peeled

1/2 cup Herb-Flavored Oil (page 382; use basil) or olive oil

Salt and freshly ground black pepper

1. Cut the zucchini and yellow squash in half lengthwise. Cut the eggplant lengthwise into roughly 1/4-inch-thick slices. Cut the onion crosswise into 1/4-inch-thick round slices.

2. Brush the vegetables all over with the Herb-Flavored Oil and sprinkle salt and pepper on them. Let the vegetables sit at room temperature to absorb the flavor from the oil for 30 minutes to 1 hour.

3. Set up a barbecue grill and preheat it to medium.

4. Grill the vegetables, turning once, until they are tender-crisp and lightly brown, 8 to 10 minutes total (the vegetables will continue to cook for a minute or two after being removed from the grill). Serve hot or at room temperature.

Moroccan-Spiced Bulgur Pilaf

Mention pilaf and a rice dish usually comes to mind. But bulgur, made from whole wheat, makes an equally fine pilaf. It's almost impossible to resist the intoxicating aroma when bulgur is laced with warm spices—cinnamon, coriander, and cumin. The grain's distinctive, nutty taste is echoed by the pistachios, and harmonizes sweetly with raisins and apricots, and is accented by the lemon and herbs. While the ingredient list may look long, the dish comes together quickly and deliciously. **SERVES 4**

1 cup bulgur wheat

$1/2$ cup raisins

2 cloves garlic, peeled

1 stick cinnamon (3 inches)

1 teaspoon ground cumin

$1/2$ teaspoon ground coriander

8 dried apricots, cut into strips
    (see sidebar, page 83)

$1/4$ cup pistachios or pine nuts, toasted
    (see box, page 98)

$1/4$ cup minced fresh flat-leaf parsley

1 tablespoon minced fresh cilantro

1 tablespoon minced fresh mint

2 tablespoons extra-virgin olive oil

Grated zest of 1 lemon

3 tablespoons fresh lemon juice

Salt and freshly ground black pepper

1. Place a large skillet over medium-high heat and add the bulgur (do not use a nonstick skillet for this). Toast the bulgur, stirring occasionally, until it is golden and fragrant, 5 to 8 minutes. Watch carefully to make sure the bulgur doesn't burn.

2. Place the raisins, garlic, cinnamon stick, cumin, coriander, and $1^{1}/2$ cups of water in a medium-size saucepan. Bring the mixture to a boil over high heat. Add the bulgur, cover the pan, and reduce the heat to low. Let the bulgur simmer until it absorbs all of the liquid and is just tender, 5 to 8 minutes. Remove the pan from the heat and add the apricots. Let the bulgur sit, covered, for 5 minutes.

3. Remove and discard the garlic cloves and the cinnamon stick from the bulgur. Add the pistachios, parsley, cilantro, mint, olive oil, and lemon zest and juice and stir to combine. Season with salt and pepper to taste. Serve the pilaf hot or at room temperature.

A bowl of fresh spearmint.

Tabbouleh
with Fresh Peas and Cumin

*O*ur Farm Stand's Organic Kitchen has put its own signature on this classic Middle Eastern salad by adding fresh basil, toasty cumin, and sweet English peas. Very young, sweet peas can be added raw, straight from the pod. Or, if you don't have tender peas, improvise with other ingredients, such as a cup of young, uncooked corn kernels or diced seedless cucumber. The main ingredient is bulgur, which is whole wheat that's been steamed, dried, and ground. Since bulgur is already partially cooked, it just needs a short soaking in hot water to make it moist and chewy. The tabbouleh tastes best the day it's made, but if you want to make it one day in advance, leave out the mint, basil, and tomatoes and add them just before serving.

SERVES 6 TO 8

1 cup bulgur wheat
1 cup boiling water
1 cup minced fresh flat-leaf parsley
$1/2$ cup fresh basil, cut into thin ribbons
2 tablespoons minced fresh mint
2 large ripe tomatoes, cut into $1/4$-inch
dice (about 2 cups)
1 cup fresh shelled English peas
(optional)
$1/2$ cup thinly sliced trimmed scallions,
including white and about 3 inches
of green
$1/4$ cup extra-virgin olive oil
Grated zest of 1 lemon
$1/4$ cup fresh lemon juice
2 cloves garlic, minced
1 teaspoon cumin seeds, toasted
(see sidebar, this page) and ground
or 1 teaspoon ground cumin
1 teaspoon salt
Freshly ground black pepper

1. Place the bulgur in a large heatproof bowl, add the boiling water, and let soak for 15 minutes. Drain the bulgur in a sieve, pressing on it with a spoon to remove the excess liquid.

2. Return the bulgur to the bowl and add the parsley, basil, mint, tomatoes, peas, if using, and scallions. Stir to combine.

3. Place the olive oil, lemon zest and juice, garlic, cumin, and salt in a small bowl and whisk to combine. Season with pepper to taste. Add the olive oil mixture to the bulgur mixture and toss to coat. Let the tabbouleh sit at room temperature until the flavors develop, about 30 minutes. Serve the tabbouleh at room temperature, preferably the day it's made.

Toasting Sesame Seeds and Spices

The flavor of freshly toasted sesame seeds and spices, such as cumin, mustard, or fennel seeds, is worth the effort if you have time. Place the seeds in a small skillet (do not use a nonstick skillet for this) and cook over medium heat until fragrant and warm to the touch, about 1 minute. If the recipe calls for ground spices, grind the seeds to a fine powder in a spice mill or coffee grinder reserved just for spices.

Rye Berry Salad

Chewy and healthy, this whole grain salad is laced with dried cranberries, raisins, and pumpkin seeds and dressed with a fresh citrus vinaigrette. Rye berries have a nutty appeal all their own. To soften them, the grain must be simmered for almost an hour. Once that's done, the salad is a snap to prepare. This makes a good winter salad because the ingredients are available year-round. **SERVES 4 TO 6**

1 cup uncooked rye berries or wheat
berries
1 cup thinly sliced celery
$1/3$ cup dried cranberries
$1/3$ cup raisins
$1/3$ cup coarsely chopped fresh flat-leaf
parsley
$1/2$ cup shelled raw unsalted pumpkin
seeds
2 tablespoons minced shallots

1 tablespoon white wine vinegar
2 tablespoons fresh orange juice
Grated zest of 1 orange
Salt and freshly ground black pepper
$1/4$ cup extra-virgin olive oil

1. Place the rye berries in a medium-size saucepan and add 3 cups of cold water. Bring to a boil over high heat. Cover the pan, reduce the heat to low, and let simmer until the rye berries are just tender, 45 to 55 minutes. Drain the berries in a sieve and transfer them to a large bowl.

2. Add the celery, cranberries, raisins, parsley, and pumpkin seeds to the rye berries and stir to blend.

3. Place the shallots, vinegar, and orange juice in a glass jar and let sit for 10 minutes.

Add the orange zest, 1/4 teaspoon of salt, 1/4 teaspoon of pepper, and the olive oil and seal the lid tightly. Shake the jar vigorously to combine.

4. Just before serving, add the dressing to the rye berry mixture and toss to coat. Season to taste with more salt and pepper as needed. Serve the salad at room temperature.

Saffron Scallion Couscous

Golden couscous, with threads of scarlet saffron and slices of green scallions, is an intriguing alternative to rice or potatoes. Couscous, a type of pasta that originated in North Africa, looks like coarse grains of sand. This method for preparing it is quick and easy. Couscous is especially delicious made with your best extra-virgin olive oil. The fruity oil will be absorbed by the couscous, greatly enhancing its flavor. **SERVES 4**

Threads of precious saffron lace this fragrant couscous.

saffron

Saffron is the world's most expensive spice, but fortunately, a little goes a long way. Nothing can duplicate the rich fragrance and golden color that saffron adds to a dish. Most saffron comes from Iran and Spain, but it is also grown on a small scale in the United States. Saffron's dark red threads are actually the stigmata from a purple-flowering crocus. The stigmata from about 14,000 crocuses must be harvested by hand to make one ounce of saffron, which explains the high cost.

You can buy whole saffron threads or saffron powder. When shopping for threads, look for long crimson strands, with little yellow or white material mixed in. Before using, crush the threads with your fingers and add them to a small amount of hot liquid to release their flavor and aroma.

Buying saffron powder is trickier because the expensive spice can come mixed with less expensive, and less flavorful, turmeric. Unadulterated saffron powder should be a deep crimson color like the whole threads. It will also be aromatic, unlike substitutes, which typically have little or no aroma. Buying from a reputable supplier should ensure that your powdered saffron is pure. Powdered saffron is easier to measure and can be added directly to food without steeping. Whether you choose threads or powder, saffron releases a wonderful scent and golden color. Finding bits of the crimson threads in light-colored dishes, like rice or couscous, is especially pleasing.

---

1 cup couscous

2 tablespoons good-quality extra-virgin olive oil

1 cup Blond Chicken Stock (page 372), store-bought low-sodium chicken broth, or water

$1/2$ teaspoon saffron threads (see box, facing page), lightly crushed

Coarse (kosher) salt and freshly ground black pepper

7 scallions, including white and 3 inches of green, trimmed and thinly sliced on an angle (about 1 cup)

1. Place the couscous in a medium-size shallow heatproof bowl or casserole and drizzle the olive oil over it. Rub the couscous between your palms until the all the "grains" are coated with oil; this should take about 2 minutes.

2. Heat the stock in a small saucepan over high heat until it just begins to boil. Remove the stock from the heat and add the saffron, stirring to blend.

3. Add half of the stock to the couscous. Keep the remaining stock warm over low heat. Stir and fluff the couscous with a fork. Cover the bowl with a plate or plastic wrap and let it sit for 5 minutes.

4. Add the remaining stock to the couscous. Using a rubber spatula, scrape up any saffron that may be stuck to the saucepan and add it to the couscous. Fluff the couscous with a fork and re-cover the bowl. Let the couscous sit for 5 minutes longer.

5. Season the couscous with salt and pepper to taste and stir in the scallions just before serving.

Chapter 8

Breakfast and Brunch

Breakfast is probably the meal that makes me feel most like a real chef. With the griddle sizzling and an eager family perched on stools at the counter, it's gratifying all around: I get to soak up compliments while my husband, son, and daughter enjoy what I've prepared for them.

I have to admit, it takes planning to pull together a hearty breakfast every morning before I head off to work, so I've developed some time-saving shortcuts over the years. When we have baked potatoes for dinner, I make extras to turn into crispy Mama Fries the next morning. With the potatoes already cooked, it takes only a few minutes to slice and panfry them to a golden brown and serve them with scrambled eggs. Leftover pasta is transformed into an egg and pasta breakfast dish my kids love called Pasta à la Mama.

Pancakes don't take long to make when I have pancake mix in the pantry. Unfortunately, most of the mixes in the grocery store include unhealthy partially hydrogenated fats, so I keep a stock of my own Quick Pancake Mix made from all-organic ingredients. The mix makes tender whole wheat pancakes, which taste great topped with fresh fruit. Adding a handful of toasted nuts provides some protein that helps keep hunger at bay until lunchtime.

But some mornings, I'm too rushed to cook anything. That's when I'm glad I have a jarful of my Maple Almond Granola on hand. Loaded with whole grains, nuts, and seeds, this granola needs only fresh fruit and some milk or yogurt to make a filling and healthy breakfast.

For more relaxed times, I've included a few special brunch recipes that can be enjoyed any time of day. Quiche satisfies robust appetites with a rich egg custard mixed with spinach, feta, and mushrooms in an herb-filled crust. Spanish Egg "Soufflé Cake," with red peppers, artichokes, olives, and cheese, is an unusual dish that looks like a Bundt cake, but tastes like an egg frittata. If you're lucky enough to have leftovers, it's just as delicious the next day.

This chapter also features our Farm Stand customers' favorite breakfast baked goods from the Organic Kitchen. The Original Morning Glory Muffin is loaded with coconut, carrots, raisins, apples, and pecans, and because they keep well for days, you can feel comfortable making a large batch. For a decadent treat, our customers line up for warm

Facing page:
Pumpkin Pecan Muffins
(page 302).

and sweet Cinnamon Nut Rolls. They take some time to prepare, but are so delicious, they're worth it.

Breakfast doesn't have to be complicated. It doesn't have to be fancy or take a lot of time. I think you'll find recipes here that make that important first meal tempting enough to lure your family out of bed, and nourishing enough to get them off to a good start.

Earthbound Farm's Famous Maple Almond Granola

When I was first learning to cook, I created my own granola using pure maple syrup and hefty spoonfuls of cinnamon. Not all of my cooking experiments were successful back then, but with this recipe, I hit the jackpot! The result is a perfectly sweet and crisp granola, with a rich amber color and a distinctive maple-cinnamon flavor, brimming with plump raisins, crunchy almonds, and sunflower seeds. My family and friends loved it so much, we started selling it at our Farm Stand, and locals and visitors from across the country have become addicted to it ever since. To keep our faraway customers supplied, we've opened an online store to make it easy for them to stock up between visits. Here's how to make the granola for yourself. If you want to avoid washing a bowl, place all the ingredients directly on the baking sheet and mix them with your hands like I do at home. **MAKES ABOUT 8 CUPS**

A cheery bouquet of sunflowers.

4¹/₂ cups (18 ounces) old-fashioned
    rolled oats (not instant)
³/₄ cup (3 ounces) shelled, raw,
    unsalted sunflower seeds
1¹/₂ cups slivered or coarsely chopped
    raw almonds
2 tablespoons ground cinnamon
1¹/₄ cups pure maple syrup,
    preferably Grade A Dark Amber
    (see box, page 280)
¹/₃ cup canola oil
1 cup raisins

1. Position a rack in the center of the oven and preheat the oven to 325°F.

2. Place the oats, sunflower seeds, almonds, and cinnamon in a large bowl and stir to combine. Add the maple syrup and oil and stir until all the dry ingredients are moistened.

3. Spread the granola on a roughly 12 by 17–inch rimmed baking sheet. Bake the granola until it begins to brown, about

25 minutes, then stir it with a flat spatula. Let the granola continue to bake until it is light golden brown, dry, and fragrant, 15 to 20 minutes longer. Stir the granola at least once more as it bakes and watch it carefully during the final minutes because it can burn quickly.

4. Place the baking sheet on a cooling rack, add the raisins, and stir to combine. Let the granola cool completely. Transfer the granola to an airtight container. It can be stored at room temperature for up to 1 month or frozen for up to 6 months. You can serve the granola straight from the freezer. It doesn't get hard and it thaws almost instantly—just pour on some milk.

F A R M   F R E S H

pure maple syrup

In Vermont, the people who produce pure maple syrup are called "sugar makers," and many welcome visitors to their sugarhouses to watch them boil maple sap, turning it into syrup.

Maple sap runs only when weather conditions and freezing temperature are just right. New England sugar makers have suffered declining syrup production in recent years because of higher winter temperatures, which have been attributed to global warming. (Canadian maple sugar production has actually increased due to the warmer climate.) Organic farming helps combat global warming because organic fields absorb carbon dioxide, a greenhouse gas, at a rate of roughly 3,670 pounds per acre. That's good news for American maple sugar makers and the rest of us, too.

The U.S. Department of Agriculture specifies four grades of maple syrup, based on the syrup's color, density, and flavor—not its quality.

■ **Grade A Light Amber**, sometimes called "fancy," is the lightest in color and has a delicate maple flavor. This syrup is usually made during the early part of the sugaring season, when the weather is at its coldest.

■ **Grade A Medium Amber** is a little darker and has a more pronounced maple flavor. The most popular grade of table syrup, it is usually made in the middle of the sugaring season.

■ **Grade A Dark Amber** has a still darker color with an even stronger maple flavor. It is usually made later in the season, when the days get longer and warmer.

■ **Grade B**, sometimes called "cooking syrup," is very dark and has a robust maple flavor, with a touch of caramel—great for baking. It's made late in the sugaring season.

Cranberry Pecan Granola

Our maple and almond granola was such a Farm Stand hit that we decided to add a second flavor. People love the subtle aroma of orange that complements the chewy cranberries, crunchy pumpkin seeds, and nuts. If you can't find dried orange peel in the spice section of your grocery store, substitute orange zest. Because the moist zest tends to clump together, make sure it's distributed evenly throughout the granola. You'll want to enjoy the lively citrus flavor in every spoonful. **MAKES ABOUT 8 CUPS**

4¹/₂ cups (18 ounces) old-fashioned
    oats (not instant)
1¹/₂ cups coarsely chopped pecans
¹/₂ cup shelled raw, unsalted
    pumpkin seeds
1 cup firmly packed brown sugar
2 tablespoons dried orange peel, or
    finely grated zest of 2 oranges
¹/₂ cup canola oil
¹/₄ cup maple syrup, preferably
    Grade A Dark Amber
    (see box, facing page)
1 cup dried sweetened cranberries

1. Position a rack in the center of the oven and preheat the oven to 325°F.

2. Place the oats, pecans, pumpkin seeds, brown sugar, and dried orange peel in a large bowl and stir to combine.

3. Place the oil, maple syrup, and ¹/₂ cup of water in a small bowl and whisk to combine. Pour the oil mixture over the oat mixture and stir to combine.

4. Spread the granola on a roughly 12 by 17-inch rimmed baking sheet. Bake the granola until it begins to brown, about 25 minutes, then stir it with a flat spatula. Let the granola continue to bake until it is golden brown, dry, and fragrant, 30 to 35 minutes longer. Stir the granola at least once more as it bakes and watch it carefully during the final minutes because it can burn quickly.

5. Place the baking sheet on a cooling rack and let the granola cool completely. Add the cranberries and stir to combine. Transfer the granola to an airtight container. It can be stored at room temperature for up to 1 month or frozen for up to 3 months.

Monkey Oatmeal

It takes a little imagination, but even ordinary oatmeal can be transformed into a nutty breakfast treat filled with protein and flavor. And it's so simple: Prepare oatmeal as you usually do. Just before serving, stir in a heaping spoonful of peanut butter. If the oatmeal needs a bit of sweetness, add a little brown sugar or maple syrup. Top the oatmeal with a pile of banana slices and a cool splash of milk.

Our Farm Stand visitors enjoy picking their own bouquets on our Flower Walk.

Apple Nut Pancakes

It's not unusual for our house to be full of guests on the weekend. Some Sunday mornings, my kitchen looks like a diner, with hungry faces eagerly leaning over the counter watching me cook made-to-order pancakes loaded with fruit, nuts, and other goodies. Apple pancakes are a popular request and can be made with walnuts—my family's favorite—as well as pecans.

This recipe feeds four normal appetites, but two starving teenagers can sometimes eat them all. See the bottom of the facing page for instructions on mixing up larger batches of basic pancakes. **MAKES ABOUT TWELVE 4-INCH PANCAKES**

Enjoying crunchy pecans is a tasty way to add healthy protein to your diet.

3 crisp apples, such as Fuji or Gala, cored, peeled, and thinly sliced (about $1/8$ inch)

$3/4$ cup toasted walnuts or pecans (see box, page 98), coarsely chopped, with some reserved for garnish

2 large eggs

1 cup milk or buttermilk, or more if desired

4 tablespoons ($1/2$ stick) unsalted butter, melted, or 4 tablespoons canola oil

2 cups Basic Whole Wheat Pancake Mix (see Note, facing page)

1 tablespoon ground cinnamon

Canola oil, for brushing the griddle

Confectioners' sugar, for dusting the pancakes

Pure maple syrup (see box, page 280), warmed if desired

1. Place the apple slices and walnut pieces within easy reach of the griddle.

2. Place the eggs, milk, and butter in a small bowl. Whisk to blend.

3. Place the pancake mix and cinnamon in a medium-size bowl and whisk to combine well. Add the egg mixture in a slow stream, stirring constantly to blend. Do not overmix or the pancakes will be tough. If you like thinner pancakes, add up to $1/2$ cup more milk.

4. Heat a griddle or large skillet over medium-low heat until a few drops of water sizzle when splashed on the surface.

5. Brush some oil on the hot griddle. Working in batches if needed, spoon the batter onto the griddle to form pancakes that are about 4-inches in diameter. Arrange slices of apple on top and sprinkle the nuts over them. Cook the pancakes until small bubbles begin to appear in the batter, $1^1/2$ to 2 minutes.

6. Carefully flip the pancakes and cook until the other side is brown, $1^1/2$ to 2 minutes.

7. Transfer the pancakes to a warmed plate and garnish with the reserved walnuts and a dusting of confectioners' sugar. Serve the pancakes immediately with maple syrup.

Basic Whole Wheat Pancake Mix

This pancake mix is so easy to make from healthy ingredients, you'll wonder why anyone buys the expensive commercial brands. Make up a batch ahead and on those mornings when every minute counts, you can cook fluffy pancakes without searching your pantry for the baking powder tin. **MAKES ABOUT 11 CUPS OF PANCAKE MIX**

A bowl of lovely pink-fleshed heirloom apples.

10 cups whole wheat pastry flour
(about 2¹/₂ pounds; see sidebar, page 6)
³/₄ cup sugar
2¹/₂ teaspoons salt
3 tablespoons baking powder

Place the flour, sugar, salt, and baking powder in a large bowl and whisk well to evenly distribute the ingredients. Stored in an airtight container in a cool, dry place the pancake mix will keep for up to 3 months.

To make basic whole wheat pancakes, using the proportions for ingredients found in the chart below, place the egg, milk (start with the smaller measure), and butter in a mixing bowl and whisk to blend. Place the Basic Whole Wheat Pancake Mix in a medium-size bowl. Add the egg mixture in a slow stream, stirring constantly to blend. If you like your pancakes thin, and the batter seems too thick, add more milk, a little at a time.

Heat a griddle or large skillet over medium-low heat until a few drops of water sizzle when splashed on the surface, then brush on some canola oil. Spoon the batter onto the griddle to form pancakes that are about 4 inches in diameter and cook until small bubbles begin to appear on the surface, 1¹/₂ to 2 minutes. Carefully flip the pancakes and cook until the other side is brown, 1¹/₂ to 2 minutes.

Note: To make 2 cups of Basic Pancake Mix (enough for 12 pancakes):

2 cups less 2 tablespoons whole wheat pastry flour

2 tablespoons sugar

¹/₂ teaspoon salt

1¹/₂ teaspoons baking powder

INGREDIENTS	SERVES 2 (6 pancakes)	SERVES 4 (12 pancakes)	SERVES 6 (18 pancakes)	SERVES 8 (24 pancakes)
Whole large egg(s)	1	2	3	4
Milk or buttermilk	¹/₂-³/₄ cup	1-1¹/₂ cups	1¹/₂-2¹/₄ cups	2-3 cups
Melted butter or oil	2 tablespoons	4 tablespoons	6 tablespoons	8 tablespoons
Whole Wheat Pancake Mix	1 cup	2 cups	3 cups	4 cups

ideas for **Pancake Fillings**

I t's fun to create new pancake combinations. Try substituting the ingredients below for the apples, pecans, and cinnamon in the apple pancake recipe (see page 282). Each suggestion makes enough for twelve pancakes. Feel free to use more or less of each filling ingredient and to experiment with your favorite fruits and nuts. It's nice to set aside some of the filling to use as a garnish for the plate. That way no one has to ask what makes the pancakes so delicious! **MAKES ENOUGH FOR 12 PANCAKES**

When blackberries are in season, they're a delicious topping for pancakes or french toast.

Blueberry Pancakes

Lemon zest provides a lively twist for traditional blueberry pancakes.

> 1 cup fresh or frozen (unthawed) blueberries
> 1 teaspoon grated lemon zest

Follow the Apple Nut Pancakes recipe but omit the apples, nuts, and cinnamon. In Step 5, arrange the blueberries and sprinkle the zest on top of the batter.

Banana Walnut Pancakes

For a special garnish, toss extra banana slices on the griddle with a pat of butter and cook them for a couple of minutes on each side. Everyone will rave about this soft and fragrant "grilled" banana topping.

> 2 bananas, peeled and thinly sliced
> 3/4 cup toasted walnut pieces

Follow the Apple Nut Pancakes recipe but omit the apples and cinnamon. In Step 5, arrange the banana slices and walnuts on top of the batter. Pour a thin layer of batter over the bananas so that they don't stick to the griddle when the pancakes are turned.

Banana Chocolate Chip Pancakes

This "breakfast dessert" is always a big hit with my kids and their sleepover buddies.

> 2 bananas, peeled and thinly sliced
> 3/4 cup chocolate chips

Follow the Apple Nut Pancakes recipe but omit the apples, nuts, and cinnamon. In Step 5, arrange the banana slices and chocolate chips on top of the batter. Pour a thin layer of batter over the banana and chocolate chips so that they don't stick to the griddle when the pancakes are turned.

Classic Omelet

A warm omelet, filled with melted cheese and bits of meat and vegetables, is a satisfying and nourishing dish that's a great meal any time of the day. The trick to making several omelets quickly and easily is to have all the ingredients handy and the fillings prepared before heating the pan. If you are making several omelets, whisk the eggs for each in a separate bowl before you start. That way you'll be ready to get the next omelet going as soon as the one before it is done. When you master the simple cooking technique described here, you'll be able to cook two or more omelets at once. **MAKES 1 OMELET**

3 large eggs
Pinch of salt
Freshly ground pepper
1 tablespoon butter
Omelet filling (suggestions follow)

1. Place the eggs, salt, pepper to taste, and 1 tablespoon of water in a small bowl. Whisk to combine.

2. Melt the butter in a small (7 inch), nonstick skillet over medium heat. When the butter begins to foam, add the egg mixture. Reduce the heat to medium-low and cook until the eggs begin to set up along the bottom and side of the pan. Using a spatula, push the cooked egg gently into the center of the skillet, at the same time tilting the skillet so that any runny, unset egg mixture rolls onto the hot surface. Do this once or twice until most of the egg has set, 2 to 4 minutes.

3. Spoon the filling over half of the omelet. If the eggs are too soft for your taste, turn off the heat and cover the skillet with a lid or aluminum foil and let them sit for 2 minutes.

4. When the eggs are cooked to your liking, run a spatula around the edge of the omelet to release it from the pan. Place the skillet at an angle against the edge of the serving plate and carefully slide the filled half of the omelet onto the plate. Using the pan to help you, fold the remaining half of the omelet over the filling. Serve immediately.

Spreading vetch and rye seeds for a winter cover crop.

ideas for **Omelet Fillings**

Here are a few ideas for omelet fillings, but don't stop here. Chunks of cheese, a handful of mushrooms, or leftover steak, ham, or spinach are all great fillings. Each of these fillings is enough for two three-egg omelets.

Bacon, Tomato, and Cheese Omelet Filling

FILLS 2 OMELETS

4 bacon slices, cooked until brown and crisp, then crumbled

$^1/_2$ cup diced ripe tomato ($^1/_4$-inch dice)

$^2/_3$ cup grated cheese, such as sharp cheddar, Swiss, or provolone, or a combination

Prepare the Classic Omelet (page 285) and add the filling ingredients in Step 3. If desired, set aside some of the fillings to sprinkle over the omelet as a garnish.

Steak and Mushroom Omelet Filling

FILLS 2 OMELETS

2 tablespoons ($^1/_4$ stick) butter

$^1/_2$ medium-size onion, cut into $^1/_4$-inch dice (about $^1/_2$ cup)

4 button mushrooms, sliced $^1/_8$-inch thick

$^1/_2$ cup finely diced cooked steak or sausage

$^1/_4$ cup grated sharp cheddar

$^1/_4$ cup grated mozzarella cheese

1. Melt the butter in a medium-size skillet over medium heat. Add the onion and mushrooms and cook until lightly browned and tender, 5 to 10 minutes. Add the steak and cook until warmed through.

2. Prepare the Classic Omelet (page 285) and add the steak and mushroom mixture, cheddar, and mozzarella in Step 3. If desired, set aside some of the cheese to sprinkle over the omelet as a garnish.

Greek Omelet Filling

FILLS 2 OMELETS

2 tablespoons ($^1/_4$ stick) butter

$^1/_2$ medium-size yellow onion, cut into $^1/_4$-inch dice (about $^1/_2$ cup)

2 packed cups baby spinach (about $2^1/_2$ ounces)

1 small ripe tomato, cut into $^1/_2$-inch dice (about $^1/_3$ cup)

$^1/_4$ cup crumbled feta cheese, at room temperature

1. Melt the butter in a large, nonstick skillet over medium-low heat. Add the onion and cook, stirring frequently, until soft and translucent, about 5 minutes. Add the spinach and cook, turning frequently with tongs, until it wilts, 3 to 5 minutes. Add the tomato and cook, stirring occasionally, until warmed through, 1 to 2 minutes.

2. Prepare the Classic Omelet (page 285) and add the spinach mixture and feta cheese in Step 3.

Brandywine is one of the tastiest heirloom tomatoes.

Spring Frittata
with Ham, Asparagus, and Herbs

A spring frittata has all the appeal of an omelet, but the preparation is more relaxed since one skillet full serves several people. And while some recipes ask you to flip the frittata over to cook the top, we've simplified the process, running the frittata under the broiler until the cheese is melted and fragrant and the eggs turn a puffy golden brown. **SERVES 2 TO 4**

Tied with twine, freshly-cut pencil-thin spring asparagus takes on a rustic look.

1 tablespoon unsalted butter
¹/₃ cup finely sliced leek
    (white and light green parts)
1 clove garlic, thinly sliced
4 spears fresh asparagus, woody ends
    trimmed (see box, page 227),
    peeled if desired
About 3 ounces ham, cut into ¹/₃-inch
    dice (¹/₂ cup)
6 large eggs
¹/₄ cup whole or low-fat milk
2 teaspoons minced fresh dill
1 tablespoon finely chopped fresh chives
1 teaspoon grated lemon zest
Salt and freshly ground black pepper
¹/₃ cup grated Pecorino Romano cheese

1. Melt the butter in an 8- or 9-inch, nonstick, ovenproof skillet over low heat. Add the leek and garlic and cook very slowly, stirring frequently, until soft and golden, 10 minutes, then set the skillet aside off the heat.

2. Meanwhile, fill a large bowl of water with ice cubes and set aside.

3. Bring a skillet of salted water to a boil over high heat. Add the asparagus spears and cook until blanched, about 2 minutes. Immediately drain the asparagus in a colander, then plunge them into the bowl

of ice water to stop the cooking. Drain the asparagus again in the colander.

4. Cut the asparagus spears into ¹/₂-inch pieces. Scatter the asparagus and ham over the leek mixture in the skillet.

5. Preheat the broiler and set the rack about 5 inches from the heat source.

6. Place the eggs and milk in a medium-size bowl and whisk to combine. Add the dill, chives, and lemon zest, then season with salt and pepper to taste.

7. Add the egg mixture to the skillet with the leek mixture and cook, without stirring, over medium-low heat until the bottom and sides have set, about 4 minutes. The top of the frittata will still be wet.

8. Sprinkle the cheese over the frittata and place the skillet under the broiler. Cook until the top puffs and turns golden brown, 3 to 5 minutes. Remove the frittata from the broiler and let it rest for 2 minutes.

9. Run a heat-proof rubber spatula or small knife around the edge of the frittata to release it from the skillet. Slide the frittata onto a serving plate. Cut it into 4 wedges and serve hot or warm.

Spanish Egg "Soufflé Cake"

At first glance, you may think this is a coffee cake baked in a decorative Bundt pan. But when sliced, you'll discover a light egg filling accented with Spanish flavors— sweet red peppers, purple olives, Manchego cheese, and pale green artichoke hearts. This unusual brunch dish tastes like a frittata, only it looks prettier. The flour that's mixed into the egg batter provides structure, allowing for a "cake" shape that slices beautifully. It isn't the sort of dish you whip up on a busy morning, but you can always make it the night before. Refrigerated overnight, it's just as good (or maybe even better) served at room temperature the next day. **SERVES 8**

2 large (about ³/₄ pound total) Yukon
  Gold or waxy potatoes (such as
  White Rose), peeled and cut into
  ¹/₄-inch dice
Salt
Butter, for greasing the Bundt pan
2 tablespoons olive oil
1 medium-size red bell pepper, stemmed,
  seeded, and cut into ¹/₄-inch dice
  (about 1 cup)
¹/₃ cup thinly sliced scallions, including
  white and 3 inches of green
2 large cloves garlic, minced
1 can (about 14 ounces) water-packed
  artichoke hearts, drained and
  quartered
¹/₂ cup sliced pitted black olives
Freshly ground black pepper
12 large eggs
1¹/₂ cups grated Manchego or sharp
  cheddar cheese (about 8 ounces)
1 tablespoon minced fresh oregano
1 tablespoon fresh thyme leaves
2 tablespoons minced fresh chives
2 tablespoons minced fresh flat-leaf
  parsley
1 cup unbleached all-purpose flour
1¹/₂ teaspoons baking powder
1 cup whole or low-fat milk

1. Bring a small saucepan of water to
a boil over high heat. Add the potatoes
and ¹/₂ teaspoon of salt and cook until
crisp-tender, about 5 minutes. Drain the
potatoes in a colander and set aside.

2. Position a rack in the center of the
oven and preheat the oven to 400°F.
Butter a 10-inch (12 cup) Bundt pan
and set it aside.

3. Heat the olive oil in a large skillet over
medium heat. Add the bell pepper and
cook for 2 minutes. Reduce the heat to
medium-low; add the drained potatoes
and the scallions and garlic. Cook, stirring
frequently, for 5 minutes. Add the
artichokes and olives and season with salt
and pepper to taste. Remove the skillet
from the heat and set it aside.

4. Whisk the eggs in a medium-size bowl.
Add the cheese, oregano, thyme, chives,
and parsley and stir to combine.

5. Place the flour, baking powder, and
1 teaspoon of salt in a large bowl and
whisk to blend.

6. Slowly add the milk to the flour mixture
whisking constantly. Add the egg mixture
and whisk to blend. Add the vegetable
mixture and stir to combine. Pour the
mixture into the prepared pan.

7. Bake the "cake" until it is set, turns
golden, and a toothpick inserted in the
center comes out clean, 35 to 45 minutes.

8. Remove the pan from the oven and
let it cool on a wire rack for 10 minutes.
Unmold the "cake" onto a serving plate.
Serve it warm or at room temperature,
cutting it into thick slices. The "cake"
can be refrigerated, covered, overnight.
Let it return to room temperature before
serving.

*The purple coneflower, or
echinacea, is used as a
medicinal herb that
provides a boost to the
immune system. And it's
lovely too.*

Bacon, Corn, and Arugula Quiche

Smoky bacon, sweet corn, and spicy arugula all share the spotlight in this delicious, rich quiche. If fresh sweet corn is not available, you can use frozen. And if you're in a hurry, use an organic store-bought crust or skip the crust entirely (the quiche bakes the same way; just be sure to butter the dish). No matter what, it will be delicious.

MAKES ONE 9-INCH QUICHE

Savory Pie Crust (page 387),
    or 1 store-bought 9-inch pie crust
    (see box, page 350)

1 tablespoon Dijon mustard

6 slices (8 ounces) thick-cut bacon,
    cut in 1/2-inch dice

8 ounces white or cremini mushrooms,
    cut in 1/4-inch slices (about 2 cups)

1/2 cup thinly sliced scallions, including
    white and 3 inches of green

2 1/2 ounces (about 3 packed cups)
    baby arugula

2 teaspoons good-quality balsamic
    vinegar (see sidebar, page 87)

3 large eggs

1 cup heavy (whipping) cream

1/4 teaspoon salt

1/4 teaspoon freshly ground black pepper

1 cup fresh corn kernels (see box,
    page 29) or frozen (thawed)

1 cup (4 ounces) grated Swiss or
    Gruyère cheese

1. Roll out the pie crust dough into an 11-inch circle and place it in a 9-inch pie plate, patting it in to fit. Trim the dough with a pair of kitchen scissors, leaving a 3/4-inch overhang. Fold the edge under to form a double layer and crimp or flute the crust around the edge of the pie plate. Pierce the crust all over with a fork and brush the Dijon mustard over it. Place the crust in the freezer for 30 minutes.

2. Meanwhile, cook the bacon in a large skillet over medium heat until brown and crisp, about 4 minutes. Transfer the bacon to paper towels to drain. Pour off all but 2 tablespoons of the bacon fat.

3. Add the mushrooms to the skillet and cook for 5 minutes. Add the scallions and cook until the mushrooms soften, 3 to 5 minutes longer. Add the arugula and cook until it wilts, about 30 seconds. Remove the skillet from the heat and add the vinegar, stirring to combine.

Touching and smelling help children learn about flowering sweet peas.

4. Position a rack in the lower third of the oven and set a rimmed baking sheet on the rack. Preheat the oven to 375°F.

5. Place the eggs, cream, salt, and pepper in a medium-size bowl and whisk to combine. Add the corn and cheese and stir to mix.

6. Sprinkle the bacon over the bottom of the pie crust and add the mushroom mixture. Pour the egg mixture into the crust.

7. Place the quiche on the baking sheet in the oven and bake it until puffed and golden, 40 to 50 minutes. Remove the quiche from the oven and let it cool on a wire rack for 10 minutes. Cut the quiche into wedges and serve warm or at room temperature.

Spinach, Feta, and Mushroom Quiche

*T*his quiche isn't shy. The rich custard base is the perfect vehicle for the robust flavors of spinach, mushrooms, and onion, topped with feta cheese. An organic store-bought crust will do, but if you want to wow your guests, make your own savory crust, with fresh herbs baked into the dough. **MAKES ONE 9-INCH QUICHE**

1 Savory Pie Crust (page 387),
    or 1 store-bought 9-inch pie crust
    (see box, page 350)
3 tablespoons olive oil
8 ounces white or cremini mushrooms,
    cut into $1/4$-inch slices (about 2 cups)
1 large yellow onion, cut into $1/4$-inch
    dice (about 1 cup)
$1/2$ teaspoon salt
5 ounces (about 6 packed cups)
    baby spinach
3 large eggs
1 cup half-and-half
Freshly ground black pepper
7 ounces feta cheese, crumbled
    ($1^1/4$ cups)

1. Roll out the pie crust dough into an 11-inch circle and place it in a 9-inch pie plate, patting to fit. Trim the dough with a pair of kitchen scissors, leaving a $3/4$-inch overhang. Fold the edge under to form a double layer and crimp or flute the crust around the edge of the pie plate. Pierce the crust all over with a fork. Place the crust in the freezer for 30 minutes.

2. Position a rack in the lower third of the oven and set a rimmed baking sheet on the rack. Preheat the oven to 375°F.

3. Heat the olive oil in a large skillet, preferably nonstick, over medium heat.

Add the mushrooms, onion, and salt. Cook, stirring occasionally, until the vegetables are soft and golden, 8 to 10 minutes.

4. Add the spinach and stir until it wilts, 2 to 4 minutes.

5. Place the eggs and half-and-half in a small bowl, season with pepper to taste, and whisk to combine.

6. Spoon the spinach mixture over the bottom of the chilled pie crust and sprinkle the feta cheese on top. Pour the egg mixture into the crust.

7. Place the quiche on the baking sheet in the oven and bake it until puffed and golden, 40 to 50 minutes. Remove the quiche from the oven and let it cool on a wire rack for 10 minutes. Cut the quiche into wedges and serve warm or at room temperature.

Savory Bread Pudding
with Spinach, Gruyère, and Shiitakes

Puffed and golden, this savory bread pudding emerges from the oven with the earthy perfume of shiitake mushrooms. Served with fresh fruit and slices of bacon or ham, it's a delicious centerpiece for a brunch buffet. It also performs double duty as an elegant side dish for a rib roast or steak. If you happen to have leftovers, they heat up well in the microwave. **SERVES 6 TO 8**

Butter, for greasing the baking pan
2 cups stale bread, cut into
    $^{1}/_{4}$-inch cubes
1 pound baby spinach
    (about 13 packed cups)
1 cup (4 ounces) grated Gruyère
    cheese
2 tablespoons olive oil or butter
8 ounces fresh shiitake mushrooms,
    stems discarded, caps cut into
    $^{1}/_{4}$-inch slices
2 tablespoons minced shallots
3 large eggs
2 cups half-and-half
1 teaspoon salt
Freshly ground black pepper

1. Position a rack in the lower third of the oven and preheat the oven to 350°F.

2. Butter a 9 by 13–inch baking pan. Spread the bread cubes in the prepared baking pan and set aside.

3. Place about one fourth of the spinach in a large, preferably nonstick, skillet over medium-low heat and cook, turning frequently with tongs, until it wilts, 3 to 5 minutes. (If you are not using a nonstick skillet, add 1 tablespoon of water to the spinach.) Continue adding spinach to the skillet until all of it has wilted.

Rudbeckia sunflowers show off the colors of autumn.

4. Spread the spinach evenly over the bread cubes. Sprinkle ¹/₂ cup of the cheese on top of the spinach.

5. Heat the olive oil in the same skillet over medium-high heat. Add the mushrooms and shallots and cook, stirring frequently, until tender, 5 to 8 minutes. Scatter the mushroom mixture evenly over the spinach.

6. Place the eggs, half-and-half, and salt in a medium-size bowl, season with pepper to taste, and whisk to blend. Pour the egg mixture over the mushroom mixture and top with the remaining ¹/₂ cup of Gruyère cheese. Use a spatula or spoon to press down on the bread pudding, making sure all of the ingredients are moistened by the egg mixture.

7. Bake the bread pudding until puffed and golden, 35 to 45 minutes. Let it sit on a wire rack until firm, 10 minutes. Serve warm.

Pasta à la Mama

Scrambled eggs with pasta, Parmesan, and mozzarella cheese sounds like a strange combination, but it makes a really good breakfast. I got the idea from Hugo's restaurant in West Hollywood, where they've had a similar dish on the menu for years called Pasta Mama. It's a great use for leftover pasta, but if the pasta is cold, zap it in the microwave for a few seconds to take the chill off before adding it to the hot eggs. I often add leftover breakfast sausage or sauteed mushrooms, making this filling breakfast even tastier. **SERVES 2 OR 3**

4 large eggs
1 tablespoon unsalted butter
3 ounces cooked breakfast sausage links (optional), cut into ¹/₃-inch-thick slices (about ¹/₂ cup)
1 cup cooked penne or rigatoni, at room temperature, cut into bite-size pieces
¹/₃ cup freshly grated Parmesan cheese (about 1 ounce)
¹/₂ cup shredded mozzarella cheese (about 2 ounces)

1. Place the eggs in a medium-size bowl and whisk to blend.

2. Melt the butter in a large, nonstick skillet over medium heat. Add the eggs and sausage, if using, and cook for 30 seconds. Add the pasta and cook, stirring constantly, until the eggs begin to set, 1 minutes.

3. Add the Parmesan cheese and stir to blend. Sprinkle the mozzarella over the egg mixture, reduce the heat to low, and cover the skillet. Cook until the cheese melts, about 30 seconds, then turn off the heat. Let the skillet sit, covered, for 30 seconds to 1 minute, then serve the eggs immediately.

Mama Fries

Baked potatoes are a favorite at our house, especially yellow-fleshed Yukon Golds. When I make them for dinner, I always throw a few extras in the oven and remove them a few minutes before they're done (see the sidebar, this page). They are perfect for these home-style breakfast potatoes my kids call "Mama Fries." When slices of baked potato are pan-fried in butter and olive oil, they come out brown and crunchy on the outside, with a tender center. The potatoes make a great breakfast side dish served with omelets or scrambled eggs, or, later in the day, with grilled steak or chicken. **SERVES 2**

1 tablespoon unsalted butter
1 tablespoon olive oil
3 medium-size baked Yukon Gold
    potatoes (about 1 pound total),
    sliced lengthwise into 3/8-inch slices
Coarse (kosher) salt

1. Heat the butter and olive oil in a large, nonstick skillet over medium heat. Add the potatoes, making sure the slices do not touch.

2. Cook the potatoes until they are golden brown and crisp on the bottom, 5 to 10 minutes. Carefully flip the potatoes with a spatula and cook them until brown and crisp on the second side, 5 to 8 minutes longer.

3. Transfer the potatoes to paper towels to absorb any excess oil. Season with salt to taste and serve hot.

A basket of freshly dug potatoes.

Baked Golden Potatoes

For baked potatoes with flesh that's more moist and creamy than that of a russet, try using yellow-fleshed Yukon Gold or Yellow Finn potatoes (about 1/3 pound each).

While the oven preheats to 400°F, rinse the potatoes but do not pat them dry. Puncture the skin in several places with a fork or knife. The tiny holes will allow the steam to escape while the potatoes cook so the skin doesn't split. Then place the potatoes in the hot oven while they are still wet and bake them directly on the rack.

For a more flavorful skin that's slightly less crisp, rinse the potatoes and dry them with paper towels. Puncture the skins, rub the potatoes with a little olive oil, place them on a baking sheet, and sprinkle them generously with coarse (kosher) salt.

Either way, bake the potatoes until they are soft when gently pressed or easily pierced with a fork, about 1 hour.

Apple Bran Muffins

A healthy muffin that's also moist and tasty is hard to come by, but this one fits the bill. Tidbits of apple make the muffins naturally sweet and delectable, while the low-fat ingredients help keep the calorie count down. Bran is nutritious, but most bran muffins are heavy and dense. These, however, are surprisingly light and tender. If you are tempted to indulge just a bit, sprinkle on the cinnamon-sugar topping for a pleasant crunch. **MAKES 15 STANDARD-SIZE MUFFINS**

2¼ cups wheat bran

2 cups nonfat milk

2 tablespoons plain nonfat yogurt

Butter, for greasing the muffin cups
   (unless using cupcake liners)

2 cups whole wheat pastry flour
   (see sidebar, page 6)

⅔ cup firmly packed light brown
   sugar

1 tablespoon baking powder

1 teaspoon baking soda

½ teaspoon salt

½ teaspoon ground cinnamon,
   plus 1 teaspoon of ground
   cinnamon for the topping
   (optional)

2 large eggs

⅓ cup canola oil

⅓ cup unsweetened applesauce

2 teaspoons pure vanilla extract

2 small, sweet apples, such as Gala or
   Golden Delicious, peeled, cored,
   and cut into ¼-inch dice
   (about 1 cup)

⅓ cup granulated sugar (optional)

1. Make the muffins: Place the wheat bran, milk, and yogurt in a large bowl and stir to combine. Let the bran mixture sit at room temperature until the bran softens, about 30 minutes.

2. Position a rack in the lower third of the oven and preheat the oven to 350°F. Butter 15 standard-size muffin cups or line them with cupcake liners (see Note).

3. Place the flour, brown sugar, baking powder, baking soda, salt, and ½ teaspoon of the cinnamon in a large bowl and whisk to combine well.

4. Place the eggs, oil, applesauce, and vanilla in a small bowl and whisk to combine well. Add the egg mixture to the bran mixture and stir to combine.

5. Add the bran mixture to the flour mixture and stir with a rubber spatula until just combined. Fold in the apples. Do not overmix the batter or the muffins will be tough. Spoon the batter into the prepared muffin cups, filling them almost to the brim.

6. Make the topping, if using: Combine the granulated sugar and the remaining 1 teaspoon of cinnamon in a small bowl. Sprinkle the top of each muffin with about 1 teaspoon of the cinnamon sugar mixture.

Note: You'll need to use two 12-cup muffin tins or one 12-cup and one 6-cup muffin tin to bake these. Butter only 15 muffin cups, leaving the rest bare. If you do not have 2 muffin tins, bake the muffins in two batches.

7. Bake the muffins until they are golden brown and a toothpick inserted in the center of one comes out clean, 20 to 30 minutes.

8. Place the muffin pan(s) on a wire rack and let the muffins cool for 10 minutes.

Remove the muffins from the pan and serve warm. The muffins taste best the day they are made. If necessary, you can store them in an airtight container for up to 3 days and reheat them in a microwave for 10 seconds or in a preheated 350°F oven for 5 to 10 minutes.

Notes: You can save time by using a food processor fitted with the grater blade to grate the carrots and apple. If you use a box grater, use the medium-size holes.

You'll need to use two 12-cup muffin tins or one 12-cup and one 6-cup muffin tin to bake these. Butter only 16 muffin cups, leaving the rest bare. If you do not have 2 muffin tins, bake the muffins in two batches.

The Original Morning Glory Muffin

Who can resist a cinnamon-scented muffin bursting with fruit, carrots, coconut, and nuts? We have our own chef Pam McKinstry to thank for this now famous muffin, which she created when she owned the Morning Glory Café on the island of Nantucket. Her recipe was published in Gourmet *magazine in 1981, and ten years later, was chosen as one of the magazine's twenty-five favorite recipes from the past fifty years. These supermoist muffins taste even better a day after they're baked. But who can wait that long?* **MAKES 16 STANDARD-SIZE MUFFINS**

Butter, for greasing the muffin cups
    (unless using cupcake liners)
2¼ cups unbleached all-purpose flour
1¼ cups sugar
1 tablespoon ground cinnamon
2 teaspoons baking soda
½ teaspoon salt
1 can (8 ounces) crushed pineapple,
    drained
2 cups finely grated carrots
    (from about 6 carrots; see Notes)
1 large crisp apple, such as Fuji, Gala,
    or Granny Smith, peeled and grated
    (see Notes)
¾ cup raisins
½ cup shredded, sweetened coconut
½ cup coarsely chopped pecans or
    walnuts

3 large eggs
1 cup canola oil
1 teaspoon pure vanilla extract

1. Position a rack in the lower third of the oven and preheat the oven to 350°F. Butter 16 standard-size muffin cups or line them with cupcake liners (see Notes).

2. Place the flour, sugar, cinnamon, baking soda, and salt in a large bowl and whisk well to combine. Add the pineapple, carrots, apple, raisins, coconut, and nuts and stir to combine.

3. Place the eggs, oil, and vanilla in a small bowl and whisk to combine well. Add the egg mixture to the flour mixture and stir until just combined. Spoon the batter into the prepared muffin cups, filling them almost to the brim.

4. Bake the muffins until they are golden brown and a toothpick inserted in the center of one comes out clean, 30 to 40 minutes.

5. Place the muffin pan(s) on a wire rack and let the muffins cool for 10 minutes. Remove the muffins from the pan to finish cooling. The muffins can be stored in an airtight container at room temperature for up to 3 days or frozen for up to 2 months. Let the muffins thaw in the refrigerator overnight and return to room temperature before serving.

Banana Maple-Walnut Muffins

Hungry kids and a bunch of overripe bananas were my inspiration for this family breakfast favorite. I turned those very soft bananas into incredibly moist and flavorful muffins. The vanilla, ginger, and cinnamon create a captivating aroma that will entice everyone to hurry into the kitchen. **MAKES 12 STANDARD-SIZE MUFFINS**

Butter, for greasing the muffin cups (unless using cupcake liners)
2 cups whole wheat pastry flour (see sidebar, page 6)
1½ teaspoons baking powder
¼ teaspoon baking soda
¼ teaspoon salt
¼ teaspoon ground ginger
¼ teaspoon ground cinnamon
2 large eggs
½ cup pure maple syrup (see box, page 280)
½ cup firmly packed light brown sugar
⅓ cup whole or low-fat milk
¼ cup canola oil
¼ teaspoon pure vanilla extract
1½ cups mashed very ripe bananas (about 4)
¾ cup chopped walnuts

1. Position a rack in the center of the oven and preheat the oven to 375°F. Butter 12 standard-size muffin cups or line them with cupcake liners.

2. Place the flour, baking powder, baking soda, salt, ginger, and cinnamon in a large bowl and whisk to combine well.

3. Place the eggs, maple syrup, brown sugar, milk, oil, and vanilla in a medium-size bowl and whisk to combine well. Add the bananas and stir to combine.

4. Add the banana mixture to the flour mixture and stir with a rubber spatula until just combined. Fold in the walnuts. Do not overmix the batter or the muffins will be tough. Spoon the batter into the

More Breakfast Delights

Don't miss these other marvelous muffins and breakfast treats:

Raspberry Corn Muffins, page 5

Raspberry Pecan Muffins, page 6

Raspberry Cream Scones, page 7

Favorite Raspberry Jam, page 9

Apricot Raspberry Jam, page 10

Cornmeal Breakfast Pancakes with Raspberry Maple Syrup, page 11

Farm Stand Carrot Cake Muffins, page 332

prepared muffin cups, filling them almost to the brim.

5. Bake the muffins until they are golden brown and a toothpick inserted into the center of one comes out clean, 20 to 30 minutes.

6. Place the muffin pan on a wire rack and let the muffins cool for 10 minutes. Remove the muffins from the pan and serve warm. The muffins taste best the day they are made. If necessary, you can store them in an airtight container for up to 3 days and reheat them in a microwave for 10 seconds or in a preheated 350°F oven for 5 to 10 minutes.

Note: You'll need to use two 12-cup muffin tins or one 12-cup and one 6-cup muffin tin to bake these. Butter only 15 muffin cups, leaving the rest bare. If you do not have 2 muffin tins, bake the muffins in two batches.

Pumpkin Pecan Muffins

The crunchy streusel topping makes these pumpkin muffins a Farm Stand favorite. The muffins are irresistible on crisp fall mornings, but are just as delicious in winter, spring, or summer. A blend of aromatic spices and tart orange zest accentuates the sweet pumpkin and pecans. And here's the bonus: With canned pumpkin puree, the muffins are quick and easy to make. **MAKES 15 STANDARD-SIZE MUFFINS**

FOR THE TOPPING
1/3 cup unbleached all-purpose flour
1/3 cup packed light brown sugar
1/4 teaspoon ground cinnamon
4 tablespoons (1/2 stick) cold, unsalted
   butter, cut into small pieces

FOR THE MUFFINS
Butter, for greasing the muffin cups
   (unless using cupcake liners)
1 2/3 cups unbleached all-purpose
   flour
1 tablespoon baking soda
1/2 teaspoon salt
1/2 teaspoon ground allspice
1/2 teaspoon ground nutmeg
1/2 teaspoon ground cardamom
   (see sidebar, page 368)
1/2 teaspoon ground cinnamon
3/4 cup chopped pecans
3 large eggs
4 tablespoons (1/2 stick) unsalted
   butter, melted
2 teaspoons grated orange zest
1 can (15 ounces) pumpkin puree
2 1/4 cups granulated sugar

1. Position a rack in the lower third of the oven and preheat the oven to 375°F.

2. Make the topping: Place the flour, brown sugar, and cinnamon in a medium-size bowl and stir to combine. Add the butter pieces. Using a pastry blender, 2 knives, or your fingers, blend the butter into the topping until it is crumbly and well combined. Set the topping aside.

3. Make the muffins: Butter 15 standard-size muffin cups or line them with cupcake liners (see Note).

4. Place the flour, baking soda, salt, allspice, nutmeg, cardamom, and cinnamon in a large bowl and whisk to combine well. Add the pecans and stir to combine.

5. Place the eggs, melted butter, orange zest, pumpkin, and granulated sugar in a medium-size bowl and whisk to combine well.

6. Add the pumpkin mixture to the flour mixture and stir with a rubber spatula until just combined. Do not overmix the batter or the muffins will be tough. Spoon the batter into the prepared muffin cups, filling them almost to the brim. Sprinkle the top of each muffin with about 2 teaspoons of the topping.

7. Bake the muffins until they are golden brown and a toothpick inserted into the center of one comes out clean, 20 to 30 minutes.

8. Place the muffin pan(s) on a wire rack and let the muffins cool for 10 minutes. Remove the muffins from the pan and serve warm. The muffins taste best the day they are made. If necessary, you can store them in an airtight container for up to 3 days and reheat them in a microwave for 10 seconds or in a preheated 350°F oven for 5 to 10 minutes.

Young Farm Stand visitors searching for the perfect Halloween pumpkin.

Cinnamon Nut Rolls

You'll impress your weekend guests when they awake to freshly baked cinnamon rolls—warm and loaded with nuts and, if you like, raisins. The Danish Pastry Dough is what makes these special; the buttery layers of yeast dough create a light, airy texture. But don't wait until the last minute to get started. At our Farm Stand, we make the dough the day ahead and form the cinnamon rolls early the next morning so they can rest for an hour before going in the oven. Best of all, if you're not baking for a crowd, you can freeze the unbaked rolls and bake them later, a few at a time. The rolls are delicious plain, but those with a sweet tooth like them topped with our sweet cream cheese frosting. **MAKES ABOUT 20 NUT ROLLS**

FOR THE NUT ROLLS

1 recipe Danish Pastry Dough
  (recipe follows)

1 large egg

2 cups firmly packed, brown sugar

2 tablespoons ground cinnamon

1 cup chopped walnuts or pecans

1 cup raisins (optional)

FOR THE FROSTING (OPTIONAL)

4 ounces cream cheese, softened

8 tablespoons (1 stick) unsalted butter,
  softened

2 cups confectioners' sugar

1 tablespoon pure vanilla extract

1. Make the nut rolls: Line 2 rimmed baking sheets with parchment paper and set them aside. (One 12 by 17-inch baking sheet holds about 10 rolls.)

2. Lightly flour a work surface, then roll out the dough into a roughly 14 by 22-inch rectangle, working so that one of the long edges is closest to you.

3. Place the egg and 1 teaspoon of water in a small bowl and whisk to blend. Brush the egg wash over the dough.

4. Place the brown sugar, cinnamon, nuts, and raisins, if using, in a small bowl and stir to combine. Spread this mixture evenly over the dough, leaving a 2-inch border of dough uncovered at the far edge and a ¹/₂-inch-wide border on each short side.

5. Starting with the long edge closest to you, tightly roll the dough into a cylinder. Moisten the far edge with water and press on the dough to seal it.

6. Using a sharp knife, cut the dough into 1-inch-thick slices. Place the slices 2 inches

apart on the prepared baking sheets. (If you want to bake some of the rolls at a later time, see the Note.)

7. Let the sliced rolls sit, uncovered, in a warm, draft-free spot until doubled in size, 30 minutes to 1 hour.

8. Position a rack in the lower third of the oven and preheat the oven to 350°F.

9. Place one baking sheet of rolls in the oven and reduce the temperature to 325°F. Bake the rolls until they are puffed and golden brown, 25 to 30 minutes. Place the baking sheet on a wire rack and let the rolls cool. If you are baking the second batch of rolls, increase the oven temperature to 350°F before placing them in the oven, then reduce the temperature to 325°F.

10. Meanwhile, make the frosting, if desired: Place the cream cheese and butter in a medium-size bowl and beat by hand until smooth. Sift the confectioners' sugar into the bowl and beat until combined. Add the vanilla and stir to combine.

11. While the nut rolls are still slightly warm, spread each with a generous dollop of frosting, if using. Serve the nut rolls warm or at room temperature on the day they are made.

Danish Pastry Dough

Layers and layers of butter folded into a yeast dough produce a light, tender texture reminiscent of pastries from the finest European bakeries. Making this dough isn't difficult, but it does take some time. While the dough can be made in one day, at our Farm

Note: If you want to bake some of the nut rolls at a later time, place the baking sheet holding those rolls in the freezer immediately after you slice them. Once frozen, wrap each roll individually in plastic wrap and place in an airtight container. The nut rolls can be frozen for up to 1 month. Let the rolls thaw overnight in the refrigerator the day before you plan to bake them. The next morning, unwrap the rolls, place them on a lined baking sheet, and continue with Step 7.

Stand we like to let it rest overnight before we start rolling and folding in the butter. Once you begin the folding process, the dough needs three separate hour-long periods to rest, so allow about half a day and make room in your refrigerator for the sheet pan. The dough can be made up to two days in advance.

**MAKES DOUGH FOR APPROXIMATELY
20 CINNAMON NUT ROLLS**

1 cup warm whole milk (about 110°F)
¼ ounce (1 packet) dry yeast
1 large egg
½ teaspoon pure vanilla extract
3½ cups unbleached all-purpose flour,
    plus more for dusting the dough
3½ tablespoons sugar
¾ teaspoon salt
1 cup plus 2 tablespoons (2¼ sticks)
    unsalted butter, softened

1. Place the warm milk in a small bowl, sprinkle the yeast over it, and let sit until the yeast dissolves, about 5 minutes.

2. Place the egg and vanilla in another small bowl and whisk to blend. Add the egg mixture to the milk mixture and whisk just enough to blend.

3. Place the flour, sugar, and salt in a large bowl and stir to combine. Add 2 tablespoons of the butter. Using your fingers, blend the butter into the flour mixture until it disappears. The mixture will be very dry.

4. Add the milk mixture to the flour mixture and stir to blend. Turn the dough onto a lightly floured work surface and knead it by hand until smooth, 3 to 5 minutes. Lightly dust a large bowl with flour and add the dough.

Dust the top of the dough with flour and cover the bowl with plastic wrap. Refrigerate the dough for at least 2 hours or up to 24 hours.

5. Remove the dough from the refrigerator and punch it down. Turn the dough out on a lightly floured work surface and roll it into a rectangle, roughly 14 by 22 inches.

6. Using your hands or a rubber spatula, spread the remaining 1 cup of butter evenly over the dough. Fold the dough into thirds, as you would a business letter (fold the left side to the center and fold the right side on top of it).

7. Roll the dough again into a 14 by 22–inch rectangle. Fold the dough again into thirds and transfer it to a lightly floured rimmed baking sheet. Cover the dough with plastic wrap and refrigerate it for 50 minutes to 1 hour.

8. Repeat Step 7, rolling out and folding the dough, then refrigerate it again for 50 minutes to 1 hour.

9. Repeat Step 7 once more, rolling out and folding the dough and refrigerating it for 50 minutes to 1 hour (the dough will be rolled out, folded, and refrigerated for a total of 3 times).

10. At this point, the dough can be used for making Cinnamon Nut Rolls (page 303). If you are not planning on using the dough immediately, cover it with plastic wrap and refrigerate for up to 2 days.

Persimmon and Date Breakfast Bread

Persimmons are one of the treasures of autumn. There are two types, but only very ripe, heart-shaped Hachiya persimmons are good for baking (for more about persimmons, see the box on page 85). The fruit gives this breakfast bread a moist texture that's laced with warm exotic spices, chewy dates, and crisp walnuts. The not-too-sweet bread is delicious lightly toasted and spread with cream cheese or honey butter. Plus, it keeps in the refrigerator for up to a week when tightly wrapped, or in the freezer for up to a month. If persimmons are hard to find, you can substitute pumpkin puree with equally delicious results. **MAKES ONE 5 BY 9-INCH LOAF**

Butter, for greasing the loaf pan
2 large eggs
$^1/_2$ cup plus 2 tablespoons canola oil
2 very ripe Hachiya persimmons, peeled, seeded, and mashed (about 1 cup)
$^1/_2$ cup chopped pitted dates
$^1/_2$ cup chopped walnuts, toasted (see box, page 98)
$1^3/_4$ cups unbleached all-purpose flour
1 cup sugar
1 teaspoon baking soda
$^1/_2$ teaspoon baking powder
$^1/_2$ teaspoon salt
$^1/_2$ teaspoon Chinese five-spice powder
$^1/_2$ teaspoon ground nutmeg
$^1/_2$ teaspoon ground cinnamon
$^1/_4$ teaspoon ground cloves

1. Position a rack in the center of the oven and preheat the oven to 350°F. Butter a 5 by 9-inch loaf pan and set it aside.

2. Place the eggs and oil in a medium-size bowl and whisk to combine. Add the persimmons, dates, and walnuts and stir to blend.

3. Place the flour, sugar, baking soda, baking powder, salt, five-spice powder, nutmeg, cinnamon, and cloves in a large bowl and whisk to blend. Add the egg mixture and stir to combine. Do not overmix or the bread will be tough. Pour the batter into the prepared loaf pan.

4. Bake the bread until a toothpick inserted in the center comes out clean, 60 to 70 minutes.

5. Let the bread cool on a wire rack for 15 minutes. Remove the bread from the pan and return it to the rack to finish cooling. Serve warm or at room temperature. The breakfast bread can be tightly wrapped in plastic wrap and refrigerated for up to a week or frozen for a month. Let it thaw overnight in the refrigerator and return to room temperature before serving.

A Hachiya persimmon.

Cinnamon Walnut Coffee Cake

Breakfasting on coffee cake scented with cinnamon and ginger, and topped with a nutty, spicy crumb topping, is a sweet way to start the day. Straight out of the oven, the cake smells so wonderful that you may have trouble waiting an hour for it to cool. Cut it sooner, if you can't resist. The topping may crumble, but it will still be delicious. **MAKES ONE 9 BY 13–INCH COFFEE CAKE**

FOR THE TOPPING
³/₄ cup whole wheat pastry flour (see sidebar, page 6)
³/₄ cup firmly packed light brown sugar
5 teaspoons ground cinnamon
Pinch of salt
¹/₃ cup canola oil
2 cups coarsely chopped walnut pieces

FOR THE COFFEE CAKE
Butter, for greasing the baking pan
2 cups whole wheat pastry flour
³/₄ cup firmly packed brown sugar
³/₄ cup granulated sugar
1 teaspoon ground cinnamon
¹/₂ teaspoon salt
¹/₂ teaspoon ground ginger
1 teaspoon baking powder
1 teaspoon baking soda
1 large egg
1 cup buttermilk
¹/₂ cup canola oil
¹/₂ teaspoon pure vanilla extract

1. Position a rack in the lower third of the oven and preheat the oven to 350°F.

2. Make the topping: Place the flour, brown sugar, cinnamon, salt, oil, and the walnuts in a medium-size bowl. Stir to blend and set the topping mixture aside.

3. Make the cake: Generously butter a 9 by 13–inch baking pan and set it aside.

4. Place the flour, brown sugar, granulated sugar, cinnamon, salt, ginger, baking powder, and baking soda in a large bowl, and whisk to combine well.

5. Place the egg, buttermilk, oil, and vanilla in a small bowl and whisk to combine well.

6. Add the egg mixture to the flour mixture and stir until just combined. Do not overmix the batter or the coffee cake will be tough.

Quick Measuring Tip

Since this coffee cake's topping and batter have common ingredients, you can trim a few minutes off the preparation time. Place the bowls for the topping and the batter side by side and then measure each dry ingredient they have in common at the same time, placing the appropriate amount in each bowl. You'll have to open the flour and sugar containers only once.

FARM FRESH

walnuts

Walnuts are unique in the nut world because they are exceptionally high in omega-3 fatty acids. Omega-3s are a "good" fat; studies indicate that they help the heart and circulatory system, including reducing hypertension and lowering cholesterol levels. One ounce of walnuts (about one-quarter cup or fourteen walnut halves) provides two grams of omega-3s, slightly more than what's found in three ounces of salmon. While walnuts are a nutritious and tasty snack, they are high in calories, so enjoy them in moderation.

7. Pour the cake batter into the prepared pan. Sprinkle the topping mixture evenly over the batter.

8. Bake the cake until a toothpick inserted into the center comes out clean, 45 to 55 minutes. Let cool on a wire rack for 1 hour. The coffee cake can be stored in an airtight container at room temperature for up to 3 days or frozen for up to 3 months. Leave it out on the kitchen counter to thaw overnight.

Fragrant cinnamon comes from the inner bark of a Ceylon Cinnamon tree.

Spiced Dried Plum Compote

Prunes, also known as dried plums, plump up delectably when simmered in a sweet and spicy poaching syrup, steeped in black tea and vanilla. For a bit of color, you can leave a few of the unpeeled orange segments in the serving bowl. This concoction is delicious on its own or served on top of plain yogurt or cottage cheese.

MAKES ABOUT 2 CUPS

³/₄ cup sugar
1 whole vanilla bean, split lengthwise
1 tea bag of black tea, such as Darjeeling, orange pekoe, or English breakfast
2 whole star anise
1 cinnamon stick (about 3 inches), broken in half
1 small orange, unpeeled, rinsed and cut into eighths
2 cups pitted dried plums (prunes)

1. Pour 2 cups of water into a medium-size saucepan and add the sugar and vanilla bean. Bring the mixture to a boil over high heat, stirring to dissolve the sugar.

2. Turn off the heat and add the tea bag, star anise, cinnamon, and orange. Let steep, stirring occasionally, for 15 minutes.

3. Remove and discard the tea bag. Remove the vanilla bean and scrape the seeds back into the liquid, reserving the pod to make Vanilla Sugar, if desired (see the sidebar on page 363).

4. Bring the spicy syrup to a simmer over low heat and add the dried plums. Cook until the plums are soft and tender, 10 to 15 minutes.

5. Let the plums cool in the syrup. Discard the star anise, cinnamon stick, and orange segments, if desired. Serve the compote warm, at room temperature, or cold. The compote can be refrigerated, covered, for up to 1 month.

Fresh Fruit Salad
with Lemon Verbena

A bowl of brightly colored summer fruit, lightly flecked with lemon verbena and a splash of citrus-flavored liqueur, makes a simply spectacular side dish for breakfast or a light finale for lunch or dinner. Lemon verbena, with its intense lemony flavor, is a favorite in our herb cutting garden, but you can also use mint. Either herb adds a refreshing fragrance, and the sweet orange liqueur ties the fresh flavors together. Berries and mango are gorgeous, but any mixture of fruit you have on hand will work equally well—especially if you choose a variety of colors and textures. Add delicate fruit, such as very ripe raspberries, just before serving, after you've mixed the other fruits. If the fruit salad isn't sweet enough for your taste, you may want to add a teaspoon or two of sugar. **SERVES 6**

$1^{1}/_{2}$ cups strawberries, hulled and
    sliced
1 cup blackberries or blueberries
1 mango, peeled and cubed
    (see sidebar, page 170)
$1^{1}/_{2}$ cups raspberries
2 tablespoons orange-flavored
    liqueur, such as Cointreau or
    Grand Marnier
1 tablespoon coarsely chopped fresh
    lemon verbena or mint leaves,
    plus lemon verbena or mint sprigs,
    for garnish

Place the strawberries, blueberries, and mango in a large bowl. Just before serving, add the raspberries, liqueur, and chopped lemon verbena. Stir gently to combine. Serve in a large bowl or on a platter, garnished with whole lemon verbena leaves.

We use biodiesel (a vegetable-based fuel) in our Carmel Valley tractors instead of fossil fuels.

Homemade Chai

The aroma of exotic spices and black tea makes chai a wonderful alternative to morning coffee. It's easy and inexpensive to make your own chai, and it keeps in the refrigerator for a week, so you may want to make a double batch. Our Farm Stand customers love this blend of spices, but you can freely change it to suit your taste. Try adding different ones, like star anise or nutmeg. You can also substitute low-fat or fat-free milk or soy milk for the whole milk, if you prefer. **MAKES ABOUT 3 CUPS**

$^1/_2$ teaspoon whole black peppercorns

1 cinnamon stick (about 3 inches)

6 whole cloves

6 whole cardamom pods (see sidebar, page 368), or $^1/_2$ teaspoon ground cardamom

1 piece (2 inches) fresh ginger, unpeeled and thinly sliced

Zest of 1 orange, removed in wide strips (see box, page 14)

4 bags of black tea, such as Darjeeling, orange pekoe, or English breakfast

1 cup whole milk

$^1/_3$ cup sugar

1. Place the peppercorns, cinnamon stick, cloves, cardamom, and ginger slices in a heavy-duty resealable plastic bag and crush them lightly with a rolling pin or mallet (or you can crush them in a mortar, using a pestle).

2. Transfer the crushed spices to a medium-size saucepan. Add the orange zest and 3 cups of water and bring to a boil over high heat. Reduce the heat to low and let simmer for 10 minutes.

3. Remove the saucepan from the heat and add the tea bags. Allow the mixture to steep for 5 minutes, then discard the tea bags.

4. Add the milk and sugar to the saucepan and bring to a simmer over medium heat, stirring until the sugar dissolves.

5. Strain the chai and discard the solids. Serve hot. If not serving immediately, allow the chai to cool to room temperature. It can be refrigerated, covered, for up to 7 days. Reheat it before serving.

Bees search for nectar among our Picotee cosmos flowers.

Smoothies

Many people think of smoothies as a breakfast drink, but they provide a healthy pick-me-up any time of day, supplying a delicious boost of nutrients. Smoothies are a great way to use up very ripe fruit, so feel free to make up your own combinations based on what you have on hand. Frozen fruit works as well as fresh, making smoothies a year-round treat.

Drew's Strawberry Banana Smoothies

At our house, Drew is the official smoothie maker. Our kids can usually cajole him into blending them almost any time of day. We frequently have ripe bananas and he puts them to good use—they add texture and natural sweetness to his smoothies. The frozen strawberries here chill the drink with less ice so the flavors stay vibrant. Sometimes after dinner, Drew adds a half-cup scoop of coconut gelato, making an extra yummy smoothie to satisfy a sweet tooth. **SERVES 2 (ABOUT 12 OUNCES EACH)**

1 large ripe banana, peeled and
   cut in half
1 1/2 cups frozen (unthawed)
   unsweetened strawberries
3/4 cup apple juice
1/2 cup plain whole milk, low-fat,
   or nonfat yogurt
1 1/2 cups ice cubes
   (see sidebar, page 316)

Combine all of the ingredients in a blender and process until smooth. Pour the smoothies into 2 large glasses and serve immediately.

Cherry Smoothies

Sweet cherries and vanilla yogurt make a tasty smoothie that's a bit unusual. You can use fresh cherries, but pit and freeze them first. For convenience, look for frozen cherries at the supermarket. **SERVES 2 (ABOUT 12 OUNCES EACH)**

1 cup frozen pitted cherries
1 cup unsweetened cherry juice
   (see Note)
1 cup frozen nonfat vanilla yogurt
1/4 teaspoon pure vanilla extract
1/2 cup ice cubes (see sidebar, page 316)
1 tablespoon sugar or honey (optional)

Place the cherries, cherry juice, frozen yogurt, vanilla, and crushed ice in a blender and process until smooth. Taste for sweetness, adding the sugar as needed. Pour the smoothies into 2 large glasses and serve immediately.

Note: Look for unsweetened cherry juice (usually from concentrate) in the fruit juice section of the grocery store.

Deep red Bing cherries, plump and sweet, are only available for a brief time in summer. Enjoy them while you can!

How to Crush Ice Cubes

Crushed ice is much easier to blend than cubes. If you don't have an ice crusher, place the ice cubes in a resealable plastic bag. Wrap the bag in a dish towel and pound it with a meat mallet or rolling pin until the ice is crushed. This is a great stress reliever, too!

A Haden mango is juicy ripe when it turns golden yellow with a red blush.

Note: Look for mango nectar in the fruit juice section of the grocery store.

Blueberry Lemon Smoothies

Lemon sorbet and lemonade perk up the flavors of this refreshing and thirst-quenching blueberry smoothie. It's equally delicious made with lime sorbet and limeade instead. **SERVES 2 (ABOUT 12 OUNCES EACH)**

1¼ cups fresh or frozen (unthawed) blueberries
¾ cup nonfat milk or soy milk
½ cup ice cubes (see sidebar, this page)
2 tablespoons undiluted frozen lemonade concentrate
½ cup lemon sorbet or sherbet
½ cup nonfat frozen vanilla yogurt

Place the blueberries, milk, and ice in a blender and process until smooth. Add the lemonade, sorbet, and frozen yogurt and process until smooth. Pour the smoothies into 2 large glasses, and serve immediately.

Strawberry Mango Smoothies

Sometimes an all-fruit smoothie makes a refreshing change. Mangos give this smoothie a thick texture without adding dairy products, and the strawberries add brilliant color. A splash of fresh lemon juice brightens their flavors. Look for mango nectar in the juice section of the grocery store. **SERVES 2 (ABOUT 12 OUNCES EACH)**

1 cup sliced hulled fresh strawberries
1 ripe mango, peeled and cubed (see sidebar, page 170)
1 cup mango nectar (see Note)
1 teaspoon fresh lemon juice
½ cup ice cubes (see sidebar, this page)
Honey (optional)

Place the strawberries, mango, mango nectar, lemon juice, and ice in a blender and process until smooth. Taste for sweetness, adding honey to taste as needed. Pour the smoothies into 2 large glasses and serve immediately.

Berry Red Smoothies

The bright color of raspberries and strawberries takes the spotlight in these smoothies, while the orange juice lingers in the background, balancing out the sweetness. **SERVES 2 (ABOUT 12 OUNCES EACH)**

1 cup fresh or frozen (unthawed) unsweetened raspberries
1 cup sliced hulled fresh strawberries, or 1 cup frozen (unthawed) unsweetened strawberries
1 cup fresh orange juice
½ cup frozen nonfat vanilla yogurt
¾ cup ice cubes (see sidebar, this page)
Raspberry Maple Syrup (page 12) or honey (optional)

Place the raspberries, strawberries, orange juice, frozen yogurt, and ice in a blender and process until smooth. Taste for sweetness, adding Raspberry Syrup to taste as needed. Pour the smoothies into 2 large glasses and serve immediately.

Chapter 9

Desserts

What is a perfect dessert? It can be a warm peach pie or a refreshing scoop of coconut sorbet at the end of a meal. Or perhaps it's a comforting apple crisp or a sweet chocolate cake, an elegant apricot almond tart, or a gooey chocolate chip cookie, fresh from the oven. A perfect dessert makes your mouth come alive. It's a mildly guilty pleasure that's both sensuous and decadent.

For me, dessert is something to be enjoyed at the close of a full day. After the dinner dishes are cleared away and my work is done, I allow myself a little indulgence. My favorites are usually simple, yet delicious and satisfying enough to make them worth the calories.

More often than not, I go right to chocolate. Many of our Farm Stand customers share this love, if sales of our rich, trufflelike Chocolate Lover's Brownie are any indication. A new favorite is a dark chocolate layer cake spread with chocolate frosting that's been enriched with sour cream. It would make a spectacular birthday cake, dressed up with ripe red raspberries. When what you want is a great cookie, our Walnut Chocolate Chip Oatmeal Raisin is a winner. The name says it all, but locals simply ask for "The Farm Stand Cookie."

For those who prefer a non-chocolate ending, there's Lemon Berry Mousse, tart and creamy, and spectacular looking when served in parfait glasses layered with summer berries. Another hot weather favorite, Nectarine Cobbler, is enticingly fragrant with juicy fruit that bubbles up around the tender topping.

But don't forget there are delicious desserts that don't include fruit or chocolate. Take ginger, for example. It's one of the world's most versatile flavors. You'll find recipes with some form of ginger sprinkled throughout this cookbook, and desserts are no exception. Drew's Favorite Gingerbread has a mildly spicy flavor that will appeal to most taste buds. True ginger lovers will adore the spicy heat of Triple Ginger Ice Cream, featuring ginger in all forms—fresh, ground, and candied.

However, I'm most proud of our bestselling Earthbound Farm Ginger Snaps, with a sugary crust and spicy crunch. They were so popular that we created their "sister" cookie, our Earthbound Farm Lemon Snaps, which

Yummy Desserts

Don't miss these fabulous raspberry desserts in Chapter 1:

Raspberry Poached Pears, page 13

Raspberry Lemon Crèmes Brûlées, page 15

Sarah's Chocolate Soufflés with Raspberry Sauce, page 16

Farm Stand Frozen Raspberry Yogurt, page 19

Quick and Easy Frozen Raspberry Yogurt, page 22

Red Raspberry Ice Cream, page 20

Facing page:
Harvest Pie with Apples, Pear, and Cranberries (page 355).

have an almost equally devoted following. Our customers have been enjoying them for years, and now you can make them at home.

When my daughter, Marea, writes papers for school, I often remind her that it's worth the extra effort to end with a strong conclusion that will make her work memorable. The same is true of desserts. A fabulous dessert can turn an otherwise ordinary meal into an experience your guests will still be talking about the next day. Whether you're planning a holiday feast, a weeknight dinner, or special snack, we hope to help you discover some new perfect treats.

Earthbound Farm Ginger Snaps

I came up with this ginger snap recipe when Drew and I were first married. We love the crackly crunch of the sugary crust that gives way to a fragrant, spicy center that's just a tiny bit chewy. We thought our Farm Stand customers might like the cookies, too. Like them? No, they love *them. Earthbound Farm Ginger Snaps are one of our perennial bestsellers, and it was a big decision to share the secret recipe. When you make them at home, consider mixing up a double batch. The dough freezes well so you can bake some now and save some for later. Just be sure to completely thaw the dough first. Once baked and cooled, store the cookies in an airtight container. They'll become crispier in a few days and keep for up to a month—but good luck keeping them around that long!* **MAKES ABOUT 30 COOKIES**

Facing page:
Our Earthbound Farm Ginger Snaps and Lemon Snaps.

12 tablespoons (1¹/₂ sticks) unsalted butter, softened

1¹/₂ cups sugar

1 large egg

¹/₄ cup molasses

2 cups whole wheat pastry flour (see sidebar, page 6)

2 teaspoons ground ginger

1 teaspoon ground cinnamon

2 teaspoons baking soda

¹/₂ teaspoon salt

1. Position a rack in the center of the oven and preheat the oven to 350°F. Line 2 baking sheets with parchment paper or waxed paper and set them aside.

2. Place the butter and 1 cup of the sugar in a medium-size mixing bowl. Beat with an electric mixer at medium speed until smooth, 2 to 3 minutes. Add the egg and molasses and beat until combined, about 1 minute.

3. Whisk together the flour, ginger, cinnamon, baking soda, and salt in a small bowl.

4. With the mixer on low speed, slowly add the flour mixture to the butter mixture and beat until the dough is smooth.

5. Roll pieces of the dough between your palms to form 1-inch balls. Lightly dip the tops of the balls in the remaining 1/2 cup of sugar. Arrange the dough balls on the prepared baking sheets, sugar side up, 2 inches apart.

6. Bake the cookies until they are very fragrant and cracks appear on top, 8 to 12 minutes.

7. Place the baking sheets on a wire rack to cool for 5 minutes. Then, using a spatula, remove the cookies from the baking sheet and place them directly on the rack to finish cooling. The cookies can be stored in an airtight container for 1 month.

Earthbound Farm Lemon Snaps

Our Earthbound Farm Ginger Snaps were such a hit, we had to work hard to come up with another cookie that's just as delicious. After months of recipe trials, we created these sunny-yellow cookies scented with fresh lemon zest and studded with chewy bits of crystallized ginger. Some people like them even more than the ginger version (see page 320), claiming to eat a whole bag in one sitting! These crisp cookies make a perfect afternoon pick-me-up with a cup of hot tea or a casual dessert paired with homemade Raspberry Ice Cream (see page 20). But lemon snap fans find them worthy all on their own, any time of day. **MAKES ABOUT 30 COOKIES**

12 tablespoons (1 1/2 sticks) unsalted butter, softened
1 1/2 cups sugar
1 large egg
1 teaspoon pure lemon extract
2 cups unbleached all-purpose flour
1/2 teaspoon baking powder
1 teaspoon ground ginger
1/4 teaspoon salt
Grated zest of 1 lemon
1/3 cup (2 ounces) minced crystallized ginger

1. Position a rack in the lower third of the oven and preheat the oven to 375°F.

2. Place the butter and sugar in a medium-size mixing bowl. Beat with an electric mixer at medium speed until light and fluffy, 2 to 3 minutes. Add the egg and beat until just combined. Add the lemon extract and continue to beat until combined.

3. Whisk together the flour, baking powder, ground ginger, salt, and lemon zest in a small bowl.

4. With the mixer on low speed, slowly add the flour mixture to the butter mixture and beat until the dough is smooth. Add the crystallized ginger and continue to beat until it is evenly distributed throughout the dough.

5. Roll pieces of the dough between your palms to form 1-inch balls. Arrange the dough balls on ungreased baking sheets, 1½ inches apart.

6. Bake the cookies until they are just set and lightly golden, 10 to 15 minutes.

7. Place the baking sheets on a wire rack to cool for 5 minutes. Then, using a spatula, remove the cookies from the baking sheet and place them directly on the rack to finish cooling. The cookies can be stored in an airtight container for up to 1 month.

These small visitors are dwarfed by our giant artichoke and cardoon plants.

Walnut Chocolate Chip Oatmeal Raisin Cookies

These chewy oatmeal cookies have something for everyone: plump raisins, crunchy nuts, and sweet chocolate chips. If someone at your house isn't crazy about one of these ingredients, simply leave it out. The super-buttery dough refrigerates and freezes so well, it's easy to bake just the number of cookies you need. In fact, the dough is so buttery that if you're too impatient to allow it to refrigerate thoroughly before baking, the cookies will come out thin and lacey. Still delicious, of course, but with a different texture. **MAKES ABOUT 36 COOKIES**

Why Choose Organic Raisins?

Raisins are a great addition to many recipes, and are also a delicious, natural snack that can satisfy a sweet tooth. Organic grapes are grown without the use of pesticides, and organic raisins stay fresh because they are kept under refrigeration.

What many people don't know is that conventional raisins are fumigated routinely while in storage to avoid mold, often with methyl bromide (which depletes our ozone in a major way).

For children who like raisins and eat them regularly, organic raisins are an especially important choice.

12 tablespoons (1¹/2 sticks) unsalted butter, softened
¹/2 cup plus 2 tablespoons firmly packed light brown sugar
¹/2 cup plus 2 tablespoons granulated sugar
2 large eggs
1 teaspoon pure vanilla extract
1 cup unbleached all-purpose flour
³/4 teaspoon baking soda
³/4 teaspoon salt
1¹/2 cups quick rolled oats (not instant)
1 cup semisweet chocolate chips
³/4 cup raisins
¹/2 cup coarsely chopped walnuts

1. Place the butter, brown sugar, and granulated sugar in a large mixing bowl. Beat with an electric mixer at medium speed until smooth, 2 to 3 minutes. Add the eggs and vanilla and beat until combined, about 1 minute.

2. Whisk together the flour, baking soda, and salt in a small bowl.

3. With the mixer on low speed, slowly add the flour mixture to the butter mixture and beat until the dough is smooth. Using a spoon or rubber spatula, stir in the oats, chocolate chips, raisins, and walnuts.

4. Cover the bowl with plastic wrap and refrigerate the dough until it is firm, at least 6 hours or up to 5 days. The dough may also be frozen for up to 2 months.

(Let the dough thaw in the refrigerator to the point that it is no longer frozen but is still well chilled before baking.)

5. Position a rack in the center of the oven and preheat the oven to 350°F. Line 2 baking sheets with parchment paper or wax paper.

6. Drop the well-chilled dough in 1¹/2-inch spoonfuls on the prepared baking sheets, arranging them 2 inches apart. Slightly flatten each ball of dough with your palm.

7. Bake the cookies until they are golden brown, 10 to 15 minutes.

8. Place the baking sheets on a wire rack to cool for 10 minutes. Then, using a spatuala, remove the cookies from the baking sheet and place them directly on the rack to finish cooking. The cookies can be stored in an airtight container for up to 1 week.

Buckets of sweet peas for sale at our Farm Stand.

Marea's Nutty Chocolate Chip Cookies

*O*ur children seem to have been influenced by my love of baking. Inspired by the Fannie Farmer Cookbook, *our daughter, Marea, created a chocolaty cookie of her own loaded with walnuts. If your family isn't as wild for nuts as we are, you can use fewer or leave them out. Cookie-baking evenings turn the rest of the family into vultures as we hover around the first batch Marea pulls from the oven. Once cooled, the cookies turn crisp, but we can't resist them while they are still warm and chewy. Marea now makes a double batch each time so she'll have some extra baked cookies to freeze. There's no need to wait for them to thaw; we all love them straight from the freezer.* **MAKES ABOUT 30 COOKIES**

8 tablespoons (1 stick) unsalted butter, softened

$^1/_2$ cup firmly packed dark brown sugar

$^1/_2$ cup granulated sugar

1 large egg

$^3/_4$ teaspoon pure vanilla extract

1 cup plus 2 tablespoons whole wheat pastry flour (see sidebar, page 6)

$^1/_2$ teaspoon baking soda

$^1/_2$ teaspoon salt

1 cup semisweet chocolate chips

1 cup chopped walnuts or pecans

1. Position a rack in the center of the oven and preheat the oven to 375°F.

2. Place the butter, brown sugar, and granulated sugar in a medium-size mixing bowl. Beat with an electric mixer at medium speed until smooth, 2 to 3 minutes. Add the egg and vanilla and beat until combined, about 1 minute.

3. Whisk together the flour, baking soda, and salt in a small bowl.

4. With the mixer on low speed, slowly add the flour mixture to the butter mixture and beat until the dough is smooth. Using a spoon or rubber spatula, stir in the chocolate chips and nuts.

5. Drop heaping teaspoonsful of the dough onto ungreased baking sheets, arranging them 2 inches apart.

6. Bake the cookies until they are very fragrant and golden brown, 9 to 13 minutes.

7. Place the baking sheets on a wire rack to cool for 3 minutes. Then, using a spatula, remove the cookies from the baking sheet and place them directly on the rack to finish cooling. The cookies can be stored in an airtight container for up to 1 month or frozen for up to 3 months.

Marea has been working at our Farm Stand since she was 13.

Chocolate Lover's Brownies

Farm Stand customers can't get enough of these intensely rich, almost trufflelike, brownies. Espresso powder adds a subtle touch of bitterness to offset the chocolate sweetness; you don't really notice the coffee taste. We always make the brownies with walnuts, but you can leave them out or substitute pecans. There's so much chocolate in the recipe that they are a bit messy to cut unless they have been chilled in the fridge for several hours, so don't wait till the last minute to bake them. Warm from the oven, they are moist and delicious—just not as easy to cut into neat rectangles. The corners and edges, which are crunchier and darker than the moist center, are delicious crumbled over vanilla ice cream. **MAKES 16 BROWNIES**

1 cup (2 sticks) unsalted butter,
    plus more for buttering
    the pan
2 1/2 cups (16 ounces) semisweet
    chocolate chips
4 ounces high-quality bittersweet
    chocolate, coarsely chopped
    (1 cup; see sidebar, this page)
1 1/2 tablespoons instant espresso
    powder
1 tablespoon pure vanilla extract
3 large eggs
1 cup plus 2 tablespoons sugar
1/2 cup plus 1 tablespoon unbleached
    all-purpose flour
1 1/2 teaspoons baking powder
1/2 teaspoon salt
1 1/2 cups chopped walnuts

1. Position a rack in the lower third of the oven and preheat the oven to 350°F.

2. Line the bottom of a 9 by 13-inch baking pan with aluminum foil or parchment paper. Generously butter the foil and the sides of the pan.

3. Pour water to a depth of 1/2 inch in a saucepan or the bottom of a double boiler and bring it to a boil over high heat. Reduce the heat to low so that the water just barely simmers.

4. Place the butter, chocolate chips, and bittersweet chocolate in a medium-size metal or heatproof glass mixing bowl or in the top of a double boiler; set it over the barely simmering water. Cook, stirring frequently, until the butter and chocolate melt. Remove the bowl from the heat. Add the espresso powder and vanilla and stir to combine. Let the chocolate mixture cool for 15 minutes.

5. Place the eggs and sugar in a large bowl and whisk until just combined. Add the chocolate mixture to the egg mixture and stir until just combined.

6. Place the flour, baking powder, and salt in a small bowl and whisk to combine. Add the walnuts and stir to combine.

Buying High-Quality Bittersweet Chocolate

The best bittersweet chocolate for baking contains 65 to 70 percent chocolate solids. High-quality bittersweet chocolate has only a little sugar, so it imparts an intense chocolate flavor to baked goods. In North America, chocolate containing as little as 35 percent chocolate can be labeled bittersweet. The amount of chocolate solids doesn't have to be disclosed on the label, but most manufacturers of the best chocolate proudly display it on the package. Look for high-quality brands of organic chocolate; they are delicious!

7. Add the flour mixture to the chocolate mixture and stir until just combined. Do not overmix or the brownies will be tough.

8. Pour the brownie batter into the prepared pan and bake until a toothpick inserted in the center comes out clean, 40 to 50 minutes. The edges of the brownies will darken and may be a little overcooked.

9. Place the pan on a wire rack and let the brownies cool completely. Cover the brownies with plastic wrap and refrigerate them until chilled, at least 6 hours.

10. When ready to serve, carefully turn the brownies out onto a tray and peel off the foil. Cut off the crisp edges (about 1/2 inch from each side) and set them aside for another use, such as a topping for ice cream. Cut the brownies into roughly 2 by 3-inch rectangles and serve.

Lemon Cupcakes

Very light and lemony, these cupcakes have more in common with angel food cake than typical cupcakes. Their nearly light-as-a-feather texture comes from the egg whites folded into the batter. The lemon glaze, sweet and tangy, is very simple to prepare. The cupcakes make a particularly lovely spring and summer dessert.

MAKES 12 STANDARD-SIZE CUPCAKES

Pink lemons have green-striped yellow skin with delightful pale pink flesh when they are fully ripe.

FOR THE CUPCAKES
1 cup unbleached all-purpose flour
1 tablespoon cornstarch
1 1/2 teaspoons baking powder
1/2 teaspoon salt
3/4 cup granulated sugar
1/4 cup canola oil
Grated zest of 1 lemon
1/3 cup fresh lemon juice, preferably
    Meyer (see sidebar, page 112)
1 teaspoon pure lemon extract
3 large egg yolks
4 large egg whites

FOR THE GLAZE
1 1/3 cups confectioners' sugar
2 tablespoons fresh lemon juice,
    preferably Meyer

1. Make the cupcakes: Position a rack in the center of the oven and preheat the oven to 325°F. Line 12 standard-size muffin cups with cupcake liners and set them aside.

2. Place the flour, cornstarch, baking powder, salt, and 6 tablespoons of the granulated sugar in a large bowl and whisk to combine.

3. Place the oil, lemon zest, lemon juice, lemon extract, and egg yolks in a small bowl and whisk to combine. Add the egg mixture to the flour mixture and whisk until smooth.

4. Beat the egg whites with an electric mixer at high speed until they are foamy, about 1 minute. With the mixer running, slowly add the remaining 6 tablespoons of granulated sugar and beat until the whites form stiff, shiny peaks, about 3 minutes.

5. Stir about one third of the beaten egg whites into the cake batter. Then, carefully fold in the remaining whites using a rubber spatula, working quickly and gently so as not to deflate them. Spoon the batter into the prepared muffin cups, filling them almost to the brim.

6. Bake the cupcakes until they spring back when lightly pressed and a toothpick inserted into the center of one comes out clean, 20 to 25 minutes.

7. Place the muffin pan on a wire rack and let the cupcakes cool for about 10 minutes.

8. Meanwhile, make the glaze: Place the confectioners' sugar and lemon juice in a small bowl and stir until smooth.

9. Remove the cupcakes from the muffin pan while still slightly warm and spread the glaze on top with an offset spatula or knife. Let the glaze harden, about 10 minutes. The cupcakes taste best the day they are made. If necessary, you can store them in an airtight container for up to 2 days.

Bouquets of fresh-cut flowers from our fields welcome our Farm Stand visitors.

Farm Stand Carrot Cake

The judges at the Monterey County Fair know a great cake when they taste one. Our blue-ribbon winner has everything you'd expect in a perfect carrot cake— heavenly spiced layers filled with nuts and flecks of carrot topped with a creamy, rich icing. Carrots make the cake super moist; covered and refrigerated, it keeps beautifully for up to a week. This cake has long been our bestselling dessert at our Farm Stand. We've recently started using the batter to make delicious carrot muffins, a new morning favorite (see the sidebar on page 332). For carrot cupcakes, just top the muffins with frosting and, perhaps, a walnut half. Either way, you'll save time by finely grating the carrots using the regular grater blade of a food processor. Otherwise, use the coarse side of a box grater. **MAKES ONE 9 INCH-ROUND LAYER CAKE**

carrots

Almost all fruits and vegetables have more flavor when grown organically, and this is especially true of carrots. Small, young carrots are typically mild flavored and tender. On the other hand, larger mature carrots are often sweeter and more flavorful. In fact, the peeled and packaged "baby carrots" found at the supermarket are actually mature carrots that were cut and sculpted to their convenient shape. You can often find real baby carrots, finger-thin with their green tops attached,

at a farmers' market or produce stand. And if you're lucky, you may also find bunches of beautiful heirloom varieties in shades of red, purple, white, or yellow.

Whatever size or color carrot you choose, look for firm ones without splits or cracks. While carrots with brightly colored orange skins may taste the sweetest, those with dark orange skins have the highest levels of the antioxidant beta-carotene and vitamin A. Avoid carrots that have black tops or "shoulders," since this is a sign of age. If you buy a bunch of carrots,

choose ones with bright green tops that look perky and fresh. At home, cut off and discard the carrot greens because they sap moisture and vitamins from the roots. Store the carrots in a plastic bag in the refrigerator.

Rinse and scrub all carrots before eating or cooking. The soil they come from naturally contains bacteria that could be harmful. Young carrots with thin skins don't need to be peeled, but larger carrots may benefit from peeling because their skin is sometimes bitter.

Note: For a fancy finishing touch, use some of the frosting to pipe rosettes on the top of the cake. To do so, you'll need a pastry bag fitted with a medium ($1/2$ inch) tip.

FOR THE CAKE

Butter, for greasing the cake pans
2 cups unbleached all-purpose flour, plus more for flouring the cake pans
2 cups granulated sugar
1 tablespoon ground cinnamon
1 teaspoon salt
2 teaspoons baking soda
2 teaspoons baking powder
4 large eggs
$1^{1}/_{2}$ cups canola oil
2 teaspoons pure vanilla extract
3 packed cups peeled and grated carrots (about 1 pound)
1 cup chopped walnuts or pecans

FOR THE FROSTING

1 cup (8 ounces) cream cheese, softened
8 tablespoons (1 stick) unsalted butter, softened
4 cups confectioners' sugar, sifted
1 tablespoon pure vanilla extract
1 tablespoon milk or water, if needed
2 cups chopped walnuts or pecans

1. Make the cake: Position a rack in the lower third of the oven and preheat the oven to 325°F. Heavily butter and flour 2 round 9-inch cake pans, tapping out the excess flour. Set the cake pans aside.

2. Place the flour, granulated sugar, cinnamon, salt, baking soda, and baking powder in a large bowl and whisk to combine.

3. Place the eggs, oil, and vanilla in a small bowl and whisk to combine.

4. Add the egg mixture to the flour mixture and stir to combine. Add the carrots and nuts and stir to combine.

5. Evenly divide the batter between the prepared cake pans. Bake the cakes until a toothpick inserted in the center comes out clean and the edges have pulled away from the side of the pans, 55 to 65 minutes.

Variation:
Carrot Cake Muffins

To make 18 standard-size muffins, position a rack in the lower third of the oven and preheat the oven to 375°F. Butter 18 standard-size muffin cups or line them with cupcake liners. You'll need to use two 12-cup muffin tins or one 12-cup and one 6-cup muffin tin to bake these. Butter only 18 muffin cups, leaving the rest bare. If you do not have 2 muffin tins, bake the muffins in two batches.

Make the batter following Steps 2 through 4. Spoon the batter into the prepared muffin cups, filling them almost to the brim. Bake the muffins until they are golden brown and a toothpick inserted in the center of one comes out clean, 25 to 35 minutes. Place the muffin pan(s) on a wire rack and let the muffins cool for 10 minutes. Remove the muffins from the pan to finish cooling. The muffins can be stored in an airtight container at room temperature for up to 3 days.

6. Place the cake pans on wire racks and let the layers cool completely, about 1 hour.

7. Make the frosting: Place the cream cheese and butter in a medium-size bowl and beat with an electric mixer until very smooth and creamy, about 3 minutes. With the mixer running on medium speed, slowly add 3½ cups of the confectioners' sugar and beat until it is fully incorporated and smooth, about 3 minutes. Add the vanilla and beat until just combined. If the frosting is too soft, slowly add the remaining ½ cup of confectioners' sugar and beat to combine. If the frosting is too stiff, add the 1 tablespoon of milk or water.

8. Run a knife around the edge of each cake layer to loosen it from the pan. Invert the cake layers to unmold them. Place one cake layer on a plate. Spread some of the frosting on top. Place the second layer on top of the frosting and frost the side and top of the cake. Press the 2 cups of nuts onto the side of the cake (see Note, page 330). The cake can be refrigerated, covered, for up to 1 week.

Quince Spice Cake

*L*ight *and not too sweet, this easy cake makes the apple-pear flavor of the quince really shine. For those months when quince is out of season, you can substitute applesauce for the quince sauce. The flavor of the cake will be less complex, but still delicious. Serve the spice cake alone as an unusual breakfast cake, or jazz it up for a dinnertime dessert with Sweetened Whipped Cream (see page 389) or Spiced Quince Compote (see page 367).* **MAKES ONE 8-INCH-SQUARE OR ONE 5 BY 9-INCH LOAF CAKE**

Butter, for greasing the baking pan
1 cup unbleached all-purpose flour
1 teaspoon baking powder
½ teaspoon baking soda
½ teaspoon salt
1 teaspoon ground ginger
½ teaspoon Chinese five-spice powder
1 large egg

½ cup sugar
1 teaspoon finely grated lemon zest
¾ cup Quince Sauce (recipe follows) or applesauce
¼ cup canola oil
¼ cup buttermilk

quince

Quince has been popular along the Mediterranean since ancient times, when it was revered as the sacred fruit of Aphrodite, the goddess of love. Europeans brought their beloved fruit to America, where it was once a common backyard fruit tree. Quince is slowly regaining its popularity.

Look for it at farmers' markets and specialty food stores during the fall.

The ugly duckling of fruit, quince looks like a lumpy, golden pear covered with brown fuzz, but it has an exquisite aroma that can perfume an entire room. In fact, most of the aromatics come from the fuzz, so don't rinse it off until you are ready to prepare the fruit. A

green-tinged quince should ripen to a golden yellow on your countertop within a week or two. Don't try biting into one, though—raw quince is hard, bitter, and astringent. Cooking transforms its taste and color, turning it into a lovely amber or rose. You'll be reminded of the most delicious cooked pear or apple you've ever eaten.

1. Position a rack in the center of the oven and preheat the oven to 350°F. Generously butter an 8-inch-square baking pan or a 5 by 9-inch loaf pan.

2. Place the flour, baking powder, baking soda, salt, ginger, and five-spice powder in a medium-size bowl and whisk to combine.

3. Place the egg in a large bowl and beat with an electric mixer until thick. Gradually add the sugar and lemon zest and continue beating at medium speed until light and fluffy, about 3 minutes. Add the Quince Sauce, oil, and buttermilk and beat until just combined.

4. Using a rubber spatula, fold the flour mixture into the egg mixture until just combined.

5. Pour the batter into the prepared pan, spreading it evenly to the edges. Bake the cake until a toothpick inserted into the center comes out clean, 40 to 50 minutes in a square pan or 45 to 55 minutes in a loaf pan. Let the cake cool on a wire rack before turning it out and serving.

Quince Sauce

Quince sauce is similar in texture to applesauce but has a more complex flavor and a brilliant amber or rose color. If you have a food mill, use it instead of the food processor to puree the fruit (see sidebar, page 31). You'll save time because there's no need to peel or core the quinces since the tough, fibrous parts of the fruit will remain behind in the bowl of the mill. Serve Quince Sauce as an unusual side dish for roasted meats or use it to make the easy Quince Spice Cake. **MAKES ABOUT 2 CUPS**

> 6 small ripe quinces
>   (about 2 pounds total)
> ²/₃ cup sugar, or more to taste
> Grated zest of 1 lemon
> ¹/₂ teaspoon Chinese five-spice powder
> 1 whole star anise
> 2 teaspoons fresh lemon juice

1. Position a rack in the center of the oven and preheat the oven to 375°F.

2. Rinse the quinces, rubbing off the brown fuzz, and place them in a small baking dish with ²/₃ cup of water. Cover the pan tightly with aluminum foil and cook the quinces until they are very tender when pierced with the tip of a knife, 1½ to 2 hours. Remove the baking dish from the oven and let the quinces sit, covered with the aluminum foil, until they are cool enough to handle.

3. If you're using a food mill, cut the quinces into small pieces (you don't need to peel or core them). If you're using a food processor, peel, core, and slice the quinces, setting aside any cooking liquid. Puree the quinces with the cooking liquid until very smooth.

4. Transfer the quince puree to a small saucepan and add the sugar, lemon zest, five-spice powder, and star anise. Cook over medium heat until the sugar dissolves, about 10 minutes. Remove and discard the star anise.

5. Remove the pan from the heat, add the lemon juice, and stir to combine. Taste the puree for sweetness and add more sugar, as needed. The sauce can be refrigerated, covered, for up to 7 days or frozen for up to 3 months. Let the sauce thaw overnight in the refrigerator and return to room temperature before using.

When our Farm Stand heirloom apples turn pink inside, they are probably ready to harvest.

Drew's Favorite Gingerbread

When our kids were young, they loved to watch the baking soda bubble and foam as I made this gingerbread. But there's a lot more to enjoy here than kitchen chemistry. This gingerbread is a favorite because it bakes up with a light texture that belies its dark, rich color and spicy flavor. Drew likes the gingerbread best with freshly whipped cream, but it would be just as good with vanilla ice cream or a lemon sauce. **MAKES ONE 9 BY 13-INCH GINGERBREAD**

8 tablespoons (1 stick) unsalted butter, softened, plus butter for greasing the baking pan
2½ cups whole wheat pastry flour (see sidebar, page 6), plus more for flouring the baking pan
1 tablespoon ground ginger
1 teaspoon ground cloves
1 teaspoon ground cinnamon
½ cup sugar
1 cup molasses

2 teaspoons baking soda
1 cup boiling water
2 large eggs, lightly beaten
Sweetened Whipped Cream (optional; page 389), for serving

1. Position a rack in the center of the oven and preheat the oven to 350°F. Butter and flour a 9 by 13-inch baking pan, tapping out the excess flour. Set the baking pan aside.

2. Place the flour, ginger, cloves, and cinnamon in a medium-size bowl and whisk to blend.

3. Place the butter and sugar in a large bowl and beat with a spoon until combined and smooth. Add the molasses and blend thoroughly.

4. Place the baking soda in a small heatproof bowl and add the boiling water. Stir until dissolved. Add the baking soda mixture to the butter mixture and beat until smooth.

5. Add the flour mixture to the butter mixture and stir until smooth. Add the eggs and beat to combine.

6. Pour the batter into the prepared baking pan, spreading it evenly to the edges. Bake the gingerbread until it is very fragrant and a toothpick inserted into the center comes out clean, 30 to 40 minutes.

7. Place the baking pan on a wire rack and let the gingerbread cool for about 20 minutes. Run a knife around the edges of the gingerbread to loosen it from the pan. Invert the gingerbread to unmold it and let it finish cooling on the rack. Serve the gingerbread warm or at room temperature with Sweetened Whipped Cream, if desired. It tastes best the day it is made. If necessary, you can refrigerate it, covered, for up to 3 days. Microwaving individual pieces until barely warm, about 15 seconds, will restore their moistness.

Chocolate Layer Cake
with Chocolate Sour Cream Frosting and Raspberries

In writing this cookbook, we tested recipe after recipe to create the perfect chocolate cake: one with moist texture and deep chocolate flavor. Our search brought us to this luscious cake with dark chocolate layers accented by a rich, but not overly sweet, frosting. For us, the secret is to use buttermilk for moisture and high-quality cocoa for intense flavor. Raspberries with chocolate is one of my favorite flavor combinations, but if you don't have pristine fresh berries, the cake is also delicious without them. It's easier to prepare than most from-scratch cakes; you don't even have to take out the electric mixer. **MAKES ONE 9-INCH-ROUND LAYER CAKE**

FOR THE CAKE

Butter, for greasing the cake pans

1 1/3 cups unbleached all-purpose flour, plus more for dusting the cake pans

2/3 cup high-quality unsweetened cocoa powder

1 1/2 teaspoons baking soda

1 teaspoon salt

1/4 cup cornstarch

1 cup buttermilk or sour cream

3/4 cup canola oil

2 large eggs

1 1/2 cups granulated sugar

1 tablespoon pure vanilla extract

FOR THE FROSTING

8 tablespoons (1 stick) unsalted butter

1/2 cup (2 1/2 ounces) bittersweet chocolate (see sidebar, page 327), coarsely chopped

1/3 cup high-quality unsweetened cocoa powder

2 cups confectioners' sugar

About 1/2 cup sour cream

FOR ASSEMBLING THE CAKE

1/3 cup seedless raspberry jam (optional)

4 half pints (about 5 cups) fresh raspberries for the filling and garnish (optional)

Beneficial insects hide among the spring wildflowers that line our organic fields—and play hide-and-seek with the children on our Saturday Bug Walks.

1. Make the cake: Position a rack in the lower third of the oven and preheat the oven to 350°F. Butter the bottoms and sides of 2 round 9-inch cake pans. Dust the pans with some flour and tap out the excess. Set the cake pans aside.

2. Place the flour, 2/3 cup of cocoa powder, baking soda, salt, and cornstarch in a medium-size bowl and sift it together into a large bowl.

3. Place the buttermilk, oil, eggs, granulated sugar, and vanilla in a medium-size bowl and whisk to combine well.

4. Add the buttermilk mixture to the flour mixture and stir to blend. Divide the cake batter evenly between the two prepared cake pans.

5. Bake the cakes until a toothpick inserted in the center comes out clean and the edges have pulled away from the side of the pans, 20 to 30 minutes.

6. Place the cake pans on wire racks to cool for 10 minutes. Run a knife around the edge of each cake layer to loosen it from the pan. Invert the cake layers to unmold them, then place them on the racks to cool completely, about 45 minutes. At this point, the layers can be stored, tightly wrapped with plastic wrap, at room temperature for up to 24 hours.

7. Make the frosting: Place the butter and bittersweet chocolate in a small saucepan and cook over low heat, stirring occasionally, until melted and smooth, 5 to 10 minutes.

8. Let the chocolate mixture cool for 5 minutes, then pour it into a large bowl. Sift in the 1/3 cup of cocoa powder and 1 cup of the confectioners' sugar. Add 1/4 cup of the sour cream and whisk to combine well. Sift in the remaining 1 cup of confectioners' sugar and stir until smooth. If the frosting is too stiff to spread easily, add 1 tablespoon of the remaining sour cream and stir to combine. If the frosting is still too stiff, gradually add just enough of the remaining sour cream to make it spreadable.

9. Melt the raspberry jam, if using, in a small saucepan over very low heat, about 3 minutes.

10. To assemble the cake: If necessary, trim the cake layers so they are flat on top (see Note). Place one of the layers on a serving plate. Spread one third of the frosting on top of this layer. Spread all of the raspberry jam, if using, over the frosting. Arrange one half of the

raspberries, if using, on the filling, splitting them in half with your fingers as you add them. Reserve the prettiest berries for the top of the cake.

11. Place the second cake layer on top of the first. Spread the remaining frosting on the top and side of the cake. Arrange the remaining raspberries in concentric circles on top of the cake. For the best flavor, serve the cake at room temperature. The cake can sit at room temperature for up to 6 hours and can be refrigerated, covered, for up to 3 days.

Note: If the cake layers are rounded on top, use a long, thin-bladed knife to trim them flat. The layers will be covered with frosting, so if they are not perfectly flat, no one will notice. Save the trimmings to eat on their own with a dab of frosting, a tasty sneak preview of the cake.

Both kids and grown-ups anticipate our late-summer pumpkin scratching event, when they go out into the fields to etch the rind of an immature pumpkin. The etching scabs over, and as it grows to maturity, the design grows along with it.

Light and Lemony Cheesecake

New York–style cheesecake makes a rich and luxurious ending to a meal, but I usually prefer a lighter, but equally delectable, dessert. This melt-in-your-mouth cheesecake uses low-fat cottage cheese in place of some of the cream cheese. And the whipped egg whites give it a texture so delicate that the top may crack as it cools. If it does, you can disguise it with a spoonful of Simple Raspberry Sauce (see page 18) or Vanilla Cherry Sauce (see page 362) and no one will know the difference. This is a great cake for company because you can make it in advance. In fact, it holds its shape best when chilled overnight. **MAKES ONE 8 1/2-INCH CHEESECAKE**

FOR THE CRUST

1¼ cups graham cracker crumbs
    (see sidebar, page 352)
¼ cup firmly packed light brown sugar
½ teaspoon ground nutmeg
4 tablespoons (½ stick) unsalted butter,
    melted

FOR THE CHEESECAKE

¾ cup granulated sugar
6 tablespoons (¾ stick) unsalted
    butter, softened
4 large eggs, separated
2 teaspoons pure vanilla extract
2 teaspoons pure lemon extract or
    lemon oil
Grated zest of 1 lemon
1½ cups low-fat cottage cheese
1 cup (8 ounces) cream cheese,
    softened
1 tablespoon cornstarch
2 cups fresh berries or cherries,
    for garnish

1. Position a rack in the lower third of the oven and preheat the oven to 325°F.

2. Make the crust: Combine the graham cracker crumbs, brown sugar, nutmeg, and melted butter in a small bowl. Stir to combine. Press the mixture into the bottom of an 8½-inch springform pan. Set the pan aside.

3. Make the cheesecake: Place the granulated sugar and softened butter in the bowl of a food processor and pulse to blend. Add the egg yolks, vanilla, lemon extract, and lemon zest and process, running the machine continuously, until the mixture is smooth, about 1 minute. Add the cottage cheese, cream cheese, and cornstarch and process for 2 minutes. Transfer the cheese mixture to a large bowl.

A variety of our Farm Stand produce on display.

4. Beat the egg whites with an electric mixer at high speed until they hold soft peaks, 3 to 4 minutes. Stir one third of the egg whites into the cheese mixture. Fold in the remaining egg whites. Pour the cheese mixture into the prepared pan.

5. Bake the cheesecake until the top is golden and just set, 60 to 70 minutes (the center will still jiggle a bit). To help prevent the cheesecake from cracking, run a thin knife around the edge of the cake to loosen it from the pan.

6. Return the cheesecake to the oven, turn it off, and let the cake cool, with the oven door closed, for about 2 hours.

7. Remove the cake pan from the oven and cover it with plastic wrap. Refrigerate the cheesecake until completely chilled before serving, at least 6 hours or as long as 24 hours. Serve the cheesecake topped with the berries.

Cranberry-Pumpkin Bread Pudding

Traditionalists may disagree, but we think this decadent bread pudding makes a nice change from pumpkin pie for the holidays. While the pumpkin puree in both desserts is spiced with the alluring aroma of cinnamon, nutmeg, and clove, the bread pudding is brightened with cranberries, and spiked with liqueur. It's quick and easy to prepare up to several days ahead of time and delicious served with vanilla ice cream or Sweetened Whipped Cream (see page 389). **MAKES ONE 9-INCH-SQUARE PUDDING**

Pumpkins come in all sizes, like these Jack O'Lantern, Jack Be Little, and Sugar Pie varieties.

Butter, for greasing the baking pan
³/₄ cup whole or low-fat milk
¹/₂ cup heavy (whipping) cream
2 large eggs
1 tablespoon pure vanilla extract
1 teaspoon pumpkin pie spice
³/₄ cup firmly packed light brown sugar
1 cup pumpkin puree
6 cups stale bread cubes (¹/₂-inch cubes from dense French or Italian bread)
¹/₂ cup dried cranberries
¹/₄ cup almond liqueur (such as amaretto) or rum (optional)

1. Position a rack in the lower third of the oven and preheat the oven to 350°F. Butter a 9-inch-square baking pan and set it aside.

2. Pour the milk and cream into a small saucepan and cook over medium heat, stirring occasionally, until small bubbles form around the edge of the pan, just before the mixture comes to a boil. Remove the saucepan from the heat.

3. Place the eggs, vanilla, pumpkin pie spice, brown sugar, and pumpkin puree in a medium-size bowl and whisk to combine. Add the hot milk mixture and whisk to combine.

4. Place the bread cubes in a large bowl and add the pumpkin and milk mixture, the cranberries, and liqueur, if using. Stir to combine. Let the bread sit, stirring occasionally, until it absorbs most of the liquid, about 20 minutes. Transfer the bread mixture to the prepared baking pan.

5. Make a water bath by placing the baking pan in a larger pan and adding enough hot water to the larger pan so that it comes halfway up the side of the smaller pan. Bake the bread pudding in the water bath until it is set and golden, 40 to 45 minutes.

6. Remove the smaller pan from the water bath and place the pan on a wire rack to cool for about 30 minutes. Serve the bread pudding warm. If you are not planning on serving the bread pudding within 4 hours, it can be refrigerated, covered, for up to 3 days. To serve, let the bread pudding return to room temperature, then warm it in a 275°F oven for 15 to 20 minutes.

Harvesting pumpkins is hard work! Every autumn, more than 100,000 pounds of pumpkins are moved from our Carmel Valley fields to our Farm Stand where our customers select just the right one to take home.

rhubarb

Intensely tart, rhubarb is an unusual vegetable that's most often paired with sweet fruits for desserts. It has long, thin ribs, similar to celery, except that they are a reddish color. Rhubarb's leaves are poisonous, though, so be sure to discard them.

Rhubarb comes in two varieties: hothouse and field. Hothouse rhubarb is a pale red or pink, while its field-grown cousin is bright red and even tastier. In some northern states, it grows wild like a weed. While hothouse varieties have a longer growing season, field rhubarb is harvested in spring and early summer, with a peak in April and May.

When buying rhubarb, look for colorful, firm, slender stalks without blemishes. Large stalks may be stringy. If so, remove the outer skin with a vegetable peeler, or pull off the strings with a paring knife. Fresh rhubarb deteriorates quickly, so store it in the refrigerator only for a day or two. If you want to keep it longer, cut the stalks into pieces and freeze them in an airtight freezer bag.

Strawberry Rhubarb Crumble

Sweet strawberries and tart rhubarb are a classic spring duo. This odd couple usually meets in a pie, but a crumble is easier and quicker to make and just as delicious. To add a little surprise, the fruity filling is studded with chewy candied ginger, and the buttery topping ties the flavors and textures together. Feel free to experiment by adding nuts to the topping, switching the ginger with the zest from one orange, or replacing some of the strawberries with raspberries. **MAKES ONE 2-QUART CRUMBLE**

FOR THE FILLING
2 pints fresh strawberries, hulled and
  quartered (about 3 cups)
1 pound fresh rhubarb, trimmed
  and cut into $^1/_2$-inch pieces
  (about 3 cups)
$^1/_2$ cup granulated sugar
1 tablespoon whole wheat pastry flour
  (see sidebar, page 6)
$^1/_4$ cup minced crystallized ginger
1 teaspoon fresh lemon juice

FOR THE TOPPING
$^1/_2$ cup whole wheat pastry flour
$^3/_4$ cup old-fashioned rolled oats
  (not instant)
$^1/_2$ cup firmly packed light brown sugar
$^1/_4$ teaspoon ground cinnamon
$^1/_4$ teaspoon ground ginger
Pinch of salt
8 tablespoons (1 stick) cold, unsalted
  butter, cut into small bits
Vanilla ice cream or Sweetened
  Whipped Cream (page 389),
  for serving

1. Position a rack in the center of the oven and preheat the oven to 375°F.

2. Make the filling: Place the strawberries, rhubarb, and granulated sugar in a large bowl and stir to combine. Add the flour and the crystallized ginger and lemon juice and stir to combine. Set the filling aside.

3. Make the topping: Place the flour, oats, brown sugar, cinnamon, ginger, and salt in a medium-size bowl and stir to combine. Add the butter. Using a pastry blender, 2 knives, or your fingers, blend the butter into the mixture until it is crumbly and well combined.

4. Transfer the filling to a shallow 2-quart baking dish. Loosely crumble the topping over the filling.

5. Bake the crumble until the filling bubbles up around the edge of the baking dish and the topping turns golden brown, 30 to 35 minutes. Serve the crumble hot or warm, with vanilla ice cream or Sweetened Whipped Cream.

Nectarine Cobbler

As this fresh fruit cobbler bakes, the natural sweetness of the nectarines intensifies and their fragrant juices bubble up around the edges of the light, cakelike topping. There's no need to peel organic nectarines for this recipe, and the topping is quick and easy to make. Depending on what's in season, you can substitute peaches, apricots, berries, or even mangoes with equally delicious results. While the cobbler is best the day it's made, any leftovers make a special breakfast treat, briefly reheated in the microwave and splashed with half-and-half. **MAKES ONE 9-INCH–SQUARE COBBLER**

4 tablespoons (¹/₂ stick) unsalted butter, melted, plus butter for greasing the baking pan
5 large ripe nectarines, peeled (unless organic; see box, facing page), pitted, and sliced into ¹/₂ inch wedges
1¹/₄ cups sugar
1 tablespoon cornstarch
Finely grated zest of 1 lemon
1 tablespoon fresh lemon juice
¹/₄ cup minced crystallized ginger
1 cup unbleached all-purpose flour
1 teaspoon baking powder
¹/₄ teaspoon salt
1 large egg
³/₄ cup sour cream
Sweetened Whipped Cream (page 389) or vanilla ice cream, for serving (optional)

1. Position a rack in the bottom third of the oven and preheat the oven to 350°F.

2. Butter a 9-inch-square baking pan. Spread the nectarine wedges in the prepared pan.

3. Place ¾ cup of the sugar and the cornstarch, lemon zest and juice, and crystallized ginger in a small bowl and stir to blend, then sprinkle over the nectarines.

4. Place the flour, baking powder, salt, and the remaining ½ cup of sugar in a medium-size bowl and whisk to combine.

5. Lightly beat the egg in a medium-size bowl. Add the sour cream and butter and stir to combine. Pour the egg mixture into the flour mixture and stir with a rubber spatula until just combined. Do not overmix or the topping will be tough.

6. Drop spoonfuls of the topping mixture on the nectarines. There may be gaps, but as the cobbler bakes, the topping will spread out to cover the fruit.

7. Bake the cobbler until the fruit juices bubble up around the edges of the baking pan and the topping turns golden, 45 to 50 minutes. Place the baking pan on a wire rack and let the cobbler cool for at least 15 minutes before serving with Sweetened Whipped Cream or vanilla ice cream, if using.

FARM FRESH

peaches and nectarines

Peaches and nectarines are close cousins on the stone-fruit family tree. Unlike fuzzy peaches, nectarines have a smooth skin. At their best, both are juicy and delicious.

Most peaches and nectarines in the supermarket come from California where the long growing season runs from May to October. Elsewhere in the country, the fruits are harvested from midsummer to early fall. The peak months are July and August. Choose locally grown fruit when possible because the most flavorful varieties don't travel well. Also, refrigeration during shipping can cause the fruits to develop a mealy texture.

A ripe peach or nectarine is fragrant, brightly colored, and gives slightly when pressed along the seam that runs down the side of the fruit. Slightly underripe fruit will ripen on the counter in a couple of days. While they may get juicier and softer, peaches and nectarines do not get any sweeter once picked.

For baking, freestone peaches or nectarines are preferable because the pits are easier to remove, although the cling varieties are delicious, too. Yellow-fleshed peaches and nectarines are higher in acidity than white varieties, making the yellow ones better for cooking. If you are lucky enough to find local white peaches or nectarines, savor their delicate flavor on their own or use them as a fresh topping for ice cream or yogurt.

Unfortunately, conventionally grown stone fruits are likely to have a high level of residual pesticides, so it's best to rinse and peel them before eating. Whenever possible, choose organic peaches and nectarines and enjoy them—peels and all—after a quick rinse.

A Field Guide to Some of Our Favorite Apples

Some people love their apples sweet and juicy, while others prefer them crisp and tart. There are thousands of varieties in the world and plenty of tastes for everyone to explore, whether baked in a pie, sliced on a salad, or eaten out of hand. Here are a few favorites from our Farm Stand apple bin.

Marea and Jeffrey demonstrate their prowess with our apple corer.

Besides being fun to operate, it quickly peels and cores the fruit, and turns the flesh into a "Slinky"-like ribbon that can then be sliced to size.

Perfect for pies, crisps sauces, and compotes— you name it!

braeburn, *a fifty-year-old New Zealand variety, is prized for its crisp and juicy flesh and sweet-tangy flavor that's excellent eaten fresh as well as cooked.*

granny smith *has bright green skin and crunchy, tart flesh, and makes an excellent cooking apple that's also delicious eaten fresh. The apple is named for Maria Smith, who was an orchardist in the nineteenth century in Australia.*

fuji *was developed in Japan by crossing a Red Delicious and the Ralls Janet, an heirloom that contributes an extra-crisp texture and sweet taste. Fuji is terrific eaten fresh or sliced on salads.*

jonagold *combines the best of a tart Jonathan and a honey-sweet Golden Delicious—a delicious combination that's great for salads and snacking, as well as for baking in a pie or crisp.*

gala, *originally developed in New Zealand, is juicy and crisp, with a mild, sweet flavor. Best enjoyed sliced on salads or eaten fresh, rather than used in baking.*

pink lady, *which is the brand name for the Cripps Pink variety, has pink-blushed flesh. Its popularity is due to a delightfully crisp texture and sweet-tart taste, as well as its pretty color.*

Autumn Apple Crisp

Just before the leaves turn red and amber, it's time to search out the first freshly picked apples of the season. Thanks to their long storage life, apples are available year-round, but fresh from the tree, they have the most vibrant taste and the best texture. They are perfect for my favorite warm apple crisp, topped with crunchy, buttery streusel and a scoop of slowly melting vanilla ice cream. This crisp is so simple to make, especially if you use an old-fashioned apple peeler and corer with a hand crank, which can be found at most kitchen stores. **MAKES ONE 9 BY 13-INCH CRISP**

4 pounds (about 10) small Granny Smith or pippin apples, peeled, cored, and cut into ¼-inch slices (see sidebar, this page)

Juice of 2 lemons, preferably Meyer (see sidebar, page 112)

1 cup whole wheat pastry flour (see sidebar, page 6)

1½ cups firmly packed light brown sugar

2 tablespoons ground cinnamon

8 tablespoons (1 stick) salted butter, softened

Vanilla ice cream or Sweetened Whipped Cream (page 389), for serving (optional)

1. Position a rack in the lower third of the oven and preheat the oven to 375°F.

2. Place the apple slices in a 9 by 13-inch baking pan. Add the lemon juice and toss to prevent the apples from discoloring.

3. Place the flour, brown sugar, and cinnamon in a medium-size bowl and whisk to blend. Add the butter. Using your fingers, blend the butter into the flour mixture until it resembles coarse meal. Sprinkle the topping evenly over the apples, but do not pack it down.

4. Bake the crisp until the apples are tender when pierced with a fork, the juices bubble up around the edges of the baking pan, and the topping is crisp and brown, 40 to 50 minutes. Serve the crisp hot or warm with vanilla ice cream or whipped cream, if desired.

Peeling Apples Quickly

If you frequently make apple crisps or applesauce, consider investing in an old-fashioned apple peeler-corer ($30 or less from kitchen stores or on the Web). It's a metal contraption with a hand crank that attaches to a countertop with a suction cup or clamp (for a look, see the sidebar on the facing page). To use the apple peeler-corer, you secure an apple on the forked prongs and position the adjustable blade against the fruit. As you turn the crank, the apple revolves around the blade that simultaneously removes the peel and slices the apple into one long ribbon while cutting out the core.

First-of-the-season apples signal that autumn's chill will soon arrive.

Summer Berry Crisp

The subtle citrus notes in the filling of this simple, homestyle favorite make the berry flavors sparkle. Blueberries hold their shape and strawberries are naturally sweet, but any combination of berries will work. The crisp really doesn't need adornment, but if you can't resist, a dollop of crème fraîche adds a pleasant tart contrast to the sweet fruit. And, of course, whipped cream or ice cream are also delicious. **MAKES ONE 2-QUART CRISP**

FOR THE FILLING
6 cups assorted fresh berries,
    such as blueberries,
    blackberries,
    or hulled strawberries
Grated zest of 1 orange
Grated zest of 1 lemon
1 tablespoon fresh lemon juice
2 tablespoons orange-flavored
    liqueur, such as Cointreau or
    Grand Marnier (optional)
$^1/_2$ cup granulated sugar
2 tablespoons cornstarch

FOR THE TOPPING
$^3/_4$ cup unbleached all-purpose flour
$^1/_2$ teaspoon allspice
$^1/_4$ teaspoon salt
$^1/_2$ cup firmly packed dark brown
    sugar
2 tablespoons granulated sugar
6 tablespoons ($^3/_4$ stick) unsalted
    butter
$^1/_2$ cup old-fashioned rolled oats
    (not instant)
1 cup Homemade Crème Fraîche
    (optional; page 389), for serving

1. Position a rack in the center of the oven and preheat the oven to 375°F.

2. Make the filling: Place the berries, orange zest, lemon zest, lemon juice, and liqueur, if using, in a large bowl.

3. Place the granulated sugar and the cornstarch in a small bowl and whisk to combine. Add the sugar mixture to the berries and toss gently to combine. Transfer the berry mixture to a shallow 2-quart baking dish.

4. Make the topping: Place the flour, allspice, salt, brown sugar, granulated sugar, and butter in a medium-size bowl. Using your fingers, blend in the butter until it is in pea-size bits. Add the rolled oats and stir to combine. Sprinkle the topping over the berries but do not pack it down.

5. Bake the crisp until the fruit juices bubble up around the edges of the baking dish and the topping turns golden, 30 to 35 minutes. Let the crisp cool slightly before serving it warm with the crème fraîche, if desired.

Apricot and Almond Tart

You might expect this strikingly beautiful tart, with glazed apricot slices fanned across its top, to be tedious to assemble. But that's not the case at all. The trick is to keep the fruit intact at the base when slicing, so that the slices spread out like a fan. Fresh apricots are usually only available for a brief few weeks in the summer, but this recipe works equally well with fresh pears in the fall and winter (see the variation in the sidebar on this page). Both fruits share an affinity for almonds; ground almonds give the crust a nutty texture, while the creamy filling contains marzipan, a sweet almond paste. Plan ahead; the sweet almond crust must be refrigerated for at least four hours before you bake it. If you're short on time, an organic store-bought crust can still look homemade if you transfer it to your own tart dish (see the box on page 350), but it won't have the same nutty appeal.

MAKES ONE 9-INCH TART

FOR THE ALMOND CRUST
$1/3$ cup confectioners' sugar
$1/4$ cup sliced almonds
$1^1/4$ cups unbleached all-purpose flour
8 tablespoons (1 stick) unsalted butter,
    at room temperature, cut into 12 pieces
1 large egg yolk
1 teaspoon pure almond extract
Ice water, if needed

FOR THE FILLING
1 package (7 ounces) marzipan (see Note,
    page 350), cut into 12 pieces
4 tablespoons ($1/2$ stick) unsalted butter,
    softened
2 large eggs
1 teaspoon pure vanilla extract
1 teaspoon pure almond extract
1 teaspoon grated lemon zest
6 to 8 small, ripe apricots
2 tablespoons apricot jam
1 tablespoon almond-flavored liqueur
    (such as amaretto), brandy, rum,
    or water

1. Make the pastry crust: Place the confectioners' sugar and almonds in a food processor and process until the nuts are finely ground. Add the flour and the butter and pulse until the mixture resembles coarse meal. Add the egg yolk and the almond extract and process until the mixture is combined, about 30 seconds. Test the dough to see if it is the right consistency by squeezing some of it between your fingers; it should hold together when pinched. If the dough is too dry and crumbly, add 1 tablespoon of ice water and process again briefly.

2. Transfer the dough to a work surface covered with a piece of wax paper. Gather the dough together and pat it into a flat disk. Cover the dough with another piece of waxed paper or some plastic wrap. Roll out the dough into an 11-inch circle, about $1/8$ inch thick. Remove the top piece of wax paper.

**Variation:
Pear and
Almond Tart**
Instead of apricots, substitute 3 medium-size pears, such as Bartletts or Anjous (about $1^1/4$ pounds). Make sure the pears are ripe but still firm and unblemished. Prepare the tart crust and marzipan filling following the instructions in Steps 1 through 6. Then, peel the pears and cut them in half through the stem end. Use a small paring knife or melon baller to remove the core. Carefully cut about nine parallel slices in each pear half, keeping the slices connected at the narrow end. Press gently on each pear half to fan out the slices. Continue with the recipe, starting at Step 8 and substituting the sliced pears for the apricots.

Note: Marzipan and almond paste are prepared with the same ingredients, however, marzipan has more sugar and a smoother consistency. If you substitute almond paste for the marzipan, use 7 ounces and add ¼ cup of sugar to the filling ingredients.

3. Use the bottom piece of waxed paper to transfer the dough to a 9-inch tart pan with a removable bottom: Turn the dough upside-down over the tart pan and carefully ease it into the pan. Peel off the wax paper. Gently press the dough into the tart pan, taking care not to stretch or tear it. Run the rolling pin over the rim of the tart pan to cut away the excess dough. Cover the pan with plastic wrap and refrigerate the crust for at least 4 hours or overnight.

4. Position a rack in the center of the oven and preheat the oven to 375°F.

5. Prick the crust all over with a fork. Line the crust with aluminum foil and fill it with pie weights or dried beans. Bake the crust for 15 minutes, then transfer the tart pan to a wire rack to cool. Do not turn off the oven.

6. Meanwhile, make the filling: Place the marzipan and butter in a food processor and pulse until roughly combined. Add the eggs, vanilla extract, almond extract, and lemon zest and puree until smooth. Set the marzipan mixture aside at room temperature.

7. Cut the apricots in half through the stem end and discard the pits and stems. Carefully cut 5 or 6 parallel slices in each apricot half, keeping the slices connected at the stem end. Press gently on each apricot half to fan out the slices.

making store-bought pie crusts look homemade

If you don't have time to make your own crust, an organic store-bought one can come to the rescue. Your pie will have a homemade appeal if you transfer the store-bought crust to your own baking dish. First, let a 9-inch pie crust soften at room temperature until you are able to remove it from the pan (about 15 minutes for refrigerated crusts or about 50 minutes for frozen ones). Carefully roll the dough out so it is slightly larger than your pie plate, baking dish, or tart pan. Place the dough in the pie plate or baking dish, gently press it in place, and trim the excess dough so it fits. If the dough cracks or tears, mend it by wetting your fingers and pressing the edges together. Follow the recipe instructions and prebake the crust, if needed, or add the filling and bake.

When selecting a premade pie crust, check the ingredient list and nutrition label on the package. Don't purchase the pie crust if you see partially hydrogenated oils in the ingredients or if the nutrition label indicates that it includes trans fats (see Four Food Choices I Live By, page xxii). Most supermarket pie crusts include these unhealthy ingredients. Fortunately, more companies are offering pie crusts with all-natural or organic ingredients, so they are becoming easier to find.

8. When the crust is cool enough to handle, carefully remove the weights and the foil. Spread the marzipan mixture evenly over the bottom of the crust. Arrange the apricots in concentric circles, skin side up, on top of the marzipan mixture. Place the tart in its pan on a rimmed baking sheet and place it in the oven. Bake the tart until the filling is puffed, set, and golden brown, 30 to 40 minutes.

9. Transfer the tart to a wire rack and let it cool to room temperature.

10. Place the apricot jam and the liqueur in a small microwave-safe bowl and microwave on high power until the jam melts, about 1 minute, depending on the microwave wattage. Or gently heat the jam and liqueur in a small saucepan over low heat until the jam melts, about 2 minutes.

11. Stir the jam mixture to combine, then using a pastry brush, lightly brush it over the top of the tart. Remove the sides of the tart pan and carefully slide the tart off the bottom onto a serving plate (or lift it, with the bottom of the pan, onto a serving plate). For the best taste and texture, serve the tart at room temperature on the day it's made. It can be refrigerated, covered, for up to 2 days.

Fresh Peach Pie

*F*resh sweet peaches dripping with juice make an incredible pie that needs only brown sugar, nutmeg, and almond extract to highlight the fruit's flavor. Select a yellow-fleshed variety; these have the most intense flavor and are best for baking. Freestone peaches, those with pits that are easy to separate from the flesh, are the easiest to slice. If you like the extra texture that peach skins add to a pie filling, there's no need to peel the peaches if you buy organic ones. And if you prefer, nectarines can be substituted for the peaches. The thin layer of graham crackers between the crust and filling here is unusual. While the taste is barely noticeable, the graham crackers absorb the delightfully runny peach filling, protecting the flaky crust from the moisture. **MAKES ONE 9-INCH DOUBLE-CRUST PIE**

Summer peaches so sweet and juicy that they are best eaten standing over a sink!

Making Graham Cracker Crumbs

W hen buying graham crackers, be sure to check the ingredient label to make sure they don't include trans fats (see box, page xxii).

Place whole graham crackers in a heavy-duty resealable plastic bag and pound them with a meat mallet or roll a rolling pin over them until they turn into even, fine crumbs. Using a resealable bag makes cleanup and storage easy and convenient. It takes about 15 whole graham crackers to make 1 cup of crumbs.

Sweet Pie Crust (page 388)
1 egg white
About 12 medium-size (2¹/₂ pounds) yellow-fleshed peaches, preferably freestone, or nectarines (see box, page 343)
1 tablespoon fresh lemon juice
1 tablespoon pure almond extract
³/₄ cup firmly packed light brown sugar
¹/₄ cup cornstarch
¹/₂ teaspoon freshly grated nutmeg
¹/₄ cup graham cracker crumbs (see sidebar, this page)

1. Following the instructions on page 388, roll out the dough for the bottom pie crust into an 11-inch circle and transfer it to a 9-inch pie plate. Press the dough firmly into the pie plate, letting 1 inch hang over the edge. Brush the bottom and side of the crust with the egg white and refrigerate it, uncovered, for at least 30 minutes or up to 4 hours.

2. Cut the peaches in half through the stem end. Peel the peaches, remove the pits, and slice each half into 4 or 5 wedges. Place the peaches in a medium-size bowl and add the lemon juice and almond extract. Toss to coat.

3. Place the brown sugar, cornstarch, and nutmeg in a small bowl and stir to combine. Add this to the peaches and stir to coat the fruit thoroughly. Set the peach mixture aside.

4. Roll out the dough for the top pie crust into an 11-inch circle.

5. Spread the graham cracker crumbs evenly across the bottom of the pie crust. Spoon the peach mixture over the graham cracker crumbs.

6. Cover the pie with the top pastry crust. Trim the top crust leaving a ³/₄-inch overhang. Fold the top crust under the edge of the bottom crust and crimp or flute the edges together to make a decorative edge. Using a small knife, cut 3 or 4 slits in the center of the top crust to allow steam to vent as the pie bakes. Transfer the pie to the freezer for 15 minutes.

7. Position a rack in the lower third of the oven and preheat the oven to 425°F. Place a rimmed baking sheet on the oven rack.

8. Place the pie on the baking sheet and bake it for 15 minutes. Reduce the oven temperature to 350°F and continue baking the pie until the crust is golden and the peach juice bubbles up through the slits, 30 to 40 minutes.

9. Let the pie cool on a wire rack, then serve warm or at room temperature. The pie can be refrigerated, covered, for 1 day. To rewarm it, bake it in a 325°F oven for 15 to 20 minutes.

Harvest Pie
with Apples, Pear, and Cranberries

Celebrate the fruits of autumn by making this pie packed with apples, pear, and cranberries. And, if you'd like, add a handful of raisins or a few tablespoons of crystallized ginger to the medley. The nutty streusel topping harmonizes with the sweet fruit filling cradled in a flaky pastry crust. It's a great holiday dessert, so consider making several pies at once. This festive pie is terrific on its own, but no one will complain if you add a scoop of vanilla ice cream or whipped cream.

MAKES ONE 9-INCH SINGLE-CRUST PIE

FOR THE CRUST AND PIE FILLING
Sweet Pie Crust (page 388)
3 crisp apples, such as Fuji, Gala, or
   Granny Smith, peeled and cut into
   ¼-inch-thick slices (about 3 cups)
1 large ripe pear, peeled and cut into
   ¼-inch-thick slices (about 1 cup)
1½ cups coarsely chopped fresh or
   frozen (unthawed) cranberries
1 teaspoon finely grated lemon or
   orange zest (optional)
⅔ to 1 cup granulated sugar
2 tablespoons unbleached all-purpose
   flour
1 tablespoon cornstarch
¼ teaspoon ground nutmeg

FOR THE STREUSEL TOPPING
½ cup old-fashioned rolled oats
   (not instant)
⅓ cup unbleached all-purpose flour
⅓ cup firmly packed brown sugar
⅓ cup chopped walnuts, pecans, or
   almonds
½ teaspoon ground ginger
¼ teaspoon ground nutmeg
4 tablespoons (½ stick), unsalted butter,
   cut into small pieces

1. Make the pie: Following the instructions on page 388, roll out the dough for the pie crust into an 11-inch circle and transfer it to a 9-inch pie plate, pressing the dough firmly into the pie plate. Trim and flute the edge of the crust, then refrigerate it, uncovered, for at least 30 minutes or up to 4 hours.

2. Position a rack in the lower third of the oven and preheat the oven to 375°F. Place a rimmed baking sheet on the oven rack.

Following the instructions on page 388 ... page 388

Buying Pears

Select pears that are firm but not hard. A ripe pear will give slightly if you press it near the stem end. Pears will ripen on the kitchen counter in a few days, but you can hasten the process by storing them at room temperature in a paper bag with an apple, which emits a gas that promotes ripening.

Note: If you prefer
a sweet filling or if
you are using a tart
variety of apples, like
Granny Smith, use
the full cup of sugar.
Otherwise, ²/₃ cup
will do.

3. Place the apples, pear, cranberries, and lemon zest, if using, in a large bowl and stir to combine.

4. Place the granulated sugar (see Note), flour, cornstarch, and nutmeg in a small bowl and stir to combine. Sprinkle the sugar mixture over the fruit and toss to combine.

5. Make the streusel topping: Place the oats, flour, brown sugar, walnuts, ginger, and nutmeg in a medium-size bowl. Using your fingers, blend the butter into the topping mixture until it resembles coarse meal.

6. Place the fruit filling in the pie crust and cover the filling with the streusel topping. Do not pack down the topping.

7. Place the pie on the baking sheet and bake it until the juices start to seep and bubble along the edge and the topping is golden brown, 50 minutes to 1 hour.

8. Let the pie cool on a wire rack for at least 20 minutes before serving. The pie can be refrigerated, covered, for up to 3 days. Let it return to room temperature before serving.

Frozen Key Lime Pie

This frozen dessert combines the silkiness of a soufflé with the sweet-tart flavor and buttery graham cracker crust of a traditional key lime pie. Its ethereal texture comes from the whipped egg whites that are gently folded into the tangy lime filling. What's unusual is that the pie is first baked to cook the egg whites, then frozen to a firm, but not hard, consistency. Plan to make this ahead of time as a refreshing ending to a cool meal on a hot summer day. **MAKES ONE 9-INCH PIE**

FOR THE PIE CRUST
1 cup graham cracker crumbs
    (see sidebar, page 352)
¹/₄ cup sugar
4 tablespoons (¹/₂ stick) unsalted butter,
    melted

FOR THE FILLING AND GARNISH
5 large eggs, separated
1 cup sugar
¹/₂ cup fresh key lime juice, or
    regular lime juice

Pinch of salt
Sweetened Whipped Cream (page 389),
    for garnish
Fresh mint leaves (optional), for garnish

1. Position a rack in the lower third of the oven and preheat the oven to 350°F.

2. Make the pie crust: Place the graham cracker crumbs, sugar, and butter in a small bowl and stir to combine. Press the crumbs into a 9-inch pie plate and bake until golden, about 8 minutes. Let the crust cool on a wire rack for about 15 minutes.

3. Make the filling: Pour water to a depth of ½ inch in a saucepan or the bottom of a double boiler and bring it to a boil over high heat. Reduce the heat to medium-low so that the water just barely simmers.

4. Place the egg yolks in a medium-size heat-proof mixing bowl or the top of a double boiler. Add ⅔ cup of the sugar and whisk to combine. Set the bowl over the barely simmering water. Cook, stirring constantly with a wooden spoon, until the egg yolk mixture thickens and lightens in color, about 5 minutes.

5. Add the lime juice and continue to cook over the simmering water, stirring constantly, until an instant-read thermometer registers 138°F, 5 to 10 minutes. Be careful not to let the mixture simmer or the yolks will overheat and scramble. The lime curd is done when it coats the spoon so thickly that if you draw your finger across it, the mark holds.

6. Let the lime curd cool for 10 minutes. To prevent a skin from forming, cover the lime curd by pressing plastic wrap or wax paper directly against the surface. Transfer the lime curd to the refrigerator to cool for at least 3 hours.

7. Position a rack in the lower third of the oven and preheat the oven to 350°F.

8. Place the egg whites and salt in a medium-size bowl and beat with an electric mixer at high speed until the whites turn foamy, about 1 minute. Gradually add the remaining ⅓ cup of sugar and continue to beat until the whites form soft, shiny peaks, 2 to 3 minutes. Do not overbeat.

9. Stir one-third of the egg whites into the lime curd. Then, fold in the remaining egg whites. Pour the pie filling into the crust and bake until the filling is set and the surface turns lightly golden, about 15 minutes.

10. Let the pie cool on a wire rack for 1 hour. Transfer the pie, uncovered, to the freezer and let it freeze for at least 6 hours. Once frozen, cover the pie tightly with plastic wrap and leave it in the freezer until serving time. For easy serving, dip the bottom of the pie plate into warm water to loosen the crust and cut the slices with a hot knife. Garnish each serving with whipped cream and fresh mint leaves, if desired.

Bearss Seedless limes, still just babies—about six months away from being harvested.

Lemon Berry Mousse

My husband, Drew, loves this luscious mousse. Not only is it a lemon lover's dream, it's also surprisingly versatile. For a dinner party, pipe the rum-spiked mousse into stemmed wine glasses, alternating lemony layers with fresh blueberries, raspberries, or strawberries to create an elegant parfait. For a casual family night, leave out the rum and simply spoon the mousse into custard cups and top it with berries. Crisp cookies, like the Earthbound Farm Ginger Snaps (see page 320), make a nice contrast to the silky mousse. But don't wait until the last minute to make this dessert because the texture improves as it chills in the refrigerator for a few hours. In fact, it holds up so well that you can make the mousse a day or two in advance. **SERVES 6 TO 8**

5 large eggs
1 cup sugar
8 tablespoons (1 stick) unsalted butter, melted
1 cup fresh lemon juice, strained (about 6 lemons)
1¹/₂ cups heavy (whipping) cream, chilled
Grated zest of 1 lemon
¹/₄ cup dark rum (optional)
1 half-pint (about 1¹/₄ cups) fresh raspberries, or 1¹/₄ cups sliced hulled strawberries, for garnish
1 half-pint (about 1 cup) fresh blueberries, for garnish
6 to 8 fresh mint sprigs, for garnish

1. Place the eggs in a bowl and beat them with an electric mixer on medium speed for 1 minute. Gradually add the sugar, occasionally scraping down the side of the bowl if needed. Increase the speed to high and beat the egg mixture until it is very light and fluffy, about 5 minutes longer. Reduce the speed to low, add the butter and lemon juice, and mix until just combined.

2. Transfer the egg mixture to a large, heavy-bottomed saucepan and cook over low heat, stirring constantly with a wooden spoon. Be careful not to let the mixture simmer or the eggs will overheat and scramble. The egg mixture is done when it coats the spoon so thickly that if you draw your finger across it, the mark holds, and an instant-read thermometer registers 138°F, 5 to 10 minutes.

3. Transfer the egg mixture to a clean bowl. To prevent a skin from forming, cover the egg mixture by pressing plastic wrap or waxed paper against the surface. Transfer the bowl to the refrigerator and let it chill for at least 6 hours or as long as 2 days.

4. When the egg mixture is cold, place the cream in a large bowl and beat it with an electric mixer at medium speed until it becomes frothy. Add the lemon zest and rum, if using, and continue beating until the cream forms soft peaks. Do not overbeat.

5. Whisk about half of the whipped cream into the chilled egg mixture. Fold the remaining whipped cream into the egg mixture to combine thoroughly.

6. Using a spoon or pastry bag, fill cups or stemmed glasses with the mousse, leaving room for the raspberry and blueberry

garnish. (To make parfaits, alternate the berries with layers of the mousse.)

7. Cover the mousse with plastic wrap and refrigerate it for at least 2 hours or up to 48 hours. Serve the mousse well chilled, garnished with the berries and mint.

Cherry Panna Cotta

You may know panna cotta *as a classic Italian dessert—milky white and delicate, with a texture similar to custard, only lighter. It's usually served with a fruit sauce, but here we've put the fruit* inside *the* panna cotta, *turning it a pale cherry color and giving it an intense cherry flavor. The buttermilk is an unusual addition, adding a hint of tartness to balance the sweet cherries. You can serve the* panna cotta *in individual molds with a dollop of Vanilla Cherry Sauce or in martini glasses, topped with a fresh cherry. This is a make-ahead dessert that keeps in the refrigerator for up to three days.* **SERVES 6**

4 cups fresh sweet cherries, such as
    Bing, pitted (see sidebar, page 362)
1½ cups unsweetened cherry juice
    (see Note, page 362)
½ vanilla bean, split lengthwise
1¾ cups buttermilk
1 package (¼ ounce; 1 tablespoon)
    unflavored gelatin
¾ cup heavy (whipping) cream
Vanilla Cherry Sauce (page 362) and/or
    6 to 8 whole fresh cherries, with
    stems, for garnish

1. Combine the cherries, cherry juice, vanilla bean, and ½ cup of water in a medium-size saucepan and bring to a simmer over medium heat. Cover the

saucepan and reduce the heat to low. Let simmer, stirring occasionally, until the cherries are very soft, about 20 minutes.

2. Strain the cherry liquid through a sieve into a medium-size bowl, reserving the cherries and vanilla bean. Return the liquid to the saucepan and cook over high heat until it is reduced to about 1 cup, about 5 minutes. Set the cherry liquid aside and let cool to room temperature.

3. Remove the vanilla bean from the cherries and set it aside. Transfer the cherries to a blender, add the buttermilk, and puree until smooth.

Vanilla beans are expensive, so when you invest in one, get your money's worth by extracting all of its flavor. You can use the whole vanilla bean to infuse liquids or sauces with flavor. Or, you can split the pod open to reveal the sticky, tiny seeds and scrape them out to add flavorful vanilla bean specks to ice cream and other desserts. The remaining pod can be rinsed, dried, and reused to flavor custards or make vanilla sugar (see the sidebar on page 363). To store a vanilla bean, wrap it in plastic wrap and place it in an airtight jar. It will keep in a cool, dark place at room temperature for up to six months.

Note: Look for unsweetened cherry juice (usually from concentrate) in the fruit juice section of the grocery store.

Pitting Cherries

The easiest way to remove cherry pits is with a cherry pitter. The inexpensive models (about $13) sold in kitchen stores or on the Web work fine, but when pitting cherries, always wear an apron or old shirt and work over a sink, just in case the juice spatters.

4. Strain the cherry-buttermilk mixture through a sieve into a medium-size bowl and discard any solids. Using the tip of a small knife, scrape the seeds from the vanilla bean pod and add them to the cherry-buttermilk mixture, then set it aside. Rinse and dry the vanilla bean pod and set it aside for another use (see sidebar, facing page).

5. When the reserved cherry liquid has cooled, sprinkle the gelatin on top and let it soften, about 3 minutes.

6. Place the heavy cream in a small saucepan and cook over medium-high heat until it comes just to a boil. Remove the saucepan from the heat. Using a rubber spatula, immediately add the gelatin mixture to the cream and stir to combine.

7. Strain the gelatin mixture through a sieve into the bowl containing the cherry-buttermilk mixture and whisk to blend. Discard any solids in the sieve.

8. Pour about ¾ cup of the *panna cotta* mixture into each of 6 individual molds (such as 8-ounce custard cups or ramekins) or martini glasses. Refrigerate the *panna cotta*, covered, until it is very firm, at least 8 hours or up to 3 days.

9. If you want to unmold the *panna cotta* onto dessert plates, remove the molds from the refrigerator and let the *panna cotta* soften at room temperature for about 10 minutes. Run a small knife around the inside edge of each mold. Hold the bottom of the mold in a small bowl of hot water until the *panna cotta* loosens, about 30 seconds. Place a dessert plate on top of the mold. Holding the mold and plate together, turn them over, shaking the

panna cotta gently to release it from the mold onto the plate. Repeat with the remaining *panna cotta*.

10. Serve the *panna cotta* immediately, garnished with the Vanilla Cherry Sauce and/or fresh cherries.

Vanilla Cherry Sauce

The warm essence of pure cherries—with traces of vanilla, cinnamon, and exotic spices—is simply intoxicating. Pour this sauce over vanilla ice cream or yogurt, dress up a buttery pound cake, or use it to sweeten Sunday morning waffles. Look for cherry juice and dried cherries on your grocer's shelves, but wait to make the sauce until fresh cherries are at their peak, when they taste the best and cost the least. Granted, pitting cherries can be a messy task, but once that's done, the sauce is simple to make, and it keeps for days. One taste and you'll agree that this sauce is well worth the effort.

MAKES ABOUT 3 CUPS

> 2 cups unsweetened cherry juice
> (see Note)
> 4 cups fresh sweet cherries, such as
> Bing, pitted (see sidebar, this page)
> 1 cup tart dried cherries
> 1 stick cinnamon (3 inches long)
> 1 whole star anise
> Seeds from 3 cardamom pods, or
> ¼ teaspoon ground cardamom
> (see sidebar, page 368)
> ¾ cup sugar
> ½ vanilla bean, split lengthwise
> 2 tablespoons cherry-flavored liqueur
> or almond-flavored liqueur,
> such as amaretto (optional)

1. Combine the cherry juice, fresh cherries, dried cherries, cinnamon stick, star anise, cardamom seeds, and sugar in a medium-size saucepan. Using the tip of a small knife, scrape the seeds from the vanilla bean pod and add them to the saucepan, then add the vanilla bean pod.

2. Bring the cherry mixture just to a boil over medium-high heat. Reduce the heat to low and let simmer, stirring occasionally, until the cherries are very soft and the liquid has thickened to a syrupy consistency, about 45 minutes. Remove the vanilla bean pod, cinnamon stick, and star anise from the sauce, discarding the cinnamon stick and star anise. Rinse and dry the vanilla bean pod and set it aside for another use (see sidebar, this page).

3. Add the liqueur, if using, to the sauce and stir to blend. The sauce can be served at room temperature or slightly warmer, but not so warm that it melts cold desserts. The sauce can be refrigerated, covered, for up to 5 days.

Triple Ginger Ice Cream

Ginger lovers will adore this rich ice cream. Intriguing layers of flavor develop as the egg custard is infused with the fresh and ground ginger. Finally, there are the chewy nuggets of crystallized ginger, added as the ice cream churns. For the ultimate ginger experience, try a small scoop between two Earthbound Farm Ginger Snaps (see page 320) for a totally incredible ice cream sandwich. **MAKES 1 QUART**

2 cups heavy (whipping) cream
2 cups whole milk
³/₄ cup (4 ounces) peeled and
　finely chopped fresh ginger
1 teaspoon ground ginger
6 large egg yolks
²/₃ cup sugar
¹/₂ cup finely chopped crystallized
　ginger

1. Place the cream, milk, fresh ginger, and ground ginger in medium-size saucepan. Cook the mixture over medium heat, stirring occasionally, until small bubbles form around the edge of the pan, just before the mixture comes to a boil. Immediately remove the saucepan from the heat, cover it with a lid, and let steep at room temperature for 1 hour. Strain the cream mixture through a sieve and discard any solids.

2. Place the egg yolks and sugar in a medium-size bowl and whisk to combine. Slowly add the cream mixture to the egg mixture, whisking constantly.

3. Return the cream mixture to the saucepan and cook over medium heat, stirring constantly, until it thickens slightly and coats the back of a wooden spoon, 5 to 10 minutes. Do not let the mixture boil or it will curdle.

4. Fill a large bowl with ice cubes and set it aside.

Vanilla Sugar

Vanilla sugar is an easy, economical way to add the delicate flavor of vanilla to foods and beverages as you sweeten them. This is an excellent way to use vanilla bean pods left over once the seeds have been removed. If the pods have been used to infuse flavor in custard or another liquid, rinse and dry the pods with paper towels or let them air-dry before adding them to the sugar.

To make vanilla sugar, simply bury a vanilla bean in two cups of granulated sugar. Store the sugar in an airtight container for at least two weeks to let the sugar absorb the vanilla flavor. It will keep indefinitely. As you deplete the supply, add more sugar or fresh vanilla bean pods, and you'll always have vanilla sugar on hand to sweeten coffee and hot chocolate, sprinkle over fruits and berries, garnish cookie tops, and more.

5. Strain the custard mixture through a sieve into a medium-size bowl and discard any solids. Set the bowl in the ice bath to quickly reduce the temperature, stirring the custard occasionally to dissipate the heat. When the custard mixture reaches room temperature, refrigerate it, covered, until it is thoroughly chilled, at least 4 hours.

6. Place the custard mixture in the bowl of an ice cream maker and churn following the manufacturer's instructions.

Add the crystallized ginger to the ice cream maker during the last minute of churning. Do not overchurn the ice cream or it could become grainy.

7. Transfer the ice cream to an airtight container and freeze it for at least 2 hours before serving. For longer storage, place a piece of plastic wrap directly on the surface of the ice cream to prevent ice crystals from forming. Covered tightly, the ice cream can be frozen for up to 2 weeks.

Bing Cherry Sorbet

Who can resist baskets of plump, fresh ruby-red cherries? They are one of summer's first stone fruits, arriving in late May, with a growing season that lasts only a few weeks. Churning cherries into a refreshing sorbet is one way to enjoy them a little longer. Fresh fruit sorbets are refreshing and light, perfect for a summer afternoon. And the sweet cherry chunks, buried like jewels in the smooth puree, make this a sorbet you'll treasure. **MAKES ABOUT 1 QUART**

³/₄ cup sugar
Zest of 1 lemon, removed in
    wide strips (see box,
    page 14)
3 cups fresh sweet cherries
    (preferably Bing), pitted
    (see sidebar, page 362)
2 cups unsweetened cherry juice
    (see Note, page 362)
2 tablespoons fresh lemon juice

1. Place ³/₄ cup of water and the sugar and lemon zest in a small saucepan and bring to a boil over high heat, stirring occasionally to dissolve the sugar. Remove the saucepan

from the heat and let the sugar syrup steep, uncovered, at room temperature for 30 minutes. Discard the lemon zest.

2. Place 2 cups of the cherries in a small saucepan. Add the cherry juice and ³/₄ cup of the sugar syrup and cook over low heat until the cherries are very soft, about 15 minutes. Set the remaining sugar syrup aside.

3. Using an immersion blender, puree the cherries in the saucepan. Or, you can let the cherry mixture cool slightly, then puree it in a blender or food processor.

Transfer the pureed cherries to a medium-size bowl and refrigerate, uncovered, until thoroughly chilled, about 4 hours.

4. Add the lemon juice to the cold puree. Taste for sweetness, adding more of the sugar syrup as needed. Place the cherry mixture in the bowl of an ice cream maker and churn following the manufacturer's instructions.

5. Meanwhile, chop the remaining 1 cup of cherries. Add them to the ice cream maker during the last 5 minutes of churning.

6. Transfer the sorbet to an airtight container and freeze it for at least 2 hours before serving. For longer storage, place a piece of plastic wrap directly on the surface of the sorbet to prevent ice crystals from forming. Covered tightly, the sorbet can be frozen for up to 2 weeks.

Coconut Lemongrass Sorbet

This creamy coconut sorbet with a subtle accent of lemon is very simple to make, but allow time for the coconut milk to absorb the lemongrass flavor. The alcohol in the tablespoon of coconut liqueur helps the sorbet freeze without becoming icy.

MAKES 1 QUART

1¼ cups sugar
4 stalks fresh lemongrass finely chopped
   (see sidebar, page 46)
Grated zest of 1 lemon
   (see box, page 14)
2 cans (each about 14 ounces)
   unsweetened light coconut milk
1 tablespoon coconut liqueur

1. Place the sugar, lemongrass, lemon zest, and coconut milk in a medium-size saucepan and bring to a boil over high heat, stirring occasionally to dissolve the sugar. Remove the saucepan from the heat, cover it with a lid, and let the mixture steep at room temperature for 1 hour.

2. Strain the coconut milk mixture through a sieve into a medium-size bowl and discard the solids. Cover the bowl and refrigerate the coconut milk mixture until it is thoroughly chilled, at least 2 hours.

3. Add the coconut liqueur, then place the mixture in the bowl of an ice cream maker. Churn the sorbet following the manufacturer's instructions.

4. Transfer the sorbet to an airtight container and freeze it for at least 2 hours before serving. For longer storage, place a piece of plastic wrap directly on the surface of the sorbet to prevent ice crystals from forming. Covered tightly, the sorbet can be frozen for up to 2 weeks.

Spiced Quince Compote

As beautiful as stained glass, quince compote will fill your house with the aroma of exotic spices while it simmers. Cooking quince with sugar turns the pale-colored flesh a brilliant amber or rose, depending on the variety. Diced quince maintains its shape and firm texture even after a lengthy simmer in the spiced syrup. It pairs well with softer apples and pears, which can be added during the last fifteen minutes of cooking. The fruit also has a lot of pectin, so the compote keeps for a long time when refrigerated. Served warm or at room temperature, this fruit topping can dress up a simple cake, waffles, French toast, or ice cream. **MAKES ABOUT 2 CUPS**

1¼ cups sugar

3 whole star anise

1 whole vanilla bean

1 tablespoon whole cardamom pods (see sidebar, page 368), crushed

1 stick cinnamon (3 inches), broken into pieces

5 whole cloves

Zest of 1 lemon, removed in wide strips (see box, page 14)

Juice of 1 lemon

4 medium-size quince (about 1 pound), peeled, cored, and cut into ½-inch dice (about 3 cups; see box, page 333)

1. Place 3 cups of water and the sugar, star anise, vanilla bean, cardamom pods, cinnamon stick, cloves, and lemon zest and juice in a medium-size saucepan. Cook over medium-high heat, stirring occasionally, until the mixture comes to a boil.

2. Reduce the heat to medium and cook the syrup until it is reduced to about 2 cups, 10 to 15 minutes. Remove the syrup from the heat and let it cool and absorb the spice flavors, about 10 minutes.

3. Strain the syrup through a sieve. Remove the vanilla bean and star anise and set them aside. Discard the remaining solids.

4. Return the syrup to the saucepan and add the quince and reserved star anise. Split the vanilla bean in half lengthwise with a paring knife. Scrape out the vanilla

Hundreds of school children visit our Farm Stand in the fall, and before leaving, choose a small pumpkin as a gift from us.

Cardamom

A common ingredient in Indian and Middle Eastern dishes and in Scandinavian desserts, cardamom is a spice with an inviting aroma and a warm, sweet flavor. Cardamom's light green pods are about a half inch long and are filled with small flavorful black seeds. You can buy whole pods (either light green or bleached white), cardamom seeds, or ground cardamom. Ground, the spice loses flavor quickly, so buy seeds, if available, and grind them at home in a spice mill or with a mortar and pestle. Cardamom is an expensive spice, but a little goes a long way.

seeds with the tip of the knife and add them to the syrup. Rinse and dry the vanilla bean pod and set it aside for another use (see sidebar, page 363).

5. Cook the quince over medium heat until the syrup comes to a simmer. Reduce the heat to low and cook until the quince is tender and the syrup is thick, 30 to 40 minutes.

6. Serve the compote warm or at room temperature. It can be refrigerated, covered, for up to 2 months. Let the compote return to room temperature before serving or reheat it over low heat until warm, 5 to 10 minutes.

Aunt Rose's Cinnamon Sugar Pecans

Years ago, when Drew's "Aunt Ro" was still alive, we would risk traveling through ice and snow to visit her in Buffalo during the holidays. I fondly remember her candied pecans as our reward. She always had a bowlful on the coffee table for us to enjoy. Not filling up on the tasty nuts between meals was always a challenge! The nuts are delicious any time of the year, but packed in a holiday tin, they make a great gift. They are a sweet, cinnamon-flavored accompaniment to a bowl of fresh berries or ice cream at the end of a meal. **MAKES ABOUT 3 1/2 CUPS**

3/4 cup sugar
1 teaspoon ground cinnamon
1/8 teaspoon ground cloves
1/2 teaspoon ground nutmeg
1/4 teaspoon ground allspice
1 large egg white
4 1/2 teaspoons cold water
3 1/2 cups pecan halves

1. Position a rack in the center of the oven and preheat the oven to 250°F. Line a rimmed baking sheet with parchment paper, for easy cleanup, or lightly oil it. Set the baking sheet aside.

2. Place the sugar, cinnamon, cloves, nutmeg, and allspice in a small bowl and whisk to combine.

3. Place the egg white and water in a large bowl and whisk vigorously until foamy. Add the pecans and stir to coat. Add the sugar and spice mixture and stir to combine.

4. Transfer the pecans to the prepared baking sheet and spread them out in a single layer. Bake the nuts for 30 minutes, then stir them with a spatula. Continue baking until toasted and golden brown, 30 minutes longer, 1 hour total.

5. Let the pecans cool for 5 minutes. Break apart any nuts that are stuck together and transfer them to an airtight container, placing pieces of waxed paper in between to separate the layers. The nuts can be stored at room temperature for up to 1 month.

Our small farm visitors find our tractors as fascinating as our crops.

Chapter 10

Basics

You've heard it before, but it's certainly worth repeating: A few special ingredients prepared in advance—perhaps a basic homemade stock, a couple of special vinegars, some roasted peppers, and maybe even roasted tomatoes— ensure that when dinnertime rolls around, you already have a good head start.

Because a rich chicken stock is so important to many dishes, I offer up two versions. One is a traditional light-colored stock with plenty of flavor. The other is dark and so full-bodied that it can be used in place of beef broth; the secret to its robust flavor is roasting the chicken parts and vegetables first.

Many of us now keep bottles of store-bought Asian teriyaki and hoisin sauces around for quick marinades, but your time in the kitchen will pay off royally when you try our flavorful Farm Stand versions. Our teriyaki sauce takes less than 20 minutes, start to finish, and you'll be amazed at how the complex flavors add so much more to a dish than the commercial varieties do. The same holds true for flavored vinegars and oil. They are easy to make and turn the simplest salad into

something special—as do homemade Slow-Roasted Tomatoes and Roasted Bell Peppers.

You may be surprised to see that I've included a recipe for matzoh meal. Matzoh balls in chicken soup are delicious, but we couldn't find organic matzoh, so we made our own. The matzoh dough rolls out easily and bakes up quickly. I've also included a couple of pie doughs—one for savory dishes and one for fruit pies, like the Fresh Peach Pie on page 351. Top that pie with luscious whipped cream or homemade crème fraîche. There are recipes for both in this chapter.

Time spent preparing a few homemade basics will feel like a most appreciated gift to yourself on those days when you crave a homemade meal, but with minimal effort.

Facing Page:
The best stocks benefit from a strong selection of fresh vegetables and herbs.

Blond Chicken Stock

Taste this rich, golden blond stock alongside the dull canned version and you'll see that there's just no comparison. If you want to make a dynamite pot of Summer Harvest Soup (see page 26), you really need a homemade stock. If it seems extravagant to use so much organic chicken just to make stock, ask your butcher to debone the breast. Or do it yourself by running a sharp, thin knife blade along the breast bone and gently lifting the flesh away. Throw the bones in the stock pot, along with the remaining chicken pieces, and enjoy boneless chicken breasts for dinner. If your knife skills are less than perfect, it doesn't matter, because any meat you leave on the bones adds more flavor to your stock. You'll also add flavor with less work by leaving the peelings on clean onions and carrots. (See page 374 for more stock tips.) **MAKES ABOUT 10 CUPS**

Bouquets of these Jolly Jester and Harlequin marigolds won a blue ribbon at the Monterey County Fair.

1 large roasting chicken, cut into
　　parts, plus enough wings, backs,
　　or legs to make 8 pounds total
2 large yellow onions, unpeeled,
　　coarsely chopped
3 medium-size carrots, unpeeled,
　　coarsely chopped
3 medium-size leeks, both white and
　　light green parts, well rinsed and
　　coarsely chopped
2 bay leaves
1$^{1}/_{2}$ teaspoons whole black peppercorns
1 bunch fresh thyme (about 10 sprigs)
4 celery ribs with leaves, coarsely
　　chopped
15 sprigs fresh flat-leaf parsley,
　　coarsely chopped

1. Rinse the chicken parts well and trim off and discard any excess fat. Place the chicken in a very large soup pot and add just enough cool water to barely cover it, about 14 cups.

2. Bring the water just to a boil over high heat, then reduce the heat to low.

Using a large spoon, skim off any foam that accumulates on the surface. Add the onions, carrots, leeks, bay leaves, peppercorns, and thyme and let simmer gently, uncovered, for 1$^{1}/_{2}$ hours. Add the celery and parsley and let simmer gently 30 minutes longer.

3. Remove the chicken and large vegetables with tongs. Set the chicken aside for another use or discard it along with the vegetables. Strain the stock through a fine-meshed sieve into a large bowl or clean pot and discard the solids. If you are using the stock at this time, let the fat rise to the surface, then skim it off with a metal spoon or ladle. If not for immediate use, let the stock come to room temperature using the quick cooling method on page 375. Refrigerate the stock, covered, until the fat has solidified on the surface, then discard the fat. The stock can be refrigerated, covered, for up to 3 days or frozen for up to 6 months.

Dark Chicken Stock

Roasting the chicken makes a dark, full-bodied chicken stock that is so versatile it can be a substitute for beef broth in a pinch. Use this dark stock in wintry stews and soups, and save the Blond Chicken Stock for lighter soups and risottos. (See page 374 for more stock tips.) **MAKES ABOUT 10 CUPS**

8 pounds chicken legs, wings, and
   backs
2 medium-size yellow onions, unpeeled,
   quartered
4 celery ribs with leaves, cut into
   1-inch pieces
4 medium-size carrots, unpeeled and
   cut into 1-inch pieces
1 cup boiling water
2 tablespoons tomato paste
2 teaspoons whole black peppercorns
6 whole cloves
1 bunch fresh thyme
   (about 10 sprigs)
Stems from 1 bunch fresh flat-leaf
   parsley, reserve leaves for
   another use

1. Position a rack in the lower third of the oven and preheat the oven to 400°F.

2. Rinse the chicken parts well and trim off and discard any excess fat and skin. Place the chicken parts in a large roasting pan in a single layer. (If necessary, arrange the chicken in 2 pans to avoid crowding, which could slow down the browning process.)

3. Roast the chicken until it begins to brown, about 30 minutes. Add the onions, celery, and carrots and continue baking until the chicken and vegetables are brown, 20 to 30 minutes.

4. Transfer the chicken and vegetables to a very large soup pot. Add boiling water to the roasting pan and scrape up any brown bits from the bottom of the pan. Pour this into the soup pot and add just enough cool water to barely cover the chicken, about 12 cups.

5. Bring the water just to a boil over high heat, then reduce the heat to low and let the stock simmer gently for 30 minutes. Using a large spoon, skim off any foam that accumulates on the surface.

6. Add the tomato paste, peppercorns, cloves, thyme, and parsley and let simmer gently, uncovered, for 2½ hours.

7. Remove the chicken and large vegetables with tongs. Set the chicken aside for another use or discard it along with the vegetables. Strain the stock through a fine-meshed sieve into a large bowl or clean pot and discard the solids. If you are using the stock at this time, let the fat rise to the surface, then skim it off with a metal spoon or ladle. If not for immediate use, let the stock come to room temperature using the quick cooling method on page 375. Refrigerate the stock, covered, until the fat has solidified on the surface, then discard the fat. The stock can be refrigerated, covered, for up to 3 days or frozen for up to 6 months.

Homemade Stock Tips

While stock values on Wall Street may rise or plunge, the stock in your freezer is always a valuable asset. Here's how to make sure yours turns out full-flavored and nourishing, whether meat, poultry, fish, or vegetable.

* Water: Stock is mostly water, so use fresh filtered water or a good-quality bottled mineral water (not distilled water). Never use hot tap water to speed up the cooking process. You'll be using water that has been stored in your water heater, which is great for bathing but not for consuming.

* Salt: As a general rule, don't add salt when making stock, especially if you are making stock to use in other recipes. Instead, add the salt when you prepare the final dish. Also, if you need to concentrate the stock by boiling out some of the water, you won't end up with a stock that's full-bodied, but too salty.

A homemade stock concentrates the rich flavors of its organic ingredients.

* Vegetables: Onion skins, unpeeled carrots, and trimmings from other light-tasting vegetables (such as leeks and parsnips) are all good additions for a flavorful stock. You can also add unpeeled garlic and dried or fresh mushrooms. If you're feeling frugal, accumulate vegetable trimmings in the freezer for the day you make stock. Just be sure that the vegetables you add to your stock are well-scrubbed and fresh.

* Flesh and bones: Poultry, meat, and fish stocks all benefit from both flesh and bones. Bones give off gelatin that gives stock a rich consistency, and flesh provides flavor. If your stock will be based primarily on bones, look for ones that still have some meat attached. If it's feasible, chop the bones and meat into small pieces so that the flavor will be released more quickly. If you're planning a chicken meal that doesn't require a whole chicken, buy a whole one anyway. Freeze the parts you don't want to eat right away for soup stock.

* Simmering: Keep a close watch on the stock, adjusting the heat to maintain a very slow simmer, with bubbles that just barely break the surface. Boiling meat or poultry stock causes the fat to emulsify, making the stock cloudy and greasy tasting.

* **Quick cooling:** To prevent harmful bacteria from developing, it's important to cool stocks that you are not using immediately as quickly as possible, before refrigerating or freezing them. If you have a large pot of stock, divide the stock into smaller containers so it will come to room temperature more quickly. Or even better, use an ice bath to cool down the liquid. Place the strained stock in a clean pot and place the pot in a pan filled with ice water until the stock has cooled down. Stirring the stock occasionally will speed up the process. Don't be tempted to put the hot stock directly into the refrigerator—the heat from the broth could raise the temperature inside the refrigerator to an unsafe level.

* **Freezing:** Freeze stock in a variety of container sizes so you'll have just the amount you need for a recipe. If your freezer space is limited, use quart-size freezer storage bags to create flat frozen packages of stock. Just be sure to seal them carefully! Also, you can freeze stock in ice cube trays for times when a small amount is called for. When the stock is frozen solid, transfer the cubes to freezer storage bags.

* **Store-bought broths:** Canned and boxed broths just don't compare to a flavorful homemade stock, so if a rich stock is the star attraction in a recipe, don't settle for less than homemade. But sometimes a store-bought broth just has to do. When buying broths, select ones that are low in sodium and without such additives as MSG. If you are concerned about the amount of salt you consume, read the labels. You may be shocked at how much salt even "low sodium" stocks

For stronger flavor, leave the skins on the onions.

have. Also check labels on certified organic broths. They won't have artificial flavors or preservatives, but they may still contain a high percentage of salt. Broth is now available in boxes (called aseptic packages) as well as cans. Overall, boxed broths have better flavor, but there are ecological pros and cons to this packaging. While less energy is used in transporting the light-weight boxes, they are more difficult to recycle than cans. Try several brands of canned and boxed broth to see which suits you best.

Slow Simmering Beef Stock
with Red Wine

It takes all day to slowly simmer a flavorful beef stock, so make this when it's cold and blustery outside. You can stay warm indoors enjoying the rich, meaty aroma as it fills the house. Then you'll have a supply of beef stock on hand for making the Merlot-Braised Short Ribs (see page 119). **MAKES 8 TO 10 CUPS**

10 pounds beef or veal bones,
    preferably with some meat
    attached
2 tablespoons olive oil
2 large yellow onions, unpeeled,
    cut into wedges
4 celery ribs with leaves,
    cut into 1-inch pieces
1 large carrot, unpeeled and
    cut into 1-inch pieces
8 cloves garlic, unpeeled
1 bottle (750 milliliters) dry
    red wine
1 can (28 ounces) diced tomatoes
1 teaspoon whole black peppercorns

1. Position a rack in the lower third of the oven and preheat the oven to 450°F.

2. Place the meat bones in a large roasting pan in a single layer and rub the olive oil over them. (If necessary, arrange the bones in 2 pans to avoid crowding, which could slow down the browning process.)

3. Roast the bones until they begin to brown, about 1 hour. Add the onions, celery, carrot, and garlic and continue baking, stirring occasionally, until the bones are deep brown, about 45 minutes.

4. Transfer the bones and vegetables to a very large soup pot or divide them between 2 pots, if needed. Add the wine to the roasting pan and scrape up any brown bits from the bottom of the pan. Pour this into the soup pot and add just enough cool water to barely cover the bones, about 12 cups.

5. Bring the liquid just to a boil over high heat, then reduce the heat to low. Using a large spoon, skim off any foam that accumulates on the surface.

6. Add the tomatoes and peppercorns and let simmer gently, uncovered, at least

Farmer Mark Marino inspects his cabbage fields in Carmel Valley.

6 hours or up to 12 hours, adding more water as needed to keep the bones barely covered with liquid.

7. Remove and discard the bones. Strain the stock through a fine-meshed sieve into a large, clean pot and discard the solids. If the stock tastes weak, bring it to a simmer over medium heat and cook until reduced by a third to intensify the flavor, 30 to 45 minutes.

8. If you are using the stock at this time, let it rest for a few minutes so the fat rises to the surface, then skim it off with a metal spoon or ladle. If not for immediate use, let the stock come to room temperature using the quick cooling method on page 375. Refrigerate the stock, covered, until the fat has solidified on the surface, then discard the fat. The stock can be refrigerated, covered, for up to 3 days or frozen for up to 6 months.

Shiitake Vegetable Stock

You'll find this vegetable stock to be more full-flavored than most, thanks to the shiitake mushrooms. If you prefer a less earthy taste, substitute white or brown cultivated mushrooms, or leave them out altogether. The fennel bulb adds a mild anise flavor, but it can be omitted if you prefer. In fact, there's no hard-and-fast rule for making a good vegetable stock, except that you should avoid adding strong-flavored or deeply-colored vegetables, such as broccoli, bell peppers, or beets. With the exception of rosemary, which is really powerful, you can substitute whatever other fresh herbs you happen to have on hand to create a vegetable stock of your own.

MAKES ABOUT 9 CUPS

2 medium-size carrots, unpeeled, coarsely chopped

3 celery ribs with leaves, coarsely chopped

1 large leek, both white and light green parts, well rinsed and coarsely chopped

4 cloves garlic, unpeeled

1 small fennel bulb (optional), sliced

2 medium-size zucchini, sliced

1 cup (about 3½ ounces) trimmed and sliced fresh shiitake mushroom caps and stems

1 pound ripe tomatoes (about 5), preferably Roma (plum tomatoes; see Note), cored, seeded, and coarsely chopped

1 bay leaf

¼ cup chopped fresh flat-leaf parsley

2 tablespoons fresh thyme leaves

Note: The fresh tomatoes don't have to be stellar for this vegetable stock to taste good. Don't be tempted to substitute canned tomatoes; they may turn your broth red.

When you cook with a fennel bulb, save its feathery tops for a delicate garnish.

1. Place the carrots, celery, leek, garlic, fennel, zucchini, shiitakes, tomatoes, and bay leaf in a large soup pot and add 12 cups of water. Bring the water to a simmer over medium-high heat. Reduce the heat to low and let simmer, uncovered, until the flavor develops, about 1 hour.

2. Add the parsley and thyme and let simmer until the herbs release their flavor, about 20 minutes longer.

3. Remove the stock from the heat and let it cool slightly. Strain the stock through a fine-meshed sieve into a large bowl or pot and discard the solids. If you are not planning on using the stock at this time, let it come to room temperature using the quick cooling method on page 375. The stock can be refrigerated, covered, for up to 5 days or frozen for up to 6 months.

Better than Store-Bought Teriyaki Sauce

Commercial teriyaki sauce doesn't come close to the full-bodied, spicy-sweet flavor of homemade. This recipe is so easy to make, you may never go back to the bottled stuff. **MAKES ABOUT 1 CUP**

Note: You can use light, medium, or dark corn syrup, but look for one that does not include high fructose corn syrup in the ingredients list (see sidebar, page 19).

1 cup soy sauce
1/4 cup pineapple juice
1/4 cup firmly packed brown sugar, preferably dark
1/4 cup honey
1/4 cup corn syrup (see Note)
1 tablespoon grated peeled fresh ginger
3 cloves garlic, minced

Place all of the ingredients in a medium-size saucepan and stir to combine. Bring the mixture to a boil over medium-high heat, then reduce the heat to low. Let the sauce simmer gently until the flavor intensifies, about 10 minutes. Let the teriyaki sauce cool to room temperature. The sauce can be refrigerated, covered, for up to 3 weeks.

Hoisin Sauce from Scratch

When we first opened our Farm Stand's Organic Kitchen, no one was selling an organic hoisin sauce. So out of necessity, we made our own. Our version is thick and rich, with a complex sweet-sour flavor. It's delicious in the marinade for Grilled Lamb Chops with Mongolian Sauce (see page 130) and the Hoisin Tofu Snacks (see page 216). While most commercial hoisin sauces are made from fermented soybean paste, we make a paste from the dried adzuki beans typically used in Japanese cooking. Look for these small, rust-colored beans in the dried bean section of Asian markets, specialty food stores, or health food stores.

MAKES ABOUT 1 CUP

Sparkler cleome brightens our lemon orchard.

$^1/_2$ cup dried red adzuki beans, rinsed

2 tablespoons toasted sesame oil

1 tablespoon minced garlic

1 cup firmly packed light brown sugar

$^1/_4$ cup cider vinegar

$^1/_4$ cup unseasoned rice vinegar

$^1/_3$ cup soy sauce

$^1/_4$ teaspoon Asian chile garlic sauce, or $^1/_4$ teaspoon dried red pepper flakes, or more to taste

1. Place the beans in a medium-size saucepan and add 5 cups of water. Bring the water to a boil over high heat, then reduce the heat to low. Let the beans simmer gently, uncovered, until they are very soft, $1^1/_2$ to 2 hours. Drain the beans in a colander and let them cool. Puree the beans in a food processor until smooth.

2. Heat the oil in a large skillet over medium heat. When it is hot, but not smoking, add the garlic. Cook the garlic, stirring occasionally, until it is soft but not browned, 2 to 3 minutes.

3. Add the bean puree and the brown sugar, cider vinegar, rice vinegar, soy sauce, and 2 tablespoons of water to the skillet and stir to combine. Bring the sauce to a boil, then reduce the heat to low. Cook the sauce, stirring occasionally, until it is thick enough to coat the back of a wooden spoon, 10 to 15 minutes.

4. Add the chile garlic sauce to the hoisin sauce and stir to combine. Taste for seasoning, adding more chile sauce as needed. Let the hoisin sauce cool to room temperature. It can be refrigerated, covered, for up to 10 days or frozen for up to 3 months. Let it thaw in the refrigerator overnight.

Ginger Vinegar

When you don't have fresh ginger on hand, ginger vinegar is a convenient way to add spicy Asian heat to salad dressings and marinades. Boiling the ginger twice gives the flavor extra strength. **MAKES 1 CUP**

1 cup unseasoned rice vinegar
   (see Note)
1 piece (4 inches) fresh ginger, peeled
   and thinly sliced

1. Place the vinegar and ginger in a small saucepan, cover it, and bring to a boil over high heat. Remove the saucepan from the heat and let the vinegar mixture steep for about 30 minutes.

2. Using a slotted spoon, remove the ginger from the flavored vinegar and place it in a blender. Add about ¼ cup of the flavored vinegar and process continually until is pureed, about 30 seconds. Return the puree to the saucepan with the remaining vinegar, cover it, and bring to a boil over high heat. Remove the saucepan from the heat and let the ginger vinegar steep until cool.

3. Strain the flavored vinegar through a sieve, pressing down hard on the solids to extract all the liquid from them before discarding. Store the ginger vinegar in a bottle, tightly sealed with a nonmetalic lid, (or use a layer of plastic wrap to keep the vinegar from coming in contact with metal lid). The vinegar can be refrigerated for up to 6 months.

Raspberry Vinegar

When we moved to Carmel Valley, Drew and I found dozens of wine bottles and gallon-size jugs of distilled white vinegar that the previous owner had left behind. We learned that he made raspberry vinegar from his harvest, and we decided to continue his tradition. We offered our raspberry vinegar alongside our freshly picked organic berries. It's easy to make your own raspberry vinegar, but don't wait until just before you want to use it, because it takes several weeks for the vinegar's flavor to develop fully. **MAKES ABOUT 2 CUPS**

2 cups distilled white vinegar
1 cup (from 1 half-pint) fresh
   raspberries or frozen (thawed or
   unthawed) unsweetened raspberries

1. Combine the vinegar and raspberries in a small saucepan and bring to a boil over high heat. Reduce the heat to medium-low and let simmer until the raspberries fall apart, about 5 minutes. Remove the pan from the heat and let the vinegar steep with the berries for 45 minutes.

2. Strain the flavored vinegar through a sieve, pressing down on the berries to extract all of the liquid from the fruit. Discard the seeds and solids. Pour the vinegar into a sterilized glass bottle or jar with a nonmetallic lid and seal it tightly.

3. Store the flavored vinegar in a cool, dark place for 3 weeks.

4. Pour the flavored vinegar through a coffee filter to clarify it. Rebottle the vinegar in a sterilized glass bottle or jar with a nonmetallic lid and seal it tightly. The vinegar will keep, unopened, indefinitely in a cool, dark place.

Tarragon Vinegar

It's easy to make your own tarragon vinegar, and it's much less expensive than store-bought brands. It takes several weeks for the vinegar to absorb the herb's flavors, so plan ahead. Tarragon vinegar makes a lovely gift, especially if you rebottle the flavored vinegar in decorative bottles and place whole fresh tarragon sprigs inside. Unlike flavored oils, the acidity of the vinegar gives tarragon vinegar a long shelf life.

MAKES 2 CUPS

> $1/2$ cup fresh tarragon leaves, plus
>   2 or 3 whole tarragon sprigs
>   (optional), for bottling
> 2 cups vinegar, preferably white wine
>   vinegar (see Note)

1. Rinse and thoroughly pat dry the $1/2$ cup of tarragon leaves. Crush them slightly with a pestle or rolling pin to release their flavor, then place them in a large, sterilized glass jar that will hold at least $1\frac{1}{2}$ pints.

2. Heat the vinegar in a pan to just below the boiling point. Pour the hot vinegar over the herbs and let steep until it reaches room temperature. Seal the jar tightly with a nonmetallic lid (or use a layer of plastic wrap to keep the vinegar from coming in contact with a metal lid). Store the vinegar in a cool, dark place until the flavor develops, about 3 weeks.

3. Strain the vinegar through a coffee filter to clarify it. Discard the tarragon leaves. Transfer the vinegar to a decorative bottle and add 2 or 3 sprigs of fresh tarragon, if desired. Seal the bottle tightly with a nonmetallic lid. The vinegar can be refrigerated for up to 6 months.

Note: If you don't have white wine vinegar, you can substitute 2 cups of distilled white vinegar.

Herb-Flavored Oil

*F*lavored oils are a simple way to jazz up a salad. Keep in mind that when you add fresh garlic or herbs to oil, it must be refrigerated to prevent bacterial growth. Almost any herb—for example, basil, tarragon, rosemary, or dill—can be used. Each will be delicious; just make small batches due to their short refrigerator life. **MAKES ³/₄ CUP**

1 cup fresh herb leaves, such as tarragon, basil, rosemary, or dill
³/₄ cup extra-virgin olive oil or canola oil

Pink rosemary has tiny pink flowers and smaller, more delicate leaves than other varieties of rosemary.

1. Fill a large bowl of water with ice cubes and set it aside.

2. Bring a small saucepan of water to a boil over high heat. Add the herb leaves and blanch them to kill any bacteria, 15 seconds. Immediately drain the herb in a sieve, then plunge it into the bowl of ice water to stop the cooking. Drain the herb again and squeeze it dry in a clean dish towel or paper towels.

3. Transfer the herb leaves to a blender or mini food processor. Add the olive oil and blend for 1 minute.

4. Let the herb oil sit at room temperature until the flavor develops, about 1 hour. Then strain the oil through a sieve, pressing down on the solids to extract all the liquid from them before discarding. If you do not plan to use the flavored oil within 2 hours, it will keep, covered, in the refrigerator for up to 10 days.

Slow-Roasted Tomatoes

Slow roasting releases excess moisture and intensifies the flavor of tomatoes so even lackluster ones are transformed into sweet, chewy morsels delicious enough to eat like candy. Because your oven will be on for three hours or longer, increase your efficiency by roasting two or three pans of tomatoes at once. Convection ovens are ideal for roasting tomatoes because the circulating air speeds the drying process. A regular oven works well, too. Just switch the pans to different racks when you turn the tomatoes, so the tomatoes will cook evenly. Don't limit yourself to roasting just pear-shaped Romas. This recipe will work with any tomato variety, but larger, juicier tomatoes will take longer to cook. Roasted tomatoes are even tastier than sun-dried in pasta dishes, salads, and pizzas. Coarsely chopped, they also pair nicely with goat cheese and crackers to make an easy appetizer.

Roma (plum) tomatoes or another variety (see Note)
Coarse (kosher) salt
Extra-virgin olive oil (optional)

1. Preheat the oven to 300°F (250°F for a convection oven). Line a shallow baking pan with parchment paper or aluminum foil for easy cleanup. Place a flat roasting rack in the pan.

2. Cut the tomatoes in half lengthwise and remove and discard the seeds. Core the tomatoes. If they are large, cut them into quarters. Place the tomatoes, cut side up, on the rack. Sprinkle the tomatoes lightly with salt.

3. Roast the tomatoes for 1 hour, then turn them over and roast 1½ hours longer.

4. Turn the tomatoes again so the cut side is up and roast them until they are nearly dry but still pliable, 30 to 45 minutes longer. Turn off the oven and let the tomatoes cool inside with the door ajar.

5. If you are not planning on using the tomatoes immediately, transfer them to a storage container and cover them with olive oil. They can be refrigerated, covered, for up to 1 month. (Freezing causes the tomatoes to lose their texture, unfortunately.)

Note: If you use a larger, juicier variety of tomatoes, you will need to allow more time for them to roast, a total of about 4½ hours. Beginning with Step 3, roast juicy tomatoes cut side up for 1½ hours, then turn the tomatoes over and roast them for 2 hours longer. Turn the tomatoes over again and roast until they are nearly dry but still pliable, 45 minutes to 1 hour longer. Then turn off the oven as instructed in Step 4 and continue with the recipe.

If you plan to roast tomatoes larger than Romas, quarter them before roasting.

Roasted Bell Peppers

Roasting accentuates the sweetness of red, yellow, or orange bell peppers and brings out their rich juices. When cut into strips, roasted peppers add color and flavor to leafy green salads, sandwiches, or casseroles, like the Grilled Vegetable Lasagna with Emerald Green Pesto (see page 188). It's nice to keep roasted peppers in the refrigerator—they make an easy appetizer when friends drop by. Slivers of pepper, especially a mix of colors, are a lovely topping for toasted baguette slices spread with soft goat cheese.

When roasting the peppers, don't walk away from the broiler. Turning the peppers frequently while their skins blister and turn black allows the flesh underneath to soften without burning. Try not to pierce the skin when you turn the peppers so that you don't lose precious juices. The charred skin should slip off the peppers easily when you peel them with your fingers. Hold the peppers over a bowl to catch any liquid that may escape. Resist the temptation to rinse roasted peppers. If a few charred bits of skin remain, they will add flavor and a pleasing rustic appearance.

Leave a little of the charred skin on the roasted peppers for added flavor.

Red, yellow, or orange bell peppers
Extra-virgin olive oil

1. Preheat the broiler and line a roasting pan with aluminum foil for easy cleanup.

2. Place the whole peppers in the pan and broil about 4 inches from the heat, turning frequently with tongs, until the skins blister and begin to turn black, about 10 minutes.

3. Transfer the peppers to a small paper or plastic bag, close it tightly, and let the peppers steam for 5 to 10 minutes.

4. When the peppers are cool enough to handle, working over a small bowl to catch the juices, pull off and discard the charred skin. Cut the peppers in half and remove and discard the stems and seeds. If you wish, cut the pepper halves into thick strips.

5. Put the peppers in the bowl with the juices and drizzle olive oil over them. Covered tightly, they can be refrigerated for up to 7 days.

Do-It-Yourself Matzoh Meal

Matzoh ball soup is a family favorite, but making it organically was impossible because we couldn't find organic matzoh meal, so, we figured out how to make our own. Matzoh meal is surprisingly easy to make, but a bit time consuming. Save this recipe for a day when the restorative benefits of kneading and rolling the soft dough would be welcome. For the matzoh ball and soup recipes, see pages 44 and 45.

MAKES ABOUT 3 CUPS

3 cups unbleached all-purpose flour

1. Position a rack in the lower third of the oven and preheat the oven to 450°F. Line 2 rimmed baking sheets with parchment paper and set them aside.

2. Place the flour in a large bowl. Add just enough warm water (1¼ to 1½ cups) to make a soft dough. Turn the dough out onto a work surface and knead it by hand until smooth, about 5 minutes.

3. Allow the dough to rest, covered with a clean dish towel, for about 5 minutes.

4. Tear off a piece of dough roughly the size of a golf ball. Stretch the dough into a small oval with your hands. Using a rolling pin, roll it into a very thin oval shape, about ¹⁄₃₂ inch thick. The dough is easy to work, so roll it as thin as you can. Place the rolled dough on the prepared baking sheet. Repeat this step until all the dough has been rolled out.

5. Bake the matzoh until it buckles and crisps, 8 to 12 minutes. Let the matzoh cool on a wire rack.

6. Break the matzoh into small pieces with your fingers. Transfer the matzo to a food processor and process until it is a fine powder. To ensure an even-textured meal, sift the meal through a coarse-mesh sieve and return any large grains to the food processor for additional processing. The matzoh meal can be stored in an airtight container at room temperature for up to 2 weeks.

A mound of kneaded dough ready to be rolled into matzoh.

Savory Pie Crust

Your guests will know this crust is homemade as soon as they see it. The lovely flecks of herbs give it a distinctive savory flavor. This easy-to-make dough is great for quiche. Mix and match the herbs to the flavors in your filling. Thyme, dill, basil, tarragon, or chives will be equally delicious. **MAKES ENOUGH FOR 1 SINGLE-CRUST PIE, 10 INCHES IN DIAMETER**

$^1/_4$ **cup fresh thyme leaves, or another chopped herb, such as dill, basil, marjoram, or tarragon, or a mixture**
$1^1/_2$ **cups unbleached all-purpose flour, plus more for rolling out the dough**
$^1/_2$ **teaspoon salt**
6 tablespoons ($^3/_4$ stick) cold unsalted butter, cut into $^1/_2$-inch pieces
3 tablespoons cold, solid shortening (see Note), cut into small pieces
3 tablespoons ice water, or more as needed

1. Place the thyme, if using, in a food processor and pulse briefly to mince. Add the flour, salt, butter, and shortening and pulse until the mixture looks like coarse meal.

2. With the machine running, add the ice water and process to combine, about 5 seconds. When the dough forms a ball, it is ready. If it is not moist enough to form a ball, add an additional tablespoon of ice water and process briefly.

3. Turn the dough out onto a large piece of plastic wrap and form it into a flat disk, patting it just enough to hold it together. Wrap the dough tightly in plastic wrap and refrigerate it for at least 30 minutes or up to 3 days. The wrapped dough can be frozen for up to 3 months. Let the frozen dough thaw overnight in the refrigerator before rolling it out.

4. Remove the dough from the refrigerator and unwrap it. If it was refrigerated for more than 1 hour, let it sit at room temperature for 10 minutes to soften slightly. Lightly dust a work surface and rolling pin with flour. Roll the dough into a round about $^1/_8$ inch thick and 2 inches larger than the pie plate.

5. Fold the dough in half or drape it over the rolling pin and transfer it to the pie plate. Press the dough firmly into the pie plate and brush off any excess flour with a pastry brush. If there are holes or cracks, patch them with small bits of the overhanging dough or press the dough back together. Trim the dough with a pair of kitchen scissors, leaving a $^3/_4$-inch overhang. Fold the edge under to form a double layer and crimp or flute it.

Note: Look for organic shortening, made from expeller-pressed palm oil, which has no trans fats (see Four Food Choices I Live By, page xxii).

Sprigs of fresh marjoram.

Sweet Pie Crust

Butter creates a light and flaky crust, perfect for fruit pies and tarts. Even though all-butter doughs have a reputation for being a bit finicky, this food processor method is surefire and quick. **MAKES ENOUGH FOR 2 SINGLE-CRUST PIES OR 1 DOUBLE-CRUST PIE, 8 TO 9 INCHES IN DIAMETER**

> 2¹/₂ cups unbleached all-purpose flour, plus flour for rolling out the dough
> ¹/₄ teaspoon salt
> 2 tablespoons sugar
> 1 cup (2 sticks) cold unsalted butter, cut into ¹/₂-inch pieces
> ¹/₄ cup ice water, or more as needed

1. Place the flour, salt, and sugar in a food processor and pulse to blend. Add the butter and pulse until the mixture looks like coarse meal.

2. With the machine running, add the ice water and process to combine, about 5 seconds. Do not allow the dough to form a solid mass or it will be tough. Test the dough by pinching a small amount between your fingers. If the dough sticks together, it is ready. If not, add an additional tablespoon of ice water, process briefly, and test again.

3. Turn out the dough onto a clean work surface and divide it in half. Form the dough into two flat disks, patting it just enough to hold together. Wrap the disks tightly in plastic wrap and refrigerate for at least 1 hour or up to 3 days. The wrapped dough can be frozen for up to 3 months. Let the frozen dough thaw overnight in the refrigerator before rolling it out.

4. Remove the dough from the refrigerator and unwrap it (for a single-crust pie you'll need one disk of dough; for a double-crust pie you'll need both disks). If it was refrigerated for more than 1 hour, let it sit at room temperature for 10 minutes to soften slightly. Lightly dust a work surface and rolling pin with flour. Roll the dough into a round about ¹/₈-inch thick and 2 inches larger than the pie plate.

5. Fold the dough in half or drape it over the rolling pin and transfer it to the pie plate. Press the dough firmly into the pie plate and brush off any excess flour with a pastry brush. If there are holes or cracks, patch them with small bits of the overhanging dough or press the dough back together.

6. For a single crust pie, trim the dough with a pair of kitchen scissors, leaving a ³/₄-inch overhang. Fold the edge under to form a double layer and crimp or flute it. For a double-crust pie, fit the dough for the bottom crust into the pie plate and trim the dough even with the rim. Roll out the second disk of dough. Place the filling in the bottom crust and place the dough for the second crust on top. Trim the top crust with scissors, leaving a ¹/₂-inch overhang. Fold the top crust under the edge of the bottom crust, and crimp or flute it to seal. Cut 3 slits in the center of the top crust with a sharp knife to allow steam to vent as the pie bakes.

A slice of Harvest Pie (page 355) with Apples, Pear, and Cranberries.

Sweetened Whipped Cream

Sweet whipped cream makes even a simple dessert special, adding a lavish touch to fresh fruit, pies, gingerbread, and cakes. While the texture is best if you use the whipped cream right away, any that's left over can be refrigerated overnight, covered with plastic wrap. The next morning you'll enjoy the special treat of adding a dollop to coffee or hot chocolate. **MAKES ABOUT 2 CUPS**

1 cup heavy (whipping) cream, chilled
3 tablespoons confectioners' sugar
1 teaspoon pure vanilla extract

1. Chill a medium-size mixing bowl and mixer blades in the freezer until ready to use (at least 20 minutes).

2. Add the cream to the chilled bowl. Beat the cream, using an electric mixer, starting on low and increasing the speed as the cream begins to froth.

3. Gradually add the sugar and vanilla and continue to beat until the cream holds soft peaks, 2 to 3 minutes. For the best texture, use whipped cream immediately, or refrigerate, covered, for up to 1 hour.

Homemade Crème Fraîche

Crème fraîche is thick, heavy cream with a slightly tart taste. It makes a delicious substitute for whipped cream on fresh fruits, pies, and cobblers. For a touch of sweetness, stir in a little honey or sugar before serving. **MAKES ABOUT 2¼ CUPS**

2 cups heavy (whipping) cream
2 tablespoons sour cream or buttermilk

Place the heavy cream in a small bowl and add the sour cream. Whisk to combine. Cover with plastic wrap and let sit at room temperature until thick, 12 to 18 hours (the sour cream or buttermilk protects the cream from developing harmful bacteria while it is thickening). Once thickened, the crème fraîche can be refrigerated, covered, for up to 1 week.

Conversion Tables

APPROXIMATE EQUIVALENTS

1 STICK BUTTER = 8 tbs = 4 oz = ½ cup

1 CUP ALL-PURPOSE PRESIFTED FLOUR
    OR DRIED BREAD CRUMBS = 5 oz

1 CUP GRANULATED SUGAR = 8 oz

1 CUP (PACKED) BROWN SUGAR = 6 oz

1 CUP CONFECTIONERS' SUGAR = 4½ oz

1 CUP HONEY OR SYRUP = 12 oz

1 CUP GRATED CHEESE = 4 oz

1 CUP DRIED BEANS = 6 oz

1 LARGE EGG = about 2 oz or about 3 tbs

1 EGG YOLK = about 1 tbs

1 EGG WHITE = about 2 tbs

*Please note that all conversions are approximate but close enough
to be useful when converting from one system to another.*

WEIGHT CONVERSIONS

U.S./U.K.	METRIC	U.S./U.K.	METRIC
½ oz	15 g	7 oz	200 g
1 oz	30 g	8 oz	250 g
1½ oz	45 g	9 oz	275 g
2 oz	60 g	10 oz	300 g
2½ oz	75 g	11 oz	325 g
3 oz	90 g	12 oz	350 g
3½ oz	100 g	13 oz	375 g
4 oz	125 g	14 oz	400 g
5 oz	150 g	15 oz	450 g
6 oz	175 g	1 lb	500 g

LIQUID CONVERSIONS

U.S.	IMPERIAL	METRIC
2 tbs	1 fl oz	30 ml
3 tbs	1½ fl oz	45 ml
¼ cup	2 fl oz	60 ml
⅓ cup	2½ fl oz	75 ml
⅓ cup + 1 tbs	3 fl oz	90 ml
⅓ cup + 2 tbs	3½ fl oz	100 ml
½ cup	4 fl oz	125 ml
⅔ cup	5 fl oz	150 ml
¾ cup	6 fl oz	175 ml
¾ cup + 2 tbs	7 fl oz	200 ml
1 cup	8 fl oz	250 ml
1 cup + 2 tbs	9 fl oz	275 ml
1¼ cups	10 fl oz	300 ml
1⅓ cups	11 fl oz	325 ml
1½ cups	12 fl oz	350 ml
1⅔ cups	13 fl oz	375 ml
1¾ cups	14 fl oz	400 ml
1¾ cups + 2 tbs	15 fl oz	450 ml
2 cups (1 pint)	16 fl oz	500 ml
2½ cups	20 fl oz (1 pint)	600 ml
3¾ cups	1½ pints	900 ml
4 cups	1½ pints	1 liter

OVEN TEMPERATURES

°F	GAS MARK	°C	°F	GAS MARK	°C
250	½	120	400	6	200
275	1	140	425	7	220
300	2	150	450	8	230
325	3	160	475	9	240
350	4	180	500	10	260
375	5	190			

Note: Reduce the temperature by 20°C (68°F) for fan-assisted ovens.

Index

Photo Credits